"Tom Reed is a born traveler and a writer's writer, who *makes* you his intimate traveling companion, on this, his personal quest for a new home in South America. Along the way, you'll be witness to his adventures and his catastrophes; you'll measure your steps in time to his, sharing moments of ecstasy and despair, probably breathless to keep up, but glad you finally did.

"His conclusions, based on a combination of his political, cultural, and environmental insights, his own spiritual awareness, and this travel experience, prove deeply satisfying. Whether you are an outdoor adventurer, an armchair traveler, or a dissatisfied *norteamericano* just looking for a better landing place, you'll find your journey to *THE OTHER SIDE* one worth taking, perhaps even unforgettable."

—Irene D. Thomas PhD,
author of *Olaf Palm, A Life in Art*,
and *The Temptation to Tango*

THE OTHER SIDE

On the Road in South America

Tom Reed

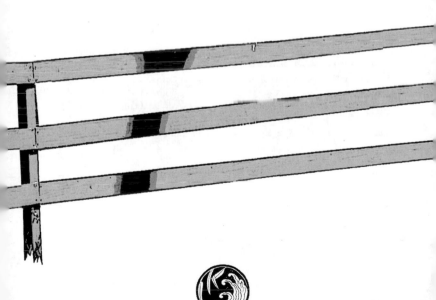

Wild Coast Media

THE OTHER SIDE
On the Road in South America

THE GRANITE AVATARS OF PATAGONIA is Tom Reed's large format book featuring full-page black and white photographs of Cerro Torre and Fitz Roy. The text of that book is an excerpt form this book. Both of these books, as well as the photographs, are available from **www.tomreed.com**

The Internet is constantly changing, so any web addresses contained in this book may have changed since publication.

ISBN: 978-0-615-49050-2

Printed in Canada
Publication date: August 23, 2011

Acknowledgements

Many people donated their valuable time to help me write this book, which, though it is the second to publish, is the first that I wrote. Three individuals deserve special mention. Sarah Wheaton took time from her busy schedule to meticulously edited and encouraged me, without pulling punches. Irene Thomas took me on as a student, spending hours with the manuscript, and giving valuable advice and support. Lauryn Axelrod, a fellow traveler, author, and media specialist, fell into the story and gave me *unending* support and encouragement to tell the story and tell it well, reminding me to return to "the quest" when I would get too far off on my beloved tangents. It is only because of these three wise women that this manuscript is fit to print. All solecisms are my intention, for the purpose of a casual or rhythmic flow of words. Two teachers provided valuable insights early in the project which allowed me to organize and present my journal in a unique yet cohesive way: Dan Imhoff helped me see the big picture, Charlotte Gullick taught me some key elements of the writing craft. Liz Collins helped by questioning me, and in the end, Lena Cruz donated her sharp eye, and proofread for me.

Thanks also go to the many people who gave their support in other ways, especially Dr. Charles Wray for providing the space to bring this work to completion, and Dixie Yeterian, who was the first to encourage me to write (and also tried to help me find my camera with her special skill). And thanks to the readers of The Granite Avatars of Patagonia, who sent in so many emails of appreciation, encouraging me to see this long work through to completion.

"The man who will go down to posterity is the man who paints his own time and the scenes of everyday life around him."

—Childe Hassam

"We do not receive wisdom, we must discover it for ourselves, after a journey through the wilderness which no one else can make for us, which no one else can spare us."

—Marcel Proust

"It was the best of times, it was the worst of times."

—Charles Dickens
(*A Tale of Two Cities*)

PART 1

THE URGE TO MIGRATE

CHAPTER 1

Fight or Flight

This trail parts chest-high chaparral with dense overhead thickets of a bottlebrush bamboo, heading south, crossing a slope that faces the rising sun, with a big lake below. It's a still and cloudless summer morning in early January, and the tingle of delight I feel entering the Andes for the first time on foot seems to buoy my full backpack.

The route passes through a burned area. The fire must have been low and hot, killing the trees by burning through the bark at the ground. Most of the trees have little charcoal on them, and the twigs are still on the branches. When the trail hits a valley that heads west, into the mountains, it follows the stream in the bottom and enters an exotic forest. Only one species of tree grows in the valley: the *lenga*, or southern beech, and they stand about sixty feet tall. The improbably dominant lenga comprises the entire forest in all of these mountain valleys, all the way up to tree line. I'm reminded of the claim that the largest living organism on the planet is an aspen grove in Colorado. I'd be surprised if all of the lenga in each valley of these mountains are not someday found to contain identical DNA, with each valley contains a single tree, sprouting countless times as the roots spread through the soils, from the quaggy bogs in the valley floors up to the desiccated scree slopes tumbling down from the eroding peaks. What is it about them that feels so exotic? The main trunk splits low into several branches which continue up, like an elm, then the leafed branches find a horizontal orientation. The leaves are small, and these horizontal layers of fine dark green leaves give the forest a Japanese feeling. "It's more Japanese than any of the forests I've seen in Japan," I joke to myself.

Proceeding up-valley, the path comes upon a small shelter made of two log walls enclosing the overhang of a huge boulder. The boulder is granite, the size of a small house. It could have ridden on top of a glacier to get here, or it could have come to rest after a violent drop from a peak above. Either way, it's been here for a long time. The little refuge, maybe half a century old, is just its current state, like a warbler nest in an ancient tree. Who knows, maybe the aboriginal Tahuelche used the overhang for shelter on occasion, or maybe all of the soot on the boulder is from fires built by hikers in recent years.

As elevation increases, the trees begin to diminish in height, revealing broken granite spires on the ridges above. Soon I'm in a sea of dense, low lenga covering the upper valley like chaparral, with a steep stream roaring in cascades beside me; then the trail makes a final lunge for the pass. Up there I find a large tarn, and where its water spills into the valley is Refugio Frey, a two-storied structure of fine cut-stone blockwork. Beyond the refugio and the tarn sits an amphitheater of several spiky peaks appropriately named "*Catedral*." The view is a satisfying reward after the climb. Not having seen any photographs of this area, I had no expectations of what I'd encounter, so I'm pleasantly surprised at the regal nature of the spires. They jut skyward like the "drizzled" points I made topping sand castles on the beach as a kid. The scree slopes around them still bear lots of snow, and this month is the southern equivalent of our July, so the snowfall must be substantial here.

The refugio was built fifty years ago and named for a local mountaineering hero. Its first floor is a rustic dining room with three massive tables and benches made of thick timbers, behind it is an even more rustic kitchen. Above is a bunkroom, able to squeeze forty people side-by-side on two long bunks like shelves, one above the other. Rock climbers are milling about, most of them Argentinean; sometimes other languages, English or Portuguese, float through the air. They tell me that a storm is coming and recommend staying in the shelter. One warns me that the snoring inside is incredible. I had planned to pass this valley today, but three weeks of sitting on buses in Chile took away muscle and stamina without my noticing. Travel is like that, the constantly changing environment and complete lack of routine, the strange food, missed meals, and increased alcohol intake all contribute to a less than optimum situation for monitoring one's physical condition. I was in shape when I left California, but I'm not now, and I'm tired. The enthusiasm I felt when I first got on the trail has dwindled. The buoy has been cut from my backpack. Sitting on a stone wall, I make a ham and cheese sandwich and consider my options. Do I want to sit in a one-man tent through the storm, or hang out at the shelter with a coterie of climbers? I decide on the tent. It's too much of a scene here. It's a one-dimensional atmosphere, like I find at international surf spots, or martial arts summer camps. If you're not a climber you're on the outside. It's one thing to be alone; it's another to be alone in a crowded room.

It takes a traverse of the entire length of the lake before finding some solitude. A tent city fills the spaces in the lenga scrub along the lake-shore. But at the far end there's a cozy alcove in the brush big enough to throw up the tent. I stash my pack in it, and take off for a walk. Making my way for the snow-covered headwall of the cirque that holds the lake, the refugio, and the climbers, I notice two huge birds cruising along the north ridge. "Fucking condors!" I blurt out. A wave of excitement rejuvenates me. It's been a hope that I would see them, but given that the California condor has eluded this birdwatcher for decades, I didn't want to get my hopes up too high.

Feeling much better without my burden, excited by the

terrain, and energized by the sight of the giant birds, I climb the headwall with the zest of a kid. Above the snow slope there is another small cirque with another tarn, this little one still more than three-quarters frozen. The granite turrets above it are pink to rust in color, but also fruity— cantaloupe, mango and persimmon in places. I make my way for the pass to catch a glimpse beyond, and meet a Belgian couple in their sixties as I begin a climb on large talus boulders. They are slowly and carefully making their way from the chair-lift to the refuge. I'm impressed. They tell me that the trail had steep drop-offs and was scary, so now I want to see it, and when I hit the pass I keep hiking north along the ridge, on the west slope of it, below the crest, following red spots painted on the rocks—and it's nothing *but* rocks. Large angular boulders lie on an angle that barely allows repose below a craggy ridge. These rocks once stood above those crags, maybe in majestic vertical displays like what remains behind me. Those spires of the cathedral have a castle-like quality, due to the highly fractured rock, which resembles block construction. Abundant fingers of rock, called *gendarmes*, decorate the towers like the gargoyles of the Cathedral of Notre Dame. I wonder where the boulder under foot once stood, in what cathedral, and in what cataclysm it came crashing down.

While traversing a buttress of the peak above, the rocks get as big as cars. I round one and see a guy about thirty feet below me, standing still, wearing a new overstuffed red pack on his back, and a big day-pack slung on his chest. I yell down, "Watch out for falling rocks," and he turns quickly and bursts into rapid exclamations about the magnificent view in Spanish that sounds like sing-song Italian. He's totally overwhelmed by the beauty, and he hasn't even seen the cathedral yet. He asks how far to Frey, and I describe the route.

In a while the chair-lift comes into view. I suppose I passed the scary part without knowing it. I still feel strong, so I leave the route and head for a peak. At over 2,000 meters the air is already getting thin for this body from sea level, and I have to stop a few times to catch my breath, but I make it to the top with no problem. The final sixty feet or so is a near vertical rock climb, up a crack and through a chimney. A spot just below the pinnacle offers shelter from the wind, which howls in off the Pacific, crossing Chile in no time, and biting my right cheek. From my perch I face south, overlooking the spectacular granite amphitheater, and turn my head to reconnoiter tomorrow's hike in the next valley to the west. Beyond my route, ice-covered Mount Tronador, the "Thunderer," looms high in the sky, marking the Chilean border, and beyond it are the lower slopes of another volcano that is probably Osorno. Its top is mantled with the weather that's moving in. To the north and south, snowy peaks and ridges continue to the horizons. The Andes are a long mountain chain—three times the length of the Himalayas. The word "Andes" is thought to have evolved from either of two Indian words: *anti*, meaning "east," or *anta*, meaning "copper."

After studying tomorrow's route with binoculars, and assessing the snowy pass to be crossed, my head turns back to the south and my eyes catch the movement of a condor closing in from the left, gliding into the wind at high speed and close range. Immediately I reach for my camera bag, but with my thumb and forefinger on the zipper pull, I stop. There's no time. If I go for the photo I'll miss the experience—and probably the photo too. The condor is only a couple hundred feet away. I see the feathers of its downy white-collar shift in the wind when it turns its head ever so slightly to look at me. Its wings span ten feet and are motionless as it cuts into the wind. It passes me at about twenty-five miles-per-hour, flying into a headwind that's thirty miles-per-hour or more, and is gone in a few seconds, becoming a flattened 'v' silhouetted against the stormy sky. Its head, described in my bird book as "bare, wattled and caruncolated," is a blue-grey, telling me it's of the southern race of the species, and the fin-like crest atop tells me it's a male. I wonder if this fin helps him soar with such efficiency. As he shrinks to a dot in the western sky I come down from the rush, and hear myself say, "Cool" out loud. A sudden feeling—that I could leave now and be satisfied with the entire trip—passes through me and takes me by surprise. Why do I feel so satisfied, so content? It's not like I came down here to see condors. I came to scout for a new place to live. Not just a new place to *live*, a place to *thrive*.

I'm an outsider in my own culture. For years I led a monastic lifestyle, working just enough to survive while focusing on my martial art training, which was mostly physical, but included meditation, reading and writing, in other words, the life of a dharma bum. While several millionaires have told me that I'm a wealthy man, something I already knew, I am financially poor. Money has never meant much to me, and so the pursuit of it has always been a low priority (ironically, this attitude requires that I make it a top priority on occasion). Luck, destiny, or good karma has enabled me to survive while focusing on things other than bank accounts and investments—what Joseph Campbell called "Following your Bliss." That same good fortune, whatever you call it, always allowed me to find some cool little cabin in the woods or in an orchard where I could live for low rent. Meanwhile real estate prices in Coastal California soared at the turn of the century, and now I find myself aced-out of the possibility of owning some property unless I decide to dedicate my life to paying for it. Life seems too short for that, but I do crave a home.

I'm low-income by choice, but a full sixth of Californians (one of six million) live in poverty due to the high costs of real estate. The bankruptcy rate has doubled since the nineties. Last year, household savings in the nation were negative for the first time since 1933. It's not like the East Coast beach town I grew up in, where the three boys across the street were raised in an impeccably-kept home by a housewife whose husband walked to the marina every morning with a bagged lunch and a thermos to earn a modest income by painting boats. Those towns don't exist in modern California.

I enjoy the little towns of the Northern California Coast, buffered by expanses of ranch land and forest, but they are no place for a martial artist to find serious students, especially because I teach a martial/spiritual path that allows no competition—my motto: "True victory is victory over self." The fact is that the culture of the entire country is not one that supports my interest.

Then there's the political aspect. I am labeled a radical. This is because I acknowledge that our political system has failed. Why that is plainly obvious to me, but not to most Americans, is a mystery. Maybe it's because I never owned a television. Somehow I escaped being brainwashed into believing that the United States is a perfect state, with leaders incapable of dealing injustice, even crimes against humanity, in order to further their private interests. I'm amazed that the plethora of evidence that points to a forty-year coup is ignored. It seems obvious to me that the powers that Eisenhower and Kennedy warned about began a takeover with the assassinations of the 60's and have recently won nearly full control by redefining our world through the barbaric events of 9/11/2001.

I only began to be politically active in response to the events of the first term of George W. Bush. After the election of 2000 was stolen I knew that our democracy was teetering, and that if they stole the vote again in 2004 it would be *history* unless the people stood up to them. I wondered if it even made sense to live in a country where an elite controlled the vote. I wasn't the only person who spoke of leaving if the 2000 theft was repeated.

In early last November I traveled to Oregon, which was considered to be a swing state, to help Move On PAC prevent George W. Bush's re-election. We were successful in that state, but of course Bush took the national election again, and Kerry didn't dispute the theft. One writer described the Bush/Kerry contest as like the Harlem Globetrotters vs. the Washington Generals—a set-up to make the Republicans look like they have an opponent.

This view is making more and more sense to me. The display of contest is what keeps the fact that there is no contest hidden.

From Oregon I drove north to visit an associate who has a dojo in British Columbia. I took a ferry across the Strait of Juan de Fuca and disembarked at Victoria, where I and a few others were chosen to be searched and inspected by the border police. Afterwards I asked the amiable officer why me. He told me that on the day after Bush was named the winner of the election, visits to Canada's immigration website were up tenfold, and that they were expecting a flood of American liberals to make a run on the border. My "War Is Not The Answer" bumper sticker, and the camping gear and surfboard in the back of my truck made me suspect.

I find myself living in a country well on its way to fascism, with a government that is not accountable to the people but to big business, and which suppresses opposition while promoting nationalism. I'm living in a country where the citizens, for the most part, take no actions to protest against the government, even when they strongly disagree with its actions. Even when the president breaks laws, violates the constitution, and breeches international agreements and treaties. As a result, my nation has allowed a group of extremely wealthy thugs to take control of the military in order to maintain economic domination of the planet. Social programs are cut so that more tax dollars can go to defense contractors (in Iraq as much as 50% of the value of such contracts is fraudulent). Much of the progress of the past thirty years has been reversed. People have such a sense of powerlessness and hopelessness that depression is epidemic, and I suspect that is intentional.

Epicurus taught not to waste time involved in political struggle, but simply to enjoy life. Maybe he was right. Few spiritual masters make any political comments. But I respect the integrity of Father Daniel Berrigan, Reverend Martin Luther King, and the Buddhist monks of Viet Nam, Burma, and Tibet who have stood up to unjust governments.

Am I to spend my life standing for what is right in a culture of apathy, dominated by a lame media, and crippled by having its only politically-heard voice, its only directive to its government, its vote, stolen? Should I sacrifice my life for a people who no longer care about my effort? Should I risk getting arrested for civil disobedience when peace demonstrators are now construed as "terrorists," and therefore may lack the rights of Habeas Corpus, possibly then jailed for life without trial—for carrying a sign? I could capitulate, but it's not my nature to shut up and join the herd. To be, or not to be? Or should I be somewhere else—exit, stage south, where a Latin American populism is growing?

"Madame, there are always two paths to take; one backwards towards the comforts of security and death, the other forward to nowhere."
                                                              —*Henry Miller*

CHAPTER 2

Choosing Chile

Most of my travel has been in Central America and the Caribbean. I never imagined I could live in some steamy banana republic, but Chile is a land that has piqued my curiosity as what I imagined to be the mirror image of North America's west coast, from Cabo San Lucas to Juneau, which I have come to love. I finally decided to close my dojo, and now that my freedom to travel was renewed after so many years of training and then teaching, my dream of seeing Chile sang to me once again, and demanded to be fulfilled. Maybe it would be like the West Coast of the fifties; with an abundance of open space and opportunity. Maybe the pendulum swing from the Pinochet era would have people in a progressive phase in which they valued what I have to offer. Like all Americans but the descendant of the natives, my genes are those of immigrants, but could I really leave this land that I love?

These were my mental wanderings when I ran into an old friend who had moved to Canada. She recommended a consultation with a particular astrocartographer. I had never heard of the title. It's a person who uses astrological charts to determine where on earth you will best thrive.

Recently a person asked me what I believe in. Not what I believe, what I believe *in*. It's that last two-letter word that changes everything for me. It indicates that you believe that something that cannot be proven is true, like God, ghosts, UFO's and magic. Why do we use this word, *in*, this way? Is it like a gamble? All your chips are *in* the pot? Is it like joining a club? You are *in* a group of believers? I'm not in. I look at the evidence, especially my own experience, including my intuition, and develop a sense of probability. Regarding astrology, my sense is that the ancient insights on which the modern study is based are profound, though much of what claims the name "astrology" today is superficial.

Once I was in a room full of Japanese, most of whom were famous Zen people. One was an intellectual. Somehow the subject of astrology came up. The intellectual stated that she could not believe that a star so far away could have any effect on her personality. The room was silent for a few seconds, until I said, "Maybe it's not the stars affecting us. Maybe it's just that we and the stars are the same thing." The room returned to silence, then a Zen person leaned forward and looked at me and said, "I like that. It's very Zen." It was one of those times when you say something you never heard yourself say before—when an attitude liberates itself from the realm of your unarticulated mental environment and finds words to use as transportation to other minds.

I think it's probably all just one reality. The planets are a reflection of you, an indicator. Maybe it's better said the other way around: you are just a reflection of the state of the universe, from when you were born onward to this moment. How do I know this if I never studied astrology? I don't. It's just how I see it, what seems probable. After all, why would such an ancient tradition persist if there were nothing to it? And who knows what knowledge was burned in the vast libraries of Alexandria, or when the Mongols destroyed the libraries of Baghdad? I read that those invaders threw so many books in the Tigris River that horses could cross the river on them. They weren't novels! We really have no idea what ancient civilizations knew. So I try to remain open and curious. I wrote down the name of the astrocartographer.

As the date of our consultation approached I found myself thrilled with the anticipation of his advice. Would he make a right-on call, a tip that would change my life? What if he told me to settle down in a trailer park in Iowa? How would Chile rate, or for that matter, the town where I live on the Mendocino Coast?

During my consultation the guy used a couple of computers as we talked and he came up with Connecticut or Rhode Island, then thought maybe New Jersey. I was cringing. I saw flat land carpeted with wall-to-wall towns. I felt anchored in a sea of concrete, a long passage from distant wilderness shores.

Sensing my disappointment he shrugged and told me it's definitely the best longitude for me, then asked if I had any place in mind, and I said I was wondering about Chile. He punched it in and asked "What town?" I gave him the name of a place on the temperate coast that looks interesting. It took a while, then he started mumbling like a creative genius coming up with a great idea—things like, "Mm-hmm," "This is interesting," "This is very good." He found it to be much better than the east coast of the United States, and apologized, saying he usually doesn't look so far south. It turns out the temperate coast of Chile is on the same longitudinal swath as the coast from New Jersey to Rhode Island. Just to be sure, he followed that swath up and checked out some places in the Caribbean, but he assured me that nothing can beat the latitudes of Chile, something about certain planets in houses. He explained that when one of these planets is in the right house it's a good place, and on the Chilean Coast I have three important planets in the right houses. Nine out of ten clients have no idea where to be, he said, but once in a while someone like me comes along and knows intuitively where they should go. The more he looked at the computer screens the more he saw that he liked. He told me that, due to the time and place of my birth, which make me a double Scorpio, the longitude of 73.5 degrees is ideal for me, and that the best time for me to visit is a two-week span beginning on December ninth, a little more than a month away. At the end of our conversation he advised me to wear a Vedic gem to help me avoid some legal hassles for the next few years.

To the degree that I remember to, I live from a detached awareness of my life, that is, from an "I" that is nonpersonal. So I often joke about life being a board game, like Monopoly, in which your little character plods along according to how the dice roll, and then every once in a while you have to draw a card. Sometimes the cards say things like: "Your husband leaves you for another woman," or "your wife tells you she is pregnant," or, "rich aunt dies and leaves you a fortune." Other times they are not definite events, but possibilities arise, like, "friend offers you cruising sailboat for half price," or "company offers you a job in Prague," or "astrocartographer tells you Chile is the best place for you to live." So I hang up the phone with that feeling you get when you draw one of these possibility cards—that feeling that the rest of your life could be very different than you thought; that feeling that you might have a big decision to make.

If we and the stars are parts of the same thing, then why would gems be excluded? Few things frustrate me more than legal hassles. This is fresh in my mind. Half of the tickets I've had in thirty-two years of driving were issued to me in the past year, causing me to attend online traffic school twice. It's not that I am a bad driver; these were for minor bendings of traffic rules observed by rookie, by-the-book cops. So I called a Vedic gemstone dealer and bought what I could afford.

Next I began to look into the price and availability of flights. I hit all the usual discounters; the best prices for flights from San Francisco to Santiago were within ten dollars of each other, averaging $1070. They were all on one airline, so I called them directly. I asked for a flight on December eighth, but it was full. Then she offered me December sixth for $811. Would I like to buy it now? Whoa, I was just checking things out, but I've said "No" in these situations before, and when I've called back to get the ticket, it was gone. So I took a deep breath, checked my intuition, and it felt right, so I bought it. When I hung up, I told myself, "I'm going to Chile in a month!" and already felt the excitement of preparing to travel.

I'm not the kind of traveler who meticulously researches his destination, and then makes scheduled plans. And my budget is tiny. I look at a map and am attracted to places. Part of this process is intuitional, and some could be on a psychic level beyond my awareness, but some part of me is fed by the sight of steep slopes plunging into water, especially if there is the potential for good surf. When I hit the ground, I figure out how to get to these areas. I need to have a quest—sightseeing gets old quickly—and I like to get involved with the people in some way.

Over the years, whenever I've looked at a map of Chile, I've been drawn to the empty spaces on the coast at latitudes equivalent to those of California, north of Point Conception. In wild coastlines I find my greatest geographic thrill, and I was excited about what might be there. My quest, however, was a bit of an aside: I had an urge to backpack in the Andes and photograph some of their spectacular peaks. When a friend returned from Argentina a year ago she gave me postcards of Cerro Torre and Fitz Roy, which implanted a subconscious homing device in my brain. I didn't realize it, but those photographs instilled a deep yearning for dramatic granite spires that would hijack my intentions to see more of Chile, and keep me in Argentina for almost half of my stay in the Southern Cone, the name of South America below Peru and Brazil, presumably named so due to the way the width of the continent and the height of the mountains both taper towards the south.

My flight left from San Francisco, then connected to an all-night flight south out of Dallas. While in that limbo between flights, I saw people with earbuds and was reminded that I had an iPod, so I pulled it out and hit the "Soul" playlist. When

I'll Take you There by the Staple Singers came on, it seemed like they were singing directly to me, and the soulful voices swept me up in the lyrics as if I'd never heard them before.

> The lead singer said she knows a place where,
> "Ain't nobody cryin'
> Ain't nobody worried
> Ain't no smilin' faces
> Lyin' to the races,"

and she said she'd take me there. Just take her by the hand let her lead the way. What a luxury it would be to have someone simply take us by the hand and lead us to a better place. I have to embark on this journey alone, searching on my own, in a strange land.

Somewhere over the Gulf of Mexico I was fading, feeling both relaxed and excited about what I'd find in Chile. As I began to drift off, I felt a small pool of anxiety. But feeling this I knew I was undertaking something worthwhile. It's a satisfying way to fall asleep.

When I woke in the morning, I was over the Pacific seeing the snowy tops of Andean volcanoes poking through the clouds, which then dissipated, revealing the coastal plains of Peru. I was feeling excited to be on the other side of the equator for the first time. We then flew over the coast of Northern Chile while taking in views of the famous Atacama Desert, the driest desert in the world, a land of exposed desiccated dirt with an occasional oasis at the confluence of a few arroyos. Soon we were on approach to the Santiago Airport.

I had no interest in dealing with the big, strange city (Santiago is about the size of Philadelphia, with a third of the country—more than five million people—living there) so I immediately rode a bus from the airport to a terminal named *Pajarito*—"Little bird?" I confirmed in Spanish, thinking it's a strange name for a bus terminal. "Little bird" the blue-uniformed woman behind the information desk answered with a nod, flapping her fingers with her wrists at her shoulders. From Pajarito I bussed to Valparaiso, only a few hours away. I chose it because I've heard of it before. Anyone who has read accounts of tall ships sailing around the horn in the 1800's has read the name of this town. It was the most famous Chilean port, and the destination of most westbound Cape Horners that sailed from Europe to California a century-and-a-half ago. It would be a good spot to rest from the long flight and get used to the new culture.

Studying the landscape on the ride, I found it dryer than expected for the latitude, which is about the same as Santa Barbara's. But the coastal range behind Santa Barbara creates more rainfall than a flatter landscape would get there, and the Planet's driest environment is just north of here, a product of the cold Humboldt Current, so the world out the window made sense. The grasses were dried for the summer, painting the landscape a buffy gold broken only by an occasional six-foot tree, dark-green and acacia-looking.

"One doesn't discover new lands without consenting to lose sight of the shore for a very long time."   —André Gide

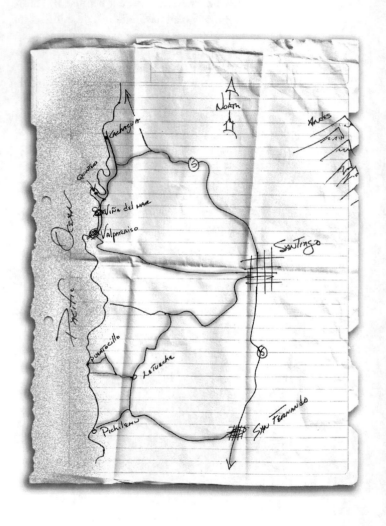

PART 2

COASTAL CHILE

CHAPTER 3

Valparaiso

Filling myself with the gumption I need when I first land in a country and have to find a hotel, I step off the bus at the Valparaiso terminal and immediately am surprised to be targeted by folks inviting me to come to their hostel. I feel an affinity for one, Patricia, a small brunette who is more assertive than the others, but more trustable and genuine also. Her place is the only one on the south side, near the old port, the market and the naval museum, all of which I have an interest in, and it's up on the hillside with a view of the entire bay. She shows me photos. I do rough mental math for the currency conversion (530 pesos to the dollar) and it's only about seven-and-a-half dollars, breakfast included. So I allow her to take me to her hostel in her minivan. We cross town to get there, and she gives me a tour. The town's got an old-world feel to it; small, crazy intersections, lots of taxis, and, of course, old—sooty and gothic in places. When we arrive I meet her husband, Luis, a graphic artist from Argentina with a cigarette and a grey ponytail. He welcomes me like he's been expecting me, like we've been pen pals or something. In his studio a few of his large portraits hang, masterfully airbrushed in a soft realism. He offers his computer at any time to check e-mail.

A steel staircase takes me from the studio up to my room, which is newly built. The room is basic, with unfinished chipboard as a wainscoting below new yellow paint, and it's minimally furnished. The important thing is that it's clean.

After a nap I descend into town. Valparaiso's up and down towns sit on a coastal bench, and the residential areas sprawl up into the *cerros*, a word that I thought to mean "peaks" (I learned the word when I climbed Cerro Cherripo, the highest mountain—an extinct volcano—in Costa Rica twenty years ago), but here it means "hills," or "heights" as we label high parts of towns in English. The choice of words probably had to do with the steepness, I think. A type of steep cable-car, or a diagonal elevator, called an *acensor*, services pedestrian traffic to each of the cerros, which are separated by canyons. This similarity to San Francisco, along with the facts that San Francisco was the next stop for many a tall ship that stopped here, and that the main church in this town is named for Saint Francis, earned Valparaiso the nickname "Pancho," which is the nickname for "Francisco."

The market is a long walk down the hill. It's a brick building that occupies an entire city block. Inside is your typical market scene: the vegetable stands, the booths filled with burlap bags rolled down to show off beans or spices, the white-tiled counters of fish and meat vendors, the circus-colored plastic container vendors, and the specialty shops. It's filled with a variation of the market aroma, less fetid than those of the humid tropics, but with similar layers of green, sea, and spice painted over a canvas of rot on wet concrete. What is different is the rotunda. The core of the building is open to a high, vaulted dome roof, and two staircases rise along the perimeter of the circular space to the second floor like the swirling Chinese symbol for the balance of the *Tao*. I climb one. About twenty-years-worth of grey cobwebs hang in the iron structural work of the dome above me. That's a rough guess. Maybe the place has never been cleaned since it was built, and the cobwebs fall every decade under their own weight. In any case it is not a pleasant site before a meal. I have been suspending judgment of the dirty streets and skinny feral dogs shitting all over the broken sidewalks, but I am forced to admit that this place is not much different from other developing nations, and a wave of disappointment floods my mind. I'm more disappointed in myself than in Chile, and the self-doubt saps my life force. After all my traveling I am still expecting to one day find a Shangri-La; a land where nature has not been raped, where wild lands meet a coast with waves that are fleeting works of liquid sculpture, and the society values art, health, and spiritual development more than wealth and ownership—a place where success is not measured by the numbers in a bank computer.

I know better than to chase paradise. It is I who often points to the fact that we are already in paradise if we can just stop our mental gyrations long enough to realize it. I am the one who speaks of all things being perfect just as they are. But I also say that truth is paradoxical; that one must at the same time accept ones situation *and* work to improve it. Life is short. If there is a better place for me, I want to know about it. "What do I mean by 'better,'" I ask myself, noting that I need to spend time with the question.

Now, climbing these stairs, I accept that it is neither my first nor my last experience of self-doubt, I find a balanced posture, paying attention to the top of my chest and the top of my head. When these parts of me are effortlessly buoyant I feel confident again. I still have a country to see. Who knows what's out there?

Short women hawking their restaurants beset me. The second floor is a mezzanine full of seafood restaurants that all sell exactly the same dishes for the same price. So, in order to attract customers, they all post one woman in an apron and chef's hat to hang out on the stairs and pull you in. Bypassing them, I circumambulate the mezzanine, but cannot find anything special about any one place, so allow the next hawker to pull me into a room with red and white checked tablecloths and filled with the scents of home-cooking. The ladies serve me a plate of fried fish, boiled potatoes and a salad of lettuce and tomato with a draft beer they call "*schop*," as I am told the Germans do. It's uneventful but satisfying, and I like the price at about three dollars, seventy-five cents. My concern about the cost of traveling here is beginning to be relieved.

I didn't know what prices to expect. Copper prices had quadrupled in the last three years, giving Chile, the number-one exporter of the metal, a seventeen-billion-dollar trade surplus. The Chilean peso gained value during this time, rising from 750 to a dollar three years ago, in 2003, to 530 now. So these days things are about a third more expensive for folks visiting from The States. So far, though, still within my tight budget.

While waiting, and then while eating, I think about the ancient Chinese curse: "May you be born in interesting times," a curse I take to mean, "May you be so distracted in your next life that you lose track of yourself and fall behind in your spiritual development." Certainly we have been born in such times. The curse could easily be, "May you be born in an interesting place." All of us born in the United States have this curse to some degree, and it is not only popular culture that is distracting (I pay little attention to it). It's our relative wealth. Here I am, a poor man from The States, but well-off compared to those around me in this room. Right now I feel spoiled. As simple and non-material as my life is, I have come to treasure some amenities that are very difficult to find in other countries. Are they simply distracting me? I wonder what life would be like without them. Could I ever choose to leave them behind? It sounds petty, but imagine living in a country where every restaurant had a cobweb-festooned entrance and served exactly the same food as all others.

After paying the bill, I climb the long hill to the hostel, which has no sign—strange, since Luis is a sign-maker. They're probably not licensed.

Some time after dark I wake from a nap and descend into town to see what's going on. Downtown I wander across one of those totally paved plazas like the Plaza de Mayo in Buenos

Aires, only much smaller. A weird sensation comes from the fascist feeling of the place, combined with the extreme vulnerability of the situation. I'm completely exposed, crossing an open plain of concrete under streetlights. Remembering accounts of the Pinochet era's violence, I monitor the Navy men with rifles guarding the headquarters of their branch of the defense department, an attractive building with a mansard roof, at the head of the plaza. The other side brings relief, and I duck into an acensor, which takes me up to Cerro Alegre, a hip neighborhood being renovated by the young and trendy. It's a poor man's version of the San Francisco Victorian neighborhoods. Wood was scarce when these pint-sized Victorians were built. In fact much of the lumber came from the west coast of the United States on ships returning to Europe after dropping off men who would become the forty-niners and those who would, by hook or by crook, take their money. Patricia tells me that termites arrived on ships from Europe and gave further cause for the abundant use of concrete and steel in the reconstruction these little Victorian houses, usually sided with corrugated metal roofing, which, according to tradition, is often painted in gay colors. I heard that an international aid organization just contributed to the restoration of these historic neighborhoods by providing the owners with paint. Then the owners sold the paint at flea markets to make ends meet.

After a hunt for something interesting, I come across a hip place called "Café Vinilo," and take a place at the bar. It's full of young people and smoke. Scratchy old American jazz plays on an antique turntable—the reason for the name, "Vinyl Café." It's kind of a Beat scene, but a bit too well-lit.

Just a week ago I realized that I'm a beatnik. Well, maybe I should drop the "nik." I'm Beat, regardless of the fact that I missed the Beat era.

I was born in the heart the Beat era, in a sleepy beach town on the tip of a barrier island in southern New Jersey. Miles Davis recorded his perennially hip masterpiece "Kind of Blue" when I was speaking my first words, but no one on that sleepy sand bar knew about this music. It wasn't on their AM radios. They were enjoying the post-war prosperity. Progress was conceived of in terms of a new car, or renovations to the house of a growing family, not in terms of new literary devices, or a rethinking of aesthetics. Wives, all mothers, didn't hold jobs. No one on the island criticized that life, questioned it, or sought anything different. Life was good.

The closest I came to the beatniks was watching Maynard G. Krebs in the Dobie Gillis show on the family black and white TV.

I had little exposure to the Beat Generation, even in college. Sure, I read Kerouac, but for pleasure, not to learn about the Beat culture.

Realizing I'm Beat was a bit of a shock. I don't know how this happened. I've just been living my life, pursuing my interests, following E.E. Cummings' advice. He wrote, "To be nobody-but-yourself—in a world which is doing its best, night and day, to make you everybody else—means to fight the hardest battle which any human being can fight; and never stop fighting." And then concluded, "Does this sound dismal? It isn't. It's the most wonderful life on earth. Or so I feel."

The realization came when I happened upon a list that Allen Ginsberg had made, characterizing the Beat Generation. Several of his items described me; ecological consciousness, questioning of authority—especially of the military-industrial-congressional complex, an interest in Zen, and a desire to liberate the world from censorship, which I would simplify to be a quest for truth. I place a high priority on the arts and aesthetics, but lack interest in pop culture and the pursuit of wealth. I have been seeking spiritual truth since I began drinking beer—about the time I began shaving. I quit shaving at nineteen.

"Jesus, I'm a beatnik," I've been thinking. It's not an unpleasant thought, I just didn't know they, uh, we, were still around. "Where are the rest of us?" Then I realized that we—assuming there are others—don't have an appearance. How could we if we are all "Nobody but ourselves?" We're invisible. I think of Maynard. These days it's the fad for CEO's to sport a goatee. It's no longer Beat. Neither are berets or sweatshirts with cut-off sleeves. Everyone wears sandals. I'm no Maynard, well, maybe a little, but you wouldn't know it to look at me. I'm no slouch. But neither was Miles. Beat doesn't mean lazy.

Twenty years ago the insight came that my personality was dominated by two aspects that could be caricatured as "the Rasta" and "the drill sergeant." Maybe Miles had a similar dichotomy, intensely hard-working, yet laid-back. The drill sergeant in me demands a hard-hitting physicality. Combine this with my love of this planet and my quest for spiritual truth, and you get wilderness traveler, martial artist. After completing my education as a geographer, I came west as young man seeking adventure and the beauty of Nature's wonders. My addiction to the ocean kept me on the coast, from Alaska to Southern California, where I found what I sought to be so abundant that I never left.

I remember the intense agony when the sergeant forced my young self to do things that I wanted to do, but which scared me. When I was still a teenager I forced myself into the Appalachians on solo multi-day trips when none of my hometown friends, mostly surfers like me, had ever even been on a hike. As I got used to my little adventures, I'd push myself farther—eventually into Alaska bear country, up on high icefields, and into the wilderness or big surf of foreign countries. That agony never really left, as the fear hasn't, but I've gotten used to dealing with these emotions when I push myself, and it has become a fulfilling way of life—even to deal with the fear and insecurity of remaining minimally self-employed as I do.

The Rasta is laid-back but not lackadaisical. I'm talking about a Rastaman *archetype*, kind of a poor and simple, easygoing, noble savage in a groove. Don't mix me up with a ganja-smoking, bible-quoting worshiper of Haile Selassie. The archetype I feel allows me to stand tall and walk with confidence in my Beat ways, the Rasta mantra *irie* being short for "I rule internally." Cummings would agree. The Rasta chant "Resistance" is a reply to the "World which is doing its best, night and day, to make you everybody else." The Rasta in me values relaxation, not as defined by American culture, but as a psycho-physical state of confident calmness, and this dovetails with the martial path. The Rasta is more of a Beat-*nik*, but the drill sergeant has a Beat dimension as well. You might say I'm looking for a southern, twenty-first century version of a Beat generation that I might thrive in. That is the "better" that I'm looking for. I realize that what I want is relief from "the world which is doing its best, night and day, to make you everybody else." I am tired of fighting "the hardest battle which any human being can fight; and never stop fighting." In the nutshell, what I seek is kindred spirits.

I don't know if the young people around me in Cafe Virilio are Beat. The music's old and scratchy and lacking soul—it's W.C. Handy—and I don't think anyone but me is really listening. I wouldn't be either if I had someone to talk to. This might be a hip hangout, but the crowd's here to socialize, not dig jazz. I have a pork chop on risotto made red with beets, garnished with chopped arugula, and accompanied by a glass of syrah. It *is* hip. I talk a bit with the blonde waitress, but the conversation is limited by my poor Spanish. I'm surprised how little I understand. Then I wander back to the hostel, taking the long way, in that mood I get in when I first enter a country—kind of a cross between "What the hell am I doing here?" and "I wonder what adventures await me?" It's a blend of alienation and doubt with curiosity and excitement.

The barking dogs, ever-present outside windows of cheap Latin-American urban hotels, don't keep me from sleeping. The next morning Patricia prepares an egg breakfast for me after asking how I like everything cooked. At the table I talk with Patricia and one of her guests, a German film-maker who is working on a documentary about this town. Then I search for the Naval and Maritime Museum, trying to take a direct route through the labyrinth at the edge of the cerros and following directions from people on the street, whom I only partly understand. I am beginning to realize that my traveler's Spanish will not allow me to understand Chileans unless they make an effort on my behalf. Few do. My last request goes to an old man with his dog at the black iron gate to his home. He gives me detailed instructions, but he has no teeth. All I understand is "Go down at the end of the dirt road." We're in a city of paved streets, so I repeat, "At the end of the dirt road?" He says yes. I thank him and take off the way his finger pointed, looking for another person to ask, but after a couple blocks, sure enough, I come to a dirt road, and at its dead end is a concrete stairway down to another street that takes me to the museum.

The Navy guards at the entrance are very kind and invite me in at no charge. It may be because today is a holiday. It's the feast of the Immaculate Conception, a vague Catholic holiday, which is often misinterpreted as honoring the belief that Jesus was conceived inside a virgin. It actually honors the belief that Mary was born without original sin, and this date, December eighth, was chosen because it is nine months before her birthday; the day of her immaculate conception. The idea that she had a conception free from original sin was first proposed about 500 years ago, but in 1854 a pope made it official dogma. Chileans may have made it a holiday then, or almost a century later when the dogma was consecrated.

Anyway, the guards are so nice that they are sweet, with a genuine childlike enthusiasm because I have come to visit. I think of the guards at the plaza last night. Maybe they were just as amiable, just doing their job. An old image reforms in my mind: that of a sixteen-year-old boy in combat gear, with an automatic assault weapon, guarding a corner by a park in Antigua, Guatemala. It was sunset, and the town was out for a stroll. At one moment I looked across the street and saw a small, young, well-groomed, Catholic Indian family standing beside the guard, waiting to cross. They were the epitome of innocence; the two doll-like children holding helium balloons by the string, one pink the other lavender. Guatemala is home to some of the most heinous atrocities I have ever heard of—acts so evil, so dark, I refused to speak of them for years. These were committed by the military (U.S. trained and funded) against those seeking freedom and human rights, by guys in that same uniform, and I wondered if that sixteen-year-old kid was capable of such wickedness, or was he just as innocent as the family beside him.

Chile is impressing me as a land of kind people with a similar innocent quality, so I wonder where Pinochet and his henchmen came from. Of course, they were enabled by Kissinger and the CIA, but they were Chilean, and they tortured and killed thousands of Chileans. Strange, this juxtaposition of the extremes of light and dark in one culture. When I saw it in Haiti I attributed it to Vodoun, a religion that seemed to be like a coin with two sides. A person could go either way and still be religious. I wonder if Pinochet and his supporters had been religious.

I enter a new addition to the old naval headquarters, now the museum. It's made of brick and has four tall stained glass windows, each in tribute to an important contributor to navigation. I can't remember which ones, maybe Galileo or Copernicus, Columbus, Magellan or Vespucci. The only one I remember is the last one: Neil Armstrong. There he was, his bust, in his astronaut suit, illuminated in stained glass with the colors of church organ music.

Continuing through the museum I see the little swords and uniforms of the little men who were naval heroes in little wars I never heard of: "The War of the Pacific" apparently was a dispute with Peru in which the Chilean Navy kicked butt, which accounts for why artifacts from the fight make up the bulk of this museum's holdings (cannonballs, pistols, paintings of naval battles, et cetera, et cetera, et cetera). My guess is that there is no such museum in Peru.

Finally I find a room dedicated to the Cape Horners, the reason I came to the museum—the "Maritime" part—but there's not much in it. It's disappointing. Some old salts must have settled here. Some ships must have been retired on this waterfront, strange that there is no obvious honor to the masters of the sea who regularly rounded the Horn, notorious for foul weather in your face. But there is one photo of this harbor filled with tall ships at anchor, and it sets my imagination off.

I can almost see the hustling, bustling waterfront of a century ago as I amble down a steep winding street with views of the harbor on my way to find a restaurant I read about in a guide book. Indeed the place has an excellent seafood stew with fish, crab, mussels and clams. I can't know, at this moment, that it will be the best seafood I will have in any restaurant for my entire trip. The waitress looks like my Hungarian grandmother when she was young. I try to tell her that, but I don't think I conveyed the part about "when she was young" very well, and I get a funny look. She avoids me after that.

Cruising the town, I find little of interest. It's a bit run-down and dirty. Not what I was hoping to find. After all, the cities name is short for "paradise valley." The architecture reveals that it was once a classy town, but the one-two combo of the invention of synthetic nitrates, which eliminated the need for Chile's natural supply (much of which was apparently the motivation for the War of the Pacific, that is to say, Chile stole the nitrate rich lands from Peru), and the completion of the Panama Canal brought this place to the canvas. Still, I enjoy imagining what it must have been like in the 1800's when so many people would stop here to recover from their round-the-horn ordeal. When I cross streets leading to the sea, a couple blocks away, I fill my view of empty water with imaginary schooners, clippers, barks and barquentines at anchor with their canvas furled to the yardarms.

My ignorance about nitrates is so extensive, that, once back at the hostel, I use Luis's computer to educate myself. It turns out that the commonly used term, "nitrates" refers to a white powdery salt the Chileans call *caliche*, actually sodium nitrate, a.k.a.: saltpeter, which is mined up in the Atacama Desert. Chile produces 69% of the world's supply. As "saltpeter," we know it as an old-time dietary supplement that lowered the libido of men on sailing ships and in infantries, and as an ingredient of gunpowder. As "sodium nitrate," we know it as a food preservative used in sausages and other cured meats, which I love, but limit in my diet because it is a known carcinogen. Dr. Johanna Budwig, the famous German biochemist, claims that, once ingested, nitrates (as well as heated oils) are responsible for the production of oxydase, which induces cancer as well as many other maladies. Sodium Nitrate is also used as a fertilizer, and studies show that Chilean farmers who are exposed to it have significantly higher rates of cancer than others.

That night I'm relaxing on the third floor of the hostel where a common room has great views. I look up from my Spanish verb book to see Aconcagua, the tallest mountain in the western hemisphere, in fact, the tallest mountain outside of Asia, looming high in the sky with an apricot alpineglow. I'm on the edge of the continent looking at the great divide. I'm on the western boundary, looking at the eastern boundary of this nation. I'm at sea level looking at a peak that is 6959 meters (or 22,825 ft.) tall. It is over a hundred and fifty kilometers, almost a hundred miles, away. No mountain below it is visible, and it floats in the heavens like a rising moon.

It is the individual's task to differentiate himself from all the others and stand on his own feet. All collective identities . . . interfere with the fulfillment of this task. Such collective identities are crutches for the lame, shields for the timid, beds for the lazy, nurseries for the irresponsible. . . .   —*CG Jung*

CHAPTER 4

Ventana

Patricia and Luis were always making sure things were going well for me. They were genuinely concerned with my comfort, and I felt so cared-for by them that it was hard to leave. It seemed like I was abandoning them, but they were happy to see me on my way to enjoy their country. Patricia gave me a ride down the hill on her way to run some errands.

I caught a bus north.

Before I left California, an old buddy from Alaska, Chile Willie, who was born and raised down here, passed through town and we met at a bar. I asked him for travel tips. He didn't have any. He only gave me a rough map of the location of his sixty acres where I am welcome to camp, on the shores of Lago Todos Santos in the Lake District. He also gave me the name of a high school friend, whose gender he reiterated to be feminine. Her name is Jose—"That's JOse, not JoSE", he instructed—she lives near the Cachagua Golf Club about fifty miles north of Viña del Mar. This information, and nothing more, he wrote on the back of a paper coaster with the logo of the beer he was drinking, a local Russian imperial stout, "Old Rasputin," which Willie pronounces, "Ras-puTEEN."

Since my intention is to spend my time south of here, I thought I'd go visit Jose first. The bus passed through the large beach resort town of Viña del Mar. A few years ago an aikido teacher who had visited Chile told me he thought Viña del Mar would be a perfect place for me to teach. He said there are five universities and no dojo. As I passed through the town, looking out the window at it for the first time, I wondered if he was right, thought about what I had experienced of Chile so far, and cringed at the size of the city sprawling before me.

The bus drops me in a little industrial port called Quintero where my guidebook says there's a cheap hotel. The "Monaco" is a flophouse that was probably once a nice place judging by its French Mediterranean architecture. Today young guys are giving it a fresh coat of red and white paint. It's on the waterfront of this windswept little town. I check in, drop my pack in a room and immediately split, asking directions for a bus to Cachagua. First I'm instructed to wait on the corner, one will come soon, but then someone tells me it won't come for an hour, so I hop in a *colectivo*—a taxi that carries four, and splits the fare four ways. The driver takes five of us, four fat ladies, and me, to Ventana, but drops me at the *cruz*—the turnoff—for Cachagua. I hitchhike with no luck until a bus comes, and flag it down. We cross land that feels like the agricultural flats between Oxnard and Point Mugu, which occupy roughly the same latitude in Southern California. When we come to some hills, the driver drops me at the next cruz, and I stick my thumb out again. A courier in a tiny red truck on a delivery run stops. We drive a small road high on west-facing slopes, with great views over the Pacific. Eventually he stops at an unsigned dirt road that he thinks leads to the golf club. It doesn't seem possible, but I hike down the road, and at the end there actually *is* a golf club. At the gatehouse I ask for Jose, and, after some deliberation, the guards tell me to take another dirt road and make a right at the stone gate. After the gate I wander up a driveway passing houses surrounded by red roses, purple bougainvillea and other ornamental flowering shrubs looking for someone to ask, and I see a thin woman with sun-bleached hair working behind a bamboo fence. I excuse myself and ask for Jose.

It's she. We have a good laugh and become friends in a few minutes. It's early afternoon now, so her maid covers the dining room
table with plates of fresh vegetables and a few hot dishes, and we
have a long lunch, the main meal of a Chilean day, talking mostly
about Alaska and her friend Willie. Before I leave the table she
invites me to stay with her. She has an empty room, in the loft of
this house that she built, which resembles a Southern California
hippie-built beach-house from the sixties, poorly, but artfully constructed. Next, I'm retracing my steps to the Hotel Monaco.

The trip is quicker now that I know my way. I reach it in
an hour, tell the girl there I don't need the room, and ask for some
of my money back since I didn't use anything. This, of course, is
an unusual request, and it creates a big stir with the young employees going to bat for me, and the older owners holding out. In
the end they refund 40% and I don't complain. Money in hand,
I dig for my wallet, but it's not in my pocket, or in the other
pocket, or in my day pack, or anywhere else. My head is buzzing,
wondering what happened, and then it hits me: my last ride to the
hotel was in a colectivo. I was the last passenger to get out. As I
opened my wallet for the four hundred-peso fare, I realized I had
that much in coins jingling in my pocket, and decided to lighten
my load. I'm too tall for the back seat, so my knees were up, and I
couldn't get my hand deep enough in my pocket to get the coins.
All I was getting was bus tickets. So I put my wallet down and
used my other hand to pull the pocket open while leaning my
knees to the side. All the while the driver was waiting and watching in the rear view mirror as I was contorting and fidgeting in his
back seat. I am still getting over the culture shock and trying not
to do the stupid things that we travelers do when we are new to a
country, and I found myself doing a stupid thing, so I hurried to
pay and get out, and in my rush I did an even stupider thing: I left
my wallet on the seat with $400, credit card and bank card, drivers
license, et cetera.

I tell the young folks that I have a big problem. I left my

wallet (I don't know the word for wallet, so I say, "My thing with my money and credit card" while forming a rectangle with my fingers) in the back seat of the colectivo. Alex, one of the painters, is genuinely concerned and offers to take me to the police station.

On the way he asks me if I can describe the driver. I tell him no, but I could probably recognize him if I saw him. He asks what the car looked like. I tell him all I remember is that it was yellow. Then he asks me what color it was—not a good sign. I'm wondering how well he understands me when we walk up to a bunch of yellow colectivos parked in a lot. I think I recognize the driver, the fat guy with the big head, as we approach. I say hello to him, but he ignores me and listens to Alex instead. I figure I must be wrong. The guy sends us off with the numbers that are on the sides of the colectivos that make the trip to Ventana, and as we are walking away he asks when it happened. I tell him it was about fifteen minutes ago and he asks where. "Hotel Monaco." He says, "I just dropped a guy off there, was that you?" and I reply that I thought I recognized him, and look in the back seat when he opens the door to see my wallet sitting there. Someone is watching out for me.

CHAPTER 5

Cachagua

I've been at Jose's house for a few days. She is a kind woman and has made me feel like I belong. My first day here was a sunny Sunday, so we went to the beach, which is only a couple of sandy blocks away. It's a wide, white sand beach bracketed by hills. The valley that runs inland from the sands is one I could live in, with flat agricultural land between chaparral-covered ridges. It could be a secret valley between Carpinteria and Montecito in Southern California. Jose's English is better than my Spanish, so that is the language we use. The subject of the upcoming Chilean presidential election gets me started on politics, and I don't let up until she asks to change the subject an hour later. I realize that my embarrassment about George W. Bush representing America to the world has created a subconscious need for me to explain. I explained our crazy voting system:

The fact that we need to register to vote a month before the elections, which, in this computer age, can be done in a few minutes.

The fact that we are not required to vote, and that less than half of us do. Those who neglect to vote usually do so because they don't want either of the two main candidates, and know that a third has a snowball's chance in hell of getting elected. In 2004, only 35% of eligible voters participated, which means about 17% of the country voted for Bush. Of 172 countries surveyed, the

United States ranks 139 in the percent of those eligible who actually vote.

That we have to vote on Tuesday, a work day, unlike most countries who vote on weekends or create a voting holiday, so it is intentionally more difficult for working people to make it to the polls.

That the two main parties, not the government, control the debates, and they don't allow a third party entry (without jumping through very high hoops).

That the candidates run campaigns funded by contributions which are mostly made by large corporations who expect to be benefited in some way if their candidate wins (and for this reason many contribute to both), so a people's candidate cannot compete.

That we do not count the popular vote of the nation, nor the popular vote of each state, but the "electoral" vote of state boards, or "colleges," the number of which is determined by the state's population. That this arcane system was devised by southern slave-holders in order to give their vote more weight due to the population of slaves who could not vote, but were counted as "population" (a black man was three-fifths of a person, as I remember) which earned electoral votes. This makes it possible to win the popular vote and lose the electoral vote.

That we have no runoff, so the candidate with the highest number of votes takes power, regardless of what percentage of the people voted for him and against him.

And, of course, that the recent elections have been manipulated by the Republican Party. In 2000 it was done in Florida by removing Democrats from the registration and by not counting Democrat's vote cards that did not have holes completely punched. I explain what a "hanging chad" is, and how no one ever heard of it before, how the issue was later used to pave the way for electronic voting machines to be used in 2004, and that the voting machine and the vote counting companies were owned by right-wing Republicans. In order to win the last election a candidate needed to win the swing state of Ohio to win the close race, but Bush didn't campaign much in that state. By no coincidence, that state had the most problems with the election. In a few towns where Bush won in an upset, they recorded thousands more votes than they had registered voters. Two towns in the same county had exactly the same number of extra votes. Famously accurate exit polls matched the vote in most states, but in a few, like Ohio and Florida, pollsters and statisticians say the exit polls were so far off that it is virtually impossible, and in every case when polls did not match actual results, the results were always skewed to Bush. Of course it is no coincidence that the man in charge of Ohio elections is an appointed, not elected, right-wing Republican who had publicly promised to deliver the vote to Bush. In his state, 3.6 million votes went uncounted. Florida's governor is George Bush's brother, I remind her, but most Latin Americans know this because Miami is usually their port-o-call.

She never heard any of this and asks how they get away with it. I explained that most Americans never heard of it either. That the media outlets are often times owned by or depend upon larger corporations for advertising. That they no longer ask "hard questions" of the government, or keep asking them until they are answered. I tell her that my guess is that 15% or 20% of Americans know what I've told her.

I feel vindicated, though the initial accusation—that I come from a society that elected George W. Bush—never existed outside of my mind. Jose is non-political for the most part. She votes because she has to, as all Chileans are required to do by law. I never cared much about politics either, but late in my martial arts training I realized that it was my responsibility to act toward the prevention of suffering. So I began to educate myself so that I could help to educate others. The people of the United States are, for the most part, good people, I tell her, and if they knew what was happening they would not allow it, but I'm not sure of that.

I stop talking and watch some of the pretty women on the beach. Chilean society is highly segmented, and I have left the common people's world for the land of the upper class. It feels like California. The next town to the north is the hot spot for wealthy Santiagans to own a "beach house," and the daughters are some of the finest looking women on the planet. One walks up and lies down near us. I swear it's the god-damned girl from Ipanema. She's about twenty years old. Probably of pure Spanish blood, a brunette with blue-green eyes and a bump on the middle of her otherwise perfect nose. No, the bump *makes* it perfect, as is her lean body. My eyes wander to the inch of air between her black bikini bottom and her flat belly in the span lifted by her hipbones, and I laugh to myself.

At the age of thirteen I realized that our human bodies are as grotesque as they are beautiful. I was taking a short nap after school, lying across my bed in the late afternoon sun with my face and arm off the bed, my hand on the floor, palm down. I woke disoriented in the way that I have only been from afternoon sleep. I opened my eyes to see my hand as it truly is. That is to say, not with human eyes. I saw the form of a manipulating extremity of a delicate-skinned creature. Below that translucent epidermis, blue ducts made their way randomly up from the digits, carrying life-blood. Cable-like tissues connected the digits to the area of a large joint that allowed the entire appendage to articulate. Where each digit hinged, at three different locations along its length, the digit widened slightly, and the skin there was baggy and wrinkled. Between each of these nodes about ten or fifteen tiny hairs stood, growing from otherwise naked skin. At the tip of each digit was a vestigial claw, with no apparent purpose; an underdeveloped part of a former beast of the wilderness, evolved.

My hand was a paw, or like the foot of a newborn ostrich, only with the central of the three toes divided into three more.

I hurried to the bathroom mirror but I was unable to

break through the genetic and social conditioning that causes us to recognize the human face. Maybe I was too awake by then.

The human form can be so stunningly gorgeous, and can arouse such intense sexual desire, but because of this experience I know that it is all a result of programming—that there is no intrinsic beauty to the human form, that my appreciation is a result of genes that have found a way to further themselves. And so, when I can remember this, I laugh. In actuality the human form before me, whose beauty evokes awe, is as grotesque as the alien of some forty-year-old science fiction movie.

Next, a couple comes walking down the beach; a tall young blonde female with synthetically enhanced mammary glands holding the hand of a short plump older male with a bald pate and a roll of dried brown leaves in his mouth, smoldering at the end. In my current state of mind this strikes my funny-bone. I remember a study of thirty-seven different cultures conducted on every inhabited continent as well as a few islands. The researcher found that, across the globe, wealth was of prime importance to women seeking a mate. Youth and beauty were most important to men. This couple is a melodramatic illustration of our genetic program at work, and the fact is that if my Spanish were better, and if my bank account had a few more zeros before its decimal point, I might be sitting beside the girl from Ipanema right now. It's all a bit ridiculous, but it seems to be what makes the world go 'round, mainly because people identify the desires that result from the presence of certain hormones to be their own personal desires, originating in their "person" that they believe really exists. So men make money because they know women want it, and women make themselves look young and beautiful so they are wanted by men—all over the planet.

I wonder about my desire to travel and see the beauty of Nature. Maybe it's the same; this planet has no intrinsic beauty, we are simply programmed to love it. Or, it could be that we are the organ creation uses to appreciate itself. Well, then, why are we destroying it? I guess our ability to enjoy the beauty of nature can be eclipsed by myopic attention to our desires. An ancient East Indian sect categorizes them into the desires for survival, sex and power. I've found that, if taken as generalities, these three cover all the motivations behind the human actions that cause suffering worldwide.

At night Jose, whose name, I learned, is short for "Maria Jose," like our "Mary Jo," has a barbecue party. She cooks a wonderful paella in a big steel pan made for that purpose set on the fire in a tall brick pit, and we drink lots of fine Chilean cabernet. As they arrive, her friends greet me, the men with sincere handshakes, the women with the customary cheek-to-cheek air kisses. I like her friends. Icha, a baldling but fit man in his fifties, was one of the first surfers in Chile. We exchange some surf stories. He is used to speaking with American and Australian surfers, so we accommodate the voids in each other's language skills and communicate fairly well. Marinela is a tiny attractive woman, half Polynesian, half Spanish, from Rapa Nui, Easter Island. She lived in Virginia for a while when she was young; when her mother moved there with an American who came to the island while working for NASA. She has traveled a bit, spending a few years in Bali, and she speaks English fairly well. Charly is a wiry guy who speaks fluent English in rapid busts of words between pauses when his brain seems to be reloading. His parents were from England. He is fascinated with martial arts, but never immersed himself in training with a teacher. He practices tai chi.

It's difficult for me to understand Chilean Spanish. It's a different language than what I am used to in Central America. I've never been to Cuba, but listening to Cuban Music I hear them drop s's and d's and anything else that requires an effort to pronounce, and that is what I hear tonight. I tell them how hard they are to understand and they are almost proud about how badly Chileans speak Spanish, which they call "Castillano." They boast that Chileans are known for "swallowing" their words. *Estoy* becomes "toy." *Pescado* becomes "pecao." *Los Estados Unidos* becomes "lo Tao Unio."

Attaching the FM transmitter to my iPod, I play reggae for them on Jose's receiver. Marinela asks if they are singing in English. She can't understand a word. Laughing, I reply that I think Chilean Spanish is like Jamaican English.

CHAPTER 6

Still in Cachagua

I'm still staying at Jose's. I can easily be out of her way by hanging out up in the attic bedroom, where machine-rounded log rafters run from the edge of the floor to the peak, supporting 1x6 tongue-and-groove planking under a funky corrugated steel roof that's nailed to the t&g with sixteen-penny nails so that nail points, an inch long, stick trough all over the low ceiling. Below is a cluster of four bedrooms behind a large, slate-floored indoor patio that is walled by salvaged windows in wooden frames. This is her living and dining area. It's decorated with, among many interesting artifacts, a few Buddhist and Hindu icons. I think it's funny when people reject their Christian upbringing by substituting these exotic statues for the ones we grew up with. Jose is thrilled with her large new Quan Yin. She tells me she's the goddess of protection. I correct her. She's the goddess of compassion.

A few days ago I took Icha's binoculars down the beach to an island where Humboldt penguins nest, and had a blast. The island is only a couple hundred feet offshore. I parked myself on the rocks by the channel and found them right away. "Fucking penguins!" I blurted out; amazed to be seeing what I thought was an Antarctic bird here in a Southern California environment. They held my eyes for an hour.

Certainly they are the least bird-like of all birds, and must be the most human-like, resembling little people as they congregate. At one time my binoculars found a crowd gathered with their backs to me. In front of them, up on a higher rock, was a single bird facing me. It appeared to be giving a speech.

One clan decided to hit the water. That meant they had to descend a steep rock slope, and they proceeded slowly, following a crack where they could get a grip with their clawed feet. The rock was slippery though, and one bird fell, sliding all the way to the water about eight feet below. What amazed me was the panic that that bird went through as it was separated from the group. They were all headed to the water anyway, but rather than relax and wait for the others, this fallen bird scrambled with severe effort to get itself up into a barnacled area when a swell lifted him, so he could climb back to rejoin the others who hadn't made a whole lot of headway in the mean time—mostly because they had stopped to watch him thrash around. Once they got close to the water, they began diving in and were transformed from stiff, slow and clumsily waddling land animals to fast and graceful sea creatures. They looked like a school of joyous dolphins as they broke the surface together in flying arcs.

Out on those rocks, oyster catchers, some exactly like the black ones in California and another species, the white-bellied austral oystercatcher, hunted for mollusks and crustaceans. The calls were exactly the same, and I remembered that last spring while building a cabin on a remote island in Alaska I heard that call and looked up from my work as a flock of a dozen flew by. Offshore, Chilean pelicans dove for fish. This is a species similar to the brown pelican I know, but more beautiful, with a black neck. On the way back to the house I cross dunes and surprise a pair of southern lapwings, a noisy relative of plovers, known here by the Indian name, *queltehue*. Their screech is part of the Chilean rural landscape.

Jose's terrier, named *Huinka*—the name for a "white man" in the indigenous Mapuche language, like the Mexican *gringo*, and the Hawaiian *haole*—has taken a liking to me. Maybe she senses that I like her. I like these kinds of little spunky, hard-bodied and bouncy dogs. I have had a few of them as friends in the past; a white Scotty named "Fogbank" in Alaska, and a Chihuahua named "Chili" in Oregon. Anyway, Huinka barks at anyone who comes to the house, but never barks at me, so Jose is at further ease with being my hostess, as if I am long-lost family.

My friends here are so welcoming that they are thinking up projects for me to do so that I will stay. While visiting Jose's landscape business partners, Alejandra and Icha, as we sat sipping fine *reserva* wine before dinner, and snacking on arugula leaves from a bowl, they mentioned that they needed a sign for their landscaping business. So I painted one. When I recommended that Jose learn to compost the yard waste she generates in her business, she was enthusiastic and asked me to build two bins. Luckily a new lumberyard had opened in the area and had lots of pallets available, which made the job quick and easy, after I overcame the objections of her maid, Mari, who protested that the compost would attract "*moka*" (*moscas*, flies). I've built many compost bins in my travels over the years, and taught their new owners how to replenish the soil. I believe this is essential knowledge. At current rates, Earth's agricultural soils will be depleted in forty years. Think about that—about what that means for the nutrition of a growing population—and what is being done about it? I think everyone who has a garden should make compost. Actually, I think everyone should contribute to a compost bin, whether they have a garden or not. For agriculture to be sustainable, the soil must have a minimum of four to 6% organic matter.

I even piss on the compost pile. If a year's worth of one person's urine is dehydrated, it will make a cubic foot of minerals, which are precious for a farmed garden.

Jose, my gracious hostess, made it easy to pass twelve days in Cachagua. Life was a blur of parties, barbecues, and beach gatherings where I enjoyed meeting the locals of this surfside getaway for Santiagans. Of course, all the while I imagined what it would be like to live here, but I remained in receptive mode, taking in all the information I could; observing, keenly—trying to keep in mind that what I am experiencing is the annual blossoming of a village that remains relatively dormant for ten months of the year.

Marinela and I got involved in a love affair that would have been real easy to hang with. She's a sweet and loving woman. I am attracted to dark women like her, but I'm six-foot-two, and she stands only five feet tall. My taste is for slender women, and Marinela is not, but her Polynesian genes allow her to carry a thin, even layer of subcutaneous fat beautifully. It makes her soft tanned skin even softer. I enjoy well-educated women. She isn't, but she has a certain kind of intelligence that is much better. She puts things in proper perspective, paying attention to what's really important in life, and not getting caught up in the rest. Wealth is not high on the list of attributes she seeks in a man. I don't know if I've ever met a more compatible woman.

Her dark amber eyes are the color of mango blossom honey. Her smile, white as the flesh of a coconut. Below her long brown hair she has flowering vines tattooed across her hips, just above her bikini line. The tattooed silhouette of a frigate bird, a wanderer of tropical seas, flies on her right ankle

The winner of an intertribal race decides the king of her island every spring. Each tribe's best athlete runs down from the top of a volcano to the sea, then swims out to a little island where the frigates nest. The tribe whose man nabs the first frigate egg of the year is the tribe whose leader becomes king. No lost votes, no stolen ones, no need for a paper trail.

Marinela has an enduring memory of camping on such an island where frigates flew so close to her as she slept in the open that she could feel the wind off their wings.

She grew up in many places. After Rapa Nui; Zapallar, Santiago, and then Virginia. But all her stories of childhood have a wild theme. Not wild as it's used these days to denote a kid who is noisy, disobedient, and generally beyond control, but wild in the true sense of the word—spending all her time in nature.

She tells stories of being a kid on the island and running into the bushes when she heard a certain kind of clucking that told her a hen had laid an egg. She'd go eat it. She'd collect snails, and then find a tin can and boil them over a fire of twigs. While listening to her, I'm reminded of the many times I have seen kids in the third world doing the same kinds of things. Most of the world's kids' play includes the fun of finding food. I first realized this while working as a deck-hand on a sailing yacht in the Caribbean. We were anchored in English Harbor, Antigua, doing some maintenance. I saw skinny kids fishing off the 300-year-old stone quay. I fished when I was a kid too, but when I caught a fish, I'd bring it home for my mom to clean and cook. When these kids caught a tiny fish they'd break into a dance of excitement and immediately gather twigs to cook it.

When Marinela lived in the Virginia suburbs of D.C., she spent all her time in the woods around a military base. She was fascinated with the forest. Her home, Rapa Nui, was once forested, but I hear that now there is not a single tree, and Santiago is too dry for a forest.

Marinela is the only woman I've ever met who loves to walk right into a cold ocean and dive in. I am especially impressed given her tropical origin and *yin* body type.

She loves the wildness in me as much as I love it in her, and she wants me to have my freedom, instead of wanting to tame it like so many women have tried to do in the past. When we got involved as lovers, it was after we both expressed our hesitation, for fear of hurting the other. I told her I was going to leave, and she told me that she doesn't have room for a relationship in her life. As a single mother, she knows she would tie me down, so she tells me that she can't get too involved in a relationship because she doesn't have time for it, between caring for her kids and hustling to earn a living as an artist and boutique owner. She set me free before our first kiss.

She's a treasure.

I had to see the Chilean coast, and couldn't miss the Andes while in the neighborhood, so I tore myself away, thanking her for letting me leave without making a fuss, while all the others were trying to get me to stay.

She gave me a ride to Santiago. On the way she told me how lucky I was to meet Jose. I agreed, and told her I thought that there may be no such thing as luck. I recounted the story about the astrocartographer and the Vedic gem, and added that I met Jose on December ninth, the day that began the best time for me to be in Chile. She told me about a healing session she had had while living in Bali in which she was covered with rocks, crystals and gems. She said she began shivering from the energy that was running through her and that the shivering kept amplifying until she was shaking so much she got scared and sat up, knocking all the stones off of her.

Marinela dropped me off at a bus terminal in Santiago. There I boarded a late-afternoon bus that arrived just after a blazing sunset in a little pueblo named Litueche. I'll travel south, reconnoitering some of the best surf spots as a way of seeing coastal Chile, then head into the Andes. I'll just let myself travel, following my interests, alert for opportunity, but not analyzing places or situations, not trying to pry an opening for myself. My approach is more intuitional; I'll take in the gestalt during this entire scouting trip, and make conclusions once I've completed my travels. My first destination is a remote left point break named Puertocillo.

"The poor farmer makes weeds, the mediocre farmer makes crops, the skilled farmer makes soil."
                                                                  —Zen saying

CHAPTER 7

Puertocillo

Missing Marinela, I lie on a blue-green nylon satiny bedspread in a little room with walls almost the same color—the color of some glacial lakes in the Canadian Rockies. My bed sits above the blaring TV at the ceiling of the first floor dining room.

Cachagua was so much like California that the experience of culture shock returns upon re-entering the real Chile. After our arrival, the bus driver showed me the only hosteleria in town, where I was received with welcome. A girl showed me to this room, and when she left, I asked for the key. She returned ten minutes later to tell me it was lost. There was a padlock already on the hasp of the door, so I couldn't use my own. When my face indicated that I thought it was a ridiculous situation, and she said something like "Hey, it costs five dollars, what do you want?" Okay, I told myself, just be careful not to leave anything valuable in the room. Chile is said to have less crime than the United States, but when I'm new to a country I err on the side of caution until I understand what crimes to expect. An acquaintance of mine got robbed on a Chilean bus when the old man sitting next to him gave him a coke spiked with a mickey. He woke up a day later under a tree with his empty wallet on his chest and a headache like an ice pick in his temple.

When I open the armoire there are someone's clothes

in it, boots and all. So I go downstairs and tell the lady in the kitchen who seems to be the boss. She talks to a guy about it and then tells me it's okay. "What do you mean, it's okay?" I'm confused. She reassures me, "There's no problem." "Alright," I think. "What do I expect for five bucks (including breakfast)?" So I inventory my valuables using the four fingers of my right hand—a checklist habit I have already developed: camera, wallet, passport and iPod are loaded into my lumbar pack, and taken with me to the dining room, where a waitress tells me what's cooking. I opt for the fried chicken. The girl brings me a draft. Chilean beers are all the same, like American beers were forty years ago. They are watery and bodiless but refreshing—what a friend of mine in Alaska calls "barley pop." So it's common here to order a beer without any mention of brand, unlike the orders that come from the barstools in the pub where I drink fine micro-brewed ales at home, where the decision is no less demanding than choosing a dinner wine at a fine restaurant. After five minutes she returns to tell me there's no more fried chicken, only some other kind of chicken that I don't understand. I tell her it's fine, and in a while I'm served a large steaming plate with a half-chicken smothered in a white sauce full of onions and peas, beside a pile of rice. Another plate is full of tomato slices covered with avocados (the rest of the Spanish-speaking world calls them *aguacate*, but here in the southern cone they are *palta*). After the meal I try to pay, but the girl gets confused and tells me to pay tomorrow. It's now midnight, and the place is as active as a North American would expect at seven in the evening. I'm told that South Americans call the time between midnight and dawn *madrugada*. I'm not sure, because the dictionary says it means "dawn," but I like the idea of having a name for the portion of the twenty-four hour day that contains the easy possibility of activity, as opposed to our "middle of the night" or "wee-small hours" which indicate a time when everyone is asleep, or should be. So I use the word to mean "midnight 'til dawn." It's not abnormal to be active in the madrugada, just as it's not abnormal to *siesta*. Earplugs in, I remember the strange realities of Gabriel Garcia Marquez, and entertain myself with the idea that the madrugada is a magical time, as it is for children who sleep through visits by The Tooth Fairy, Santa Claus, and the Easter Bunny; a time when things inanimate come to life, when an enchanted world is accessible to those who choose not to sleep. And I drift off on my springy bed.

The next morning I'm up early and out on the road after tea and toast. When I leave, the boss lady, who I suspect is "Tia Louise" from an ad I saw in Icha's Chilean surf magazine, asks if I ate dinner last night. I tell her I had chicken and a beer. She pauses and studies the ceiling and, as if it spoke to her, gives me the round figure of seven thousand pesos for everything. I pay, get directions to the road for Puertocillo, grab my pack and head out into the cool clear morning. Men sweeping the streets direct me up a hill where I hike out of town filled with that totally free feeling when you first set out on the road. I wonder how long it will last. When it's gone I'll return home and enjoy the opposite feeling—the comfort of refuge, like a ship making a harbor after a long sail—the one you have when you are so happy to be home and don't want to go anywhere. I come to a cruz with a steel bus-stop shack. Thinking this must be the road to Puertocillo, I drop my pack and begin listening to Spanish lessons on my iPod. After a few minutes a twenty-year-old kid comes up and begins hitching with me. Only a few vehicles pass in fifteen minutes, so I ask if he thinks I can get a ride to Puertocillo, and he says yes.

Puertocillo has a left point break. Most of the famous waves in Chile are the same. The waves come up from the Southern Sea where the "Roaring Forties" and "Furious Fifties," the relentless high winds of those latitudes named by seafarers, generate monstrous swells for nine months of the year, but this is the first of the quiet months. The waves work their way up the coast of South America, and when they find the right coastal topography they peel off in perfection. If someone stops for us, I may see how perfect it is in Puertocillo.

After a half-hour, a semi with an empty flatbed stops and we climb up into the high cab. My pack gets dumped behind the seat. We drive for a while, and pass what, recalling the map, I think is probably the cruz for Puertocillo, so I check with the kid and he says I can get there the way we are going. There must be a road that's not on the map. Along the way we drop the kid off at a cluster of a few farmhouses. The driver and I continue, and eventually roll up to a giant wooden gate—like a swinging wall. He uses his cell phone to call the gatekeeper who comes out and opens the thing. It reminds me of the big gate in the original "King Kong" movie, minus the drums, torches and chants. He verifies that I can get to Puertocillo this way, and we proceed into a paradise of a huge ranch, most of which is hills wooded with pine and eucalyptus plantations, but which has pastoral bottomlands. Over the years, Chile Willie has told me about his childhood in Chile. He has described the big old ranches, *estancias*, that were owned by one family, but which were home to the workers who spent their whole lives there: attended the ranch school, played on the ranch soccer field, worked all aspects of an almost self suf-ficient ranch, got old and died there. One of the reasons the CIA helped Pinochet eliminate Allende was because the socialist was dividing these ranches up and giving lands to the people who had worked them for generations whether the people wanted them or not. In the case of Willie's family ranch, the people turned down the land, preferring instead to live under the benevolent lord—Willie's grandfather—to keep things in order. Nevertheless, the government eventually forced the issue, destroying decades of ag-ricultural organization.

We work our way down the slopes and find a cluster of barns, workshops and houses there. The driver says this is as far as he goes, and that I can get a ride with a pickup from here to Puertocillo. In the shade of a big eucalyptus I drop my pack and continue Spanish lessons. An hour later all that has passed was a walking woman and a wandering dog, so I figure I better try to get out of here the way I came, back to that cruz that I thought probably went to Puertocillo. I begin walking east, but see a mechanic in a workshop, so I walk over to ask him how to get to Puertocillo. He tells me to take the road west. I ask how far it is, and he says it's only five kilometers. I don't understand his directions, but his hand motion indicates that it is over the hill to the north, so I take off on foot. Some kind of camelid grazes in a small pasture. A guy meanders down the road on a bicycle. Ten minutes later two surfers drive out in a sedan with boards on top, then I hit a fork. I take the right, thinking that the forks are the same road, and will rejoin soon. It's that kind of situation: an area of old dunes where it's likely that soft sand would cause someone to create a new route, but I am wrong, I realize, and doubt my choice after a hundred yards, so I cut through the brush for the other fork. On it I see the meandering bicycle tracks. They are not covered by car tire tracks, so, to be sure, I follow the bike tracks to the fork where I see them get covered by the car tires. Confident that my first choice was the right one, I get moving up and over the ridge.

The ridge is covered with an "Oregon pine" plantation. This is a tree I have never heard of, and that makes me wonder if I am getting Alzheimer's disease. I've studied dendrology, the taxonomy of woody plants, of North America. I search my memory banks, but that name isn't there. It's planted for lumber, as a fast and straight growing alternative to the curvy, slow-growing hardwoods that are native.

At the crest I get a view of the large bight in the coast. The slopes dive steeply down to the sea. On the brink of the slope I get a better view and see the tiny fishing town on the north end of the bight, and the left point break on the south end. An inviting beach stretches between them for a couple miles. On top, I'm in pastureland. Giant thistles bloom with flowers like round purple brushes that someone might use to wash pots and pans. The plants are head high, with dark artichoke leaves. There are blackberry thickets too. It could be Northern California, but there is no poison oak. It doesn't grow in Chile. There are no rattlesnakes either. I miss neither of them, nor would I ever miss the Great White Shark that is common beyond Northern California surf, and which takes a taste of a surfer now and then. The Whities are here, but I am told that they stay well offshore for some reason. The idea of a California without these plagues is more than comforting, it's almost utopian.

At the toe of the slope I make a hard left and hike along a sandy road to the surf camp. Icha told me to go there and tell the owner he sent me, so I drop his name when I meet the guy. We talk a bit, and then a truck full of his friends arrives. In Chileno style I meet them all and kiss the cheeks of all the pretty young girls. The gist of the conversation is that he is about to leave for Christmas in Santiago and they have no food for me, but some surfers might share their fresh-caught fish and other food. I'm not into bumming food, and the surf is small. I've seen the place. That was my main interest—just to see how it is. After ten minutes of watching the waist-high waves peel off the point, I know I would like to return with a board and wetsuit. So when I see a truck heading out, I hustle over and ask them if they are headed to Litueche. They aren't sure where it is so we talk a little about it, and then a woman in the back asks me where I'm from, and I answer, "California." "So are we," she says in English, and we all laugh at ourselves for assuming the other was Chilean.

They are a family of surfers heading to Patagonia after surfing Peru and Chile. They give me a ride south through more tree plantations to the cruz for Pichilemu, where a bus has just stopped, and I run across the street and board it.

"One of the great dreams of man must be to find some place between the extremes of nature and civilization where it is possible to live without regret."   —Barry Lopez (searching for ancestors)

CHAPTER 8

Pichilemu to Pullehue

In Pichilemu, Chile's most famous surf town, I found a hotel and grabbed a room even though I wasn't thrilled with the price. I wasn't in the mood to pound the pavement looking for something better. I dumped my pack on the bed and took off exploring the streets making my way to the point. It was a perfect summer day. The wave looked even better than Puertocillo, kind of a mirror image of "Rincon" in Southern California, which is famous for its long rights, except this point has a long sandbar trailing off of it. A little surf shop near it rents a board and wetsuit for 6,000 pesos, but I declined, since the lulls between wave sets were long and the crowd was young and excited. These are the ingredients for a competitive session, which I'm rarely in the mood for. The point has a good view of town, which reminded me of the Pismo Beach of many years ago, with that central California feeling; dry, but forested. Of course, the "forest" was an Oregon Pine plantation that will be harvested some day. That means one day the view from town will be of clear-cuts.

Back in town I found a place to eat fried fish with a schop while locals watched the big college soccer championship on TV. The schop made me tired after my long day, so I went back to the vacuous hotel—not another guest in site—and took a nap.

When I woke I opened the window wide and a yellow-jacket flew in and buzzed me. Normally it wouldn't concern me,

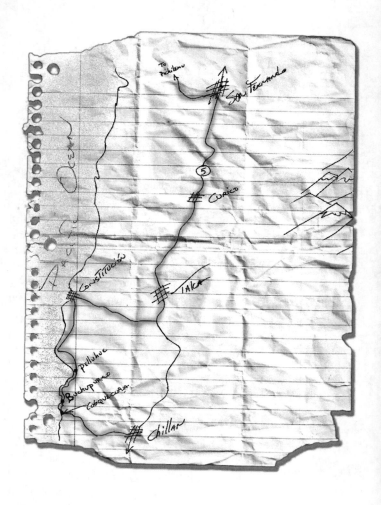

but my last encounter with one is still fresh in my mind. A four months ago I was backpacking in Big Sur and suddenly felt a needle poking my sternum. I looked down, and there, trapped under my sternum strap, was a yellow-jacket. I don't imagine it took more than a second-and-a-half to get it out of there, but I got stung pretty bad. I've had several stings in my life and none were of any seriousness to recall. But this time, after ten minutes more on the trail, my ear began closing and my throat got scratchy. Then, all the hair on my body began to itch. An hour after the sting my partner and I made camp by a river about ten miles back in the woods. When I took my pack off I checked my tingling hips. The hot skin under my hip pads was covered with welts. I searched for the strange word for them— hives. I'd never had them before. Assuming they were caused by heat, I waded up to my navel into the cold river and stayed until my feet began to ache. Then I got into long underwear and my sleeping bag and rested, telling my friend that if my esophagus swelled and closed, to take my knife and pierce my skin at the notch between my clavicles, cut into my esophagus, cut the tube from his hydration bag and insert it in the incision to allow air to pass directly to my lungs. He responded with a nervous laugh, hoping it was a joke.

A week later, when the swelling on my sternum finally went down, fifteen stings were revealed. I cannot understand how it was possible for that bug to sting me so many times in a few seconds, but there were the red welts, each topped with a pinhead scab, to prove it. I looked like someone with good aim had used me for a dartboard. My sister, a family nurse practitioner, told me I had to carry an EpiPen with me always. She said that I could die from the next sting now that I've had such an allergic reaction. Maybe it was the number of stings (yellow jackets have smooth stingers that they can use multiple times to inject venom, as opposed to a bee's barbed stinger that is left in the skin), or the fact that it was so close to my heart, or maybe it was because I was still getting over exposure to some poison oak while hiking on the Lost

Coast the week before, and my histamine levels were already high. Anyway, now I look at wasps and bees a different way.

Right now, this yellow-jacket hovers in front of my face, as if looking me in the eye, and I am flooded with an acute awareness of my mortality. I do have an EpiPen with me, but my mind disregards it. I tend to this mind state, focusing on it, and become grateful. As a martial artist I have been around live samurai swords. A bare sword held in another's hand brings this same feeling, this cognizance of the frailty of flesh. The reason I am grateful for the feeling is that it reminds me that life is happening now; that I will die, and I don't know when. In a sense, we live our lives postponing too much. I've tried not to, but of course I haven't been fully successful. At this moment, facing the insect that could be my end, I am fully present, and it reminds me to pay attention.

Paying attention is the very thing that I postpone. I need this reminder. I recall a parrot in a utopian novel by Aldous Huxley, his last novel, entitled "Island," that reminded people by squawking "Pay attention!" It has been twenty-five years since I read that book (time to read it again) and I have never come across a better phrase in all my studies—well, another one comes close. It is the inverse. I saw it on a friend's refrigerator. It was written in a calligraphy that, as I remember, was Tibetan. I asked what it said and she stated, "Do not be distracted." I burst into robust laughter. There it was, the key to life, written in an obscure language, taped to an old refrigerator in a California ranch house.

The yellow-jacket buzzes at eye level and seems to give me these admonitions.

Out on the street again, now in a state of acute awareness called *kensho* in Zen, I seem to have no history. The present moment is my entire world. I feel the cool air on my skin, and the organization of my body as I walk, enjoying the colors of town in the golden light of a setting sun. The smell of fresh empanadas seems to dance on my tongue and plunge into my empty belly, stopping me in my tracks, so I duck into the source and place an order I'm handed a ticket, so I ask how long it will take because no other customer is there. "Only five minutes," the girl tells me. A five-minute wait is a good time to spend paying full attention.

The next morning I descend for complimentary breakfast. I'm the only guest in a large dining room with three central pillars. It must have twenty tables, covered with cobalt-blue cloths and topped with the Chilean bouquet of square paper napkins arranged in a spiral of white corners pointing to the ceiling inside of an aluminum cone, shaped like a little pilsner glass. The woman who checked me in cooks and serves me the typical scrambled eggs in a tiny metal pan.

Her name is Maria. She is the only other person I've seen in this building. She speaks clear Spanish, and is very helpful. She tells me the bus to San Fernando stops on the corner just fifty yards west of the hotel door, and calls to check on the time. I pack and am out on the street fifteen minutes early, but the corner is such a non-distinctive one that I am confused, so I check with people who assure me that the bus does indeed stop there. Time to shrug and trust again. Why would a long distance bus stop on this corner where an abandoned, windowless old building is on a little dirt street, across from a vacant lot? Fifteen minutes later the bus comes, stops, and in a minute I'm on the nicest bus of my life—reclining chairs, a water station and bathroom, and a soundproof door separating the cabin from the driver.

I want to head south on the coast, but the roads going south get smaller and smaller, so the best way is to go inland to San Fernando in the central valley, head south to Talca, then come back to the coast.

In San Fernando it's impossible to find a bus to Talca. I don't understand why, and don't try to. I just grab a ticket for a bus to Curico, which is on the way. I have a forty-five minute wait, and sit on a bench out by the bus docks. A man in his fifties sits beside me, and starts talking my ear off. I understand about a third of what he's saying at best. It's all mumbles. Then I realize he has no front teeth. He's a nice guy; a furniture repairman waiting for a bus out to the countryside where he will cut a Christmas tree. A janitor paces back and forth in front of us pushing a mop that is damp with something that smells like diesel over the smooth concrete. I see no one from another country. The station is full of people on their way to visit family for the holidays.

In Curico I walk off the bus and directly to a window for a line that advertises "Talca," buy a ticket, stash my pack in the cargo bay, and am seated in five minutes. I continue down the central valley, where the level land is covered with Cabernet vineyards and punctuated by big rivers running high and fast with Andean snowmelt the color of *café con leche*. Occasionally I get a glimpse of snow capped peaks in the east, and a look at the natural landscape—a savanna with head-high acacia-like trees covering from twenty to 50% of the dry grassland. If I were to see a giraffe out there, it would fit in.

We pass a few billboards and I notice that they are owned by ClearChannel, the right-wing media corporation from the United States which owns something like 1200 radio stations, distributed in all fifty states—more than half of the pop stations in the country. They're the nation's largest broadcaster and concert promoter, owning well over a hundred concert venues, various radio research companies, radio trade magazines, and regional news networks. ClearChannel plays hardball with the music industry. Musicians need to be heard on the radio for their music and concerts to sell, but if you don't book your concerts with ClearChannel, they won't play your music. If you sing an antiwar message, they won't play your music. The vice-chairman, a Texan, has long and strong financial ties with the Bush family. In 2003, when cities like San Francisco had 200,000 marching against the invasion of Iraq, ClearChannel sponsored pro-war rallies in the Midwest, but they had only a tenth of San Francisco's turnout. The power of media control cannot be overstated. I wonder what they're up to here in Chile. Most of their billboards advertise universities. Apparently there has been a recent surge in small private universities in this country. When I see ClearChannel's name on the billboard it makes me wonder who owns the universities and what type of education they are offering. Using the media is one way to brainwash folks, using school is another. But then, just because they buy ad space doesn't mean anything.

In Talca I disembark and see a bus for Constitución, which is en route to my next coastal destination. I ask the driver if he's going there (a precautionary habit) and he says yes and invites me aboard, opening the cargo door for my pack, and giving me a claim check ticket. The ride crosses an expanse of Oregon pine plantations. These tree farms are beginning to bother me, as I have been looking forward to seeing the natural forests that I imagined to cover the blank areas of the maps I have wondered about over the years. Constitución, being a mill town, is of no interest to me. Icha, the veteran surfer, told me to skip the nearby beaches because they are polluted from the mouth of the Río Maule, which drains the central valley's agricultural lands near Talca before its waters are used by the lumber and pulp mills here.

Rivermouths can be excellent spots for waves due to the build-up of sandbars where sediment-laden waters slow upon hitting the ocean's deep, still water. Waves are best when they run diagonal to the bottom that makes them break, and a river can deposit a triangular "delta" shaped bar pointing to sea, with a right peeling off the left side and a left across the river. Historically, rivermouths have been fertile waters full of fish, the result of all the freshwater nutrients as well as detritus, plants and animals that are discharged there. In the old days surfers would be wary of sharks here, but these days we need to be more aware of the water quality, as many people see a river as a toilet that will flush away trash, sewage and other effluents. This view, when extrapolated to the industrial level, is the reason so many rivers are polluted by industrial waste.

Agricultural waste is less intentional, but can be equally deadly. The Mississippi Delta was once one of the most productive chunks of liquid real estate on the planet, but it drains the American "Breadbasket," and all the runoff from 41% of the contiguous forty-eight states. The nitrogen in agricultural runoff fertilizes the water causing intense algal blooms that then die in such volume that their bacterial decomposition uses tremendous amounts of oxygen in the water, causing a hypoxic condition in which fish cannot "breathe." This water, deficient or even void of oxygen (anoxic), then floods the seawaters of the rivermouth, making it impossible for fish to inhabit. The waters off the mouth of the Mississippi are now the largest dead zone in all of North American waters. An area of coastal water almost the size of New Jersey is basically void of life. There are about 150 such places on Earth (one-third of them are around the United States), almost all of them rivermouths.

Eighty percent of Chinese rivers are too polluted for fish to live. Unregulated industry in many developing nations poisons the rivers with chemical waste that goes largely undocumented. To the degree that multinational agricultural supply corporations are successful in convincing a country to use its products, residues of insecticides taint the waters. Trash kills too, for example sea turtles mistake plastic bags for jellyfish and eat them, usually dying from the meal. It's reported that 100,000 marine mammals die each year from eating plastics in the North Pacific alone.

So when I arrive at the Constitución terminal I search for a bus south to Buchupureo, where Icha told me there is a good wave. My map shows a road, but it begins to become evident from the answers I get at ticket counters that the road on my map is less of a road and more of a path. There is no bus, but one guy in a little office is helpful. I am getting less than half of what he is saying, even though he has teeth. He puts me on a bus to the small coastal town of Pullehue, and we cross more miles of Oregon pine, then it opens up: ranches, grain fields, potato patches, pastures—there's a feeling of the Sonoma coast of California. Then, at an intersection a sign points east to Santa Rosa, with wild mustard and fennel blooming in the fields behind it. It's what I imagine a flashback must be like— you feel like shaking your head—like your eyes are stuck on the wrong channel. It all looks exactly like California; I have to tell myself where I am.

Once again the driver drops me off at the cruz, and I begin hitch-hiking, but soon a beat-up old bus rounds the corner and stops for me. I ask if he goes to Pullehue and I don't understand a single word he says— not a single word, no matter what I ask. So I just laugh and hop aboard. After a few minutes I'm feeling like I better be sure where he's going, so I walk forward and tell him I want to go to Buchupureo. This time I understand that he's going to the plaza in Pullehue.

By the time we arrive it's getting late, so I use internal radar to decide which way to search for a hotel. I find one quickly— a motel arrangement, around a courtyard framed with huge hydrangeas instead of the parking lot of a motel. It's an ancient adobe place, and it's a wreck. A grape arbor leads to a passage to a terraced lawn high on a bluff overlooking the ocean, but the grass is overgrown and the stone wall is broken down. A few pieces of junk lie around. "Good place for photography" the old man says. I wonder what it was like when this place was new. Was it a hip and trendy place in its day? Were there elegant cocktail parties here on the cliff-side terrace full of wealthy lumber barons arriving in model-T Fords?

I am the only guest again. I bargain for a low price and get one. Somehow these places always have one room that is a special discount. They show it to me and I take it. But neither the old man nor his son, the owner, can find the key. So they move me next door. I pay, but they don't have change, so the old man has to run into town for it. When I turn on the shower there is no hot water (which was part of the deal we made), so I tell the guy. In five minutes he reports that he fixed it, and I try again. Still cold.

I go out and tell him, but he doesn't believe me, so he comes to the bathroom and tests the shower water before he hurries around back, turning squeaky valves, banging on tanks, lighting burners, then returns and tries it again. Still nothing, so he moves me to a nice room—for this place—where there is hot water. The old guy teases me about being from the United States and needing hot water. He just takes cold showers, he says. I tell him I could just go jump in the ocean; it would be a lot cheaper. The thick adobe walls are painted mint green. There are no windows. I duck under the five-foot high lintel over the doorway to the bathroom and get a scalding hot shower, then head out on the street to find a restaurant. The town has four. Not one has a single person in it. I return to the first one and am welcomed. My roasted chicken comes to my table in less than ten minutes. This surprises me, but then I realize that there is a roasted chicken take-out place next door, so they just went out the back door and bought one. It was good though, with French fries and the typical lettuce, tomato and avocado salad. And with a schop it was less than five bucks, and good prices always satisfy me.

CHAPTER 9

Buchupureo

Adobe walls and no windows make for a good sleep. I dozed all morning till the owner's TV came on. Then I got on the street and found a corner café for tea and empanadas filled with *pino*, which, I learned, is beef and onion, and if you are lucky, olive. I wasn't lucky.

It's Christmas Eve, but nothing seems too unusual. Of course, I have no idea what *usual* is here. Two six-foot strands of tinsel garland are festooned from randomly-located wads of scotch tape. One is stuck on the glass of a framed watercolor print of fishing boats, which is the only other thing on the yellow adobe walls. While enjoying my morning tea, I study the napkin holders. They're made of the bottom two inches of a liter coke bottle turned upside-down and trimmed with lace, with the top five inches of the bottle also turned upside-down and glued to the bottom and trimmed with red ribbon. I decide they are not for the holiday, but are for "everyday use." Same with the flower vase on the red-and-white checked tablecloth. It's the bottom two inches of a green two-liter bottle filled with plaster with a plastic red rose stuck in it.

My attention goes to a four-foot-long stick standing in the corner. It's got a half-liter soda bottle stuck on the end, and a red ribbon wrapped around the bottle. Is it covering some special tip for playing a game or fishing? I get up and take a look. It's just a stick. A kid must have been playing with it and left it there. I wonder how often things thrown together by kids have been exhumed by archeologists only to cause their confoundment. "It must be a ceremonial object because it has no obvious use."

In a short while I'm walking across town under the burden of my pack and feeling good; feeling rested and strong, and ready to see Chile. In no time I'm hitchhiking and soon get a ride from two friendly guys in a little red pickup. I ride in the back, the cold coastal fog condensing in my hair and chilling my bare arms. We arrive in some little town and they drop me off. I cross town on foot, and as I'm heading out the other end they come by and stop again, laughing. Eventually they drop me off when they turn into a little farm community. I keep walking. It's a beautiful morning. I could be in Arcata, California in June. Dandelions cover emerald rolling fields on a coastal bench. A big bull lies near an ancient low barn in the sun that is burning off the morning fog. That fog lingers over the coast, but the brightness of the whitewater of breaking waves pierces through it, touching my eye. People have planted potato patches, strawberry patches, and it's even warm enough for cornfields. Yellow lupines blanket the hillsides.

Before long, a silver mini van stops, and three young guys make room for my pack and me. They only go a kilometer, and I walk a few more miles after that, then rest in the shade of a big tree watching swallows dart after insects. A bee passes and reminds me I could die at any moment. There's no traffic at all. Then a guy in a little yellow Chevy pickup comes up the road and stops. He's another good-natured local. I'm beginning to understand why this country has a reputation for friendliness. His language resembles Spanish, but I understand about 15% of what he says, so I guess the rest and tell him what I think he's saying and he says I'm right; that I can get to Buchupureo this way, but he's only going a little farther. After the next turn the road becomes a dirt logging road, the next bend puts us in the middle of a clear-cut. We meander through fresh clear-cuts and replanted ones for a few miles, then drop into a precious little valley with an ancient adobe hacienda—white walls and red tile roof. Around the corner is another one. I wonder how old they are and who built them, under what circumstances. It seems like a perfect place. I ask what the weather is like in the winter and he tells me, "A lot of rain...a lot of wind too." We climb out of the sweet valley and at the crest of a forested hill he stops and says this is as far as he goes. I'm confused because there is nothing around. He tells me he is going to the hacienda we just passed, and that he just wanted to help me climb the hill. "Buchupurco is eighteen kilometers," he says. Pointing south. I thank him, figure three one-hour hikes will get me there, and take off with long strides.

I'm on a plateau covered with Oregon pine and nothing else. The road is good; rocky, but good, and I'm moving fast. Then the bees arrive. These big black things with rusty hairy backs zip up to me and orbit my head. Sometimes there are two or three of them. I never kill animals unless it is for self-defense or food. Feeling under attack, I swat one to the ground and it bounces and flies away. I imagine if a giant did that to me. I'd be dead instantly. I'm throwing punches at them and letting my loose wrist flick so I backhand them with my fingertips. My fingertips are traveling fast when they hit. What *are* these things? I figure they are hornets, and that they can kill me. They come and go, but I have a few around me constantly. I think of the story of the "killer bees" of South America as I walk south with the sun at my back, watching their shadow over my head to see if they try to land on me.

After a few kilometers I see a big valley ahead. As I drop into it, I realize it's a big ranch, and runs to the sea. The road crosses the mile-wide valley in a straight line that passes through wildflower-filled pastures, the sound of surf detonating in the distance indicates that it's a surge, slamming a steep beach. At the south end of this flat-bottomed valley, red Peruvian lilies flank a stream crossing. A friend has them growing as a nuisance at his home on the Mendocino Coast. After the stream the road climbs up and over more hills, and down into another broad, flat valley on the coast. This one has a little Indian village named Pullay. At the south end of the village I drop my pack and sit on it, in the shade of a tree, finishing my water and listening to the unfamiliar birdsongs. My mind opens to the possible perception of the *biophany*, or the symphony of this ecosystem. As I listen keenly, some fishermen drive into town selling crab out of the back of a pickup. An old red jalopy log truck carrying poles passes by and doesn't stop. Three Indian guys fill the cab and they have no room. The map says Buchupureo is not far, so I get going again. My feet are hurting. I have lightweight low-cut hikers on, but the weight of my pack pushes the rocks right through the soles. I push on, and finally see the ideal Buchupureo valley, filled with farms. I have "hit the wall," and am weak, so I stop to rest, and take in the vista of the valley, which has a reputation for its fertile soils as well as its long left point break. They say the best potatoes in the country come from the farms below. This latitude, thirty-six degrees, is the same as the Big Sur and San Simeon areas of California—an inviting latitude.

As I survey the valley I naturally imagine living here, and wonder about the sea-level rise that meteorologists, climatologists, oceanographers and geographers predict. How high will it rise, and how soon? It's another flat-bottomed valley, and looks to be mostly below fifteen feet of elevation. How much of it will be inundated in my lifetime? How much of it will be left unfarmable by salt-water intrusion?

The word is that we have ten years to make the radical changes necessary to drastically reduce the production of greenhouse gasses; beyond that we will be past the point of no return. And so far not much is being done. Meanwhile, as permafrost melts, arctic marshes spew volumes of methane, a more efficient greenhouse gas than carbon dioxide, into the atmosphere, and speed the warming process. The warming process is accelerating while humans try to make just a bit more money before they absolutely have to change. Maybe also by people like me who want to travel before it becomes too expensive. The sea level will rise. We don't know how much or how fast, but we know coastal paradises that are within a few feet of sea level will be taken by Neptune. The impact will be huge, as much of the world's population lives near the ocean. In the United States, 51% of the population lives in coastal counties. Other countries like Bangladesh and some low-lying island nations will disappear almost entirely. As attractive as this valley is, it may not be a wise place to settle. I wonder why nobody lives up here on the bench. Wind? Winter storms? No water?

Luckily, a little pickup comes and stops, giving me a lift to the valley floor where the farmer turns inland. I take off for the beach, pass a jumpy old man hoeing weeds outside his fence, and ask him if there is a place where I can eat. I don't understand a single word that comes out of his hippopotamus mouth (he's only got two teeth on either side of his mouth). I'm tired. I look at the fork in the road ahead and ask If I should take the right side and he says yes. Who knows if it is the way to a restaurant. The road takes me to a beach with no buildings. Two teenage boys are standing in the road talking and I scare them when I walk up to them to ask questions. They point to a restaurant, but it's on the other side of the river. It's possible, I learn, to walk down the beach and cross on a footbridge, so I do, stopping to soak my poor feet in the surf's edge. I slug my way across the soft sand and cross the narrow, rickety footbridge that zig-zags from one set of undersize piling to the next, and find "El Puerto," the restaurant. It's a big place, clean, with lots of windows but no customers. I drop my pack and get a menu and water. The waitress answers my questions, saying yes, the salmon is local and fresh, so I order it with more water and a beer. In a while she brings poorly cooked, frozen, and most likely farmed, salmon, and I devour it and the excellent potatoes and salad, and have another beer. When I ask if they are open tomorrow, they explain that they don't open till 12:30 because it's

Christmas Day.

When Marinela was visiting California with her Chilean friends, they met a local in Santa Cruz who gave them a place to stay. The same guy is building a surf resort here in Buchupureo, and she told me to visit him, so I ask about him, and am told that he lives at the next house around the bend. I find him in his yard getting ready for a Christmas dinner party at a friend's house. He gives me directions to a tiny beach out on the point, and lets me fill my water bottles from the yard spigot while he voices his concern about his water quality suffering from saltwater intrusion. Then I hike out to my hideout. It's a rocky nook that gets plenty of sun and has a good view, but it's hidden from town. The famous wave would be breaking in front of me if there were a swell. I bathe in the cold ocean, then have a good rest in the sun watching kelp gulls and these little accipiter-like hawks, which I identify as a small caracara called a *chimango*. They are abundant all over Central Chile.

All night the small surf breaks and swashes up the sand and back in a rhythm that makes sleep more satisfying, like it is for an infant sleeping at mother's breast.

In the morning it's foggy, so I stay in my tent, meditating. After the sun breaks through the coastal fog I check my clock and it's already one, so I decide to break camp and get a bite to eat at El Puerto. By the time I get there it is 1:30, but they're closed, so I turn and climb into the forested hills between here and the next town south. At the top, a little truck comes along and stops for me. The guy squeezes me in the back seat with a bunch of boxes and bags. He takes me to Cobquecura, the next coastal town, connected to the central valley city of Chillan by asphalt. It sits in the bottom of a valley wider than all the others I've crossed in the last few days. When I ask if he knows where there is an open restaurant, he asks if I like seafood, then delivers me to a place, and lets them know that he brought me. I enter the pink building and sit at a table with a hot-pink tablecloth. A dozen people are inside, at three different tables, having Christmas lunch, surrounded by hot-pink walls. There is nothing special on the menu for the holiday, though. It's the same as any other menu on the coast. You have your choice of fish, rice and salad, or fish, potatoes and salad. The type of fish varies. I order grilled corvina and boiled potatoes, which they call "natural" potatoes. When the meal comes I ask for some butter for my bread and a glass of white wine. The corvina is fresh and delicious, and you can't beat the potatoes. I'm almost finished eating when the waitress brings the first bad wine I've had in Chile   very sweet, so the timing is right. It's dessert. The butter never comes. While waiting for the bill, I study the building. Log rafters painted glossy black hold up an orange-stained wood panel ceiling.

The road south of here dwindles, so I decide to bus to the central valley again in order to keep moving south. This stretch of coast invites me, and if my pack wasn't so full I'd buy food and continue south, but with all the gear for the mountains, books, street clothes, and other "things I might need" on my back, I cringe at the thought of adding food.

When I leave I ask a guy hangin' out by the door if he thinks there is a bus to Chillan today. He says he believes so in clear Spanish, and he sends me to the plaza, which is several blocks across town to the east. At the plaza, it's dead quiet. One little poor Indian guy is sitting on a bench. When I approach him he gets scared. I ask if there's a bus, and I don't understand a thing he says before he hurries away. I wonder why they're so skittish around here.

I'm not into waiting and hoping (too much travel experience for that), so I study the place and see a street sign a block away pointing the way to Chillan. If I can wait for a bus at the edge of town, then I can hitchhike while I wait. The only problem is that the sign points west; Chillan is east. I follow it, skirting the north edge of town, expecting to cross a bridge or find some similar reason for heading west. On my way I keep asking people and they tell me to keep going. I'm all the way to the beach before I'm told to turn left, and I cross town again, this time from north to south, passing within a couple blocks of the restaurant where my search began, and find the place where the road begins its climb up the crest of the ridge on the south side of this valley. As I arrive, two Mapuche Indians in their traditional bold, black, red and white rugby-striped ponchos ride into town on horseback. They are well dressed—for the holiday, I imagine—with silver spurs, and the Chilean campesino straw hat that has a flat top and a very wide circular brim.

A half-hour of hitchhiking leaves me in the same spot, and then a bus enters town. I expect it to rebound soon, but another half-hour later, no bus. Then a pickup with a surfboard in the back stops. I walk up to the window and choose English, "Howzit goin'?" I get a confused look. "Vas a Chillan?" "Si." I throw my pack in the back and get in. Most pickups in Chile are "crew-cabs" that have a back seat. The couple in the front seat look like they could be from the States, but I assume they are Chilean since they didn't understand my English. We speak Spanish for a few minutes before the woman realizes my Spanish is not so great, so she asks if I am Chilean. Immediately I know she is not Chilean, or she'd know. We switch to English. It turns out that her husband, the driver, is an engineer, and they came from France to build a plant to process chicory into a no-calorie sweetener. We talk about that—the sweetener, the job, the country, but inevitably the topic lands on George W. Bush. They are especially curious about Bush's religiousness and the conservative Christian agenda. They are shocked that such a thing would be happening in the States.

I tell them that most Americans (I can use that word to describe people from the United States to a Frenchman, whereas South Americans rightfully consider themselves to be Americans) have a very poor grasp of American History. Most have never read the Constitution either. So when the Christian Conservatives tell them that our founding fathers intended this nation to be a Christian State, they believe it. By intention, there is no mention of God or Bible in the constitution. Our founders were adamant about the separation of church and the federal government. Of course, being an educated European, he knows most of this. The United States has been a model of government and creative success, so many Europeans study our government and society at some point in their education.

I begin with radio, since the ClearChannel billboards are still on my mind. I tell him about all the Christian Radio being broadcasted in my nation. One company, Salem Communications, owns over a hundred stations and broadcasts to almost two thousand affiliate stations—not just in the rural South, but in major progressive cities like New York and San Francisco. The affiliation is one of the keys to their power. Even though they may have different names to their churches, they are united in what they oppose. For example, they all condemn gay marriage and abortion, some to the degree of calling for the death penalty for those guilty. I cannot consider someone sane who wants to kill a person for loving someone of the same gender, but who expends endless effort in preserving the life of a human embryo smaller than a sesame seed, or of a person who, having been in a coma for years, has been diagnosed as brain dead.

The French couple agree, and understand that there is a level of cooperation that is never seen in the competitive business world. I continue to explain that the other key to the power of the religious right is the fear/guilt trip that they capitalize on. People are so afraid of going to hell, and want so much to do the right thing, that they feel they must contribute heavily to these on-air preachers. The income of these radio stations is staggering. Not only do most of the preachers live in the lap of luxury, but more importantly, there are enormous amounts of cash to expand their influence by buying more stations and by buying politicians and legislation. Over the last twenty years legislation has been passed that paved the road for what is happening now. Before 1987, the

Federal Communications Commission required radio broadcasters to provide equal time to political opponents. No more. A decade later, the FCC eliminated ownership caps with the Telecommunications Act. Today Salem is so big that it is one of the largest political donors in the business, and almost all of its funds go to Republicans. These days, one-third of Americans listen to Christian radio all across the nation, an increase from less than a quarter only five years ago.

My view is that the Republicans courted the Christian vote in order to gain numbers when they saw liberals losing their foothold with devout Christian Democrats. I joke about Bush's approval rating being the same as the percentage of conservative Christians—it can't get any lower because they *believe* in him.

I tell the French couple about the evangelicals expecting Armageddon—what some call "The Rapture." It's not something I fully understand, and the scary thing is that *most* political progressives don't. The reason it's so scary is because one-third of the electorate believes in it, and most of the remaining two-thirds are not even aware of it. According to Bill Moyers, back in the nineteenth century, some preachers twisted the Bible a bit to come up with the prediction that when Israel occupies the biblical lands, "legions of the antichrist" will attack it. Non-converted Jews will be burned, and "true believers" will be lifted out of their clothes and transported to heaven to be seated at the right hand of God, from where they will watch the rest of us suffer plagues—you know, things like frogs and boils—for several years. We'll know when the rapture happens because they will all disappear; presumably their clothes will be left in a pile where they stood a moment before.

The Frenchman is having a hard time believing this. "One-third?" he asks. I tell him it is hard for me to believe also, and most people on the two coasts aren't aware of this phenomenon because it is not in the news, and they have no exposure to it. I explain that most of the media exported to France originates on the two coasts. I leave it like that, although I know it is not entirely true.

Last year, when I drove up to Vancouver Island, and went up the coast of Washington, which I had never seen before, I was astounded at the extent of the deforestation. The land has been completely raped everywhere but in Olympic National Park. In fact, when you cross the park boundary it's like hitting a wall of trees. In one tiny logging town surrounded by clear-cuts as far as the eye can see, sat a little old church with a banner strung over the front door reading "Rapture Ready." This was my first and only direct exposure to this segment of the American population. I imagined that these people, having worked so hard to denude the landscape of their very source of income, see that it's all over, and would just as well leave their clothes in a heap over their footprint as pack them up and move to a place where they could destroy another forest. Former secretary of the Interior James Watt was quoted saying that, "After the last tree is felled, Christ will come back." Maybe these loggers on the Washington coast agree. In fact, environmental destruction is seen as a precursor to the Rapture. It's like Bob Marley sang, they think great God will come from the sky, take away everything and make everybody feel high. The Frenchman laughs and puts a Bob Marley CD in the dashboard player.

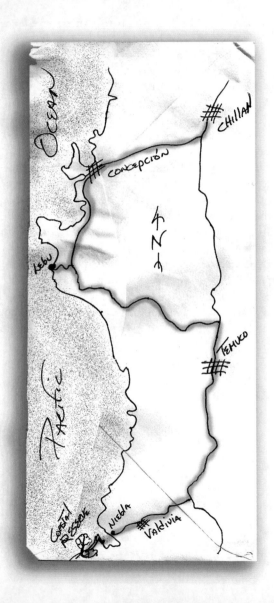

CHAPTER 10

Lebu

The French drop me off at Hospedaje Sonia Segui, which I found in my guidebook, and chose because it's near the bus terminal. The place is a dump, but my room is clean, and it's only seven bucks with breakfast. I'm the only guest again. When signing in I see that no one has been here in a few days. Some Germans and Canadians and one girl from Santa Cruz stayed here last.

The owners light the on-demand hot water heater, which is in the stairway, so I can get a shower. I get undressed, and go to the shower, but there's no water. When I tell them, a big confusion ensues. I realize that they were all sleeping off a midday holiday drunk when I showed up. Finally the man of the house announces that there is hot water. I undress again, enter the shower, but it is too hot. The cold-water handle is missing. How can you run a hostel with no cold-water handle? I leave a trail of wet footprints back to my room and get my Leatherman pliers, return to the shower, and adjust the water temperature. The shower feels good. Afterwards I reach for the little blue hand towel they gave me. When it touches my face it reeks of cigarette smoke. It's hot here in the valley, so I wait for it to cool off before heading out for food.

It's Christmas Day, so most places are closed, but otherwise there is no indication of the holiday. Americans spend eight billion dollars each year on Christmas decorations. That's about a third of Bolivia's GDP. Because of the closures, I miss some interesting looking restaurants, and have to eat at a fast-food beer and sandwich place called "Schopdog." The name is cool, but the food is bad. I fight a tough steak with a sheet-metal knife.

Walking back to my flophouse, I see a kid with a skateboard stop to adjust his earphones. He's got the right idea. This is the first time I've traveled with an iPod, and I'm still getting used to the ability to listen to music any time I want to. I put Jason Miles on the iPod. Miles is a smooth jazz musician these days. I hate that sleazy stuff, but in the eighties he spent some time with Miles Davis, and this album, "Miles to Miles," is very much in the funky feel of the late trumpeter's last albums. The music is an electronic recreational drug that makes the dull walk through blocks of urban neighborhoods fun. A person wearing headphones, or in this case, "earbuds," inhabits a secret audio world that no one is privy to, and in this case no one around me has ever heard. It gives me a connection with home, where our musical banquet is exploding with diversity. I listen for a while in bed, then enter the dream world.

Chileans are not early risers, but at 6:30 in the morning there's a hell of a racket outside my window—Mexican style mariachi music. I'm groggy and doze for a while, but after about twenty minutes I get up to look out the window and see some steaming stainless steel vat on wheels being delivered by a pickup with three guys in fluorescent orange highway vests. The oom-pa blares from the truck radio with a piercing accordion and a booming polka bass. I grab my earplugs, but I've woken and can't get back to sleep, so by eight I'm packed-up and descending the stairs. The family is asleep still, so I enter the kitchen, fill a water pot and put it on the stove. There are no matches to light the burner. I'm looking all around for a match when a girl walks in. She gets scared when she sees me. I say good morning and ask for a match. She can't find one so she goes and wakes her aunt, the owner, who tells her there is a lighter in the fruit basket. She hands me the lighter, and I ignite a flame under the pot. She is surprised at my reason for needing a match. I guess most adults in her life wake up and light a cigarette in the morning. Her aunt takes over and kicks me out of the kitchen so she can make me breakfast: the little metal pan of scrambled eggs with Italian bread and butter—with a heavy, serrated steak knife.

At the terminal I buy a ticket to Concepción, another coastal city, hoping to find buses from there to a town further down the coast called Lebu that Icha said has a good break. The man at the counter tells me the bus arrives at 9:30 out back. It's 9:10, so I go out and wait. Fifteen minutes later a woman who is also a waiting passenger comes out to tell me that the bus will now be arriving out front on the street instead, so I thank her and carry my pack through the station to the curb out front, where the bus arrives on time. Soon we are driving through endless pine and eucalyptus plantations in the coastal range. As we crest the range we are in a drizzling heavy mist, then we descend to the industrial port city. I have no interest in Concepción, and soon I'm on a bus which passes the cruz to Lebu. It's another comfortable bus and I relax with some straight-ahead jazz on the iPod, watching the pine plantations go by. Most people are asleep as usual.

I haven't seen a natural forest yet, and it brings a sad feeling to know how much of it must have been destroyed, and all the species of wildlife, herbs and flowers—gone with the forest. Environmental devastation on this scale must surely have driven many species to extinction, and I feel grief for them. Both pine and eucalyptus drop leaves that change the chemistry of the soil with their oils. This, along with the dense uniform canopy of a plantation, makes it difficult for anything to grow under them, so there is no food or cover for wildlife. It must be part of the reason that 23% of Chilean mammals are threatened with extinction. I have traveled the southern equivalent of the latitudes from Los

Angeles to San Francisco, and have seen no forest but the mono-culture plantations.

The driver drops me off in Cerro Alto at the cruz. Across the street I ask a guy at a bus stop if he is waiting for the bus to Lebu. He responds to my gringo accent by replying in careful English that he is proud of. "Yes, where are you from?" I tell him and he says, "Welcome." The bus takes us twenty-five kilometers to Lebu. It's a wooden Wild West town—a fishing, coal and log port, except there's no coal left, I don't see any log tucks or mills, and I assume the fish are declining, since they are everywhere in the world. What I'm saying is that it is poor.

It's a grey, cold, windy day and I've got to search for a hotel because Lebu is not in the guidebook. Everyone tells me the same thing: there is one hotel—the big gold one. It's easy to find: with three stories, it's the biggest building in town, and sports a new coat of Dijon mustard paint, and the sign, "Hotel Central" is visible from three blocks. I enter and find my way through the labyrinth of hallways with tall ceilings and old, well-worn wooden floors that roll like swells on a confused sea. The place is silent except for the thunder of my Vibram soles meeting the floorboards under the weight of my pack. If anyone is in the building, they hear me walking: *da-doo, da-doo*, as my toe follows my heel in the stiff boots I've been wearing since punishing my feet on Christmas Eve. I'm wondering if I will be the only guest again in this ghostly, drafty echo chamber. The office is empty but further exploration leads to the kitchen, where three maids sit talking. When I make the usual request for a cheap room, the older woman, who is probably only my age, guides me upstairs and shows me a large well-lit room with a bed and night table for nine dollars. I make sure it's the cheapest and take it. I already know I'm on the first bus outta here in the morning, but this place is so strange I'll spend the night.

Another, younger, woman joins us, and those two have a conversation, every single word of which eludes me. Then they pick up the wooden bed, turn it sideways, and take it out the door and down the hall. When they turn it again, to take it into another room, the bed falls completely apart. They collect the pieces and dump them in the room, take one of the six beds in that room, and carry it down to mine. The older lady had one of her front lower teeth, but still I can understand only a few words—unfortunately not enough to know what she is saying. I ask her to speak slowly and clearly, and, making no secret of her frustration with my inability to understand her, she speaks faster and louder. All I get is something about when I cancel. I can't figure out what I need to cancel. This is like a crazy dream, where all these strange things happen, and the other people in the dream act like it's perfectly normal. At this point if I were to walk through the door and find myself in my fifth grade classroom it wouldn't shock me. The woman is complaining to her assistant about my not understanding her. Suddenly I realize that she wants me to cancel my debt, so I ask her if she would like me to pay, and I make her day.

She gives me a hundred-year-old key, a towel and a roll of toilet paper, and shows me the bathroom down the hall, which has an electric heater on the showerhead. The wiring is not too bad though. I've seen much worse in Central America—bad enough to scare you out of taking a shower. My room is a surreal setting. It contains a bed, a little night table, and a dining-room chair, with a clear-glass bare bulb sticking out of a socket in the flexible conduit running up the wall. That's all that's in the large room. The dull yellow walls were probably last painted in the twenties. I wonder what they have seen. They are twenty feet square with an eleven-foot high ceiling. A square room with a wood floor and plaster walls and ceiling make the acoustics about as bad as possible.

Out on the street, I seek a restaurant, but can't find more than a little sandwich shop. As I stand on a corner, wondering which way to go next, two young guys in white shirts and ties walk across the street, and one waves. Since he initiated, I walk over to him and ask if he can steer me to a good place to eat. He asks in fluent English where I'm from. Then, without using the

"H" word, asks me what the hell I am doing *here*. He must be from the States—a missionary—but I don't ask. I just note his directions to a café.

I take a seat and joke with the waitress because I never heard of anything on the menu. She doesn't think it's funny. I'm getting the feeling that I have entered a sub-culture here in this strange town. My choices are chukrut, colaciones, pichanga and barro luco. I'm hungry. I ascertain that pichanga (which I only know as the Cuban word for the Cuban music we call "charanga") is not a sandwich, and it's the most expensive thing on the menu (at three-and-a-half dollars), so I order it. Soon she delivers a little clay bowl filled with French fries with hunks of beef, chicken, sausage and hot dog, wedges of tomato and avocado, and topped with more French fries and melted cheese. It's not bad, but I need more.

First I stop by a little shack with a lop-sided broken-back wooden awning that has a sign saying, "internet." I check e-mail for forty-five minutes and pay seventy cents. Then I stroll to the harbor, which is in the river. It's still a grey day with a cold wet wind coming in from the ocean. All of the wooden fleet follows a red, white and blue theme. They carry flagged buoys, so I know they're either crabbers or long-liners, but I see no traps or drums, so I take a closer look. Some of them are well-built. Others are square and boxy with a ninety-degree angle where the topsides meet the transom, straight lines in the hip, a hard angle about two-thirds forward, then a straight line to the bow. The planking above deck, typically the "garboard" which is a continuation of the hull, is, on these boats, more of a fence, full of wide gaps between planks.

I am temporarily absorbed into the evil image of the tattered black buoy flags on the tops of clusters of old bamboo poles fluttering and clattering in the wind below a dark sky. There is something batish about them, and the driven damp chill pierces my fleece and jeans. But it is only the image and the weather. I sense no evil in the air. Why do they use black flags? I wonder.

There is a bin full of green fifteen-millimeter line on one

boat's bow deck, so I'm guessing long-liner, but how do they get the line aboard? Then I see that each has a hydraulic capstan forward of the house and to starboard of the keel. Still, I can't figure out how it crosses the gunwale, so I ask a deckhand. He tells me they put a roller on the gunwale when they haul the line in.

I wonder how these fishermen are doing. I read one of Julia Whitty's excellent articles in Mother Jones magazine that said that deep-sea long-liners are now catching one-tenth of their former catch. This Lebu fleet is not made of deep-sea boats, but they are surely catching less these days. Those pelagic long-liners make sets up to sixty miles long with thousands of hooks catching all sorts of fish, 25% of which are "by-catch," unwanted fish that get thrown back in the sea to die. They are thought to catch 40,000 turtles and 300,000 seabirds a year, most of which eventually die from the damage of being hooked and then having the hook ripped from their mouth or throat.

But long-liners are not as damaging as trawlers, which drag the ocean floor with nets. The "tickler" chain that scrapes the bottom to scare fish into the net is responsible for destroying anything in its path that cannot escape. Corals and other delicate organisms growing on the bottom are razed over an area 150 times that of the area of forests clear-cut on land. Obviously trawlers catch more species than they want. When I worked aboard a shrimper one winter in the early eighties in Alaska, we'd bring in crabs that would run into corners on deck, and we'd throw them back (once an octopus showed its intelligence by immediately reaching up for the rail, and pulling itself up and over, back into the water). The fisheries management agencies goofed and allowed us to drag Kachemak Bay one day during the week of the crab molt. Due to our malpractice, we brought up hundreds of crabs with shells like wet cardboard that were crushed under the weight of the shrimp in the dragnet. Many fin-fish were able to survive, and swam away after a minute of recovering from the ordeal. But crabbing as well shrimping in that bay, one of the most productive on the planet, has been closed for almost all the years since.

As destructive as they are, trawlers mainly stay on the continental shelf. Driftnets, however, are set across the oceans. Pelagic driftnets can be up to an incredible 150 miles long. Occasionally weather causes a boat to lose or abandon one of these non-biodegradable synthetic nets, and the nets go on "fishing" for years, catching fish who attract predators who get caught and attract more. Now only10% of the big fish that filled the seas a few hundred years ago are left, and those survivors are smaller than their ancestors, due to overfishing. Fish is the primary source of protein for one-sixth of the world's population, and the pressure on the seas—the largest public domain, or "commons" on the planet—for food is not about to let up. Since the turn of the century, the global catch has been shrinking while the population is growing. If measured per capita, the catch is down to the levels of the mid 1960's, and dropping.

The "nurseries of the sea" are dying too. The U.S. loses 20,000 acres of coastal wetlands each year. Twenty percent of the world's coral reefs are damaged beyond their ability to recover. Fifteen percent of the world's seagrass beds are gone, having died in the last ten years, and kelp beds are going too.

It's not looking good. People need to eat fish. Fishermen need to catch fish. Few are demanding that things change.

I continue along the river, out to the point. On the way I find two boats being built out in the open. They seem like cypress on oak. The details are rough, but the overall project has nice—sweet lines. They're about thirty-six feet long, maybe they're twelve meters, with a wide belly and a twelve-inch-wide, twenty-two-inch-deep keel behind a ten-by-ten for a bow stem. Scraps lie around where they chain-sawed natural knees from curved, thick oak branches. These will be stout vessels. I wonder about their future. Will they catch enough fish? Will the prices allow the crew to earn a living after they pay for the boat and the fuel? One thing in their favor is that this part of the Pacific has less human impact than most coastal waters of the world.

At the point, a reef trails from a rock that is home to the harbor light at the south side of the rivermouth. A big swell must barrel along it. Who knows what the normal conditions are. My one glimpse of it is uninviting: a dark choppy sea whipped by a cold wind, and no swell. I try to imagine a sunny, glassy day with clear green overhead hollow lefts marching across that reef one after the other. It's difficult to do.

It's a long tramp back to town, past the boatbuilding yard and some stray dogs. Chile is full of stray dogs. I read that people like to cuddle them when they are puppies, then cut them loose to fend for themselves. In general, I have an aversion to stray dogs, having been attacked a few times over the years, but I've been amazed how friendly Chilean dogs are. They never even bark at me. It may reflect the kindness of the people. Today is different, though, and one tiny, little Jack Russell-ish mutt barks and charges, but it's easily scared off. In town I decide on one of the three or four sandwich shops that are the only restaurants I can find. Inside, a young girl comes and asks what she can serve me. I request a menu. She doesn't understand me. This is basic traveler's Spanish that has never failed me—or anyone, I would guess. When I ask again, she has that worried look of a teenage girl on the first day of the job when the only gringo who has ever been in the shop walks in and keeps asking for something she never heard of. So I ask for a list of things to eat, and she goes to the guy behind the counter—maybe her dad—and he gives her a menu. She returns to my table, folds the menu in thirds and shows me one side, saying that is all they have. Most of it is juices and ice cream. I decide quickly, ordering "Sandwich # 10-5" which is one of two shown, the other being "Sandwich #10-4," and sit back to enjoy the atmosphere. The walls are pink again, but not hot. Disco music is blasting. A life size poster of Marilyn Monroe in a red gown covers a door that has been sealed shut.

My sandwich comes. The menu described it as "bird" with mayonnaise, tomato, avocado and a fried egg. The egg is on top, its yolk peering up at me through a hole cut in the top of a hard roll. Immediately I see that it's impossible to eat as I expect to eat a sandwich. Usually travelers don't have this experience in Latin America, it is reserved for more exotic lands in Asia, Africa and Oceania. A few eyes are on me, only because I am unusual. I don't think they are wondering if I know how to eat "Sandwich #10-5." I decide to take a bite. As predicted, the yolk erupts from the hole like a volcano. I use three napkins to wipe my fingers and the tip of my nose, then attack with knife and fork. I glance around, and am relieved that no one is paying attention. When my plate is clean, I pay and leave the girl a hundred pesos. This confuses her again. She asks me to take my change. I tell her it's for her. She doesn't get it.

Yes, this is a subculture here in Lebu. In a few hours of walking around, I have come to the conclusion that when this Wild West town was in its heyday, there was lots of work and money, and as in the Pacific Northwest, the loggers, miners and fishermen patronized drinking establishments often. Then work began to dry up as the natural resources were depleted. Things got sour, happy drunks turned into brawlers and bums. Families were down and out, and religion came to the rescue. On garage doors, walls and fences you find quotes from the bible, or "Preparate, Christo Viene Pronto" painted in a neat but untrained hand. I suppose no one can afford to eat in a restaurant. But I have no idea what is really going on here. The dialect is beyond my comprehension. I can't find a beer in this town, maybe it's dry. I *do* find a bus depot and decide to be on the 6:45 AM to Temuco, in the central valley. This is how I have to proceed south, because once again, the coastal road diminishes to something smaller than a bus route. I'm headed for the town of Valdivia. I hear it's an attractive university town.

If these coastal towns were not so backward and if travel

along the coast was easier, I'd love to spend more time seeing the entire stretch, but I don't want to get stranded. I feel like I will find other places where I'll be happy to have extra time to hang out—where the possibility of kindred spirits will be greater.

On the way back to the hotel I glance into a window and see a bar, so I stop in for a schop, which helps me get to sleep early.

CHAPTER 11

Temuco

In the morning my attempts to be quiet are useless. It's like I'm stomping down the hallway to the bathroom, stomping back, then the clacking of my key in the lock echoes through the hall. The pack on my back makes me stomp even louder down the stairs to the front door. It's braced shut by a five-foot length of a sapling wedged to the front of the bottom step in the foyer. I remove the stick and step out on the street. I'm acoustically liberated, and proceed to the depot in the cool air of pre-dawn twilight, in the last moments of the madrugada.

It gets light all of a sudden, as if a giant curtain were opened. The driver arrives at the little depot just after me and sells me a ticket. We leave on time, but the bus is a local, and unlike the cruisers I've been riding which have reserved seats, this one picks up as many as can fit standing in the aisles. Tradesmen, laborers and secretaries are using it to go to work along the route. It's a long, slow trip to Temuco. In the first hour we pass a coastal plain at the mouth of a river valley that is full of farms. I love coastal farms and enjoy looking at this sweet place. I think of some of California's coastal farmland that has been lost, like the rich soils of Carpinteria, Ventura and Oxnard that are being covered with housing tracts, shopping malls and car dealer lots. It seems criminal to me. In the United States, 400,000 hectares of farmland are lost each year to urbanization and development. That's the equivalent of a one-kilometer-wide swath of land stretching from New York to San Francisco. It's a huge amount, but less than half the amount lost each year in China. This loss of food source is occurring wherever cities are growing, and that's all over the world. Arable soils are a limited supply on this planet. Not only are they being covered with concrete and asphalt, they are also being lost to desertification at a rate of fifty million acres a year. They are being eroded as well. Around 90% of cropland in the U.S. is losing soil to erosion at thirteen times the rate it can be rebuilt. Some of the worst erosion is of the richest soils. The soil that took thousands of years to build in what is now Iowa is eroding thirty times faster than the building process. Half of the soils of the nation have been lost already, just since the Europeans arrived.

The standard time requirement for building soil is 500 years per inch. Currently, an inch of soil is being eroded every seven to twenty-four years, depending on the location and farming practices. Simple math tells me that this is going to cause big problems soon, since the world population is growing rapidly. In the last forty years it has doubled. Right now one-third of humanity, that's two billion people, are chronically malnourished, and they're not all in African villages. Since George W. Bush took office, there's been a 22% increase in U.S. households experiencing hunger due to poverty. In the small town where I live on the California coast, the population is about 6,200. The local "Food Bank" feeds an average of 1400 people a month in 768 households. Not all of those receiving aid are residents within the city limits, so it must be about 15% of the people in the area. I read those figures three times when they came in the mail in a letter asking for donations. It was hard to believe. While Chileans lack many fine aspects of modern life, food is not one. So far I haven't seen anyone starving or even panhandling. I think the low population and ample supply of arable land create a healthy ratio. While the average American family throws 14% of its food in the garbage, 11% of us are never certain they will have enough to eat.

Even people who are getting enough to eat are developing mineral deficiencies due to the loss of minerals in the soils. Some essential minerals are present in only a third or a quarter of the amounts that my grandparents ingested when they ate fresh vegetables. When small farmers rotate crops, they can grow plants that reach deep into the earth with their roots. These roots can pull up vital minerals, and the farmer can plow the crop back into the field. Modern industrial agriculture doesn't take this time. There's no money in it.

At the head of this valley lie a series of lakes where hundreds of elegant black-necked swans congregate. In this area I'm happy to see a few small patches of native forest—the first I've seen of it. I think of all the country I've passed through, and the endless plantations, and now finally a glimmer of what Mother Earth created in this land. It appears similar to oak and beech, but that is a guess about unfamiliar species observed from a moving bus. The undergrowth is lush and dense, with climbing vines. It's beautiful. It's what I've wanted to see—what I expected to find in the huge open spaces on the map. Instead I've been disappointed by pine and eucalyptus plantations; endless tracts of dull monoculture that is grown rapidly and harvested in its youth. Until today I had not seen anything in a lumber mill yard or on a lumber truck that was bigger than a 4x4—usually it's 1x4's and 2x4's. Today I saw a truck with 2x6's and 2x8's, but the rings showed that almost every one was cut from the very center of a seven to nine-inch diameter tree.

If native forests are special to me, old growth forests are sacred. Have you been in one? They are rare these days. Each of the lower forty-eight of the United States once had primeval forests. Basically, they grew everywhere but in the deserts and prairies and chaparral. But today extensive tracts remain only in protected areas of Northern California, the Cascades of Oregon, along the border of Idaho and Montana, northwestern Wyoming, and below the highest peaks of Colorado and Arizona. The East, from Maine to Texas, Wisconsin to Florida, was one giant forest of ancient trees. Now, there are a few museum-sized pockets of specimens. In some regions only a half of a percent of the original forest remains, in other regions there may be as much as 6%. The accepted figure is that, overall in the lower forty-eight, 4% of old-growth forest remains, and I wonder what is the percentage of the population that has stood in such a forest.

After five hours of sitting on the rough bus, we finally make Temuco, landing in a small street-corner terminal for a single bus line. Luckily they have a bus for Valdivia, my next destination, and it's supposed to leave in five minutes. I buy a ticket but can't find the bus at the docks. Then I see it over in the corner of the lot, and approach the driver, but he won't let me on, telling me it's too early. So I look for a bite on the city street, carefully enter a tight convenience store with my pack on, get a couple empanadas of beef and onion, and eat them in the parking lot, keeping an eye on my bus. Just as I finish the greasy pastries the bus pulls forward and begins to take passengers. It's another comfy "Marco Polo" from Brazil. I can't figure out how they can have nicer busses than in the U.S., pay more for gas, have two employees on board, and still charge about a fifth of the price of a U.S. bus. But they do it, and I like it. Getting around in Chile is *way* easier than anywhere I've ever been. I don't know how long that will last though, with the peak of global oil production predicted to happen some time in the next few years. Oil will get more and more expensive. It has to. It's the law of supply and demand. Oil has already gone from twenty to seventy dollars a barrel in the last four years. We are living in the good old days of the future, or, as peak-oil analyst Richard Heinberg says in the title of his book, "The Party's Over."

When U.S. oil production peaked in the seventies, we began importing more and more of it. When global oil production peaks some time in the next decade (some say it's already plateaued), there will be no other planet to import it from. Production and availability will decline at the same time that demand is increasing due to rising populations, especially those of industrializing countries. The wind will be taken from the sails of civilization as we know it, leaving us becalmed in a doldrums of history. Our only option is to find new sources of energy. If we begin now we can lessen the impact, but not much is being done yet. Brazil's strategy has been to dedicate half of its sugar crop to the production of ethanol for powering its cars, but that has led to a doubling of sugar prices worldwide. In the U.S., one-sixth of the grain production is going into ethanol production, and Malaysia has big plans to produce huge amounts of biodiesel from palm oil.

The question is: if there are already over 400 million people dying of starvation each year (WHO estimates that one-third of the world population is starving), and if we are losing farming soils so rapidly, then how can we afford to grow crops to run our cars?

This is the concern of Lester R. Brown, president of Earth Policy Institute, and author of *Plan B.2*. Brown doubts the wisdom of growing enough grain to feed a person for a year just to convert it into enough ethanol to fill the tank of an SUV, especially now that we have seen six of the last seven years in which world grain consumption has exceeded production. Grain reserves are now the lowest in thirty-four years.

Future transportation will most likely be very different here in Chile as well as the rest of the world. I'm not just talking about the transportation of people, but that of food and goods. In Mendocino County people are organizing, taking a serious look at the approaching problem, and seeking self-sufficiency and localization, but here in Temuco, I doubt anyone is paying attention... yet. I wonder how hard humanity will be hit, and where people will be hit the hardest. Undoubtedly, the people who will suffer the most will be those who fail to plan for the day of 150 or 200-dollar-a-barrel crude.

CHAPTER 12

Valdivia

The ride is luxurious compared to the last bus from Lebu. I have come to accept it as my karma that if there is a whiney kid on a bus, he will be right behind me, kicking the back of my seat and pulling my hair, hanging his head over the seat and screaming. That's just the way it is—one of those mysteries of life, like when you choose the shortest of two checkout lines in a store, only to end up behind someone who has some problem that holds you up, while people who arrived after you and decided on the other line are already out the door. It used to drive me crazy, but after so many occasions, I get it. It's a cosmic joke—a divine prank—or it's karma. So I try to laugh at it these days. Still it's a relief to be off of that Lebu bus.

The kids on this bus are quiet, watching an 'R' rated murder mystery from the States called "One Way Out," which is translated as "Sin Salida"—literally: "Without Exit." So many people down here tell me they learned to speak English from watching movies, I don't know how they can do it with this kind of translation—and then there is the foul language conversion. When Jim Belushi calls someone an asshole, the subtitle reads "Stupid." Learning English this way could eventually get you in trouble. But in the short term, the foul language problem is taken care of, but the kids remain fascinated with the sex and violence. They're quiet.

The land changed once we got south of Temuco. If I were an inland type—and a flatlander—I'd say it was heaven. The feeling of this land is pastoral, from the Latin word *pastor*, meaning "shepherd," and I wonder what it is about a shepherd and his flock that is so comforting. There is something about this kind of landscape that brings psychological ease. The gently rolling grain fields, pastures, and vegetable plots are separated by rows of giant hardwoods. I heard that Valdivia is the rainiest city in Chile. The land is obviously well-watered. There is a sense that it will provide, like a father, nurture, like a mother.

In most native religions the people are provided-for by some form of earth goddess, and I wonder if that influence is the reason why every roadside shrine I have seen is a grotto or cave housing a statue of Mary, the mother of Jesus. Many of these shrines are set inside of a natural hollow, but some are constructed to look like a grotto or cave. In the Chinese sense of yin, the mother resides in the feminine environment: hollow, dark, damp, fecund.

I wonder if I could ever live away from the sea.

From the Valdivia terminal, I go directly to a little hospedaje that my guide book map shows as being close-by. The owner is an amiable man in his seventies with slicked-back hair, a limp, and a polite manner. They have one room left, he says as he leads me up a narrow wooden staircase. He shows me some kind of a shack added on to the building, but this is the second floor. I don't know what is under me, but I take it. It comes a thousand pesos cheaper because it doesn't have a TV. He apologizes that it's all he has left, but it's what I want. He shows me two spotless bathrooms, and says that one doesn't have hot water right now, but he is about to fix it. And he does.

After a shower, I walk into town. It has a pleasant feeling. It seems clean, but maybe that's because it gets well-washed by rain. There's an abundance of college kids around, as there's a state university here as well as a few tiny private schools. So there are a few hip hangouts, and I visit one for a Middle-Eastern lunch and a schop. This is the first offer of anything beside standard Chilean fare I've seen since a sushi shop in Zapallar (just north of Cachagua), the exclusive beach resort of the wealthiest Chileans, and it's the hippest spot since Café Vinilo in Valparaiso. It's a treat to eat different food in this big old Victorian house with a spacious deck for dining and hanging out. Even though people are smoking out on the deck, it's a relief from the typical smoky indoor restaurants.

I stroll back to the hospedaje via the riverfront, which takes me on a circuitous route, but the riverfront's the highlight of this town. The market sits by the river. Near it a bridge crosses from town to an island. Students cross on foot to attend the university, which is no more impressive than an average large high school in the States. Pedestrians heavily traffic the bridge, and an occasional rowing shell passes below in the flooding waters draining all the well-rained-upon land from here to the crest of the Andes, eighty miles east. All the water gives the city a fresh scent that's occasionally punctuated by diesel exhaust. A few of the downtown buildings are capped with towers, and some of them fly colorful pennants, giving the place a charming old-world appeal. While I walk the riverside my bladder swells from the beer. My pace quickens, and I find great relief when I make the hospedaje, and then take a nap. Amazing, how sitting on a bus all day can wear you out.

A few hours later I'm back out on the street to see what goes on in this town, but I see a sign that says happy hour ends at eleven o'clock, so I realize I'm not going to be seeing the local crowd. The place probably picks up around twelve-thirty or one. Conforming to the nocturnal habit of the South Americans is beyond my willingness to "do as the Romans do." I choose a workingman's bar: "*Bomberos*," literally "Pumpers," but meaning "Firemen." The only women in the place either work there or are half naked in beer posters on the wall. But it's a clean place. A TV plays a sports channel—the ESPN South America channel, showing soccer games.

Schop is often dispensed from taps radiating out of a large white ceramic head on the bar. I suppose the thing has a name and may be a common item in some parts of Europe, but I can't remember seeing one before. They probably have them in Bavaria. I order a schop from the one here. A guy down the bar orders empanadas. They look good, so I get a half-dozen myself. Empanadas are that kind of food which is different everywhere you go. Sometimes they are big, sometimes small, some are baked, most are fried. Some are folded, giving them a geometric outline, while others are curved half-moons or crescents with crimped edges like a pie. The ones here are little fried crescents filled with beef and onion. I salivate when they are set in front of me. They're delicious. Funny thing about deep fried food—no matter how much you know about it being unhealthy, it always tastes great.

A guy built like a fireplug comes to the bar and asks me if I am Chilean, and we have a good interaction. A few minutes later he invites me to his table where he and three friends are drinking. After he learns that I'm from the United States, political subjects arise.

Educated Chileans all know that the CIA brought Pinochet to power on a tragic day, September 11, 1973. They suffered under a brutal dictatorship for seventeen years. Conservative estimates are that 3,200 people were killed and tens-of-thousands tortured and disappeared by his regime. The United States, enabled by the work of Henry Kissinger, who covered up U.S. information about the atrocities, turned a blind eye to the human rights abuses, and maintained strong ties with Pinochet because he killed the first publicly elected Marxist in the world, his predecessor, Salvador Allende. A few years after that assassination, while George H.W. Bush was Director of the CIA, Allende's foreign minister and ambassador to the U.S., Orlando Letelier, then living in D.C and working with the Institute for Policy Studies, was murdered, along with his North American colleague, Ronni Moffit. We now know that Pinochet's intelligence chief, Manuel Contreras, a paid asset of the CIA under Bush, ordered the planting of the remote-controlled bomb which ripped apart Letelier's car in D.C. George W. Bush's father had the CIA leak a false report that cleared the Pinochet regime of any connection to the murder. Chileans who pay attention to the United States know this, as my host does, so when I tell him I think George Bush is a bad man, I am accepted as a friend with a big smile.

The others at the table are not participating in the conversation. My host explains that they are "political mummies." I tell him I know exactly what he is talking about—that I know plenty of mummies back home—too many. Then a troubadour enters—a Jewish-looking man dressed in black with a vest and a fedora to match—and begins serenading each table, improvising his songs according to the names of those seated at the table. Our table is the most receptive and he serenades us for an hour. He asks me if I like Bush, and I say he is very, very, very bad. This allows him to sing his next song knowing he will not insult me. Unfortunately I don't understand the song, but I enjoy his folksy-flamenco, nylon-string style. By this time these guys have been buying me one beer after the other for a couple hours, only allowing me to buy one round. Then they decide to end the night with a fine wine. I hate to mix beer and wine, but I want to be polite, so I do, then go use the bathroom where, in the old style, you piss on a tile wall below a perforated pipe with water trickling out of it. I say goodnight to the guys and stumble back to the hospedaje in the first hour of madrugada. I cringe when ringing the bell, hoping I'm not waking the elders up. When they let me in, they ask with a smile what time I would like breakfast.

Of course, a dog barks relentlessly below my window, but I'm getting used to it, and the alcohol melts the rough edges of the grating yaps, and I drift off.

People are up early the next morning, but I'm a little hung-over. I force myself to get up and to the breakfast table at the time I told them I would eat: 8:30. I'm in a fog while steeping a cup of black tea. The matriarch of the house, Eliana, brings a few slices of ham and cheese with bread. Chilean bread is like some I've seen in the Caribbean, called "Johnny cakes" there. I heard that the name is a bastardization of "journey cake," because the little hard rolls travel well. They are the size of a small hamburger bun, and have the consistency of a dry sponge. Not too bad though, when fresh, with butter. In three or four seconds I compare them to the "California Complete Protein" sprouted multi-grain bread I eat at home, cognizant that such a healthier bread is nonexistent here.

It is my morning ritual to drink several cups of tea, using the same bag, before I eat, but first I have to wait for the tea to cool. In the mean time I am sitting and staring out of the fog in my head like a sailor at a harbor-mouth waiting for it to clear. The gentleman who gave me my room, Roberto, enters, and his wife, Eliana, tells him I'm just sitting there not eating or drinking. She's wondering what's wrong with me. Turning in my chair, I explain that I just like to drink tea first, but I have to wait for it to cool. She is embarrassed and relieved at the same time. Every morning must be a minor adventure for her as strangers have their breakfast in her house. In summer, we come from all over the world. She tells me about a Chinaman who spoke not one word of "Castillano." I marvel at the feat of traveling without one word of the local language.

A Swiss couple comes down and joins me. I understand their Spanish well, but, of course, they speak English. Not being a language person, the abilities of European travelers always amaze me. We in the United States are really pitiful when it comes to language. I can only think of one non-Hispanic friend who is even close to being bilingual, though I do have some bilingual acquaintances. Now that we know languages are easily learned before the age of seven, I am astonished that none of the parents I know have placed their young children in a language-learning environment early in their schooling. Europeans humble me with their ability to speak three or four languages. When I hear of scholars who speak twelve, sixteen, or even twenty languages I feel hopelessly provincial.

Eliana joins us in conversation, but never takes a seat. I am beginning to wake up, and enjoy the interaction. She tells us stories of her childhood in the countryside, beginning with her parents sailing around the horn from Spain, seeking a better life. I can understand more than half of it—enough to follow along—because she speaks slowly and clearly, as she knows she must for us, and she's not missing a single tooth. I thank her for speaking this way. She laughs and says her son teases her about speaking like a robot. The surprising thing I learn over the two hours at the table is that my Spanish speaking is as good as the Swiss couple's, but they understand much more than I do. They have developed an ear for other languages, while my ear still hears something very far from a fluid reception of communication. For me it is more like having to frantically decode incoming messages racing against a stopwatch. I decide to work at receiving entire thoughts, phrases, ideas, and concepts, rather than grabbing at each word and translating it. I have minor success. Eliana encourages me. She is happy to rattle on and on to allow me to practice. She's as kind as she is verbose.

When we break from the table, the Swiss are off to the riverside market to see the sea lions there. The big beasts swim a few miles upriver to see what they will be offered from people at the market. Declining the offer to join them, I explain that I surf with sea lions all the time in Northern California. Instead I head for the tourist information office which, it turns out, is right next to the market, and request information on a reserve of natural coastal forest that I heard about. It's an unusual request, and the ladies decide they can't help me after almost ten minutes of discussion among themselves. They send me to the CONAF office, which is just like the Forest Service in the U.S., a branch of the Department of Agriculture. I bypass the CONAF office three times before I see it—right at the address I was given. It's a house set back off the street with a green shrubbery-filled yard in front, anomalous on this city block. I enter an empty office with cheap dark paneling, loiter, look at posters of trees until finally a secretary enters. Again, I make my request. She takes out a huge black ring binder and pages through it for a minute, then, saying, "Ya," as Chileans do when something is produced or completed, she opens the rings, takes out a single sheet and hands it to me. It covers sixteen points very briefly, some extremely briefly, like: *1) Catagorica de manejo: Reserva Nacional de Valdivia, 2) Provincia biogeographica: Valdivia, 3) Proteccion Legal: Total*, et cetera. Basically, it's useless information.

I'm thinking, "Okay, I got what I asked for, so I have to ask for something different." I explain that I would like to go hiking there and I need to know how to get there and what the rules are. She looks at me like I'm telling her I want to move in and live here. Just then, she is saved by a forest biologist who walks by. He's a German-looking guy in his fifties. She tells him what I'm asking and he turns and looks at me over his bifocals that he pulls down his nose, and says in English, "It is not so easy. Please, em, come to my, em, office." I follow him back to a small room full of stacks of papers and surrounded by bookshelves sagging under the weight of their overload. He's very welcoming, searching for English words that he probably hasn't used in a decade, pulling out maps of the reserve and showing me the routes of access. Obviously he is very endeared to the reserve, especially the groves of Alerce— similar to Sequoia, but actually a close relative of Cypress. These trees are smaller than Sequoias, but live longer—to 3600 years or more. He tells me that all the forests north of here are one huge ecological disaster. I let him know, I've seen it, and agree. Then he reveals that his reserve is not open to the public, and I'm thinking that this is a dead end when he says that they can make an exception for someone with my level of interest. It turns out that no one has ever come to this office with my request. He is happy that someone, especially someone from the States, actually cares about his reserve. He says that he can arrange for me to accompany the guard patrol that hikes through the place every week. He's got my interest, and starts showing me all the high mountaintops in the reserve. I admit my confusion; I thought it was a coastal reserve, but there's no coastline on his map. He looks at me, takes off his glasses and says that I'm speaking of a private reserve. He digs through his bookshelves and finds a brochure and gives it to me. On the back is the address of the Nature Conservancy Office in Valdivia, only a few blocks away. I thank him and he wishes me good luck.

A secretary answers the doorbell at The Nature Conservancy office, which shares an elegant house with a few other environmental groups. I repeat my request. She invites me in and asks me what exactly it is that I want to know. I tell her "Everything. I don't know anything." I ask her if she speaks English and she says in English "No, wait a minute," and she walks to the offices in the rear. I hear her telling someone in Spanish, "A man is out there who says he wants information on the reserve and says he doesn't know anything." A guy comes out and says hello. In a few seconds I realize he is fluent in English, but something about his speech makes me wonder where he is from, so I ask. "Milwaukee, Wisconsin." He has been working for TNC for twelve years in South America, so his speech has picked up a "Latin tinge" as a jazz musician would say.

We talk, and after a while he says I need to speak with Pancho, and asks me to wait. He comes back with Pancho, a cool Chilean in his thirties with a bald head and a goatee, fluent in English, who explains that I can't backpack in the reserve because 1) they are afraid of fire, and 2) they have no trails, though they are hoping to build some this year. I ask if he needs help, and he lights up and asks if I am qualified. I tell him I have a degree in geography, years of surveying experience, and a lifetime of backpacking experience. Pretty soon he's telling me about all the exceptions they could make to their no-backpacking rules for someone who knows what he's doing. He asks me to return at 4:30 and he will have more information about what needs to be done and when.

Back on the street I look for lunch. I find myself waiting on a busy corner beside a gorgeous blonde. As we walk across the street there is an intense vibe between us. At the other corner we exchange smiles when we cross paths. First I think that I should have asked her to lunch, then, laughing, "Ah, she's probably married to some millionaire."

I can't remember where I ate, but I *can* tell you it was nothing eventful. Chilean restaurants never are—at least the working class restaurants that I eat in. I have no doubt that I had beef, chicken, pork or fish with potatoes and a salad of lettuce and tomato, maybe with some avocado, but I'm not complaining. The food's good. It would just be nice to have some vegetables, or some kind of variety. This is Chile's hippest college town, outside of Santiago. I compare this to the same situation back home. There I'd have my choice of cuisines from all over the planet. In the end, it's not the variety of nationalities that is as important as the variety of foods. It's fine to eat nothing but Chilean food for the rest of your life, as long as you eat a wide variety of vegetables, grains, fruits and meats. The Japanese Government's dietary guideline recommends eating thirty different foods each day for health. I know it's important, and suspect that many Chileans have a diverse home cuisine. The markets are cornucopias. I ate well with my friends in Cachagua. It's the restaurants that are stuck, like a vinyl record with a scratch.

A Chilean was quoted in a travel book saying that Chilean "Society doesn't see diversity—it doesn't see anything except itself. There's no such thing as multi-culturalism in Chile." It makes this country sound boring, and without much of an opening for a man of the Japanese arts.

At 4:30 I return to have a five-minute meeting with Pancho. He explains a few possible projects, and asks me to come back at ten in the morning to meet with the reserve manager who he says is very happy that I want to help. These guys like their appointments and mini-meetings.

I leave the office and cross the bridge to see the university. I'm thinking that if I were to live in Chile, I'd prefer a college town where people are more progressive and things are happening. Roofs cover the walkways entering campus—a bad sign—they don't do that for the shade. It indicates that it rains more often than not, but it's better than a water shortage. I find the gym, thinking I might be able to get a workout. It's essentially a basketball court. I look around and can't find anything else. A guy is watching me. I don't know if he's a coach or a janitor, but I ask him if there is a weight room, and he gives me directions. On the second floor is a vacant room with an ancient universal gym. I used one of these in 1973 when I was a high school oarsman. It was outmoded by 1980 and I haven't seen one in fifteen years. I learn that they have no pool. I'm a bit disappointed as I leave the grounds to wander through the botanical gardens. The gardens are not impressive, few of the plants are flowering, but I'm happy to see a small redwood tree thriving in this hospitable climate—it makes me feel like I do when I run into another traveler from my home town: "Hey, what are you doing here?" I want to ask the tree.

As I leave campus I see a kid pushing buttons on an mp3 player. These kids always have to remind me that I have music with me. On the way back to town I listen to Ernest Ranglin's fresh "Modern Answers to Old Problems." Crossing the bridge, I see a single and a pair paddle lightly away from the rowing club dock. If I lived here I would row. I kinda like this town, but want more. Again I face the fact that I am spoiled.

Little things we take for granted add up to make life in California seem to be in a future century. I'm talking about things that seem ridiculous by themselves. Simple things are fresh in my mind like the availability of organic and international foods and state-of-the-art nutritional supplements, smoke-free restaurants and bars. And now, leaving the University gym, I appreciate the health club were I work out and swim. But the list is long when you take the time to make it. Did you ever fully appreciate express or priority mail? In many countries, the mail is a crapshoot that takes weeks. In Mendocino County we have excellent public radio, which gives us diverse sources of news and entertainment not spewed forth by a media corporation. This is a rare and precious thing in the world.

Downtown I discover a restaurant called "El Campesino," and it has country style cooking, which, around here, has a lot of German influence. In the middle of the nineteenth century, Chile invited Germans to settle this area. Almost 20,000 accepted the offer, and then procreated. I enjoy German meatloaf with boiled potatoes and fried bread with the old lettuce and tomato salad—and a schop, of course, a small one, a bit of the hair of the dog…

Then I call it a day.

The meeting goes well in the morning, but they say I can't start until January sixth, when the crew comes back from holiday vacation. I agree, but afterwards I wonder what I'm going to do for a week. While sauntering across town I stop at an office supply store and buy a new pen, then decide to search out the municipal pool that people at the university told me about. So I jump on a number sixteen bus as instructed, and ask the driver if he goes to "Piscina Agua," the name of the pool. He does. We go through poor residential neighborhoods making several turns at unimportant corners so that I am thoroughly lost, and eventually stop at the municipal pool. I have no idea what it is doing here, but here it is. I enter and ask if I can look first before paying. As I'm taking a peek, a guy I take for the pool manager realizes I'm a foreigner and offers me a tour. They have a bag-check counter so theft is not a concern, and if I pay extra, there's a sauna. The water looks cloudy, but acceptable, so I pay the high price (for Chile)—four dollars—to swim. When I check my bag, they give me a claim card on a rubber band that goes on my wrist, and a spandex swim cap that is mandatory. When I get in the water I realize it's way more than cloudy. It's green with algae, with less than a ten-foot visibility. But I'm here, so I swim. After a mile I stop, stand, and turn to see everyone in the place looking at me. I suppose it is because I know how to swim.

On the bus I realize that it's only the downtown area that is relatively clean and attractive. Most of the ride is through poor neighborhoods. From the bus I beeline for El Campesino. The swim made me hungry. I order *"asado de ollo"* thinking I'm going to get some kind of a beef stew in a clay pot. The waiter brings a pot roast. Of course. It's like home cooking, and I thoroughly enjoy it.

After paying, I'm out of small bills. This is something I've always had a problem with when traveling in countries less developed than the U.S., and it is something I have never been able to understand.

When you land and change money at the airport you are given large bills and it becomes your task to pay attention to where you are, where you are going, and what you have in your wallet, so that you pay with large bills whenever you are at a large or expensive place, and save the small ones for when you are in little places or out in the country. If you fail to do so you will be left unable to buy something—like a bus ticket—because you only have a 10,000-peso bill (about eighteen dollars) and they don't have change. I have been paying attention, but not well enough, I suppose. Actually, I think I've just been visiting small, cheap places.

So I visit a bank on the plaza. As I enter, a uniformed "Private Vigilante" (the title on his shoulder patch) jumps in my path to ask what I want. When I tell him he sends me to the second floor. I wait five minutes for one customer to complete business with the single teller, and reduce my 20,000 peso note to two fives and a ten. Next I need to break the five, so I go to a big drugstore on the corner, across the street and they help me.

The thing I don't get about all this is that you can be in a busy restaurant, with twenty people eating 2,000 peso plates, and they don't have change for a 10,000-peso bill. What do they do with the money? Either I am the only one paying for my meal, or they take the money out of the register every fifteen minutes. I've been in hotels that are full and I can't pay for a 4,000-peso room with a 10,000-peso bill. This is crazy to me, but no one else I've talked to seems to notice, which makes it even crazier, and it's always been like this for me in Latin America.

Now it's possible for me to go to the internet place and pay 300 pesos an hour to check e-mail. I finally remember to Google "Oregon pine," and to my surprise I learn that it is Douglas Fir. The joke's on me. I never took a close look at one. It's humbling to know that I, like my countrymen who I find unfathomable, can simply believe what I'm told without using my own powers of observation.

CHAPTER 13

Chaihuin

When I left Cachagua, Marinela gave me a list of people she knows in southern Chile who could help me learn about the place where they live. One of them was in Valdivia; a guy named "*Pollo*." "Chicken?" I exclaimed when reading her list. She explained that in Chile many little kids get a nickname for the animal that they look like, and the name sometimes sticks with them for the rest of their life. I accept the explanation and try to imagine a kid looking like a chicken. "Poor kid," I think.

Anyway, I'm hanging in Valdivia, so I decide to give the bird boy a call. He answers his cell phone and soon shifts to very good English, telling me he is on the road coming home from a meeting in Puerto Montt, a port city to the south, and will be home at six. I give him the hospedaje number and he says he'll call when he gets in and we can have dinner and a few beers. At five to six I return to the first floor salon to be near the phone. While waiting, I talk to Eliana for an hour, then call him again. He says he'll call me in ten minutes. Eliana continues our conversation. She is a conservative woman. She tells me about Chilean Christmas traditions, and then her various experiences with foreign travelers and their wide-ranging levels of ability to speak Spanish. After two more hours I call him again. He tells me he got hung up with work in Osorno, and will be home at 10:00, and I should call him at 10:30. By now I am starving, so I step out to a nearby restaurant—a simple one with no décor, just chairs and tables—where I try the Chilean standard, "Lomo de Pobre"; a flank steak with two fried eggs on top, and a side of fried onions and potatoes. Of course, I have a schop.

At 10:30 I leave the restaurant and find a phone booth to call Pollo. He says he's just arriving to Valdivia, and asks where I am, and says he'll pick me up in five minutes. So I wait for a half-hour sitting on a concrete wall, watching a pack of stray dogs, still fascinated by their friendliness.

In order to convey my emotional state, first I will say that I am extremely punctual. Martial arts training first taught me never to be late for class; then very soon it became obvious that if I came early I could learn more by practicing before class. Later came the realization that I should arrive earlier to help my teacher get everything prepared. This all may sound like the drill sergeant talking, but in the end I realized that to be late for any meeting is rude, as it shows a lack of value for the other person's time. Time is what a person's life is made of, and should be valued. That's Rasta.

But, while I think it's rude of him to be doing what he is doing, I acknowledge that I am an equal participant in this stringing-along. I can disengage at any time, and I have chosen not to. I am assuming there is a reason for this insanity, which may be as simple as the cultural attitudes towards time and punctuality. I give it a half-hour and am in the final minute of waiting, about to leave, when he drives up and invites me into his car, like nothing ever happened. Okay, I forget it and enjoy talking to him learning about this area and what he does here. He takes me to a lively night spot called "The Bunker," named after Adolph Hitler's last redoubt. I'm not sure of the nuance of the humor. It's full of people eating and drinking and smoking. It's a popular spot, not a hip one.

He tells me about his business. He's part-owner of a fleet of fishing boats that go out for king crab and a bottom fish with a name I don't get. The thing is caught on long lines set at 3500 feet down. I double check on that depth. He flirts with the waitress who has no interest in him (he doesn't look much like a chicken any more, but with his thin features, I can see how he once did). Pollo insists on paying the bill and I let him by way of compensation for my time that he wasted. He takes me downtown for a nightcap, but it is still before midnight, and no one is out yet, so we grab a last beer at a "Jazz Bar" that is playing acid jazz. When we part, he tells me to call him at 11AM to make plans to have lunch with his family.

I sleep late and then hang around the breakfast table talking to Eliana. At eleven I call Pollo, and he tells me to go to "La Casa," a big old yellow Victorian house by the river that his wife owns. She rents rooms as galleries, boutiques, and a café. I arrive on time, at 1:30, and of course, he's not there. So I have a look at the art, which is not interesting, then put the iPod on and relax on the veranda listening to bossa nova. At two his wife arrives and I introduce myself, explaining that I'm waiting for Pollo. She calls him and he tells her that he's on his way. I return to the music for another half-hour, then leave.

The waiting makes me realize I don't have time to waste with him, and it makes me realize that I don't have the time to wait for the Nature Conservancy crew to get back from their holiday. So I march over to TNC's office to tell them this, but it's Friday afternoon on the last workday of the year, and only the secretaries are in. I decide to make a trip out to look at the job in the morning, to suss it out and get an intuitional hit. Then I'll take off for the Andes.

Back at the hospedaje I meet Harold, a German landscape architect. He's a good guy, and I feel like having company, so I talk him in to going out to the Kunstmann Brewery for dinner. I laugh about dragging him out for German food, but he's a good sport. The beer is probably the best Chile has to offer. A golden ale named "Torobado," literally "beige bull," was named for the farm that was here before the brewery bought the property. It's a brew head-and-shoulders above the typical barley pop, with a rich flavor and full body. The prices of the food are high, so I have a forgettable sandwich. Back in town we hit the jazz bar for a nightcap. A Buddha bar groove throbs out of the speakers while we talk. I don't understand why the euro-techno-lounge-music, also called "acid jazz" can be considered jazz. I like the groove, but it has little to do with jazz. The minstrel who played on my first night in Valdivia was the only live musician I've come across so far in Chile. It seems to be a rarity. In any small college town stateside, there will be some live music several nights of the week. Even on the isolated Mendocino Coast it's that way, and an occasional big name passes through. I like to travel three-and-a-half hours to the San Francisco Bay a few times a year to hear my favorites play in person. My memories of the concerts are sweet. I wonder how life would be if I never went to another Latin jazz concert, never attended another reggae festival. The musical quality and variety is another amenity of the United States that we take for granted.

Harold's not paying attention to the music. He isn't conservative, but he's not a liberal German. He's a bit on the timid side—middle of the road. He gets his news from mainstream corporate media, and it interests me that while he is better-informed than most people in the States, it's not by much. But I'm not in the mood for politics so I stay with the light topics of his type of traveler. Stories of past travels are enough to keep the space between us filled with words.

The next morning's breakfast is with Harold and a dreadlocked guy from the Basque region of Northern Spain who intends to hitchhike through Argentina, down to Punta Arenas in the extreme south of Chile. Eliana lets me go without a long conversation, as she knows I'm on a mission. At the market, I find a colectivo that goes to Niebla, a little town by the river-mouth. The driver delivers me to the tiny ferry port, and I step right on to a little passenger boat with a cabin forward, canopied benches on the aft deck, and a new red, white and blue paint-job. We cross the river, passing between two old stone fort walls with parapets, one on either side of the river. This defense strategy made it difficult for invaders to enter the river to take Valdivia from the Spanish. In the middle of the river a few terns pass overhead. There are ten species of terns found in Chile, and I cannot identify this one for sure, but I suspect it's an Arctic tern, which migrates from the Arctic to the Antarctic and back every year—the longest migration known. I muse about possibly seeing this very same bird in Alaska while sailing on Kachemak Bay, when the tern was headed for the Arctic shores. I remember the time I was surveying section lines out in the wilderness in the foothills of the Alaska Range about a hundred miles northwest of Anchorage. It was spring. The ice had thawed, and there were ponds in the rolling landscape where, during the thaw of the last ice age, large chunks of ice had been buried in the sediments deposited along the meltwaters. These chunks, sometimes bigger than a house, subsequently melted, leaving a kettle—a pond in a depression with no outlet. These kettles were full of frogs that were most likely mating and calling for mates, given the time of year and the intensity of the clamor. Flocks of Arctic terns were taking an overland short-cut to the shores of the ocean that men named them after. They had come from Antarctica, up the pacific, but rather than fly west around Alaska, they went right up Cook Inlet, and continued north across land. Here they were, about to cross the mountains, screeching excitedly while hovering over these ponds, diving and filling up on frogs to fuel their final flight. For the frogs it was the terror of death from above. I wondered how long this has been their annual pit-stop. How many generations of terns have eaten frogs in the spring at this kettle? How many men know about this?

In Corral I ask for a bus to Chaihuin, but the answers are not easily understood. I gather the general whereabouts of the bus station, then locate the little turquoise building, but it's an hour's wait for the bus to Chaihuin, so I hike out the road to the edge of town, and put my thumb out. Only a few vehicles pass before a young Indian couple in a black pickup stops, and I hop in the back. I'm on my merry way to Chaihuin, wrapping around the corner of the coast at the south side of the river-mouth on a beautiful sunny New Year's Eve. The landscape reminds me of the Mendocino Coast back home, but the coastal bench here is not as wide. Twenty-foot tall wave-washed rocks look like slate. The dark grey strata is laid back towards land as if the waves had knocked it over. Indians raise sheep here. They seem to be very friendly with each other. Everyone waves as we pass. Then the truck dies.

The driver can't get it started, so he lifts the hood. I jump out, feeling funny just sitting there in the back. He decides that it's not getting gas, so he disconnects the gas line and sucks a mouthful of gas and spits it into the carburetor, and tells his wife to try it again. He repeats this three times. The third time I instruct his wife not to put her foot on the gas—I'm taking a guess. It might be flooded, so it's either that or floor it. I can never remember. I'm not much of a mechanic.

Just then a mini van comes along-side us, and the driver asks if we're okay. He's told we are. Meanwhile I'm trying to figure out if he's a colectivo or not. He has two couples in the back, and they look like they are traveling even though they look local—if that makes sense. I ask if he is going to Chaihuin and he invites me to ride with him. Everyone is very nice and polite. So much so that I sense—maybe due, as well, to their conservative dresses with a little lace—that they are Christians of some devout style. The girls are pretty Mapuches, in their twenties, with long clean and well-combed black hair falling down their backs and long noses extending down their tan faces. They might be sisters coming home to be with family for the New Year.

The driver asks where I'm going, and delivers me to the Reserve. I'm still not sure if he is a cabby or not, so I offer money, but he declines with a big smile. People have to get out to allow me to get my pack from behind the seats. While waiting I see that the young husband beside me has one of those big black hornets with the rusty hair sitting on his shoulder. I send a backhand at it and am an inch off in judgment, stinging him with flicked fingertips. I cringe, but he never even bats an eye or looks at me, he just keeps smiling and talking with the others.

In a few minutes I'm talking with Alfredo, the reserve manager, who seems well-educated but doesn't speak a word of English. He is surprised to see me, but I explain my desire and he accommodates me, sending me out to see the valley with a slight Indian park guard named Enrico. We walk along a dirt road beside a river, and are set upon by the hornets. I kill one and look at it. Surprised, I see that it's a fly. That's good. It won't kill me. No doubt it's a relative of the "green-head" that I grew up with on the coast of Southern New Jersey. I've heard them called "deer flies" and "horse flies" but don't really know what they are called, which I find amusing, given my interest in nature. It shows how we tend to ignore insects. I have field guides to birds, mammals and trees of North America, but never bought "Reptiles of North America," and never even *heard* of "Insects of North America." Enrico teaches me its name, *tabana*. I ask with a laugh why there are more around me than him, but he takes me seriously, explaining that they like the colors blue and black. I'm wearing a blue t-shirt and am carrying a black lumbar pack. I inquire about their bite, and he assures me that they leave no big welt. I tell him about the flies that come out of the East Coast salt marshes and how strong the bite is. A kilometer later we see a huge tarantula crossing the road. It's wearing the same outfit as the tabana—hairy, with black and rust colors. I stop and play with it with a stick, and ask if it's dangerous. He says no. "That's good," I tell myself.

Wild fuchsias grow along the river side of the road, five or six feet tall, and full of pendulous flowers, hot pink on the outside, purple inside. Opposite them, hanging over the road-cut, is *nalca*, he teaches me, an edible plant that's probably part of the rhubarb/celery/cow parsnip class, Magnoliopsida. It has those kinds of leaves, but they are three feet in diameter, dark, wrinkled and hairy. We pass some foxgloves blooming. I inform him that they are native to Europe, but they grow wild in the woods where I live too. I wonder if the blackberry we see is the same species that is native to the Pacific Northwest. If so, how did it get here? The thistles are clearly a different species than ours, but a very similar species, just a bit more dramatic in appearance. I question him about poisonous plants, and he is confused. I tell him about poison oak, which is plentiful at this same latitude in California. He is amazed. He never heard of such a thing. "That's good too," I tell myself.

Before bushwhacking in these woods I present one last question: "Are there any dangerous animals at all in this forest?" Enrico gives me the negative. No snakes, no venomous insects, only the puma, which I know from California to be fairly shy, and sensitive to size—not a concern for a man over six feet tall. I've only ever seen the ass end of one running into the bushes.

We get to the valley, which runs south from this road that winds along the south side of the west-flowing river. Enrico finds something resembling a trail, and we enter the woods. It disappears after a hundred feet, and I'm snagged by bamboo vines, which loop over various appendages as I attempt to proceed. It's unbreakable, so I retreat and fall in behind Enrico, who is wielding a machete. We cross a muddy area with little vegetation, and holes in the ground. I want to know what made the holes. After ten minutes of explanations and further questions to clarify, I finally understand that they are made by land crabs, which they call "birds." You can imagine the source of my confusion, and the Abbott and Costello routine that we went through. I never expected a land crab at this latitude.

The woods are broad-leafed, dense, and impenetrable, with an unyielding understory, including various vines and occasional thickets of a bamboo they call *kila,* which can be over an inch thick. The ground is damp, and he tells me it floods in winter. I realize the best place for a trail is on the side-slope, maybe six or seven meters above the bottomland. On the steep slope the earth is hard. It's difficult to get a bite even with my Vibram soles. Not much covers the ground besides fallen leaves. I still cannot see out of the canopy to get a view of the lay of the valley, even when I climb a tree. Navigation might be difficult, but there is moss on the south side of the trees, so it would be hard to get lost. The forest looks tropical, but we are almost at forty degrees of latitude. Enrico offers little, but answers all my questions. In winter it occasionally snows at elevations over 1500 meters, and valley bottoms flood after heavy rains—the same as the Mendocino Coast.

I have an idea what I'm getting into, so we head back. On the road-walk I try to make conversation, talking about all the similarities and differences between this forest and the one where I live. I find it interesting that this forest has nothing like poison oak, and fill him in on how bad it can be.

I had a case once, which would have had me in the hospital if I had had health insurance. I take care of *myself*—I'm my own doctor—but this time I was getting a little worried. My arm looked like a log; swollen beyond recognition with no indication of the contours of wrist and elbow, and covered with scab that was broken like mud-cracks. Golden fluid oozed out of the fissures. The normally loose, wrinkled skin over my knuckles and elbow had become domes, turgid with fluid. I couldn't stand without a powerful ache from my own blood pressure. And there was nothing to do but wait, unless I were to take a chance with a cortisone injection, which I've refused ever since I talked to a guy in the gym. He was obviously recovering from some trauma. I asked, and was told that when he had poison oak, he received a steroid injection, which caused the deterioration of both of his hip joints and he had to have them replaced with artificial ones when he was in his thirties. He just had to have those artificial joints replaced, only five years later.

On this particular occasion I did, however ask a friend for a prescription for oral steroids—prednisone. When the pharmacist saw me she insisted that I go to the hospital, but I talked her out of it somehow. Then the next day it got worse. The thing with poison oak is that you never know how long it will continue to get worse, and when it will turn around. I promised myself that if it was worse in the morning I would go to the hospital, and luckily it turned in the night and I saw minor improvement when I woke. I was due to travel to Japan in a week and was e-mailing my friend there telling him I might have to postpone. Poison oak clears amazingly fast though, and by the time I landed in Fukuoka, the only indication of my suffering were the pink blotches of new skin on my arm.

Next I tell Enrico about rattlesnakes, then bears, answering his questions about the times I've been chased by bears and how many people get killed every year by them. The look on his face changes to one you might find on a kid watching a horror movie. He's overwhelmed with the abundant dangers of the North American woods.

I realize that I have frightened this young, innocent, gentle Indian with tales of an exotic forest full of dangers, and I remember the scary movies I watched as a kid. Someone would be in the South American forest. There were strange serpents with potent venom, vampire bats, tarantulas crawling on a sleeping man's pillow, piranha devouring a man in the river. I change the subject.

We round a bend and a crested caracara is sitting in a tree maybe thirty meters away. "Caracara?" I ask. "Carancho" he answers. Later I learn that they are the same bird, and that many animals have local names in South America. This large bird looks kind of like a cross between a hawk and a raven, but is actually a close relative of the falcon. I've only seen one before, and that was in Curacao.

Back at the headquarters I confirm that they will provide

housing when I come to work, and they tell me groceries will be provided as well. I promise them I will return in a few weeks, thank them with handshakes and leave. I have some time before the four o'clock bus, so I cross a quarter-mile of dunes to see the beach and the waves. It looks like a well-formed right might peel off the sandbar at the rivermouth, but the swell is too small to know. I walk barefoot in the swash to the south end of the cove and back, flailing my shirt to keep the tabanas at bay. Then I catch the beat-up old bus.

On the way to Corral the driver stops for people on the roadside who don't board. They give him money and requests. I don't understand a word of the Indian patois, but imagine they are asking for simple things like rice or cooking oil. One guy asks for beer. There is a section of coast on this drive that is a gem: pastures on a coastal bench sit above surf-battered rocks. I am inspired to build a home here.

Back in Corral little fishing boats fill the cove. As if they were all owned by one person—which may be true—they are all painted the same colors: yellow with orange on the inside. All are double-enders. Some are little flat-bottomed rowing dories, others are about twenty-foot with nicely curved lines and a sail mast and boom. On the way to the ferry dock I spot a large red-necked grebe, which I later determine to be the great grebe, locally called a *huala*. It resides all over the Southern Cone.

Back in Valdivia it's New Year's Eve, so I pick up a bottle of cabernet before returning to the hospedaje. I anticipate that Eliana may invite me to join the family for dinner, and if not, it will make a good birthday gift for her, as she turns seventy in four days.

I am invited. As I rest in my room I smell the slow-cooking dinner scents drift into my window. Dinner is at "10:30, mas o menos."

"There is that confidence that there is a better place than the present
environment, which seems of so torn and ragged a nature. There is
that sense that there is a way to live and a way to be that rings truer
and goes deeper and finds more of the true self within it than the way
of being and doing that is taught by your culture."

—The Q'uo

CHAPTER 14

Crossing the Andes

Dinner was fun, though it wasn't served until midnight. I figured that the "mas o menos" meant mas, so I allowed an extra fifteen minutes before descending to the dining room at 10:45. Harold the German figured that it meant 11:00 so he came after me, and a tall, blond-haired gardener from Northern Italy who spoke only a few words of Spanish, but understood a lot just because of the common Latin root of both tongues, knew that it meant more like 11:15, his culture being more similar to this one in reference to time.

Roberto gave me the honor of opening a bottle of champagne two minutes before the hour, and after a toast, all men shook hands and hugged, everyone else kissed cheeks. Roberto and Eliana's daughters, a son-in-law, and cherubic eight-month-old granddaughter were all there. The baby (called a *wa-wa* in Chile) was always happy every time I saw her, and tonight was the same. We all told stories and had a good meal of roasted pork and potatoes with some tasty special salads. The Italian seemed to have a dialect that sounded like Argentinean Spanish; there were lots of *sh* sounds replacing *s*'s ("cinco" was "shinko") and the soft *g* sound left his mouth often as he attempted to communicate, all the while laughing at himself.

At nine the next morning, I was awake and thinking of getting on a bus. I went through my entire pack and separated out a few things that I hadn't been using, and gave up my big heavy Spanish verb book. From now on I'd be carrying food, so I had to make room. Everyone was still asleep when I went to the terminal to see what my options were.

I learned that there were buses directly to San Carlos de Bariloche, the famous Andean resort in Argentina, and inquired about the schedule. I should have known when I heard "19:00" as the arrival time, that the clerk was using military time, but I didn't make the leap. When he said, "*trece,*" dropping the final *e*, I thought he was saying "*tres.*" This led us directly into another Abbott and Costello routine in which I thought he was telling me that the bus left Osorno at three, and after a six hour ride, was in Bariloche at seven. Amazingly, he kept his cool. I guess he's used to this stuff. So am I, though the cause of the problem is usually with me, so I take a few seconds from time to time to do things like look at the ceiling, scratch my head, and take a deep breath. Finally the gentleman wrote the schedule on a piece of paper, and I saw the problem immediately; the bus leaves at 13:00, not 3:00. I told him what I thought he was saying, but he was only slightly amused. He was, however, genuinely happy that I finally understood.

Back at the hospedaje, I enter and Roberto, always the first to rise, comes to the door. I tell him I'm thinking of running for the 10:30 bus to Bariloche. He suggests that I just go to Osorno. I *am,* I say, but he mumbles something about not having to go so early, and gets on the phone to the "Cruz del Sur" bus line, and verifies that the bus from Osorno to Bariloche doesn't leave till 1:45, and since there are many busses to Osorno, a one-hour ride from here, I had time to sit down and have breakfast. So we sat down, and Eliana joined us.

At this point, after only five days, I'm feeling like these people are my aunt and uncle. We talk about my plans to hike in the Andes and return in a few weeks, and after a couple hours

I excuse myself to get ready. In my room, the clock tells me that the last bus that will get me to Osorno in time leaves in thirteen minutes, but I remember coming in here last night during the midnight countdown and noticing that my clock was two minutes fast, so I know I can make it. In just a few minutes my pack is on one shoulder and I'm stomping down the little staircase. Poking my head into the salon, I kiss Eliana goodbye and give her a bag of my culled belongings to hold, then stride across the street. Hearing "Hey!" I turn around to see Roberto jogging across the street with no cane. He always uses a cane when he leaves the house. He comes running up to me and says I don't have to go to the terminal, that the bus will come up the street to the corner and pick me up there, so I won't be late. He walks me to the corner and we wait a few minutes. I'm trusting. He's getting just a little nervous. Then the bus comes up the street and stops at the light across the big boulevard from us. Roberto walks out in the street to ask the driver, with sign language, if he is turning and we get an affirmative signal. The bus turns and stops, and I'm on, thanking my friend Roberto again while climbing the stairs.

The bus heads southeast through many wetlands. My Valdivian family just explained the origin of these swamps a few hours ago, but it was in the madrugada, after a few bottles of wine, so all I remember is that it was a cataclysmic event involving an earthquake and a flood of water charging down from the Andes. Or was that another disaster? It seems they also told about an earthquake causing a landslide into a lake that created a wall of water full of trees running downriver and hitting Valdivia at some time in the past. I see those orange Peruvian lilies that grow in my friend's yard at this same latitude, and the exact opposite month, on the California coast. As we arrive in Osorno, olive-green and ochre "black faced" ibises, a bird the Chileans call *bandurria,* forage on a lawn.

When I buy my ticket to Bariloche, the clerk asks for my passport. It's the first time I've used it to get a bus. Obviously, they want to be sure you can cross the border to Argentina. The new passports in the USA will have a radio frequency device implanted in the cover that will contain more information about the bearer than most would want available to security guards, just out of a simple preference for privacy. By the time you read this, a new passport will allow customs agents in the U.S. to know all about you as soon as you're in the vicinity. You have to wonder who else will procure the reading technology. In some ways it'll be worse than our nationwide exposure to thirty million security cameras. I wonder if this electronic loss of privacy will ever come to Chile. The technology costs money, but as long as it comes from North American companies, my government will probably give it away as foreign aid in the battle against terrorism. Columbia will gobble it up, but the leftward trend in the rest of South America may lead to nations declining to join the U.S. course towards a police state.

Like the proverbial frog in the pot of gradually heating water, we are losing our liberties so slowly that we don't demand them back. Little by little, the freedom and privacy we once enjoyed is lost. Soon we are scheduled to have a national ID card, the details of which are not public yet. It could also have an RFD, like the passport. It gives me the creeps to know that sensors anywhere will know so much about me. I wish I could wake up from the nightmare that is happening in my homeland. It could be enough to drive me out of the country.

It's another short wait in the terminal, listening to 60's pop music from the States on the loudspeakers. Eric Burdon and The Animals sing,

"We gotta get out of this place,
If it's the last thing we ever do.
We gotta get out of this place,
'Cause, girl, there's a better life for me and you."

And I wonder, if there will be an exodus of freedom-loving people from the United States in the near future, or will they stand up for their rights, or will they become frog soup?

Then, after a few minutes, I'm on another deluxe cruiser heading east through perfect farmland, towards the Andes, and listening to my country/folk-rock playlist. The music is comforting. There is something homey about it that relieves the strain of always being in a strange place, in a strange culture, speaking a strange language, and now heading towards another strange country. The stress had accumulated without my knowing until listening to this music brought a contrasting and comforting calm. It's a good stress, *eustress*, but still it's necessary to escape and recover from.

A light rain falls and the clouds are low. The verdure of the fields is that lush, glowing green that you only see in the rain, when no glare reflects off the leaves. It reminds me that the ancient Greek word for green literally meant "wet." Flocks of bandurrias pass in formation overhead, honking. If I weren't addicted to the coast, I might live in a place like this where I could learn to grow productive gardens yielding bushels of food, and I wonder about Buchupureo and the predicted sea-level rise again. The prudent man would not live there.

Environmental catastrophe has been predicted since I became a teenager, since the time I was able to comprehend such predictions. And though we certainly are on the brink of it now, even those of us who are concerned hesitate to change our lives in anticipation of the forecasts. Are we afraid to be a Chicken Little, or are we the townspeople who have heard the boy cry "Wolf" a few times too many? If scientists only knew with some accuracy what the future will bring, then we could trust their prognostications. But anyone with an IQ higher that their body temperature can read that all the implications of global warming, combined with the death of the oceans, population growth, peak oil, the agricultural crisis, the general decline of so many natural systems, and the general unsustainable quality of so many human endeavors that we depend on will spell trouble, and soon. And then there are the predictions of ancient peoples like the Mayan and Hopi who say big changes will happen in the next few years, maybe in

2012. Still, I can't quite bring myself to go into survival mode. Maybe I'm afraid of all the fun I'd miss. Are we all insouciant fiddling Neros?

As we enter the foothills, diagonal slopes, which must be the flanks of volcanoes, occasionally appear above the forests in the distance, their snow-capped peaks penetrating the dark wet ceiling. I listen to "Box of Rain" and relax. "It's all a dream we dreamed one afternoon, long ago."

Long bus and plane rides provide an opportunity to daydream. When we daydream our brain waves slow to the *alpha* range. The parts of our brain that allow creativity and problem-solving are actually more active than normal. When we "zone-out," we can access deep wisdom, inspiration, and insight. But on this ride, I get no answer to my question about where to live.

At a spot on the road where there is a vista across a large lake, we pull over, and the conductor crosses the road for *a jabali* sandwich. From the sign I gather that it is wild pig—"Comida Campestres," and a silhouette of a javalina-looking boar.

We enter Vipuyehue National Park. Layers of dark misty clouds hang weightlessly in the valleys as if they are snagged on the treetops of a primeval forest. The shape of the trees is one unseen in North America, except in Southern Mexico. (Just where is the boundary between North America and Central America, I wonder? Politically, Mexico's border, zigzagging across the southern Yucatan peninsula, is the answer. But geographically, a line following the river valleys that make the shortest connection from the Bahia de Compeche to the Golfo de Tehuantepec is a more rational boundary. Of course it's not possible to use this line, as it would place the southern extreme of Mexico off the continent.)

This is a tropical-looking forest, draped with vines and choked with bamboos, one of which grows leafless to a man's height, then has a leafy chimney-brush top. I constantly refer to mental images from the same latitude north, and imagine the lower slopes of Mount Shasta hosting such a jungle. It's fascinating. The obvious guess is that the isolation of the Southern Cone provided a cool weather niche for the tropical trees of the Amazon to descend into, but it turns out that this is wrong. Though 80% of South America is tropical, these forests are isolated from the tropics to the north by the vast deserts of Northern Chile and the dry pampas of Argentina. These trees are descendants of the ones that grew on Gondwanaland, the ancient southern continent that broke up and drifted apart, becoming South America, New Zealand, Australia, Africa, and India. Their ancestors found a nook to survive in during the last ice age, when most of this Southern Cone was under ice. Their closest relatives are in Australia, but 90% of them are endemic species.

This forest of the Southern Cone is known as the Valdivian Forest. It once began on the Pacific shore and ran over the great divide until it tapered off in the dry valleys of the eastern slopes. Now 80% of what grew in the small coastal range is gone, and 90% of what once covered the central valley has been razed. Half of the entire forest has disappeared, and if deforestation were to continue at the same rate, all of it would be gone by 2025, but I have faith that the many large national parks and reserves will save some of it.

At road-cuts, layers of charcoal-colored lava, frozen in mid-flow, are revealed. Nalca, with its umbrella-size leaves, hang over the cuts. It turns out this is a special plant in that it's part of a nitrogen-fixing symbiosis with cyanobacteria, and it is also highly invasive.

As we approach the pass, purple lupine appears for the first time. It reminds me of Alaska. Until now, all the lupines have been yellow. The light green moss we call "Old man's beard" hangs from the tree branches. At the pass we're just below tree line.

Entering Argentina is easy for us. A golden retriever explores the luggage bay for interesting scents, while we get our passports stamped. Some of the passports I see are from the States, Germany, and the Netherlands, as well as Chile, and Argentina. I buy an empanada in the cool, light rain while waiting for the others to get on the bus. We are out in the middle of nowhere—just this border crossing here. But in Latin American style, there is a little stand where you can buy a snack.

Snack foods are omnipresent in all of the Latin American countries I've visited. Cookies, crackers, candy, crunchies, chewies, and cheesies as well as sweets of all kinds can be found in any public place. I haven't eaten any of them in many years, preferring my hunger to the poisons—mainly sugar, hydrogenated vegetable oils and artificial flavors and colors.

Sugar causes a spike in my blood sugar levels that my pancreas must balance with a spurt of insulin production, ending in the "sugar blues" when the insulin has done its job and blood sugar levels suddenly drop. It's a ride I don't enjoy. Nor do I care to feed intestinal yeast with it, or lower the strength of my immune system. It is a non-food to me, but not my countrymen. The United States grows a lot of corn. I mean a *lot*, and about half of it is processed into high fructose corn sweetener that accounts for about a sixth of the average North American's caloric intake, and it's responsible for the current epidemic of obesity. Even though they are high calorie foods, the energy intense series of processing stages that these corn sugar foods go through ends up using ten calories of energy input for every calorie of snack food produced, diminishing other nutrients at the same time. Most of this energy input comes from the energy of oil, so I wonder if these foods will continue to exist when oil prices soar. High oil prices may improve people's diets.

I avoid hydrogenated oils mainly because they interfere with the body's ability to metabolize good oils, causing deficiencies of certain fatty acids. Artificial flavors and colors are not food—for anyone. Never were, never will be. One study found widespread nerve damage that was due to the synergistic toxicity of MSG, aspartame, and food coloring when combined. I expect future studies to reveal that it is these kinds of combinations that have been killing people with all the new diseases and deteriorations that plague modern people. And the deadly combinations may not all be purely chemical. At some point the influence of electro-magnetic fields and microwave transmissions may be known to alter our internal environment. I also suspect the waste products of yeasts, molds and fungi that seem to thrive in a body fed on junk food.

It took some time, and I am still learning, but the transition I see that I am making is one from eating for gratification to eating for nutrition. Snack foods are typically gratification and little if anything else. I've lost interest in them. I'm not suggesting that we eat solely for nutrition, though some would argue we should. My appreciation for a fine traditional Italian dish preceded by an appetizer and accompanied by a dry Chianti and fine olives is too strong to deny. A good Japanese meal can be an equally sensual pleasure and usually even more nutritious. The gratification and enjoyment of indulging in our sense of taste and oral experience of texture is a pleasure that, if you ask me, is part of the reason we are here in the physical realm, but part of the gratification should be an appreciation for the nutritional value of wholesome foods.

I try to avoid fried foods too, but it's not that easy on the road, especially here, and I have a weak spot for empanadas. I enjoy these types of pocket foods of all cultures, from the little African samosas to the giant Italian calzones, especially when home-made.

While wiping the grease from my fingers I watch what look like juncos finding crumbs near the empanada stand. They are Patagonian sierra finches beautifully colored like an oriole; an orange back, golden breast, grey wings. Their *heads* are what remind me of juncos. The male has a black head, and his mate's is slate grey.

Now in Argentina, the forest has changed. It's of a single species, beginning at tree line and extending down into the valleys.

The bark looks a bit like black birch or cherry. We're at the western edge of Nahuel Huapi National Park, descending through valleys below occasional granite walls that thrust up into the clouds.

Soon we're low enough to begin passing little resort towns with tasteful rustic architecture that includes a heavy dose of peeled, gnarly, hardwood logs. We pass the north side of the lake with the same name as the park, and wrap around it to the southeast shore where we arrive in Bariloche. The roadsides are planted with lupines of all colors—ones I have never seen before. It's quite beautiful, as this is one of my favorite wildflowers. There are all types of blue, from a deep dark inky purple to baby blue with white tips on the petals. The pinks range from the lightest rose you can imagine to the color of a Chilean cabernet. Somewhere in that range you can try to fit in a few shades of salmon.

PART 3

ARGENTINA'S PATAGONIA

CHAPTER 15

Bariloche

I'm in a German-style café in Bariloche. It's full of chocolates and chocolate baked goods. People say this town is known for its chocolates. A young couple walk in and I'm reminded that a friend once told me that chocolate contributes to endorphin production, creating a chemical environment suitable for the emotion of love. That's why so much is sold on Valentine's Day.

I ask for "toast with ham and cheese" and tea with a pot, an *olla*, of hot water. I'm corrected. On this side of the Andes the double '*l*' is no longer a '*y*' sound as it is in all of Latin America. It's now a soft '*g*' which we cannot write in English, except as the phonetic notation "/zh/," or in the inconsistently spelled word *pleasure*. But it's an easy sound to make, as long as you can remember to. Anyway, I ask for an "ozha" of hot water in Argentinean style, and the waitress is now able to accommodate me. When the order comes, it is two very large and extremely thin toasted ham and cheese sandwiches (a typical South American breakfast) with a small pot of hot water and a teacup on an oval tray meant for espresso. The water in the pot is only a third more than the volume of the cup, so I ask for more very soon, making sure to pronounce "olla" as she wishes. Ten minutes later the waitress comes by and busses a table near me. There are only three couples in here besides me—no pressing need to bus, as the place is four-fifths empty. But still I have no hot water. So I flag her down and ask again. About three minutes later she brings the water. Harold the German warned me about the bad service in this town.

So far, the German's warning about the poor service is understated, and I'm surprised. An Argentinean waiter is the epitome of excellent service in my imagination, but so far the service has been beyond poor, to the point of idiotic.

Yesterday, upon arrival at the terminal outside of town, I tramped into the city under the weight of my backpack for the exercise. I had asked a guy on the bus to see his guidebook, as I don't have one for Argentina. I wrote a few notes and then tried to find the places while walking the streets. Peak season began yesterday, the first of January, so I knew getting a room might be a challenge.

At the first place they had a space in a dormitory room for eight bucks. I've never stayed in a dorm and didn't want to, so I moved on. The next place was forty bucks for a room with three beds. Then I found a sweet spot: a little house up on the hill set back behind a high stone retaining wall with a narrow stone stairway and gardens blooming with fragrant roses. A "full" sign was in the window, but I knocked anyway because it was the last address on my list. An old lady came to the door and tried to shoo me away, pointing at the sign, but I told her I wanted to ask her some questions, so she opened the door a few inches and asked where I was from. My accent or my nationality or both caused her to say, "I think English is best," but her accent was so heavy that I thought she said, "I think George Bush is best," and I was stunned for a second. "What?" came out of my mouth in Spanish with a tone that asked, "Are you crazy?" We worked that out quickly and she invited me in, told me her rates and where I could find a room, and about the great hiking in the mountains. She was very kind and very old, but I imagined her in her prime, hiking in the high country with woolen knickers, or maybe even lederhosen. I'm sure she came from some Germanic European country, and was an athletic blonde in her day.

At Albergue El Gaucho, a friendly, masculine, English-speaking blonde named Ingrid, a much younger version of the woman I just left, checked me into a dorm room. I didn't want to look or walk any more, and I liked her. She gave me directions to a cash machine. It always amuses me to use that word—"machine." It seems so archaic, more appropriate for some oiled contraption with levers and gears from the industrial revolution. But it is our word of choice. When I bought my first telephone answering "machine" in the eighties, it came with a booklet to explain how to operate the "Message Recording Device." A reasonable name, but I knew no one would ever use it. Still, I respected the manufacturer for refusing to call it a "machine."

For the first time in my life, I got cash from one of these things in a foreign country. I had always relied on traveler's checks, but they have gone the way of the great auk. It was a relief to know my card worked. I had a full wallet and an empty stomach, so I set out searching for a good restaurant, which was not easy, given that it was New Year's Day. Most places were closed, but eventually I found a clean, well-lit place. It was not a warm atmosphere, more like a deli, but it was open and cheap. I took a table for two against the wall, sat facing the door, and studied the menu. The prices were easy since the Argentinean peso is three to a dollar—lots easier than the Chilean 530:1. After a few minutes a couple came in and sat at the next table. A few minutes after that the waitress came and took their order. Remembering what the German told me, I turned and flagged the waitress. I thought I would have an empanada to start.

"No hay" she said.

"Okay, Pollo Portuguesa con arroz."

"No hay arroz."

"Okay, papas fritas, y ensalada mixta."

"Y beber?"

I let her know I wanted a beer, but it's my first day in Argentina, so I don't know the beer. I asked which one is good.

"They're all good," she said. "Okay, which is better *Quilmes Regular* or *Quilmes Imperial?*" Her answer contained so many soft *g*'s that I was lost. I ordered the regular in a medium size.

After ten minutes she returned to tell me "No hay Pollo Portuguesa." She said they have grilled chicken, and I agreed to that, and asked for my beer. Five minutes later two waitresses came to tell me they don't have dark beer, *negro*, they only have regular, which the one girl held in her hand. A bit impatient at this point, I told them I didn't ask for negro, I asked for regular, pointing at the bottle in her hand. She opened the bottle and walked away in a huff.

Meanwhile, three young Argentineans entered and sat at the front window. After ten minutes and no service they began waving with increasing dramatic effects. Soon they appeared to be stranded on a desert island, the waitress, their passing ship. They saw me watching them with amusement, knowing what they were doing, and we began smiling at the situation.

I finished my 650 ml barley pop in about fifteen minutes. They finally got a liter and it was gone in no time between the three of them. So then we were all waving and laughing, and they invited me to their table. Naturally the first thing we did is chuckle about the service, then we did the name and where-are-you-from routine. They were two guys from Buenos Aires and a woman from Neuquen. They asked how long I had been waiting. "Forty minutes" I admitted, and we laughed. After a few minutes my chicken came, but with no potatoes. We laughed again, even harder. Then, the waitress came to the front door beside our table, and locked it. People began rattling the door because she didn't change the sign in the window from *abierto* to *cerrado*. This continued for a while, then, when two people exited, the door was left open and a couple walked in. They sat down and waited, and soon resorted to flagging the waitress down. She came and told them something, and they got up and left. She locked the door behind them. Assuming that the place was now closed, I got up and changed the sign. People then stopped rattling the door. I told my friends that I expected someone to come up to me and tell me I'm on candid camera, and they had a good laugh.

Finally the waitress came and gave me my potatoes, and went to the door and opened it, changing the sign back to open. About ten hungry people rushed in immediately. This struck our collective funny bone and we exploded in laughter. I was in tears. It was one of those times when just to look at another person at the table would cause you to lose control. The laugh was so hard that it hurt, my stomach and cheek muscles tiring from the constant contractions. Then we realized that the waitress was pissed-off at us, which made us laugh again, just because we were witnessing the worst service we could imagine and it was making our night, while she was the one who was angry. Oh well, I guess I shouldn't have changed the sign. We left and bought a few liters of beer at a convenience store, and went back to their hotel to drink and talk about politics and lifestyles. I felt at home with the Beat nature of my first Argentinean friends.

While the other two were absorbed in a day-old romance, Eduardo wanted to know what people were like in The States—what our lives were like, and why we allowed our government to invade other countries. First I explained that there *is* a peace movement that has been active, especially since the winter when Bush was threatening to invade Iraq. But, I admitted, it needed to be much larger and stronger, adding that most people had good hearts, but that they were too easily influenced by the mainstream media, and too wrapped-up in their materialistic culture.

He wanted to know specifically how people live in such a way that they ignore their government's actions. He is probably in his late twenties, so all of his adult life he has been in a culture of rebound from fascist inclinations, exploring alternatives such as *horizontalism*. I explained that the United States is a big country, that people live differently in different regions, but that the primary pursuit of owning a home has become quite an endeavor for many who live in desirable areas. From my perspective on the Mendocino Coast, it seems that, due to the high mortgage payments, it's the rare husband and wife who are not both employed full time, even when they have kids to raise. This situation leaves little time after household and parenting activities, and after personal time for recharging one's spirit, for any political inquiry, like searching the internet for real news, let alone for political action—and this is the situation for people who really *care*. Even when people are well-informed and motivated to act, it is another step to risk getting arrested for civil disobedience when the paycheck is so necessary. Then there are those who do have the time, and who might care, but not so much that they would risk rejection by peers, alienation in the workplace, and loss of clientele (if they are a business-owner or self-employed) if they were to make bold political statements by raising the issue with others, or posting a bumper sticker or sign. Instead of a Gestapo enforcing compliance, we have a media that makes people too frightened to uniquely and genuinely differ.

Those who tell Bush what to say have designed his speeches to foment a nationalistic support of the military that allows no questioning without having one's patriotism doubted. In this situation it is easiest to remain uninformed, to minimize internal conflict—so that one's heart has no chance to extract oneself from the comfort of the norm. Much of the nation simply remains in denial of the truth, like the people who use an old-growth redwood tree as a logo for a business or event on the Mendocino Coast. There isn't an old-growth redwood around for forty miles. It would be more accurate to use a redwood *stump* as a logo, but we love to hang on to the images of the grandeur of the past. The once-majestic coastal range forests have been decimated. In their place are hundreds of thousands of acres of second and third growth trees that will never see maturity because of a scheduled date with a chainsaw, yet we cling to the myth that the giant trees are still here because we are in love with the grandeur of the past, and don't want to face the sadness of acknowledging what has happened. Only 4% of the old-growth redwood forests still remain, and hardly any of that is in huge Mendocino County.

So it is with this nation. We cling to the idea that we lead the world in freedom and democracy, and that we only fight "good wars" in which we arrive in a cavalry charge to save the day. Psychologists call it a belief in "American Exceptionalism." People have been brainwashed into supporting the government, especially the President in a time of war, as an act of patriotism, when in fact, the founders of the nation specifically called on future generations to constantly question the acts of government and to express patriotism by purging the government of people who do not act in the public interest. In the nutshell, it could be said that the problem lies in the mistaken belief that the government acts in the best interest of its people. And so we deny the facts, dismissing them as left-wing nonsense, and consider it blasphemy to state the truth that our democracy has faltered and succumbed to the financial elite who are in the business of using coercion and military intimidation or protection to increase multinational dependence on their products.

Eduardo asked me to speak of the average citizen. The bulk of society, I said, is composed of prisoners behind the bars of a dollar sign. Success is spelled "$ucce$$." They are the citizens in a nonstop, insatiable scramble for material comfort. They've been bribed by a bounty of belongings, and abundance of appliances, a cornucopia of commodities into a willingness to believe a President, no matter how obvious his lie, to wave a flag in a nationalist rah-rah no matter how many innocent foreign civilians die, and to remain generally ill-informed, in an easy state of denial.

He nodded with lips pressed together indicating that it all made sense—a sad state of affairs that is difficult to remedy, and poured another round of Quilmes.

"You know what Bob Marley said, a hungry man is an angry man," I said, "Dem belly-full."

When I left, Eduardo told me "Taste" in English, with a sincere look, as we began moving in opposite directions on the sidewalk. The gears of translation were grinding in my head as I attempted to grasp his meaning. *Sabor* means "taste," but it is used in the Caribbean to indicate soul—when music has a kicking groove, the right spice or flavor. I was lost trying to apply it in the current situation, but I assumed "sabor" is a way of telling a person you are a kindred spirit, or that our time together was enjoyable, so I replied "The same." We'll never see each other again.

Walking up the hill to the albergue, I thought of the sad situation in my country—how patriotism has been hijacked to serve those who are stealing our democracy. Abraham Lincoln said, "To sin by silence when they should protest makes cowards of men."

"It is no measure of health to be well adjusted to a profoundly sick society."
— Jiddu Krishnamurti

CHAPTER 16

Entering the Andes

After breakfast, I visit the "*Club Andino,*" the mountaineering club, which sits on a tiny triangular block between the intersections of three streets. A couple of young guys who work there are extremely helpful in deciding on a route for a backpacking trip and they sell me a map. The word *backpacking* isn't used here for multi-day hiking trips. The word is *trekking*. I hate it. It creates the mental image of some yuppie with a gaggle of sherpas carrying all his crap on a long circuitous route in the Himalayas. I can't bring myself to say it, like the men in comedies who can't force the word "love" out of their mouths. I go to great lengths to describe the activity, and then they say, "Oh, you want to go trekking," and I'm forced to admit that I do. Anyone carrying his or her belongings onto buses in a backpack is now called a backpacker. The word is used to define the travel-on-a-shoestring crowd, which I cannot avoid being a part of.

Pre-trip excitement is building as I shop for food, finding everything fairly quickly. Some dried foods, such as soup and milk, are quite common, as is salami, cheese and bread. Then I decide on a big meal before heading out, so I go to a steak house for lunch. The Argentinean words for meats are new to me, so I guess and get a big plate of beef, which smells good, roasted over a wood fire, but is only a little more tender than a shoe. I don't recognize the cut. Each piece has a few ribs in it. I ask for mashed potatoes and a salad (my choices are very limited), and am served about five mashed spuds in a stainless steel mixing bowl, and a big platter of lettuce tomato and onion. The place must be geared towards family-style dining. Intent on consuming the beef, I chew with tenacity and patience, and eat as much of the potatoes and salad as I can.

Back at the albergue I pack my food, then head back out on the streets to find a hiking staff and some lightweight sandals. I'm old school. Years of practice in the dojo with a five-foot staff makes me very comfortable with one, and I prefer it to the new trend of "trekking poles."

I set out on a tour of the hardware stores of Bariloche. Years ago I was stuck in San Jose, Costa Rica for a day with a friend. A big storm had come in off the Caribbean and caused road closures on the way down the lush mountain slopes to my surfing hangout near the Panamanian border. We spent hours at the task of finding a three-meter length of stainless steel rod, having it cut in thirds, and then machined to accept fishing spearheads that we found in a sport shop. We also searched for PVC pipe and surgical tubing to make a Belizean sling—a kind of underwater bow-and-arrow that locals taught me to use years ago on the barrier reef of Belize. It was this day in San Jose that showed me the value of such a mission. You learn words, meet people outside of the tourism industry, and learn how they make the city work. So I will go to great lengths for something like the perfect wooden handle, and at the end of the day it will have been good, even if I don't find one, which is the case today. The shovel handles are all too fat and heavy, and the broom and mop handles too skinny and weak. Cheap sandals in my size are elusive too, and the search for them is not as much fun. The stores that sell them just aren't as interesting as hardware stores, where you find all sorts of strange things to ask the shopkeeper about.

My gums ache all day from the chewy lunch. The taste of blood prompts me to check a few times in a mirror to see if they are bleeding.

Just as the stores are closing I spot a pair of light flip-flops—"*sandalias hawaiianenses*"—at a sports store for the young and fashion conscious. I am forced to buy them for seven dollars, twice what I'd pay in the states. The yakuza-tattoo koi motif on the sole is okay, since it is black on black, and invisible when covered by your foot anyway. I buy a liter of beer and head back to the albergue, where I cut off the red logo glued to the sandal straps.

In the dining room the film, "Groundhog Day" plays on the TV, so I fill a seat behind a single viewer, a guy from Barcelona. The audio is English, the subtitles, Spanish. It's a profound comedy, in which the main character wakes up every morning to repeat the same day. At one point we both crack up laughing, and he turns, surprised that I know that it's funny, and asks if I can read the subtitles. I tell him I don't have to, I speak English. The next time we laugh, he asks me again. I try different words to tell him that I simply understand what they are saying. I don't know if he gets it. When the movie ends, he goes out on the town, and I go to bed.

At seven the next morning, I pack in the empty dining room while sipping yerba maté, then sit down to a bowl of corn flakes with sliced banana and peach. The peach is excellent. Oscar, the albergue attendant, walks by, sees my bowl, and exclaims, "*Desayuno de campeónes!*"

I hop on the 8:15 bus to the ski area; it's filled with workers making their commute. The guy dozing beside me didn't bathe yesterday, and maybe not for a week. I'm the only hiker on board. At the ski slope parking lot, my feet hit the ground and I check my photocopy of a hiking guide to the Andes. It says the trail leaves the south end of the lot, so I head there and see a wooden sign, which reads "*Frey*"—the name of the *refugio* about four hours in on my route. The dirt road beside the marker heads south and becomes the trail I was on when I began this story. I hike up past the bamboo and the burn, through the enchanted lenga forest, and make camp across the glacial tarn from the climber-filled Refugio Frey. I climb a peak, and as I sit on top, my mind is blown by a giant condor passing at close range. It's the kind of situation that would have made my mother gasp.

One might think an event like that would seem to last forever. I took it in as best I could. The detailed image of the downy white collar feathers shifting in the wind is burned into my brain. It may be that I *wanted* it to last forever, which is why it seemed so brief.

In just a few seconds the great bird shrinks in the western sky. "Cool," leaves my mouth as I come down from the rush, and I feel a deep satisfaction relax my body— like I could leave now and be satisfied with the entire trip—and this takes me by surprise. Like I said, it's not like I came down here to see condors. But, I realize now that I have always had a desire to see one since I began bird-watching when I was in college. Back then, I'd page through "Birds of North America" memorizing birds so I'd know them when I saw them. I'd come upon the ten-foot-wide California condor on the vulture page and daydream about what they must be like. Later I backpacked into the Sespe Wilderness, and other areas of Los Padres National Forest where they live, but never had the fortune of seeing one. So I suppose I came here with about thirty years of subconscious anticipation. Sitting on top of this mountain, I feel like I'm sitting on top of the world.

I didn't expect to come this far from camp. I have no food, and am rationing what little water I have left, taking occasional small sips. I'm feeling the elevation. It's a problem I've always had. If it's my first day in the mountains, I begin to notice it at about six-and-a-half thousand feet. My elevation is 2163 meters. That's 7,095 feet, and it's been a hard day. I head back to camp, traversing the length of the ridge, crossing the pass, and as I hit the snow on the east slope I see the excited Argentinean far below. He's slipping and falling in the snow. In a few minutes I'm beside him. Now he is seeing the amphitheater for the first time, and in a loud voice he goes on and on about how beautiful it is, like an Italian art critic who's looking at the finest masterpiece he has ever seen. Suddenly he switches, with equal gusto, to describing the difficulty of descending the snow slope. I show him how to stomp his heels into each step, and suggest that he follow me, placing his feet in my tracks. He does, and begins exclaiming about how well it works. "Perfecto!" Soon he realizes he doesn't need to follow my footprints, and goes off with another round of superlatives now that he can descend on his own. This guy is loving life. I wonder if he has ever backpacked before. I wonder if he has ever been in snow before. I wonder about his plans to make his way all the way to Pampa Linda, at the base of Tronador, maybe forty miles from here. I think he is in for a rough trip, maybe getting lost a time or too, but he'll probably love it, as long as his injuries are minor.

I see that he is okay on his own, but ask him, to be sure, then leave him. I glissade down the slope, angling towards the headwall of the amphitheater where there's a stream flowing out of the bottom of the snowfield. He is hooting for me, so I stop at the bottom and yell to him not to do what I did. I get a good icy drink that makes my esophagus ache, fill both water bottles and wait for him. When he arrives I explain that a beginner should never glissade without an ice axe, especially when there are such sharp rocks below. Then I show him the water. He likes the idea to *carga el agua*. I tell him to always get water as far upstream as possible, then I take off down the valley.

At my tent I make a fast tuna sandwich, and eat it ravenously. What looks like a little olive-golden warbler visits, but then the male joins her and reveals that they are black-chinned siskins, what they locally call *cabecita negra austral*—"southern black littlehead." This is textbook habitat for them: the forest edge.

I head down to the refugio to check the scene. As expected it's crowded with climbers. I have a beer and a bowl of roup, and talk with the Belgian couple I'd met on the way up to the pass, offering to e-mail the photo I got of them. It should be a good one, I predict; they will be two little dots in the snow below three towers of the cathedral: Torre Piramidal, Torre La Lechuza, and Torre Principal.

Back at the tent I brush my teeth and go to bed, falling asleep in no time. In the madrugada I wake to the sound of rain falling, and it falls all night. Otherwise it's quiet and good sleeping. I wonder what chorus of snores is rumbling in the refugio.

It rains all morning and I sleep late. During a lull in the rain I pee and then re-enter my bag and listen to an old rock mix: music I heard on Honolulu FM radio when I lived on the North Shore of Oahu in '79. Tunes from Pink Floyd's "The Wall" are the morning's favorite. The wind howls, driving a fine rain against the tent, but it's bone dry inside. This is the first true test for this little one-man tent, and I'm impressed. I'm cozy in my "dry pod" listening to my iPod as the storm intensifies. The next playlist sends me off into memories of a Puerto Rican lover. It's an album I first heard while driving her sports car on the freeway in Oakland on our way to hear Chick Corea at Yoshi's. Her sound system was good, and I had lots of questions, but she had no answers about the music. An old boyfriend had given it to her, and it lived in her dashboard as "DISC 5." The next morning I retrieved it from the car: Little Louie Vega's "The Elements of Life," a persistent Latin groove with lyrics that celebrate the human experience. I remember her while listening. She was a tall, beautiful, intelligent and athletic mulatta from New York City. Like me, her personality *also* put a roof over two sub-personalities. They were her versions of the Rasta and the drill sergeant. But in her case, they had their own rooms, that is, each dwelled in a separate hemisphere of her brain. The problem was that they didn't co-exist in harmony. They were adversaries, and, of course, the drill sergeant dominated. She was actually a graduate of West Point. Her right hemisphere pushed her to a doctorate from Cornell. She ran, and often won, races as a way of expressing the drive of that half of her brain. But in the left brain was a repressed apathetic couch potato who resented being bossed. The drill sergeant resented having to constantly crack the whip if anything was going to get done.

My strongest and most fond memory of her is of the time I took her backpacking on the Sinkiyone Wilderness coast. We moved quickly together along the tops of forested bluffs that stood with their feet in the Pacific. At a creekmouth I took her out to the pristine beach, where we sat feeling like grains of it's sands compared to the immensity of the wild coast. I was silently taking in the majesty of the place, not responding as she described the beauty around us. Her mind normally idled at higher rpm than her car, but this one time she slowly quieted to a complete rest, and after a few minutes, softly said, "There's nothing to say." She finally understood. No commentary was necessary. It was a precious moment. Of course, once back in the buzz of the fast life, she forgot. I wonder if, every once in a while, she remembers. Lao Tzu wrote, "The greatest revelation is stillness."

After a few hours of music, the rain lets up and the tent brightens to a glowing olive-green. Outside the weather looks promising. Clouds are whipping by the towers, opening here and there to reveal a deep-blue sky. The sun is still high, so I consider breaking camp. I could make it to the next valley, but it's not as dramatic as this one, and the photography will be better here if the light is right. So I grab the water bottles and take off for my water source at the head of the valley. The sun comes out and I shed a layer. Down the valley, several climbers stagger out of the thickets of dwarf lenga, where their tents are hidden. They stretch and look at the sky. I detour up the talus to the base of the towers, seeking a photo composition. About a quarter of the way up, the wind switches 180 degrees, coming from the northeast, and brings the rain back on us instantly, all the while the clouds high above still race in from the southwest, past the tops of the towers. I carga el agua and make for the dry pod.

CHAPTER 17

Jakob

In the evening the rain broke again, so I wandered down to the refugio to see what was going on. I thought I might try their food, but was early for dinner, so I hung outside. It started raining, and a guy ran out to get his sleeping pad that was drying in the wind. On his way back in he passed me. I asked if it was still dry, and when he said, "More or less" in English, we began talking. He is another Belgian—a mountaineer around my age who is on his eleventh trip to the Andes. He's here doing some rock climbing. We ended up having a spaghetti dinner together, and sharing a bottle of wine. Also at our table was a dim-witted mountain guide from Colorado, a few years older than me. On a hunch I asked him if he knew a climber I was on the icefield with last summer in Alaska, who worked as a Colorado mountain guide in years past. He did, and was happy to remember him. I think they smoked many joints together.

It began raining so I waited, but it wouldn't let up. So I had to scramble the length of the lake in the dusk and rain. I was wet and it was dark by the time I got to the pod. I crawled into my bag wearing my damp clothes in order to dry them. The night turned warm, and I woke up clammy when the shit hit the fan. Rain came down in sheets, the drop size changing from fine, creating a loud hiss on the fly, to large, which sounded like corn popping. The wind slammed the tent hard, but it remained taut.

I was lucky that my clove hitches to the low lenga branch and root held through the violent snapping of the lines. There wasn't a drop of condensation. I have never seen that in a storm like this. My congratulations to the designer of this Mountain Hardwear tent. The unique thing about it is that the fly has the tubes in it for the long rods that create the frame. The tent walls are suspended from the fly. This is ingeniously simple. All other tents I've ever seen had the rod tubes in the tent wall, making the tent taut, with the fly stretched over it, but the fly could sag in wet weather. When the fly lies on the tent, the tent can't breathe, and you get condensation. In this tent the fly is always tight, and the tent hangs from it, creating air space for it to breathe. Why didn't I think of that?

This morning it's still raining. I slept well, but now I'm listening to the iPod again, wondering if the rain will stop. In the middle of the Eliades Ochoa playlist the rain stops. Outside I see patches of blue charging eastward. It looks promising, but I remember what happened yesterday and am hesitant to break camp for a false promise. I wait a while and busy myself by photographing some geese that are grazing nearby. I wonder where they weathered out the storm last night. I have the feeling that they've been standing there in the open on one leg with their bills tucked under a wing the whole night. They're pretty, and unusual, like a cross between a goose and a guinea hen, with a grey head and back, black and white variegation on their flanks, a wide rusty collar, a white belly, and a small bill. They are the ashy-headed goose, or *cauquen*. They never leave their range in the southern cone. I get quite close to them, making them nervous but not causing them to flee.

The weather keeps improving, so I make the call and break camp. Just as I get under way, a young couple comes towards me and the girl asks in gringa Spanish for the way to San Martin. "San Martin?" I ask, "Jakob?" I'm thinking that maybe it has two names. It does. They want to go to Jakob, where I'm headed. To get there I have to follow the same route as on my first day when I went to the pass. I tell them in English that I'm going there, I know the way, and they can tag along if they want, and they do. They are from Dallas. I never met a traveler from Texas before, and I laugh and tease them about it. It turns out that the guy's parents work for an airline so they got a cheap adventure, but don't have a clue what they are doing—a great experience for them.

Once we get within site of the pass, they decide my pace is too fast, so I make sure they understand where to go. I explain that on the scree slope on the other side of the pass, they need to be careful not to knock a rock loose that could hit the person below, and I'm on my way. In the pass the wind is howling. My ancient anorak and my nylon fly-fishing pants are breaking it well. I find a Dutch couple hunkered down behind a huge boulder, and yell to them at a distance of five feet, joking with them about the wind. Then begins the descent—the worst scree descent of my life—okay, the second worst, but the longest. It's endless—at least a mile, with no trail. I could use a hiking staff now. I can't believe the two couples behind me have to do this. Neither of them have the equipment or the experience. To be doing it for the first time near home is one thing, but out here is not a good place to begin. It seems like this place is full of beginners, though; I'm getting the idea that the refugios attract "trekkers" sauntering off with a day pack and sneakers on a presumed walk to the inn.

At the bottom of the scree, the paint marks on the rocks lead me to a steep dry creek bed, and when that gets choked-off by lenga, a trail takes off into the woods. Once inside I find another out-of-place couple. They are from Columbia. After the descent, they are licking their wounds and wondering what they have gotten into. The trail continues on through a wonderful forest made of large lenga on undulating bottomland. Then it hits a fairly raging stream crossing. The rains have it at flood level—all whitewater—but only about ten feet wide. An eighty-foot waterfall is roaring above. I find a stout, low lenga branch that touches another from the far bank and make a hair-ball move in the thicket, grabbing handfuls of stems and walking on the branches as a bridge. I make it across dry. None of those behind me can do that, and I'm a bit concerned, but maybe they will all help each other. A mile later I hit another crossing, and decide to have lunch on the sunny bank. After food I search for a crossing, find a downed log in the water, and cross it using two branches to steady myself, staying dry again.

Soon I leave the forest and climb, zigzagging up slabs of exposed granite between lenga scrub, up into tundra, then snow. The pass offers a dramatic view of the cathedral, mostly because of the patchy light hitting it periodically, between the shadows of the breaking storm clouds racing by overhead. On the other side of the pass is another killer scree slope, with no trail markers past the first two, which are bamboo poles. So I ignore the bamboo, and descend the soft slope of sand and gravel, avoiding rocks, following the most well-worn and fresh tracks, hoping that this is going to work, because I surely do not want to climb back up this thing. At the bottom the tracks take me into another dry creek bed, and I find a trail. I'm relieved; then in a hundred feet, it disappears. I'm fucked. I check the map. Below, the valley steepens to a gorge, and I refuse to go back up, so I have to traverse almost a half-mile to the lake, where the refugio is. And, no doubt, the six behind me will follow my tracks. Crossing alpine brush thickets is not new to me, which is precisely why I'm grumpy. It's not too bad to go down through them; going up is harder but still doable. Going sideways is insane. Alpine brush grows down-slope to shed snow and avalanches, so crossing it is a nightmare, especially with a backpack. The only good thing I can think of is that I don't have skis on my pack, as I often do in this situation while ascending to or descending from an Alaskan icefield.

I adopt an attitude and attack—the only way that works for me. Anything less than an aggressive bent will have you falling and crawling and generally stymied. My progress is not too bad.

Occasionally I get a glimpse over the canopy, which only averages about eight to ten feet high. Seeking the path of least resistance, I use clearings when I see them, to make some progress upstream and uphill, as I've allowed myself to drop too much to get around the horizontal branches. The next clearing I find is not so pleasant. It's a swamp on a side-hill. Something I've never seen before. The mud is swallowing my boots, and if they were untied they'd be sucked off, but I suppose I must prefer it to the brush, as I remain in a series of bogs for about a quarter mile, until my arrival at the lake where the map shows a stream crossing. It may usually be a simple stream crossing, but after the rain it is thigh-deep and moving quickly. There's no alternative, and I'm filthy with mud, so I unbuckle my pack (in case I fall, so I can get out of it and breathe) and go for it, facing upstream and moving slowly and surely, wishing again that I had a staff.

On the other side, a trail takes me a few hundred yards to the refugio. There wardens greet me—red-haired Willie and a brunette named Luciana. They ask me how the trail was. I ask, "What trail?" I recount my descent following the fresh tracks and my bushwhack across the lenga. They say everyone is doing the same thing. We're supposed to traverse to the left from the top of the pass, following the bamboo poles. I tell them there were only a couple of poles. They don't seem to believe me. Probably they don't *want* to believe me because then they may feel they should go mark the route. Searching through the lenga thickets, I grab a good tent site and make camp, then return to the refugio to hang my boots over the wood-fired cook stove in the attractive rustic building of stone and timbers. Outside, Luciana is commenting on the two tiny dots coming down the scree slope: "Mas perdidos," and shrugs it off. She warns me that fifty kids are due into camp soon. Back in my camp I cook rice and green pea soup with some salami in it. Then the couple from Dallas arrives, looking like they've been dragged here; muddy, bloody and tired. I can't resist teasing them, before welcoming them and suggesting a good tent site. It's a relief to see they made it and I congratulate them. They will dine at the refugio, so they invite me to join them and we share a couple bottles of cabernet—their treat, as thanks for my guiding help. We converse, at times yelling, over the cacophony of fifty fourteen to sixteen-year-olds.

It rained lightly all night. Sometime in the madrugada I awoke to a kid yelling "Hey!" "Teenagers fooling around," I thought, but after a while he began yelling "*Ayuda!*" ("Help!"). I waited a couple of minutes, hoping his chaperones would help him—not wanting to leave my cozy bag for the dark cold rain to assist the little nut—but eventually I did, and of course those responsible for him reached him a minute before me. His light had broken on the way back from the outhouse and he couldn't see. Obviously a city kid. The mountains are full of this kind of project in the summer, especially here at the refugios—the ol' get-the-city-kid-out-in-the-woods routine. With the refugios, the kids don't have to carry a tent or more food than a couple lunches. At least no one is fool enough to take the kids from refugio to refugio—over the passes. They come up the valleys from the road to the refugio and then go back.

The next thing I know the sun is hitting the tent, and I'm up having el desayuno de campeónes after some maté. The Patagonian sierra finches are all around camp. Even though I know they are finches, my mind registers them as very colorful juncos. This is the opposite of "Shoshin," the Japanese concept of "beginner's mind," which I honor. The human mind has a tendency to label things and then deny them full attention afterwards, thinking that, because it is labeled, it is known. We often feel we know activities well even though we've never studied them. Take, for example, what I am doing out here; walking. We have walked so much that we feel we know it, and so stop paying attention, but with beginner's mind we can discover a lot about our habitual muscle use, and the self-expression in our gait. We miss volumes when we live with this kind of closed mind. It engenders a "been there, done that" attitude that prevents us from experiencing the magic of life, and it is a barrier to learning on a deeper level. I take a breath and wake up to the present moment, which is entirely new, as are the finches.

I zip-up camp and hike to a high cirque with a frozen lake. On the way I cross galleries of exposed bedrock that are works of art in that meaty color of jasper with white quartz veins and the black grains of something like biotite, magnetite, or hornblende. It looks like a slab of beef, marbled with fat and sprinkled with black pepper, ready for the grill.

Again, the breaking storm makes for dramatic lighting, and I try, waiting for an hour at various vantage points, but am unsuccessful at capturing the beauty of the place with my camera. Eight waterfalls splash down near-vertical granite walls that ring the lake—a turquoise tarn about three-quarters covered with ice, but revealing large trout, hungry for the first flies of spring, in the open areas

While I'm sitting, the Texans arrive. They have some questions about what's around here, and where the route is to Laguna Negra, the next refugio. So I take out the map and show them, explaining that there is too much snow to make it to Laguna Negra without the proper equipment, which even I do not have with me. In the process of showing them the map, the next valley to the west draws my attention. They take off for camp, miserable in this chill, damp wind, and I traverse a south-facing slope for that valley. It's an enjoyable jaunt crossing tundra and small scree slopes, then I drop a little at the pass to walk on flat ground. This is the route to Pampa Linda, and a glacial erratic the size of a Volkswagen is topped with a pile rocks to make a giant cairn sitting in the center of the pass like some Pleistocene monument. I don't see a single footprint the whole time. The next valley is stunning, with granite walls and waterfalls. I find a perch and hang out for a while, taking it all in, then head back to camp.

Three big, cheap dome tents have been pitched beside

my pod. I find it rude—an invasion of my space—I feel robbed of my camp. I wonder if it is a cultural thing, a youth thing, or both. I wonder if I do things that an Argentinean would find rude, while I am clueless about my inappropriateness.

My stomach needs food, but I need my space, so I break camp as fast as possible. The kids—teenage boys—are fascinated with me, and one becomes their spokesperson. He asks if I like The Simpsons. I let him know I don't have a TV, and he reports to the others. He asks if I like the Rolling Stones. I say I do. They like that. He asks if I have a girlfriend, and, anticipating their reaction, I tell him I have many. That makes their day. Loaded up, I stomp out of camp, and as I pass the refugio, they come running down the trail behind me, asking if they can have their picture taken with me. I oblige, let go of my feelings and laugh with them for a photo. Crazy kids.

The trail follows the gorge that was below yesterday's final scree descent—the one that made me bushwhack. The little river flows to the north, through Arroyo Casa de Piedra down to Lago Moreno, which is beside the big lake with the same name as this park, Nahuel Huapi. After enough of a hike to make me feel separated from the camp, the trail passes a promontory overlooking the gorge. Three young hikers are having lunch here. They are from the States. I request to join them for lunch, and we talk a bit. It turns out that one is a college friend of the daughter of a woman who was a clown in Alaska. I painted her mom's silhouette in a mural of performing artists I did back in the mid-eighties, when these kids were just a few years old.

We don't know what to expect at the river crossing ahead. It may be handy to have some help so we hike there together and find a bottleneck of a half-dozen young Argentineans coming at us. The crossing is easy and hairy at the same time. It's easy because there is a big steel cable strung across the river. It is hairy because it crosses the top of a forty-foot waterfall. One slip could easily be an ugly death, which accounts for the bottleneck. People are taking their time. I wear my boots, but remove my socks and insoles. Once across, I take off on my own while the others dally. It's a beautiful hike. In a section of tall forest, some of the lengas are four feet in diameter. There are views of the snowy high route to Laguna Negra, which doesn't look too bad—from here. I come upon three male Magellanic woodpeckers, in Spanish called "giant black carpenters" (*carpintero negro gigante*). Red crested heads, with feathers so fine that the bright sky behind them reveals the silhouette of their skulls, atop their black bodies. This bird is a close relative of, and about the same size as, the eighteen-inch-long ivory-billed woodpecker which may still be fighting extinction in its final redoubt—the deep, bayoued forests from eastern Texas to southern Arkansas. Or, it may be extinct, a victim of deforestation.

Passing through a bamboo thicket where the trail has been recently brushed, I score a nice, stout six-foot bamboo staff, and see a yellow-bellied robin, called the Austral thrush. Thrushes have some of my favorite bird songs. It is among my greatest pleasures to sit on the balcony of my Alaska cabin early on June's first mornings to witness the songs of thrushes and sparrows claiming nest territories. There I open myself to the perception of what Bernie Krause calls the *biophany*, short for the "biotic symphony" of that ecosystem. He says, "In any healthy habitat the creatures vocalize in relation to each other, much like instruments in an orchestra. The creatures have learned to do this. In order to be heard, they have to stay out of each other's way. They sing for territory and mating. If they can't be heard, they'll die out, so each voice has its own niche. When the creatures' voices are in conflict, that means there's trouble in the environment." My hunch is that Krause is on to something, and I find it fascinating to receive all the songs of the robins and hermit thrushes and fox sparrows as I would receive the notes of the rhythm section of an Afro-Cuban jazz ensemble. Each has its timing, and its contribution to the overall symphony. But this Austral thrush's tune would be disappointing. According to the book it doesn't have much of one. It's a mystery to me why one species would evolve to sing such an exquisite song and its close, maybe its closest, relative has evolved to be silent. There's a topic for a wildlife ecologist's PhD thesis.

The route leaves the big trees and climbs a little, entering dwarf lenga. It's strange, and I'm wondering about it when I get a view up the valley. I see that the glacier that made this valley scoured deeply upriver, then rose. I figure the tree size is a function of the soil depth. Where there was once a lake, the sediments are deep and the lenga grows large. Where the bedrock that created the dam of the lake was scoured by ice, the soil is still thin, and the lenga grows dwarfed. This hypothesis gets confirmation after re-entering a grove of large trees. When exiting from it, I get a view to see that the grove is growing at the terminus of a large landslide, where the soil is deep, piled up on the thinly soiled granite dam.

The trail crosses the little river using a classic suspension bridge. Four rusty old steel cables hold a rickety path of 2x6's, with missing boards, and a few rotten ones threatening to break under the weight of the next big man with a heavy pack. The three Yankees behind me don't show up while I dry my insoles, which have absorbed all the remnant waters in my boot from the last crossing.

Thoughts come of the litigious nature of the society I am from. What national park in the States would have such a cool bridge, or for that matter a river crossing like the one I made a few miles back? Memories of Japan return. In the city of Kyoto there are pedestrian river crossings made of concrete stepping-stones. At one shrine I followed a trail back to a sacred waterfall that used a series of eight-inch-wide steps cut at uneven intervals in a diagonal path up a steep mossy slope above a stream. What quality of life is removed when every path meets government safety specifications? What toll does insulation from risk take on the psyche of citizens? It would never cross my mind to sue someone over my mistake or clumsiness, and I abhor that aspect of my own culture. I've read that it's an aberration of the American dream. The original dream was simply to own a house, but has involved into the dream to be wealthy, and now almost any get-rich-quick scheme is acceptable. This could be the result of a weak cultural tradition in our young nation.

I change socks and cross the bridge. My feet feel good and I descend quickly into a mixed hardwood forest with occasional meadows that are home to wildflowers: Roses, Peruvian lilies, and a spray of others. The funny thing is that there are no butterflies, and no bees, which *originated* on Gondwanaland. Bees are more prone to extinction than any other animal, but I don't want to get carried away with such ideas after seeing just one meadow. Maybe it's the wrong time of day. It's already evening. As I descend the river grows, with turquoise waters flowing below tall hardwoods of substantial girth. Bird songs become more plentiful and diverse. Bamboo thickets grow so dense that ten feet inside it's dark as night. A bird chortles three notes very close to me on several occasions, but I never find it. Unless it can throw its voice, I know it's only ten or twelve feet away, and I cannot see it. Adding to my amazement, the sound of its call indicates that it is about the size of a robin. A Chilean flicker passes overhead. Its local name comes from its call; *Pitio*.

CHAPTER 18

Bariloche Again

At the gravel road, I check the map and begin walking towards Bariloche. A bus comes along, going the other way, but I stop him and ask if there's a bus to Bariloche. He says he goes there on the return trip, so I board. You gotta love the South American bus system. The sun is going down, it's nine in the evening, and I'm about twenty miles from town on a gravel road. The biggest town around is Colonia Suissa, which may be home to 300 people. And there's a bus running by.

"Cuba Linda" is my selected iPod playlist. Cachao and others play traditional *mambos, danzons, sons* and *guiros* as we drive to Colonia Suissa, and then turn around, heading for Bariloche. As we pass the trailhead, the three young hikers from the states flag us down. They too are pleased and amazed that they got on a bus.

In town, I make an unusual decision. Normally I don't listen to music in situations where I might interact with people, but the music is so good, I leave the iPod on and hike up the hill listening to "Prisonero de Amor" with my new bamboo staff hitting the concrete in time. At El Gaucho there is one bed left and I nab it, get a shower and go out for a steak and a schop.

The steak does my body good after the exertion of the hike. I would *prefer* to be a vegetarian. I tried it for eight years, but I was training hard at the time and, after three different acupuncturists insisted that I eat meat, I returned to an omnivorous diet and benefited. It was my muscles, including my heart, that responded most obviously, and I learned to eat meat without guilt after I realized that it's not my fault that my body needs meat. I didn't make it that way. One day, when I am old and inactive, maybe I can go back to the vegetarian diet, but as long as I'm working hard, I need meat to do my best. Apparently not everyone is like this. If you take stock in the blood-type theory, then you will acknowledge that I need meat because of my type O blood—the blood of the hunters and gatherers. If that theory seems crazy to you, maybe you can let me off the hook some other way. Though I no longer feel guilt, I do apologize.

I don't apologize to people for the killing—that's between me and the animals—my diet is certainly a contribution to their suffering. I apologize for the environmental and humanitarian ramifications of my eating habits. Ranching is the main cause of deforestation on the planet. A growing population demanding meat also demands thousands of new acres of pasture each year. But the pasture is only part of the problem. Livestock is also fed grain. David Pimentel, a Cornell ecologist, crunched some numbers. He concluded that eight hundred million people could be fed by the grain that U.S. ranchers feed to livestock, and that the seven billion livestock animals in the United States consume five times the grain that the entire human population consumes directly. (This beef in Argentina's Patagonia is most likely grass-fed, from the pampas). He also determined that grain-fed beef production takes 100,000 liters of water for every kilogram of food.

After ingesting all this biomass, cattle fart methane, which is twenty times more effective a greenhouse gas than carbon dioxide. And they do it in volumes so vast that they're responsible for18% of the gas-emission causes of global warming—a percentage greater than of all transportation combined. So it seems to me that meat eaters should cut back on their carnivorous habits, if they can, for the sake of the planet and our fellow hungry humans.

The next day my body is tired. Luckily, it is raining, so there's a good excuse not to do anything. I go out and grab a cheap omelette in a hip little cafe, and go on a search for boot wax, which I find relatively easily in the third shoe store I try. The omelette was tiny, so an hour later it's time for lunch at last night's place, *La Esquina*—a burger, fries and a draft for ten pesos. The "Big Mac Index" of the Economist Magazine rates the cost of a Big Mac in Chile at 5% below the cost in the States, while Argentina registers at 26% lower. The low food prices must have something to do with the fact that Argentina has the fourth-highest foreign debt, and the eighth-lowest cost of living in the world.

When I leave the restaurant, it's time to return to the albergue for a siesta. After a good rest, I clean my pack, wax my boots and wash my clothes, hanging them in the boiler room to dry. Then I remember I lost my knife—well, it's not lost, I know right where it is—at my lunch spot at the second river crossing in the valley between the refugios. Anyway, I undertake a search for a knife. A knife is just the sort of thing a rich guy will buy to make himself feel like he's ready for the wilderness, making it hard to find a reasonably-priced one at an outdoor store in this tourist town, so I'm back on the hardware store circuit. I finally find the store I've been told about (when I ask, I am always challenged by the word for hardware store—*ferreteria*, which demands a loose rolling tongue), but it's closed on Saturday afternoons. I guess they siesta later than I do. A block away is a barbershop. I've been wanting a haircut, but all the places I've found so far have been unisex *peluquerias*, where the guys inside seem a little too happy to see me when I look in the window. This is the good ol' workingman's part of town. So I drop in to the empty barbershop.

The barber is about sixty years old. He's sitting in the barber's chair, watching the soccer game. At twenty pesos for a haircut, and five for a beard trim, it's about twice what I had in mind, but all the conditions are right, so I go for it. I pay with a hundred-peso bill and of course he doesn't have change, so I offer him all the money in my wallet besides that bill, which is twenty-three pesos, and he's happy. Too bad I can't tip him; he did a good job.

On my way back to the albergue I continue my hunt for the knife. A knife has always been la *cuchilla* in the countries I've visited, but in Argentina it is masculine, and of course the double *l* is the soft *g* sound. *Cuchillo*. It's not easy to say, and the people are constantly confused by my request. Finally I learn that a pocketknife is called a *cortepluma*—a "cut feather?" I think, then realize it's a "pen-knife." Luckily, the last try—the closest place to the albergue—has a cheap knife, a switchblade—for twenty-five pesos.

On the way up the hill, I see a pack of stray dogs. They are common here just as in Chile, but it's cooler here, so they don't lie around sleeping so much. Still they lack aggressiveness as much as their Chilean neighbors. They seem happy and well fed. The streets of Chile and Argentina are lined with variations of a basket atop a four-foot pole, which is where people put out their plastic bags of trash, so dogs can't get into it before the trash collector comes. I've never seen a dog trying to get into the trash in these bins, so I imagine people feed the dogs. They may even "own" them, feeding them regularly but letting them roam at will.

When I arrive at El Gaucho, Oscar pretends that he doesn't recognize me because of my short hair. An Australian named David had been asking about backpacking, so Oscar sends him to me. I get him oriented with my map, and we become friends. He has a vibe that lets me know he is a thoughtful, caring, and compassionate man. Sure enough, I learn that he has degrees in environmental science and law and is here volunteering for a human rights organization in Cordoba. He's trying to get a deep understanding of world banking and the mechanics of the multinational corporations that play in concert with them. I suggest he see a documentary entitled "The Money Masters" to get himself on the right track. I tell him what I learned from the film—about the Rothschilds, the Bank of England, and the Federal Reserve in the United States. I suspect Australia has a similar system, in which a private bank is contracted to issue currency, and the government pays interest on that new money to the bank. Macro-economics is not something I fully understand, so we go to the computer and in a few minutes we learn that indeed Australia's currency is issued by a subsidiary of the Reserve Bank of Australia, a private corporation, and that the printing agency was formerly a subsidiary of the Commonwealth Bank which was established in 1913 to print bank notes for the country. The U.S. Federal Reserve got that same power on December 23rd of the same year, when all but three members of the senate had gone home for Christmas, without having adjourned the fall session. Those three senators remained in Washington so that they could take advantage of the still-open session to pass the Federal Reserve Act, making it necessary for the government to begin collecting federal income tax within a year so that the American people could begin paying the debt to the Federal Reserve.

I doubt it's a coincidence that Australia and the U.S both fell to the central bankers within months of each other. I tell David it's my guess that it's the heirs and successors of those who were behind all these events that are now calling the shots in world banking. They decide the fate of nations.

We exchange e-mail addresses, hoping to get together for some future mountain or surf trip.

The next day he takes off on the same trip I just did. I stay in town another day, still a bit tired; besides, rain is predicted. Erica, from England, enters the albergue, and I like her right away too. She works for an NGO in Central America, and has a good heart. We take a bus out to the Llao Llao peninsula, and talk about finding a job with an NGO. I've tried several times to find a job working in the field, but all the jobs on the internet are to fill a desk chair in D.C., San Francisco, or the Big Apple. She tells me most people get hired after they volunteer for a while. Out on the Llao Llao, we go for a short hike in the forest full of noble trees, some that remind me of California's madrone, only more gnarly and with golden bark instead of orange. That chortling bird is messing with me again, calling out from bamboo thickets just a few feet from me, but it avoids my eye. On our third search Erica detects a movement, then, what looks like a wren with a rusty throat and eye stripe hops out of the dark interior of the thicket. It is a *chucao*, a type of *tapaculo* found in the Patagonian beech forest. It *is* robin-sized, but resembles a large wren because of its short, erect tail. Apparently, it is famous for its ability to throw its voice.

The hike is just the right amount of exercise for me to loosen up, and we hitch-hike back, catching a ride in the back of a little red Chilean pickup, stopping at a few tourist sites on the way. Erica has decided to head south. It is a big decision for many travelers, as the bus rides are long—really long—and at this time of year they're full. I have been wanting to see the big granite towers down there, but my butt has been arguing with my heart, protesting the endurance bus trip. She feeds me all the information she has collected while we have a five o'clock lunch, then she heads to the terminal to buy a ticket for tomorrow's bus.

At Club Andino I visit my friends and collect all the info I need to know for my next backpacking trip, then go buy some penne, ground beef, salsa Portuguesa, and a bottle of cheap wine, then head back to the albergue. Peter is packing in the dining room. He's an electrical engineer from the Czech Republic who has been traveling for a few years. He worked for a while in New Zealand designing radios, but had a hard time making friends, so he came to South America and has been here for fourteen months enjoying the mountains and the people. He leaves tomorrow to go skiing in the Pyrenees of Spain. He encourages me to go south.

The dining room slowly fills with people. What many travelers like about this kind of hostel is the friendly, social atmosphere on occasions when the chemistry of the guests is conducive. Tonight it is, and a party evolves with a few college girls from Buenos Aires, a hippie girl from Calgary, Alberta, and an Argentinean couple. Eventually the conversation arrives at George

W. Bush, and I begin answering questions. The room goes silent like a classroom. These people are intensely interested in knowing what's going on in the States. Most of the educated world is.

They want to know why we elected such a bane to humanity. The education level of my audience allows me to speak English. I explain that we didn't elect him, but still I have to explain why the election was close enough for the Republicans to steal. I tell them about the corporate money behind Bush, and the psychological con on the people, I mean the employment of what is called "public relations techniques," which is another phrase for "lying." After taking office, Bush spent $250 million in his first term on "public relations," that is, he spent those government funds to fool the public into supporting him and his programs. This has been the trend in recent administrations, but Bush is spending twice as much as Clinton did. Of course, Clinton had a budget surplus, while Bush gave us the largest deficit in history, which, for me, is like rubbing salt in a wound.

Then I tell them about our lame media—the "corporate media"—which rarely challenges the administration. The U.S. Media is ranked fifty-third in the world for freedom of the Press—that's tied with Botswana and Croatia. Progressive people and the independent media have theories about why this is so, but part of the problem has to be media ownership.

I explain the best I can how our major media outlets are mostly owned by just a few companies, all of which were heavy contributors to Bush's campaign. As I remember, in 2000, CBS was owned by Westinghouse, whose board of directors was led by Frank Carlucci, former Secretary of Defense, former Deputy Director of the CIA, and also chairman of the board of the infamous Carlyle Group who employed Bush's father as a Senior Advisor. At that time, Westinghouse had the third-largest weapons contract with the U.S. government. I tell the hostelers that most people who watch the CBS TV news, or listen to it on their several dozen radio stations, don't know this.

The room is attentive. I can see their minds working, putting the pieces of the puzzle together. So I continue. General Electric owns NBC. They don't just make light bulbs. They make "military hardware." This company contributed over a million dollars to Bush's 2000 campaign, then paid no taxes from 2001 to 2003, while receiving $33 million in tax rebates from the government. In these two years they made almost $12 *billion* in profits. The Political Economy Research Institute rated GE as the fourth worst polluter. All this goes unreported for the most part, certainly by NBC, which owns 13 TV stations.

Now they are whispering to each other while I keep talking about all the big media outlets being part of huge conglomerates. Besides news, they decide what movies are shown, what is in magazines and newspapers, even what is printed in history books. Fox News is owned by the same company that owns Harper Collins books. "Harper Makes History" is the title of their e-newsletter. The scary fact is that it is true to a large degree. As Winston Churchill said, "History will be kind to us because I plan to write it."

What history book will tell you that Prescott Bush, heir of a steel and arms manufacturer, and member of a secret society built on opium trade fortunes, married the daughter of Nazi money-launderer George Herbert Walker, worked with him, and ascended to an elite level of society? None. Then in November of 1934, Prescott Bush conspired with other elites (Morgan, Du-Pont, Remington) to hire a U.S. marine general to usurp FDR in military coup in order to establish a fascist state. The coup never happened because the marine, Smedley Butler, was only playing along with them, and when he had enough evidence, he went public. Even then, the group had sufficient control to suffocate the story, escaping the scrutiny of the nation, and that Bush maintained enough wealth and power to put his son on track towards the oval office.

Some of the younger girls want to know what they *do*

say in the news. I laugh because it reminds me of what John Kennedy said, so I quote him, "The (North) American people are the most entertained and the least-informed people on the face of the Earth." I tell them that our corporate media avoids important questions, and keeps the people in a state of fear of terrorists while feeding a sense of super-patriotism that is essentially nationalism. I describe the system of colored alerts we have in our airports. The seemingly perpetual orange alert makes people so afraid that they are willing to surrender their constitutional rights and freedoms because they are told it is for their own protection.

"What do you mean by *important questions*" they ask. The two most important ones that come to mind concern the stolen elections and what really happened on 9/11 in 2001. I back up, describing two concepts that are prominent in U.S. culture: one is that the media is liberal, and the other is that anyone who questions the validity of an "official story" is a "conspiracy theorist," which equates to being a paranoid schizophrenic—I suspect these concepts have been surgically implanted into our culture, but I have no information on which to base my suspicion. So, the conservatives are able to discredit and downplay any real reporting as being another absurd bias of the liberal media. Any questioning of an official story is immediately associated with mental imbalance. Subsequently, even famous progressive reporters treat the questioning of the 9/11 Commission Report exactly as they would if the subject were UFOs. They are afraid of being labeled, losing their credibility, and losing the small influence that they have. Only a few have had the courage to brave the "conspiracy theorist" spotlight, and the funny thing is, those people *have* no conspiracy theory. They only have questions. It's the official story of the 9/11 Commission that's a conspiracy theory. There is no proof, for example, that nineteen Arabs hijacked four planes and flew three of them into buildings. There are hundreds of reasons why the official story does not hold water. Then I have to backtrack once again to explain the English phrase, "holding water." The official story has so many big holes in it you couldn't even use it as a sieve. I continue with how World Trade Center Building Number Seven collapsed into its own footprint at slightly over free-fall speed (actually attaining free-fall speed for the distance of eight floors), as the twin towers did. That is to say, these buildings fell in just about one second more than the time it would take to drop a brick off the top of them—a physical impossibility, given the resistance of the eighty or ninety intact stories below the crash levels. And I remind the listeners in the room that no plane hit Building Number Seven. The only possible explanation is demolition, but the media avoids the question as if sacrilegious. A large percentage of the U.S. population doesn't even know Building Number Seven collapsed—never even heard of the building.

I stop. The room slowly fills with small conversations about the topics covered in my little exposé. Eventually, these conversations grow and evolve to lighter subjects so that the festive mood returns—kind of a metaphor for life in the States.

The bad thing about this kind of hostel is that when a party does happen, you better enjoy it, because you will not get to sleep until it dies down, so I join in and cook a big pasta and meat-sauce dinner and share my mediocre wine.

The First Draft of History, *a forum*

Funded by ExxonMobil, Boeing, and Booz Allen Hamilton among others, "Bringing together Journalists, policy makers, academics, and business leaders... hoping to arrive at a first draft of the history of our time." —*from a promotional website*

CHAPTER 19

Italia

In the morning it's socked-in and raining. Another day in town does not sound so good. In the dining room I sip maté, wondering what to do. At 9:30 the clouds break, at 9:50 I make the call to jam for Refugio Lopez, and at 10:00 (checkout time), I'm packed and out the door. The bus driver stops at the cruz for the trailhead, and I hop out with a couple of young, intense German hikers along with two young Argentinean women. We all try to figure out where the trailhead is. The map shows it to the west, but there are two signs with arrows pointing to the east. The Germans and I trust the map, the girls follow the arrows. We find the trail in two minutes by stopping at a roadside hot dog stand –out in the woods, with nothing around it—and asking. Of course, the stand is there because of the trail and the beautiful creek that it follows for a short while. The Germans take off up the trail. I think about ordering a *pancho*—the nickname for *Francisco*, and also for frankfurter—but decide on a *lomito*, a cheese-steak sandwich. The women have disappeared.

Not far along the creek the trail goes up. I mean *up*. It's steep, and I pass winded tourists who will soon turn around. Eventually there are some lovely views of the lake, and its islands, framed by the lenga branches. I finally realize what it is about this tree that is so striking, so exotic, so Japanese. I remember visiting the Silver Pavilion, a Zen temple in Kyoto famous for its gardens. There, gardeners were pruning a pine tree, clipping any needles that hung down from the branch so that all those remaining reached for the sky. The tarp on the ground under the tree was full of culled needles. These longa grow like this, naturally. All the leaves are on the tops of the twigs. All the twigs are on the tops of the branches. I wonder how those gardeners would react to seeing this forest.

Higher up it begins to rain. There are more views of waterfalls and spires of rock. I feel good with a light pack, having decided to take advantage of the refugios for the first time. So far, so good. This steep trail is easy without tent, stove, pots, food, fuel, and sleeping pad. I'm carrying a sleeping bag, clothes, rain gear, and lunches, as well as the usual junk—first aid, tools, toiletries, sunglasses, et cetera, et cetera. I am trusting that the refugios will live up to their name, and provide a dry bed and hot meals.

I finish the hike in shorts, t-shirt and rain jacket, thinking that the refugio may be good on such a day, when hikers might have cancelled their plans to hike up here. I walk in the door to find a large steaming room full of kids, and I mean *full*. They arrived yesterday for a two night stay. The attendants tell me the best thing is for me to go back down, but when I say I'm headed for Laguna Negra, they take me up to the top floor, to a relatively quiet room called "*El Clandestino*," where the teachers find refuge from their kids. Since the teachers are mostly with the kids, however, I have the place to myself for stretches of time. I sit on the concrete floor and make a sandwich—Yeah, concrete. This place has a jeep trail to it, and the whole thing is concrete. Not all that attractive, but it has an exceptional view of Lago Nahuel Huapi, which means "Tiger Island" in Mapuche. The place is functional, but lacking the rustic charm of Frey and Jakob. The walls are painted yellow, the floor, blood red. The second floor has large rooms with rows of bunks, one just above the floor, the other about chest high. The third floor's rooms are smaller. This building will sleep one hundred people tonight, like sardines. I escape the noise with some new Latin Jazz downloaded just before I left home.

The storm has intensified and at times the steel roof covering the boards above my head gets lifted and rattles and jumps in the wind. The teenagers are zooming, maybe from sugar, maybe from maté, probably from both. In the next room they are shouting and laughing, occasionally breaking into a soccer fan-song accompanied by a driving rhythm that they must be banging on the roof from the top bunk. There is no other wood surface except the slats under the bunks.

There are wet blue jeans and sneakers hanging from anything and everything that one can suspend cloth from. The humidity in the place is 100%.

I wipe the condensation off the window and look out to see a blue plastic twenty-two-gallon drum hanging from ropes to bolts in the rock in the middle of a high cascading stream below a Couloir. A black waterline leaves the barrel bottom and meanders toward this place. I have complete trust in the water.

At the dinner hour I descend, and they make sure I have a place at a table, and serve me spaghetti with bread and beer. That takes care of the grain portion of the food pyramid. The din in the dining room is deafening.

I ascend to my refuge-within-the-refuge, and take further refuge in my music, continuing with the same playlist. When I begin to fade, earplugs replace earbuds, and have a good sleep.

Early in the morning I'm in the dining room before anyone else, preparing my pack for the trail. Since the whole place is asleep I may not get breakfast, so I dig into my lunch bag to see what I might have. Then an Argentinean comes down, and asks where I am going. I tell him Laguna Negra. He says he is too. His name is Mauro, he is young, broad-shouldered and fit, and seems to have a good head, so I suggest we hike together, and he agrees it's a good idea. Outside the storm is breaking, but the wind is howling and the temperature is around freezing. There is ice where puddles formed last night. We share maté from a gourd, talk to a refugio warden about the route, and take off.

It's a steep climb, straight up, in typical Argentinean style—no such thing as a switch-back on these "trails" between refugios—but this is good because it keeps us warm. As we approach the saddle the sun breaks out for a few minutes, and I stop to shoot a peak. I tell my friend, Mauro, that good mountain photography requires either the luck of being in the right place at the right time or—he interrupts, finishing my thought, "The ability to wait."

I'm not interested in waiting. In the col the wind is howling. Snow blasts us from the side. Mauro surmises that the wind-chill factor is about fifteen to twenty degrees below zero Centigrade. He is in training to become a mountain guide, so he asks how to say "wind-chill factor" in English. Due to the conditions, we descend immediately. As you might guess, the route is straight down a scree and talus slope. Mauro gets ahead when I stop for a few more shots, so I become quite cautious. He's just far enough down that if I were to knock a talus chunk loose, it could pick up so much speed before he had time to react that it could easily kill him if it hit his head or heart. These "trails" and the people I see in the refugios don't mix, but for the most part people do not travel from hut to hut. If they did, the mortality rate would be incredible.

I try to move off to the side so he's not in my fall line, but I can't. The slope is funnel-shaped, and no matter where I go, he is directly below me. I'm happy when I hit the bottom. I can end my vigilance of every step, and stretch out my legs on the tundra. We follow red marks on occasional rocks, and when we hit a little stream he stops for water. He doesn't carry it. Nor does he carry a filter. I suppose the relative lack of wildlife here makes waterborne pathogens like giardia rare.

We have a snack. Argentineans eat crackers on the trail. I don't know how they keep them from breaking into crumbs. At home the only bread-food I take into the backcountry is bagels.

They're bombproof. But here I have small loaves of bread that do well. And they taste pretty good too, reminding me of the fine Italian breads of South Jersey. We snack at the very edge of tree line. At the upper limits of their range, the lenga become natural bonsai. These evoke even more Japanese aesthetic, because the size of the leaves are in proportion to that of the tree, making them ideal for bonsai. Some of the specimens are stunning—worth several thousands of dollars if it were possible to transport them, and maintain them in Japan. There is one near our snack site that is so remarkable I have to photograph it, and I end up crawling on my belly on the wet tundra to try to get the right angle—good entertainment for Mauro.

From there we descend and cross the shallow valley, busting through a thicket of dwarf lenga flanking a stream; then we take a direct route to another col. We pass through one of those hillside swamps, and Mauro teaches me the name, *mallin* (remember, double *l* is a soft *g*); it sounds enough like "machine" to make it easy to remember. He teaches me that a cairn is a *pierca*, and explains the difference between *nieble,* the fog we see ahead, and *nubes,* clouds, as I was calling the fog. Then he yells. I turn back and see him pointing to two condors gliding into the strong wind. They enter a fog bank, disappear, then exit and cross the valley without ever flapping a wing.

When we make the col, Mauro says it's a shame ("*que lastima*") that it is so cloudy. Normally, he says, we'd have a dramatic view of Tronador from here. Every time I hear that phrase I remember where I learned it—while beginning the climb of Cerro Chirripo in Costa Rica, when a high-elevation dairy farmer asked us where we were from, and after our answer he said it was a pity that our astronauts had just died in an Apollo explosion.

From that col we traverse a slope on large, loose, sharp granite talus rocks the size of furniture that teeter when stepped on, and ring when banging together. We come to another col, this one leading to the valley containing Laguna Negra and the refugio there that is named "Italia." It sits as Frey does, beside the spillway from a high tarn to a cascade falling into the valley below.

The route is not straight down. The slope's too steep. First we climb over the small peak to the west, and then we descend the crest of a rocky spur pointing straight down into the valley. At the bottom we glissade down on the north side of the spur in perfect conditions, as it is a few degrees above zero now, and the morning sun is shining and warming the northeast-facing slope we are on. A thin layer of corn snow sits above a firm crust. My bamboo staff comes in handy.

The trail circles the tarn, taking the long way around to avoid the sheer cliffs on the south shore. There are a few tricky moves as the trail traverses rock walls, but nothing too dramatic. Still, a slip would have you plunging into the icy drink twenty feet below.

Soon we enter the refugio. It's another built of concrete. I have no idea how they got the concrete in here, but I have to assume it was by mule or horse, via the valley below. It's an odd shaped building—some strange kind of wedge shape, maybe designed to deal with avalanches, or high winds, or both.

As I step in and am greeted by the wardens, I instantly fall in love with the cook. She is a young and beautiful woman of Spanish blood, a brunette with eyes the cool green color of the tarn beside us. She is soft-spoken and hard working, obviously happy to be spending the summer high in the mountains. Her name is Cintia. I do my best to remain sane.

Mauro and I have lunch inside, sitting on vertical log shorts at a table of heavy timbers, out of the intense wind that seems to get angrier when it's bottlenecked here at the mouth of the cirque. Afterward, the sun shines for longer periods than before, so I ask Mauro if he wants to go outside. We look around and yell to each other at a distance of four feet, occasionally stumbling when the wind causes us to lose our stance. I begin to talk about what to climb, and he realizes I'm crazy, and says he's going in to read a book. So I solo up a little peak to the north and am rewarded with an outstanding view. "*Increible!*" I say out loud to myself as I summit and see what's on the other side. I hang out for a half-hour, taking photos and waiting for Tronador to peek out from the clouds, or for the condors across the valley to swing by. Neither do, so I descend, grabbing a heart-shaped rock on the way for Cintia.

My solo time up here has given me some perspective. I have met a few people in my life who have at first-sight pierced my soul, and she is one. I've come to think that these people are probably souls that I have had experiences with in a past life, so I try to acknowledge this bond, honor it, and make a commitment to loving them as purely as I can, stepping outside of the personal façade that appears in this current incarnation. Some say we keep returning to this physical realm until we learn how to Love.

It's an opportunity to practice unconditional love. I can do it in this kind of situation, and could maintain it even if she were to suddenly become a raving lunatic. What I am having trouble with is extending that kind of love to all others even though I doubt there is a more worthwhile endeavor than learning to do so. But I take this opportunity to practice.

Back in the refugio I have another sandwich. A few hikers have arrived by hiking up the valley below, but the place is empty compared to my other refugio experiences. Later, Cintia serves me a risotto dish and I buy a bottle of wine ("Aberdeen Angus," a cabernet) to share with Mauro who has made himself some instant soup with hot water off the woodstove. Two of the hikers join us. They're graduate students from Buenos Aires, one a historian, the other a cellist. Then a computer programmer from Boston arrives. He doesn't speak Spanish and doesn't slow his English down for the Argentineans, so they can't understand him. Mauro leans over and asks me if he is from a big city. When I nod, he says he could tell by the guy's rapid speech and inability to relax. I turn the cellist on to Maurelenbaum2/Sakamoto playing bossa nova on my iPod.

When everyone hits the sack, I stay up and help Cintia clean so I can talk to her. If she speaks a word of English she doesn't let me know, so I struggle with her Spanish. She uses lots of unusual words. Maybe it's some Buenos Aires vernacular. Mauro says she's a *Porteña*, which I take to mean she has an accent from the coast of Buenos Aires.

I'm intrigued. It's not often that you find such a beautiful woman alone in the mountains. It's not just her appearance—this is a beauty-in-the-eyes-of-the-beholder situation; I'm certain that my psychic attraction makes her appear more beautiful to me that she is to others—but it's the gentle heart I see in her eyes that adds to her beauty. It's not common in Latin cultures for a good-looking young woman to ignore the riches offered by wealthy city men. Cintia prefers to live in the mountains and wants to become a guide. It's a rare occasion when I have such an interest in a woman, and I'm not free of loneliness, so I try to get to know her, but I don't think she has any interest in me. It's another joke in the divine comedy; when you meet the woman you've been seeking for twenty years, you find yourself twenty years too old for her. The problem is that I keep forgetting how old I am.

When she tries to light the countertop propane stove with matches, they won't light, and she blames it on the fact that they are made in China. I burst into laughter, and get a strange look, which I deserve. If you are old enough, you remember back in the sixties when cheap plastic things were made in Japan. Back then, when such an item would break, we'd curse the Japanese. In the mid-eighties I was surfing a big, hollow, reef break in a little village in Central America and living in a cabin that an Indian named "Danny" was care-taking. Danny and I would sit around an open fire on the broken concrete floor of the kitchen and tell stories in Spanish all night. The man had the patience of a rock. It would take me a half-hour to tell a five-minute story, and he'd help me with the words. Anyway, one day Danny was combing his hair and his plastic comb broke. He got angry and growled,

"*Puta Japonesas.*" I cracked up. By that time, the Japanese were making fine products, often better than American-made ones, but the idea of the "fucking Japanese" was just catching on down in the jungles.

So when Cintia complained about the Chinese matches I had a good laugh. I try to explain it to her, but, well, I guess you just had to be there in Danny's cabin. I'm sure I lose points with her by telling my story, but she accepts the heart-shaped rock with delight.

The weather moves in and it howls all night. I was thinking of a pre-dawn climb to get some photos—hopefully of Tronador—in the first of the sun's rays, but I kept rolling over and re-entering the dream world after I'd wake and hear the weather spraying the steel roof just over my head.

Mauro and I are the early risers again. He teaches me the procedure of making yerba maté. Beginning with a raw, dried gourd, the inside is first scorched by rolling hot coals around in it, then you coat the inside with sugar, then fill it with fresh maté and water every day for four days, letting it sit between the changes. When you are ready to use the gourd (also called a maté) you fill it with maté—the dried and chopped leaves of a tree in the holly family—and put your palm over the top and shake it upside down. Only the fine powdered maté sticks to your palm and you blow it off. You do this three times, afterwards leaving only the coarse dried herb piled against one side, then fill the gourd with hot water that has not boiled, insert a metal straw with a filtering sieve, called a *bombilla*, at the bottom, and pass the drink to your friend. The first round is strong. When a person finishes the few sips, he passes it back to the server, who typically has a thermos full of hot water. This continues for several rounds. You don't say *gracias* until you don't want any more. I enjoy the ritual.

Mauro nibbles on giblets—some chocolate cereal from Nestle—right out of the bag. It looks like dog food. I've been wondering how this guy's pack is so small, now I understand. He starves himself, running on mateine, mate's version of caffeine (the herb is also rich in magnesium and potassium), cracker snacks, and evening instant soup.

There's a bus schedule posted in the refugio, and the whole place takes off to make the one o'clock bus, including my friend, Mauro. I have the feeling we'll hike together again. I'm in no hurry to leave, and I'm hoping the weather will break, allowing me to get some photographs, so I decide to hang out and leave later to catch the evening bus. The weather never improves, but I get to spend a little time with Cintia. The two male wardens have to hike down to the road almost every day to carry food and fuel up because someone stole their horses, left in a field by the road. Since the Argentineans are so fond of crackers and cookies, I imagine that half of what they carry up is just that. I have been in Argentine supermarkets where both sides of entire aisles are dedicated to crackers. Anyway, the shuttling is getting these guys in shape.

Over the years I have carried a business card with a quote from Bob Marley's song, *Wake Up and Live,* that I give to people who would appreciate it. It reads:

"Life is one big road with lots of signs

So when you're riding through the ruts, don't you complicate your mind.

Flee from hate, mischief and jealousy

Don't bury your thoughts, put your vision to reality."

I give one to Cintia, translate it, and she puts it on the center post of the counter where guests sit.

It's a four-hour walk out, so after noon I get ready to leave, and find that my bamboo staff is broken in two, the fibers still keeping the two halves connected. The feeling of insult rises, showing my ego. It was a good staff, but more importantly it was *my* staff. I ask Cintia and she tells me one of the wardens broke it. I can't understand why. It's pointless. I shrug it off. Cintia plays some music with juice from a solar-powered battery—a Jorge

Drexler CD that is a sweet bossa groove with some DJ scratching. She gives me a driftwood staff from the woodshed, I give her a hug and tell her I love her which causes a puff of air to burst from her lips in disbelief that I could say such a thing after our brief encounter. My sense is that she's heard it a hundred times. I laugh, and tell her not to worry, my love for her is unconditional, like she's a sister. I turn away and descend deep into the forested valley on steep switchbacks beside the tall cascade falling hundreds of feet at a time from the tarn, wondering if I will ever see her again.

I begin meeting hikers who always ask the same questions. First "How far is it to the refugio?" Second, after they hear my accent, "Where are you from?" I get a view of the descent below the high route coming to Laguna Negra from Jakob. It is a steep and narrow scree slope entering a tight valley. Not inviting, but I imagine I may do it some day. This is impressive country.

It's an easy walk out on a gentle grade, following the river. The sky is cloudy, with an occasional shower. I catch movement in my peripheral vision, and look just in time to see a huet-huet walk into the night of a bamboo thicket. Its white eye-ring, rusty crown and belly, large feet and erect tail are enough to tell me what it is, with the help of a book, of course. But when I see a little bird with a golden eye-stripe acting like a chickadee or a nuthatch, I can't find it in the book. There is only one possibility, but it's a finch that lives several hundred miles to the north. Birding is like that; you have to know when you don't know. Once I told that to a friend I was introducing to the avocation. She is a physician's assistant, and she told me I'd be amazed how many doctors need to learn to admit that they don't know. She said some doctors lack powers of observation, which cause them to miss what is obvious to a more sensitive eye, and they immediately misdiagnose instead of saying, "I don't know." "I don't knows" don't go over well in the hospital. For me, they are words of wisdom. It is clear to me that the fear of not knowing is at the root of many of the world's problems. So simply stating that truth can be profoundly liberating.

Once I was walking along a narrow beach on the Carib-bean shore of Central America. A few dugout canoes, hewn from single giant hardwood logs, were parked in the brush at the top of the steep beach, under coconut palms. The bow of one cantile-vered over the sand, and its name was painted in a crude hand; "I dON't KNOW." It sent a jolt through my body that I will never forget. It was like a shaft of light penetrated to my core self and revealed a grain of enlightenment.

Why do we have religion? I think it is because we are ter-rified of not knowing—not knowing if there is a God, not know-ing if life is meaningless or not. Why is there violence between religions? My hunch is that it has to do with the fear of being wrong. Once we have decided to cover our fear of not knowing with religion, once we have dedicated ourselves to a religion, to a God, the last thing we want to learn is that we made the wrong choice—that we are fools who have submitted our very lives to a manufactured non-entity. So we must prove that we are right, and all others are wrong. How many of the world's religions follow totally different rules given to them by the one true God or gods. Think about it. They can't all be right when they say their God is the only God. They can only all be right if they admit other gods exist. As strange as that may seem, I think this is possible. I think that all the gods of mankind might all be lesser gods, below an ultimate unifying intelligence. But then, I don't know.

I see a parade coming and step off the trail. A group of kids in their late teens pass. They just keep coming around the bend like cars of a mile-long freight train. There are thirty-two of them plus a bunch of adults. Judging from the looks on the faces, this is a hoods-in-the-woods program. These kids have gotten into some kind of trouble, and this is part of their therapy. Some are pureblooded Indians; one is a tall, thin, blonde, Germanic boy whose cheek and brow structure looks swollen. He is dressed in brand-new camo fatigues that still hold the fold creases. He's got shiny new black combat boots on, and one of those big-ass knives lashed to his shoulder strap (what are these adults thinking?). He looks like he could end up studying at the School of the Americas (now renamed the "Western Hemisphere Institute for Security Cooperation") at Fort Benning, Georgia.

The School was established in Panama in 1946 and moved to Georgia, in 1984. Over the years it has trained over 60,000, mostly military officers from Latin American countries. Over 600 of the graduates have been convicted of, or linked to, everything from heinous murders and massacres to crimes of human rights abuse in every country to which they have returned. This is the reason the SOA is frequently referred to as the "School of Assassins." The Pentagon's reply is to shrug it off, saying that it's only 1% bad apples. But the Catholic priest that leads a huge protest of the school at Fort Benning every November asks us if we can imagine some big university with 30,000 students whose graduating class each year includes seventy-five (1% of each class) serial killers a year. "They'd be shut down in a heartbeat," says the priest.

Ten of the school's students later undemocratically seized power in Latin American countries, one being Panamanian dictator Manuel Noriega.

Here in Argentina, there was turmoil from 1976 to 1983, what is called "The Dirty War," when the military conducted coups, "disappeared" enemies, and tortured political prisoners. Two SOA grads, Viola and Galtieri, were ruthless dictators during this period. In 1998, when Spanish attorneys charged Pinochet with crimes against humanity, they also called for the indictment of thirty of his high-ranking officials. Ten were SOA graduates.

So this kid could have easily been a candidate for a round trip ticket to Georgia, but luckily Argentina just withdrew its participation in the program, as have Venezuela and Uruguay. Chile and Bolivia may soon follow.

CHAPTER 20

El Gaucho

Near the road, families have hiked in for picnics on wooded bottomlands by the stream. A thicket full of wild pink roses blooms beside the trail. The two wardens from refugio Italia pass by. One is carrying twenty-five kilos of flour in his pack; the other has a large tank of propane in his. No crackers. They smile and greet me by name, and I don't mention my broken staff. The trail crosses private property before it hits the road, so I duck under a cyclone fence that has had its bottom pulled up so many times it has permanently taken a new shape, the bottom curving up to a height of four feet, looking like a chicken-wire sculpture. The trailhead is inconspicuous, so, thinking it is likely that I will return to hike more in this beautiful park, I make a mental note that it is seventy-five paces east of a green steel bridge decked with wooden planks spanning a picturesque gorge of the river. I'll make a note on my map later. Now I stand on the bridge and take in the beauty of the turquoise waters flooding fast and deep below mature trees that lean over as if to protect the precious life-giving liquid.

The road heads east, toward Bariloche, and I begin hoofing it. In a few minutes it starts raining, so I take shelter under a big tree, and give my thumb to passing cars, but they are all full. Then a little red Peugeot stops. It's a couple with two kids in the back and a full trunk, but the guy re-arranges things and magically makes enough room for my pack in the trunk. The hatch locks on the first try. After we get introduced and they know where I'm from, they compliment me on my "*Castizhano*." Like Chileans, Argentineans claim to speak *Castillian*, not Spanish. They say Spanish is spoken in Spain, but, ironically, back in the old country "Castillian" is what I'd call "The Kings Spanish"—the most prominent of six regional languages of Spain, none of which are called simply "Spanish."

Their compliment is overly generous, which, along with the way they picked me up, reveals how gracious they are. We discuss the difficulty of learning a foreign language. The guy says he's learning English from watching subtitled movies. Thinking of the poor translations I've seen in movies on the buses, I warn him to be careful. They teach me that in Argentina *vos* is used instead of *tu*, the familiar form of "you." I'm amazed that I've been here for ten days and haven't figured that out yet, which shows how poor my skill is. When people have been saying, "vos," I thought they were saying "*voz*," "voice," and I couldn't understand why people were always referring to me as my voice. They teach me that in this country, "re" as a prefix it means "very." For example, *re-cansado* is "very tired." They give me another word, *boludo*, which they use for "bum" or "knucklehead," like the Chileans use *huevon*, which is literally "big egg," but also "big gonad," and is used frequently among friends. Finally, I learn *Barbaro*, literally "barbarian," but in Argentina, it's "cool."

In Bariloche they drop me off right at the front door of the El Gaucho because it's raining. I thank them and enter. Luckily I made a reservation. It's full. When I walk up to the desk, the new blonde woman knows who I am even though I've never seen her before. She shows me to my room, and helps me retrieve my stash from a locker in the garage. She speaks English, and after I tell her where I've been, she says she's a friend of Cintia's. When I admit that I fell in love with Cintia, she swears, with a hint of complaint, that all the men fall in love with Cintia. Even her own boyfriend did.

I immediately dig for my shampoo and razor, and get a hot shower. Then I'm off for "La Esquina," where I have become a regular for the good beef and cheap prices. The tables are full, so I take a stool at the bar between an older local and a German tourist who's reading a novel in English. They're both smoking and sharing a big wooden ashtray, but they are kind enough to push it away from me. I greet them, and the old guy notices my accent and says, "English?" I say yes, and order a draft. The Chilean "schop" has turned into the local "chop." When it comes, I order a "Bife de Chorizo." A week ago I thought this was beef sausage, but time in a place allows you to begin to learn the colloquialisms. I have no idea why, and there probably is no good reason for a steak to be called this, but it is.

The bar is a bit of a museum, and there are foreign coins glued to the log post at the corner. There are about a hundred of them. The older man is leaning away from me so I can see the coins. I point to a U.S. quarter and tell him that it's from my country. He protests that I said I was English. "No," I correct him, "I *speak* English." A thick silence ensues. I break it by pointing to the bell behind the bar, and explaining that in Alaska, when a person rings the bell it means he's bought a round for the house. He says that here it's for last call. The German is eavesdropping and joins us, in Spanish coated with a thick German accent, and without the use of his upper lip, adding that in Germany it's a round for the house, too.

My steak comes, and it's delicious. The bill is less than eight dollars with two drafts. I like this place. On the way home, I buy eggs and beer, and when entering El Gaucho, I poke my head into the downstairs *comodor* to see what all the noise is. It's a big party instigated by a Belgian, and my friend David the Australian is there. He and I trade stories about our trips, then he leaves and I get absorbed into the crowd at the table. A seventeen-year-old Argentinean girl tells me in English that she and her girlfriend are sleeping with me. I raise my eyebrows. "In my bed?" I ask. "No, no, no, in your room."

We all drink and talk. Someone is passing a notebook around with commonly used phrases and sentences written in Dutch, Portuguese, and Spanish. I guess this is what the Euro "backpacker" crowd does. They ask me to add English. I work my way down the page, and come to the slang and foul language, which begins a new discussion.

A woman wants to know what is "Holy Crap!" I explain that it's used by someone who is afraid to say, "Holy shit!" It's for when you are surprised; for example if I walked around the corner and saw a flying saucer in the sky, I'd say, "Holy shit!" The seventeen-year-old girl says, "Holy shit! I am sleeping with an old man!"

"What old man?" I ask.

"You!"

I laugh hard at the surprise, realizing that subconsciously I've been anticipating, with dread, the first time that a girl would call me an old man. It's hilarious, though, at the same time, a bit painful. I think of Cintia and wonder if she would agree. Later I go to the bathroom to piss, and look in the mirror. God damn it!

Even though I'm pushing fifty, it's only been in the last few years that I have begun to slow down. During this time I witnessed my mother's slow death in which she seemed to age a decade in month. Generations used to seem static. Now I'm seeing older people as the aged young. For the first time, I have a strong sense of the physical deterioration that is always happening, and see it in my own generation, even Deepak Chopra. For the first time, I'm forced to face my attachment to my physical abilities— I enjoy them tremendously, and refuse to let them go without a fight.

For the first time, I'm realizing that I'm too old for some women, and there's nothing I can do about it. This past summer I fell in love with a twenty-six-year-old kayak guide in Alaska. Then

I got my heart broken when she left me because she didn't want to get too involved. She told me she was afraid of being widowed when she was only sixty. Cintia is only a year older than she was.

Men have a genetically programmed attraction to beautiful young women, but these days I'm beginning to wonder where I need to draw the line. The really strange part of it all is that when I've had relationships with young women in recent years, I've noticed a new kind of love emerging—a fatherly kind, which is powerful, but gets tricky in two ways. One is in managing the voice of experience—it's hard not to give advice when someone you love would benefit from it, but constant advice-giving is hard on a relationship. The other is sorting out the scramble of emotions that arise in a sexual relationship that also carries tones of a father-daughter relationship.

In working with people in the field of somatics and mind/body integration, I was amazed to learn how many female clients had suffered sexual abuse from fathers, uncles, and big brothers. It opened my eyes to a dark world that I couldn't understand. It was beyond my comprehension how a man could do that. But after experiencing heights of arousal with a young woman who occasionally drifts into the space in my heart reserved for the daughter I never had, I can grasp first-hand the root of the crimes these men commit.

I remember reading Thich Nhat Hanh in the eighties. At the time, my lover was a Kuna Indian girl who was almost my age, but about five-two, and a hundred pounds. Her almond eyes, dark skin, and straight black hair gave her the look of a Southeast Asian girl. Hanh wrote a poem in which he claimed to be many different kinds of criminal. The poem's meaning eluded me until he claimed to be the pirate that rapes the twelve-year-old Thai girl in the straits of Malacca. Suddenly a wave passed through my body. Because of my passion for my lover, I understood him, and then understood the entire poem. I was capable of all of the most heinous crimes. Somewhere inside of me was the tendency for each.

It was an important step in my ongoing cultivation of compassion and forgiveness.

By the time I figure all this out, it will be due to the obvious fact that I am indeed an old man.

The bedroom sleeps five. I stumble in before the girls, and two beds are occupied already. I left my earplugs in my bunk at Refugio Lopez, but the party is downstairs and it's not loud in this upstairs room. At dawn an alarm goes off. Then the snooze alarm wakes us all every five minutes. Just when I'm finally angry enough to say something, the guys get up. They are completely inconsiderate, and, as they dress, I learn why. After filling the room with a fog of deodorant, the ritual of clicking and snapping, the process of checking the pistols and utility belt compartments tells me they're some kind of cops. It's pure arrogance. The final insult isn't when they turn on the light to check for forgotten belongings, it's walking out and leaving the door open. I close it, and the girls and I got a few more hours of sleep.

I wake up to the blue sky I had been waiting for in the mountains. There is snow covering the peak to the south. It will be a good morning for photography.

After a *zhanki desazhuno* of eggs, which always horrifies Argentineans who nibble on a cracker or two with their maté, I bus to the terminal and buy a ticket to Rio Gallegos, a city on the Southern Patagonia Coast. There I can get a bus into the mountains to see those granite spires I've been lusting after ever since my friend gave me postcards of them a year ago. I've been weighing the decision for a few days, but I was convinced by the Czech when he told me it really wasn't a bad trip. Complaints filed by my butt dwindled and my heart took over the show. The English woman, Erica, said that the buses going down along the foothills of the mountains were booked far in advance, and the coastal route was the only choice on the spur of the moment, so that's what I'll do... with only slight dread of sitting for thirty hours.

The day is spent washing clothes, drying gear, waxing

boots, et cetera. Then I undertake a quest for new earplugs. A pharmacist recommends new silicone ones that I never saw before, On the way home I pass the lakefront outdoor pool, and, thinking of a workout before the ride, I enter to inquire if I can swim. The six employees tell me I can, and that the water is fourteen degrees. I make a rough conversion in my head, guess fifty-seven degrees Fahrenheit, and laugh. "No wonder the pool is empty!" I joke, and leave.

Later, I find a trendy little restaurant. The waitress efficiently takes my order of ravioli, serves it with a glass of good wine, and then ignores me. Finally I flag down a waiter for a salad, and sit content with watching a gorgeous girl—tall, thin and dark— with her date seated right in front of me, and the entertaining musings about my age that follow.

Back at El Gaucho I drink *fernet*, kind of a Jagermiesterish after-dinner drink, with three young guys from Buenos Aires who are preparing to go out. I drink it straight. They mix it with coke. I tell them coke is not healthy. They correct me: it is the *fernet* that's not healthy. I correct them: the extreme acidity of coke disrupts the acid/alkaline balance of the human body, which must maintain itself within a certain Ph range to survive. In Chile and Argentina both, it is common to see people carrying coke around instead of water. Coke is also commonly set on a dinner table, as an after-dinner drink. But the United States is the largest consumer of soft drinks, drinking over thirteen billion gallons a year. The phosphoric acid in coke makes it as acidic as vinegar, but it has enough high-fructose corn syrup in it to mask the acidity. The phosphorus demands that the body balance it with calcium. The acid needs to be buffered, and calcium can do that, so the net effect of a drink is the robbery of calcium from the bones, making coke drinkers prone to fractures and osteoporosis.

When they learn that I am more than ten years older than they thought, they all toast me, but they will never stop drinking coke.

After I decline their third invitation to join them as they head out into the madrugada, they allow me to go to bed, and then they wake me in the morning light when they return, and the fat one begins to snore. Sleep becomes impossible with the rumble, so I get up and, after maté, put all my food into a skillet and make a breakfast destined to blow an Argentinean mind: a scramble with several eggs, ground beef, cheese, onion and green pepper, and a loaf of bread. Afterwards, I check out, stash my pack, and take a long walk along the lake with Paz, a twenty-six-year-old environmental policy worker from Buenos Aires. I met her late last night while she was playing cards with Oscar. After we walk and lounge on a lakeside lawn, she wants to have lunch. I need cash, so we go to the bank. The "machine" allows me to proceed through the entire transaction, and then rejects my card as invalid. I tell a bank employee what happened, wanting to be sure that the transaction was not recorded. She reassures me and asks me to try another "box." It doesn't work, and neither does the third. I try a different bank with no luck. My bus leaves in a couple hours, and my wallet is empty. I tell Paz I have to deal with this, and say goodbye.

Back at El Gaucho, Mercedes is on duty. She is the only employee who is by-the-book, and the only one who does not speak English. It takes a while to talk her into allowing me to use the phone, assuring her that I use a calling card and that there will be no fee billed to the hostel. I refer to a list of phone numbers written in the back of my notebook in case something like this happens, but I cannot contact Wells Fargo Bank. Finally, a London-based customer-service operator for the international calling card that I use tells me that U.S. toll-free numbers cannot be called from outside the country. All my numbers are worthless. Using the hostel's computer, I pull up the Wells Fargo site. But when I click on "Debit Card Help," the page is not accessible with the browser in the computer. It offers four new browsers to download. I quit and go to my webmail to send an S.O.S. to my father, sister, and two friends, asking for a regular toll number for Wells Fargo. Then I decide to try the phone again. I go through my pleas with Mercedes, then call, and it doesn't work, so I try customer-service again. The same woman answers and recognizes me. She has time and compassion, so she goes to a Wells Fargo website and finds an MCI number to call inside Argentina. I thank her, beg Mercedes to continue using the phone, ignoring her body language that makes her look like she is waiting for a busy bathroom with a bursting bladder. When I call the number the woman on the other end tells me I need an MCI calling card to connect to Wells Fargo. I ask if I can buy a card. She says yes, if I have an American Express card. I have a Visa. They don't accept it, by Visa's request. I get back on the internet, and find the same site the operator in London saw. The numbers are the same and there are no others, so, on my knees with Mercedes, I call again. This time a guy answers. I tell him I need to call an 800 number in the states. He says, "It wouldn't happen to be Wells Fargo, would it?" What, is this guy psychic? At this point I am so flustered (the bus leaves in an hour) that I don't even try to figure it out. I just say, "Yeah!" I give him the number and while he is connecting me I realize they have a special arrangement with Wells Fargo, which is why the number is on the Wells Fargo website. The other operator didn't tell me this.

I get connected with the bank, and the guy tells me my account has been closed.

I'm stunned. Not only is there no possibility in my mind for this reality, it means my lifeline has been cut.

He asks if there is another signer on the account. Oh shit. It hits me. Ten years ago, I put my father on my account so that he could help me if I had any problems while I was on a long trip in Venezuela and the southern Caribbean. Now he is eighty-nine years old and getting forgetful. I call him, but it is 9:30 am at his place, and he is already out shooting pool at the senior center, so I leave a message, then get back on the computer to e-mail him the details—all the numbers he'll need to know to get my account active again. I copy the e-mail to my sister and two friends, asking them to call him and make sure it happens. The bus leaves in thirty-five minutes, so I rush down to the corner and luckily the right local bus comes immediately. It arrives at the terminal ten minutes before my departure time. I try to change the few Chilean pesos in my wallet at a kiosk in the terminal, thinking that because Bariloche has direct connections to Chile, someone in one of the terminal shops may help me. They do, but rip me off pretty badly in the exchange, giving me only four Argentinean pesos per thousand Chilean. I give them five thousand, take twenty, and board the bus with the equivalent of almost seven dollars, making the decision to relax and trust that it will all work out.

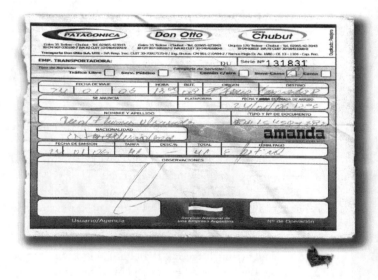

CHAPTER 21

Down the Atlantic Coast of Patagonia

It's fifteen hours to Comodoro Rivadavia. That's the name of a city. In Argentina they include a hero's rank when they name a city after him. It would be like our naming the capital "General Washington." There we will make a two-hour layover, then continue down the Atlantic Coast to Rio Gallegos. On the way, we travel south through valleys on the east slopes of the Andes, stopping in a little town called Bolsón, considered to be Argentina's enclave of mountain hippies—reminiscent of some tie-dye hamlet in Colorado. As we approach the next stop, I get a glimpse of spectacular blue-grey granite peaks thrusting skyward among glaciers at the far end of a sweet valley. We stop in a little village, and I'm wondering where we are. The woman beside me asks what the name of this town is. She saw what I saw. While passengers are loading luggage below, I step out to stretch, and ask an Indian girl the name of the town. "Laopue," she says. I repeat it in my head until returning to my seat, and then tell the woman. She says she knows. I guess she asked around while I was out. We take off and when we pass the back of a sign on the left, I turn to read the other side: "Lago Puelo" with an arrow. How am I ever going to understand what these people say if they leave half the letters out of their words?

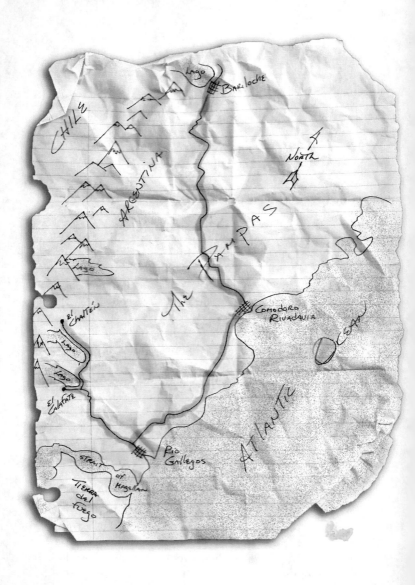

The bus cruises south along the edge of the Andes for another hour, then strikes out across the pampas. Here the grasslands cover rolling hills—the toes of the foothills. I imagine at some time of year they are green, but now they're dry. I'm searching for wildlife, specifically the *rhea*, a large flightless bird, but see no animals. The sun of early evening illuminates the pampas with golden light, and as we pass a small pond, the bus jumps a flock of parrots. It's astonishing—the equivalent of seeing a flock of parrots in southern Saskatchewan. It's the Austral Parakeet, southernmost parrot in the world (okay, technically a parakeet, but at thirteen inches long, I'll call it a parrot). It probably inhabits the highest latitude in the world as well, as I cannot imagine a species exceeding forty degrees of latitude in the northern hemisphere, and its range here extends to fifty-two degrees south. This green flock remains in a tight group as they zigzag away from the road, flashing the orange underside of their tails.

An hour-and-a-half later we see the last of the sun's rays. My search for rhea continues while I admire the light on the hemispheres of golden flowers that remind me of brittlebush, especially the way they are accented by long blue-grey shadows. As we pass a small slough, I'm stunned to see a few flamingoes. It's the Chilean Flamingo that ranges as far south as that parrot. They're a very light rose color. As I remember, their color varies with their diet. The more shrimp they eat, the more pink they are. I recently read that the flesh of salmon varies in color for the same reason. The article said that farmed salmon are fed fish pellets, so feed suppliers offer the farmer a color wheel to choose the color of flesh he wants his fish to have. The feed formula will contain the dyes necessary to customize the color of the salmon meat, which is normally colored by the crustaceans in their diet. It went on to say that the feed pellets are composed of caught fish, and it takes three pounds of those fish to produce a pound of farmed salmon, so this process is a losing proposition in bioproduction. It's a losing proposition environmentally as well; the fecal matter from the densely populated fish pens creates pollution problems, and diseases spread easily through the overcrowded fish, eventually infecting wild salmon. It's widely believed that damage to the wild stock from the farms could cause their extinction in this century.

Flamingoes. I remember driving in Port-Au-Prince, Haiti. As we passed a ramshackle ghetto of extreme poverty right on the waterfront, my Haitian friend, Evelyn, told me that when she was a little girl, this coast was lined with palms. Beyond dry land it was a shallows that would seasonally be covered with vast flocks of flamingoes. Then it became a refuse landfill, now the poorest people were building huts and lean-tos on top of the trash. Amazing, where the mind can go from the sight of a flamingo.

Now a fat full moon ascends slowly, as if it is too heavy to get airborne, from the flat eastern horizon. I think of friends who will be watching it from other lands, and recall memorable moonrises: those I saw rising out of a glacier from my Alaska cabin, one from the western shore of volcano-ringed Lago Atitlan in Guatemala as the sun set, and one through the bare branches of a hardwood forest while snow fell on a cold night in the mountains of Kyushu, in Japan.

We pass through a flat-bottomed valley with steep walls as we cut through the Sierra San Bernardo, a small mountain range sitting in the middle of the vast pampas. The bus stops briefly at a terminal in a town that seems to be a military outpost. Strange place for it, but a good place to hide, I suppose. The landscape feels like New Mexico.

When we pass the fort, I see jet fighters, probably made in the U.S. I know that my country accounts for 48%, damn near half, of global defense spending, but it is also the leading source of military aid. It was only last year that I realized that foreign military aid comes with the stipulation that about 80%t of it be spent on weapons made in the United States. I always assumed, without thinking about it, that the U.S. gave money to foreign governments to help run their military. Really, it is the U.S. government paying U.S. defense contractors to manufacture weapons and ship them overseas. The U.S. has provided over eighteen billion dollars in foreign military aid in recent years.

Back out on the barrens of the pampas, we enter a tiny, poor town with miniature houses and a few bare light bulbs on skinny poles, insufficient to be called streetlights. The place looks fake, like we have magically entered a village on some clerk's basement model train platform, or maybe a town that is about to be destroyed by a giant lizard (that is, a man in a lizard suit) in an old Japanese horror film. When the bus makes a turn and I see the village below the still-low moon, I finally and instantly understand an Ansel Adams photograph that has until this day puzzled me. The light of the moon on the pampas, and the shapes of the ramshackle houses—shadows here, moonlight off a steel roof there—is enchanting. Of course, I cannot explain it any more than I could understand the photograph, "Moonrise, Hernandez, New Mexico," before this moment. I would look at collections of his work and see awesome mountains, images from forests, and then this anomalous night shot of a little town. It was his most popular photograph, maybe the most popular of all fine art photographs, but I never got it. Now I feel like I was there with him. It's the light.

Waking at first light, I search for a grasp on reality, and remember I'm rolling into a city called Comodoro Rivadavia, on the Atlantic Coast of the Argentine pampas. It's dawn on a Saturday morning, and I have less than seven dollars. I fall back asleep, and wake to tapping on my foot hanging in the aisle. The biggest Indian I have ever seen south of Tucson is the conductor, and he instructs me to leave the bus so they can clean it. I begin my two-hour layover by walking down to the sea, just to check in with the Atlantic. Flat mesa-lands stop, and at the base of fifty-foot bluffs, a flat ocean continues to the horizon.

I find an ATM, give it a try, and am rejected. I skip

breakfast, thinking I will probably need every penny for intra-city buses, taxis, phones, and internet access to straighten the bank thing out.

It's a long day on the bus south along this deserted coast. The "groove" playlist is the soundtrack for a nonproductive search for rheas. It's not listening-music, just a groove, that Buddha Bar stuff. It's relaxing. I ignore all three movies that play on the overhead screens.

On several occasions we pass coves with beaches, but there is never a wave. I imagine that the famous *pamperos*, the winds that blew off this land and aggravated the tall ships bound for the Horn, wearing on them before the real trial had even begun, must keep any swell from surviving all the way to this beach. Then I remember that the continental shelf here extends beyond the Falkland Islands. The edge of the shelf is about 600 miles out in the Atlantic, maybe the widest shelf extending into open sea anywhere on the planet except for one in the Arctic Ocean. Predominating winds south of here are westerly, so most ocean swells run in that same direction, away from this coast. Individual storms may arise that could send a swell this way, but traveling across this wide shelf, it would no doubt dissipate in the relatively shallow waters.

The view reminds me of the Baja coast of the Sea of Cortez, except that this place is flatter, featureless, and far cooler. I never see a rhea.

We pass a few small towns and stop in one or two. In the towns there are pigeons—the same rock dove we have in North America. How the hell does a pigeon get to a place like this? Do they follow people, are they brought by people, or do they stow away on some vehicle like rats on a ship?

It's sunset when we arrive in Rio Gallegos. The Czech was right, it wasn't a bad trip. My butt's fine. I take a deep breath for the adventure that lies ahead, and descend the steps. While waiting for the crowd to disperse from the cargo bay of the bus,

I see a German-looking guy fussing with his pack at the curb of the concrete peninsula between *darsenas*, or bus berths. A bus is pulling in and its low rear-view mirror is going to hit the guy in the head, so I quickly walk to him and tell him in English to be careful, ready to yank him out of the way if he doesn't respond. He steps aside as the mirror glides by silently. We talk. He and his friend are German, and have reservations at "Hotel Paris" downtown. They found it on the internet, and it's only forty-nine pesos for two. It sounds just right for me. I need a place that will accept a Visa card. I get a map and bus info at the tourist office and catch a bus downtown. An ATM is right where the tourist map says it is, but my card still doesn't work. Then I walk a block and turn the corner to find the front door of Hotel Paris. There, in the front window, is a Visa decal.

Check-in is quick and easy. The room is nothing to write home about, but cheap for being right downtown. I explain my situation and ask if I can get some cash with my Visa. The owner is too old to know how to use the card "machine," and tells me to return to the desk after ten; the man on the night shift will give me an extra hundred pesos. While finishing my business at the desk, a woman comes up and asks for a room, but they tell her it is full. I got the last one.

The hip internet spot I had heard about is just block away. I suppose it's labeled "hip" because it's modern and has a fast connection. There's nothing really hip about it. I check e-mail. My dad writes, "Did you get your money yet?" That's it. Nothing more. I have no idea what he's talking about. I write back asking and let him know the name of my hotel and the town.

Weak from hunger and fatigue after the thirty-hour trip, and confident that the hotel staff will help me, I go to the supermarket and buy a bag of bread, cheese, tomato and avocado, and a beer, all for seven pesos—that's one-third of my money. Back in the room I eat several sandwiches with the beer, then undress for a shower. After showering, I fall asleep.

When I wake I assume it's after ten, so I go down to the desk, a bit groggy. The clock behind the desk says it's 11:50, so I explain my situation to the night clerk. He's expecting me and jumps into action. As he's running my card, the phone rings. He answers and waits about ten seconds, then says, "No spik eenglish." After another five seconds he hands me the phone. I say hello and the woman asks if I speak English. I say I do, but I don't work there, I just happen to be at the desk. She says, "Tom?" It's my sister.

She tells me what happened. My father went to the bank to make a withdrawal, and the young teller asked him which account he wanted to withdraw from, not noticing that one account was a dual account under my name and address, six hundred miles away from his. So my father simplified his life by closing the account that he didn't even know he had—mine. After receiving my e-mail and phone messages, he was able to re-open the account, so all should be okay.

I get the hundred pesos from the clerk, a helpful and kind man, then go back to my second-floor room, and think about a plan as I sit on the bed and stare at the floor. All of a sudden I notice that it is made of Douglas Fir. I'm sure it was brought around the Horn from Oregon or Washington before the construction of the Panama Canal. This whole building is probably built of it, as there is no forest within hundreds of miles from here.

The hotel is quiet, so I sleep well. But in the morning it sounds like a herd of elephants are playing soccer in the hallway. This place is like that hotel in Lebu, Chile, where every step echoed through the entire building. When someone walks in the next room the floorboards ring, and if I'm too close to the wall my mind reacts with concern that they might step on my toe. A key turning in the lock of a door down the hall sounds like it is in the night table beside my bed. The acoustics, with plaster walls and ceiling, are incredibly live. What's more, my room is beside the marble staircase. I open the door to see the elephants, but see a maid gandy-dancing down the hall with a five-gallon bucket of water and a mop, wearing hard-soled shoes with those kind of blocky wooden heels that my Hungarian grandmother wore. I think flamenco dancers wear them too.

Breakfast—tea and croissants—comes with the room. I ask for more hot water three times but my requests are not appreciated by the waitress. There is a Swiss guy nearby who is on a one-and-a-half-year, round-the-world trip. I assume he has just been to Ushuaia, the southernmost city in the world, located at the bottom of Tierra Del Fuego, where many a cross-continent bicyclist begins or ends a trip. From here he will go north all the way to Alaska, overland. Then he will cross to Siberia somehow and take the famous railway west. I give him my e-mail address in case he needs help in California or Alaska.

At the ATM, still no luck, so I call the bank. They tell me my account is fine, but the bankcard, once cancelled, is done so permanently and irreversibly.

I call my father and tell him that I am okay, and that I will try to get cash with my credit card at a bank tomorrow.

I'm stuck in a place that's a cross between some Nevada mining town and a wind-swept seaport in Newfoundland. It's flat and ugly on a cold and windy Sunday, with everything closed. The relationship between my ability to access numbers in a computer in California and my ability to maintain and fuel my body is glaringly clear. I feel as if someone has unplugged me from my source of sustenance. I'm reminded of the characters in film "The Matrix" who, having entered the false reality of the matrix, have their cranial plugs pulled from their real bodies back on board their ship, and collapse lifeless on the spot in the cyberworld. I'm alive, but without access to the digits in the Wells Fargo computer, my lifeline is cut. I feel like a homeless person with no money, job, or acquaintance, let alone friend. But I have a credit card.

On a hunch, I walk north. The phone and power lines howl and whistle in the wind, sounding like ghosts in an ancient castle on the Scottish moors. Trash and leaves swirl in eddies by corners of buildings. Dust gets in my eye. At least I'm on land. Again thoughts come of the sailing ships that fought these winds. When steam was overtaking sail, a little more than a hundred years ago, the canvas-driven boats could no longer afford the luxury of putting into this port to wait for the *pamperos* to die. They had to push on towards the Horn to make headway in the race against steam. The last days of sail were the most miserable for the sailors, and the only ones who stubbornly refused to quit were the masters of the profession. Many of them went down with ships that should have been waiting out a storm. I can only think of it as a decision to go down as a master seaman rather than live as a nobody. If they surrendered to steam, they'd have to take demeaning work on a steamer, somewhere between those shoveling coal into the boiler and those barking down tubes to the engine room. To them, even the captain of a steamer was a nobody, because he gained a port by dominating the sea under the power of coal. There was no finesse, no playing of the wind-dealt hand, no need for skills earned from a life at sea. Steam cheated Neptune, their worthy and respected opponent. It just wasn't right.

I find an open restaurant and leave the wind. Steam basins full of pasta and sauces take the center of a room with mauve walls. A classic waiter, with a pink shirt, a pink and black striped apron, slicked-back black hair and a big mustachio stands with arms folded in the corner. He doesn't move a muscle, but when I ask if there is a special, he answers in a deep voice, deepened by years of smoking cigarettes. There is—all you can eat for twelve pesos, with bread. "*Bueno*" is all I say. I don't tell him he is going to lose money on me. I ask for wine, and he brings me a stainless steel carafe containing about three glasses of cheap sweet wine.

I get to work on ravioli with a cheese and ham sauce, lasagna, stuffed manicotti, and fettuccine with a marinara sauce while watching the news on TV. It's all about Buenos Aires: a hotel fire, floods, bank robbery, and a road jammed by picketers and "antipicketers."

For some reason I am confident that my money situation will be corrected soon. At the internet spot, I call off my calls for help, then catch a bus to the terminal, listening to the reggae playlist. The Maytones sing "Money Worries."

"Anywhere you go, it's the same cry, money worries, money trouble."

At the terminal I buy a ticket to El Calafate, a town at the foot of the Andes, for thirty-three pesos. Back in town I spend forty-seven pesos on dry food provisions at the supermarket. With the fifteen pesos at the pasta shop, that's ninety-five of the hundred pesos I got last night, so I'm broke again.

I suppose the situation is stressful only because I still haven't recovered from the bus trip and food fast. I feel relaxed, but I am still fatigued. When I get to my room I have trouble unlocking the door. The key is one I've never seen before: a paddle-shaped thing that is inserted horizontally. But I'm still so out-of-it that I can't realize I need to turn it the other way, and have to ask for help. This creates further distance between me and the staff, who see me as a crazy gringo, traveling with no money.

The silicone earplugs allow me to take a nap. In the evening I blow half of my five pesos on a call to Marinela. I laugh at the pleasure of hearing her sweet voice. Leaving the phone store, I'm reminded of a TV show I saw many years ago in which a British anthropologist explained that the high voice of a woman is attractive to males because the male is genetically programmed to respond to the needs of his young, who have high voices. A woman's high voice insures that she will be provided for as well. Just before seeing that show, I had read in Newsweek that hormone balance determines various mental abilities. High testosterone levels allow a person to excel at map-reading—something that I had, till that point, taken pride in. These two events helped me to realize that what I thought was distinctly *me* is, in fact, mostly a result of genetic programming and the chemistry of hormone levels.

While I wander the streets southward, I think about this, and about the cultural programming that I allow to color my experience here. A Visa decal in the window of a café draws me there. It's a corner shop with a modern décor. The three glass walls and tile floor create a cold atmosphere. The men working there appear sleazy with their greasy slicked hair, but that's my programming again—cultural, not genetic. They're kind and helpful, accommodating me by charging more than the bill so I can have the extra amount in cash. I have a big hamburger and a Stella Artois Belgian beer—a treat, head and shoulders above Argentinean beer. Outside the window, a gypsy wagon is parked on the median strip. A sign indicates that it is a tourist office. This town is really putting an effort into tourism. I suspect that they're trying to get people to stay a few days instead of just passing through on their way to Tierra del Fuego to the south, or El Calafate to the west. They bill themselves as "El Ciudad de los Pinguinos," because those birds are the only thing that a tourist would want to see here. Since the devaluation of the Argentinean peso, the numbers of foreign tourists have multiplied, and my guess is that Rio Gallegos is trying to harvest its share of the foreign money, but it doesn't look like the fish are biting. Still, the effort is admirable and appreciated, at least by me.

The café fills up with friends meeting for a cafecita and a cigarette. People at window tables wave to friends walking or even driving by. The full body of the Belgian beer feels good on my tongue. The TV news is on—more on the floods in the north. I see that the water going down the storm drain is turning counterclockwise. Folk legend has it that, down here, water goes down drains in a clockwise direction due to the Coriolis effect—opposite of the northern hemisphere. But while the idea is correct—that the Coriolis effect causes free-flowing objects to bend to the left in the southern hemisphere—any container with a drain has many other influences in it that over-ride the faint Coriolis force. It is interesting to me to see that even the water approaching this storm drain in open country is subject to forces, maybe a slight current, that overpower Coriolis.

The congenial greasy guys sincerely wish me well when I take the twenty pesos with the change.

I go to the phone shop and call Wells Fargo to order a new bankcard sent in care of the old folks at the Valdivia hospedaje, then e-mail their son-in-law so they are expecting to receive important documents for me. Back at the hotel I charge camera and iPod batteries and get packed for tomorrow's trip to the mountains.

CHAPTER 22

The Banks of Rio Gallegos

In the morning I shower, have tea and sweet croissants, store my backpack in a little closet under the stairs, and head for the nearest bank. It's Monday morning and a line waits at the door, fifteen minutes before they open at ten. I hustle over to another bank—Banco Patagonia—where I find the same situation, so I get in line with the locals. After they open, the three tellers, young men in white shirts and ties, go into action stamping documents, and it sounds like a flamenco dancer imitating Thelonius Monk, amplified in the acoustics of the marble and glass room. When I get to the counter, I make my request to get money with my Visa card and they tell me they don't deal with Visa, and send me to Banco Tierra del Fuego. Once there, I wait in line again and repeat my request through a little hole in the glass window. I'm told to see the woman at the first desk, who tells me to go to Banco Francais. I ask her to call them to verify so I don't have to wait in line again, only to be sent somewhere else. She calls, then tells me to go to BanSud instead. At this bank I go directly to a woman at a desk and tell her the entire story. She says that the only way to get money with a Visa card is to use an ATM. I tell her I have never needed to do that, so I don't have a PIN. I ask what is the difference between the ATM and the bank. She gives me a long detailed explanation, but between her soft-spoken words, the room with its poor acoustics, echoing telephones ringing and stamps pounding paper, and, of course, my poor ability to understand Spanish—let alone Argentinean bankers lingo—I don't get it. I ask for the routing number of the bank, thinking I can have money wired. She leaves and returns five minutes later with several pages of instructions for electronic transfers. She keeps pointing to one line that is very important, but I don't understand the key banking terms in it. I ask her how long it will take to receive a transfer and she says five to six days. I'm frustrated, but thank her and leave. All I have accomplished so far is to learn that they use the word *clave* for PIN. Clave means "code"; I know it as "keystone," which is why it's also the name of the hardwood sticks that, when clicked together in a specific rhythmic pattern, form the foundation of Afro-Cuban music.

Out on the street I decide to give Banco Francais a shot. I enter and see three cubicles with desks. Only one is occupied. I take a number—twenty-three. After ten minutes of waiting, the teller calls out "Number fourteen." I leave.

I return to the hotel and ask the morning clerk to hold a room for me. He says he'll hold it for an hour. When I tell the clerk and the owner the story, they send me to Western Union. It looks like a little old bus station—worn out and dirty. The guy who is obviously in charge is a no-nonsense type, keeping things moving. I tell him that I want to receive money from the United States, and need to know how to do it. He says I just need to have the money sent to Argentina. All I need is my name to collect it. I grab an instruction brochure and am walking back to the hotel to call my father, when, as I'm crossing the main street, I read that you need a Western Union card to make the transaction. I turn about-face in the middle of the street, and walk back to the office. When I ask if I need a card as it says in the instructions, the Western Union *jefe* asks me where I read that. When I point, he marks a big *x* over the part about needing a card and gives it back to me. I ask if there is a limit. He says 500 pesos; if I want more I have to go to Banco Hipotecario.

At Banco Hipotecario there's a short line, so just for the hell of it, I try asking the teller for money with my Visa, and am turned down. So I ask if I can receive money by Western Union and am sent to a mild-mannered gentleman at a desk who has a black eye with blood in his eyeball behind his glasses. He has a welt on the side of his head. Someone must have clocked him. He sends me to a pleasant middle-aged woman in a room with no windows. She shows me the form, but won't let me take it. When I begin to write down all the info I need, I realize that it really *is* just the name of this town and my name as it appears on my passport. Can it be this easy?

At the hotel, the morning clerk is still on duty. I pay for the room and ask him if I can get some cash with my Visa, he tells me he can't do it without the owner's permission, and the owner will be back at three. I tell him the owner doesn't know how to use the credit card machine. That's news to him. He's trying to learn English from a little book so he can help tourists, and asks me to check a few phrases he has written. One says something about "Behold the glacier," and I tell him that word is for poets, and he should use "see."

I'm back out on the street waiting for the bus to the terminal. The 'B' line winds through the northwest quarter of town—through barrios, warehouses, vacant lots with plastic bags flying from the occasional bush like a white flag from the aerial of a speeding car, past numerous concrete and brick houses in various stages of construction, waiting for their owners to get more money together (none of them are being worked on). Once we leave the main street, the whole trip is on washboard gravel that makes the bus vibrate violently. The stress on all the fasteners must be intense. I imagine that bolts and screws must break regularly. My first time on this route, I followed the map I had just gotten at the terminal so I would know where to get off. The route is so twisted and convoluted that I got turned around by ninety degrees. Now I just listen to the reggae playlist and watch things go by the window with no concern about my location.

A tiny circus is in town, the "Cirque de Sol," with its tent set up across the boulevard from the terminal. When I see the tent I know I'm close, and begin to anticipate dealing with the nasty little girl who sold me the ticket yesterday. When I walk up to the ticket window, I see her walking out the back with a big bag. I'm lucky. I tell the other girl that I can't go on the two o'clock bus because of bank problems. She is friendly and kind, and issues me an open ticket good for ninety days, extinguishing all my concerns about needing to make a reservation. "Whenever you want," she says with a smile. I thank her and get back out on the street. The same driver picks me up on his return trip. When we get back into town he stops at a corner, and a new driver boards and takes over. I've taken this bus five times and three of those times the bus changed drivers, and each was at a different time of day. I've never seen this tag-team bus driving anywhere else in the world.

In town I go to the phone store. There are a couple of these on every block, but I found one run by a kindhearted lady, so I always go there. I call Visa. A man answers, and I ask if he speaks English. "No, I do not speak English" he says in clear English. I ask if there is a person there that does. "Wait one minute please," he says in perfect English. After a few minutes of violin music, I remember that I only have six pesos to pay for the call, so I hang up. The bill for the call is six pesos, and so I am pesoless.

Hunger returns, so I walk for a half-hour looking for a visa decal. I'm lucky to have this credit card. Without it, I suppose I would be looking for work. I have never gone hungry except when I've fasted for health reasons; I don't know what it's like to go hungry involuntarily. It really is astounding to fully grasp our need to put so much fresh organic matter inside our bodies every day to survive, and that so many of us succeed in doing so for our entire lives. Humans take 40% of all the plant biomass harvested on the planet in a year. Two-thirds of that is the wheat, rice and corn that we grow. A small fraction is the vegetables and fruits we eat; chainsaws and bulldozers eat the rest.

I think of all the people on the planet who go hungry most of the time. It seems to me that the number is going to grow, maybe dramatically. As the world population grows, it grows mostly by poor people, and it's predicted to increase by 40% in the next fifty years. At the same time, rising sea level will drown many acres of our arable land, climate changes will make farming impossible in some areas, and soil loss will slow production in general. Rising oil costs will make food grown by "green revolution" style farms more and more expensive. And the oceans are running out of fish. What the hell are the next billion people going to eat? What are you and I going to eat? People concerned about coming food shortages say we better start gardening now if we're not already. Some say it's time to return to the country and farm; the image of the lush fields below Chilean volcanoes returns to my mind. I think we need to address the population growth, but no one is doing that. This is simply amazing to me. It makes me feel like I come from a different planet. Isn't it obvious that the exploding human population is one of the greatest threats to this planet? Yet every major voice calling for change ignores this issue as if it is forbidden territory. I have to assume that they see it as an ethical question, the answer to which is not clear. One thing is perfectly clear to me: if we ignore population growth, billions more people will suffer in the next few decades. Many more species will become extinct. Global warming will be impossible to stop.

I find an interesting restaurant that only accepts Master-Card, and a sandwich shop, which accepts Visa, but has no tables. So I return to the corner place where I ate last night. As I walk in, I see last night's waiter sitting at the bar so I walk over to say hello. When he asks how it's going, I tell him the story. He offers another thirty pesos on my card, and then checks with me, to be sure that I *am* going to "consume" (in Spanish). I never heard that one before, but I tell him yes. I'm tempted to ask if I can behold the menu, but let it go. After the meal I immediately spend twenty-five on a notebook and pen.

I check e-mail. There's one from Gangaji, a woman who confirmed that a sudden realization I had had nineteen years ago was indeed profound. Back then, a perfect storm of events led to my complete surrender of self, so that I fully experienced that the person I had identified myself as, this ego I call Tom, is little more than a mental construct, the main character of my continuing story. I was without the small self, but my teacher at the time did not understand what I was experiencing, and because I trusted him so much, I doubted my insight for ten years. Once I began to grasp the profundity of the experience, I met Gangaji. Now I receive occasional emails from her foundation. She writes, "If you will take a moment to recognize the peace that is already alive within you, you then have the choice to trust it in all your endeavors, in all your relationships, in every circumstance of your life." I smile.

I e-mail my sister, asking her to send money via Western Union, and give her the instructions. But I've learned never to rely on one avenue of service in countries where the gap between what is promised and what is delivered is wider than in the USA. So I go to the web and search for a Visa international help number, but all I get is information on their corporate structure. Finally I realize there are phone numbers right on the back of my card. I am such a neophyte at using these plastic cards! I decide to try one of the numbers from the hotel, since it's a toll-free number specifically for calls from outside the U.S. The clerks are cool with letting me use the phone, but the owner's petulant wife is on duty. When I ask if I can use the phone she gives me a look like I just stuck a pin in her ass, wrinkling her nose, baring her top teeth, and squinting. I bend over to get the number out of my pack, which is on the floor, and when I stand up she's gone. I wait. After five minutes she returns and I ask her if I can use the phone; she tells me it is too complicated for her, making the same pained face. So I go down to the phone store, and the kind lady smiles and tells me I don't have to pay to make a toll-free call or a collect call. I call Visa collect and ask them to give me a PIN, and am on the phone for a half-hour. They insist that I can only get a PIN if I am calling from my home phone. It takes ten minutes to explain why I need it, answering all their questions, and then I'm transferred to the supervisor. We go through the whole thing again and she consults the security department. They won't bend the rules. They keep telling me to just go to the bank and ask for money, so I tell them that this is Patagonia; I think these people are still recovering from the heists of Butch Cassidy and the Sundance Kid, who operated in this province. Finally they say they can send me money. They connect me with another agent, but he doesn't know where the money will go or how long it will take. I give up.

At Hotel Paris I get my key, haul my backpack out from under the stairs, and re-enter the room as if for the first time. It's beginning to feel like "Groundhog Day."

It's dusk. I've worked all day and my two accomplishments were to email my sister asking her to send $500 by Western Union to "Argentina," using my full name, and to exchange my bus ticket for an open one. Both achievements took a total of nine minutes, yet I've been at it for eight hours. I lie down, but sleep is impossible with all the stomping and door-slamming in the hall. After an hour-and-a-half it is time to feed myself again. When I come down the stairs the bitchy owner lady is there at the desk. Remembering "Groundhog Day," I give her a big smile when handing her my key.

I try the east side of town this time. While beating the streets in search of an attractive restaurant behind a visa decal, I come across a hardware store. Inside they have tool handles that are almost perfect for a staff—just over an inch, maybe thirty millimeters, in diameter—a tad on the stout side, but light. The owner says they are strong. They look like their made of some kind of pine (the owner doesn't know the wood), and cost five pesos. Not a single peso is in my pocket as I continue down the street in a new rhythm, with the staff knocking the concrete on the backbeat of my footsteps, between every third step, inviting an Afro-Cuban 6/8 bell pattern. I guess I still have "clave" on my mind.

In just a few blocks there's a new Chinese restaurant, which makes my intestines grumble, remembering bad, greasy ones of the past, but I walk over to it anyway. There's an all-you-can-eat buffet going on, and the window displays a Visa decal. The waiter is super-friendly and the price is right. The roast beef is excellent, but iceberg lettuce is the greenest thing I've had in weeks, and I'm craving vegetables. I'd expect a Chinese restaurant to have some, but can't find them. Then I see what I guess is tempura green beans, and I take a big pile of them. At my table I bite into one and discover it is a whole, batter-dipped baitfish. I eat them all.

Back at the internet spot, mail from my brother tells me that my sister could only send $300 because it's Martin Luther King Day and the banks are all closed. $300 was all she could get from an ATM. She'll send $200 more tomorrow. I reply "NO!" in capital letters, and tell them I can't wait here any longer; I'm out of here as soon as that $300 comes.

In the Paris, the night clerk is surprised to see me. I tell him the story. He gives me my key and a bill for the room. The bitchy lady is trying to bill me twice. I learn the word *Factura*—"invoice," but my dictionary says it also means a roll, biscuit or muffin. While I show him my receipt for today's payment, my mind goes through a list of words like "pay-roll," "bank-roll," "dough," and "bread," wondering about the connection. He shrugs and throws his invoice in the trash. I put in my earplugs, and get a good sleep. When I wake, I look at the clock. "Ground-hog Day" again.

The maids are causing a ruckus in the hall. I go to the bathroom at the end of the hall and shower. Thinking of the movie puts me in good spirits. I'm fully present with my emotions. The bathroom's head-high white tiled walls are trimmed with blue masking tape. The ancient floor tiles fit together in groups of four to create filigree designs using abstract pineapples in maroon, pink, green, gold, and grey. I shave, and watch the water go down the drain counterclockwise.

When I leave my room, I ask the maid if she wants me to leave the door open. She says, "Yes, are you leaving?" I tell her I hope so, and laugh. I'm still smiling when I enter the dining room. The waitress is the same every morning, but she acts like she never saw me before. After I finish my tea, I flag her down (even though there are only four of us in the dining room) and ask for more water. She gives me the pain-in-the-ass look for the third morning. I immediately notice my emotional reaction to her, which makes me smile even more. The croissants are too sweet, so I give them to a young British couple two tables away.

I'm at the bank early, and waiting. A nerdy guy in a sweat suit comes up and says, "Nia," which I can now interpret, given the context, to be "Buenos Dias." He sits beside me on the brick windowsill. At two-and-a-half minutes after ten the doors open, and I beeline to the lady in the room with no windows. She smiles, remembering me, asks for my passport, and walks out. In a few minutes she returns to inform me that all they have is pesos. I tell her that's perfect. She gives me 900 pesos, and I inquire if there's a Western Union office in El Chaltén, a little town in the mountains where I am headed. She doesn't think so, but gives me a brochure with a phone number. At the phone store I call the number and finally have a phone conversation in Spanish without a single problem. Phones are difficult for me because I can't watch the speaker's mouth. At least that's why I *think* it's difficult. It could also be that the phone on my left ear sends a signal to only one hemisphere of my brain—the right—which may have more trouble with language than the left. There *is* an office in El Chaltén. They give me the address. I cross the street and e-mail that to my sister, asking for another $150 which will surely be below the 500 peso limit of small offices, but ask her to try to validate that there is indeed a

Western Union office at the address I gave her in El Chaltén.

With all loose ends tied, I leave there feeling the joy of being released from bondage and captivity. Back at the Paris, the morning clerk is happy to hear I got the money. We talk about learning English a bit, and I encourage him to practice with travelers. I grab my pack from under the stairs and get on the B-line for the sixth time, through the bumpy labyrinth, past the circus, to the terminal where the sweet girl is at the counter. I tell her happily that I can go today and she smiles and asks "At one?" "Yes." I get a ham and cheese sandwich—the special "primavera" one, which has a piece of lettuce and a paper thin slice of tomato in it—for a dollar. It's not too bad.

A guy with a "Sitka, Alaska" T-shirt passes while I'm walking to the trash can with my plastic sandwich wrapper. Yes, he is from there. I tell him I once lived near the town of Homer. He tells me he was in Homer once and had trouble with his bankcard. He was stuck with only two dollars, so he spent it on a fishing lure and caught a silver salmon and ate it for three days while he waited for a wire transfer that took five days to arrive. I can tell it's become a fond memory now. He introduces his wife and kids. They're on a seven-month tour, but I don't get any stories, or tell mine, because their bus comes. We exchange e-mail addresses.

A young couple with an eight-month-old baby sits beside me, and I begin goofing with the little boy, making faces at him and getting him to laugh. An old man with some disability limps to a seat near us and sits down with a "primavera." He puts the sandwich on his lap, but his fingers lack the dexterity to open the shrink-wrapped cellophane, so I help him and serve him the sandwich on the little Styrofoam tray.

I feel good. I didn't feel this good yesterday, but I worked at being happy anyway. Now that all the frustration is gone, I'm super-happy. It reminds me of the doughnut on the baseball bat when I was twelve years old. It was my last year in Little League. I was a good player, but no star. Still, I made the all-star team. The all-stars had a different coach, and he gave us a "doughnut" to put on the bat when we were on deck. A doughnut is a weight that looks like what it is named after. You drop it over the handle of the bat, and it weights the bat while you take practice swings. After I began using it, I began hitting home-runs. My regular coach asked me what was going on, and I told him it was the doughnut. Practicing with the extra weight made the regular bat feel super-light.

CHAPTER 23

El Chaltén

When the bus arrives, I'm delighted to see it's a five-star double-decked cruiser (music, TV, bathroom, heat, air conditioning) with the added bonus that the seat beside me is empty. I learn the word for "armchair"—*butaco*, spread out, and pick up where I left off in my reggae playlist with "Jah Can Do It," one of my favorites by Dennis Brown.

I'm on to Rico Rodriguez's "Fu Man Chu" when a flock of rheas appears out the window. At last! It's a thrill to see these birds in the wild. They stand about four feet tall, and keep together in a flock as they flee from the bus. When we pass a scarlet-breasted bird standing on a fence post, I consult my field guide and guess that it's a long-tailed meadowlark. Only a few minutes later there's another flock of rheas, and they're huge. I assume the birds in the first flock were all immature, as several adults in this flock stand six feet tall, but then I realize that it's possible, and I would guess likely, that they are two different species. The Greater Rhea is not supposed to be this far south, but there it is, right outside the window—I see six-foot tall birds—so the smaller ones may be the Lesser Rhea, which is native to these southern pampas. They run across the pampas, frightened by the bus. I'm tapping people on the shoulder to get them to look out the windows, wondering what it would be like to be out there on the ground with them as they charge across the grassland. The image reminds me of the scene early in the film "Jurassic Park," in which the ostrich-like dinosaurs stampede by the humans. Rhea males impregnate several females who all contribute eggs to his nest, which he defends while he incubates them. During this time he can be aggressive in his defense of the clutch, and the sharp claws of a man-sized cock charging at thirty-five miles-per-hour is close enough to Jurassic Park that I would be sure to avoid them in spring.

Not long afterwards I see my first herd of wild *guanaco*s. These are large camelids with golden backs and white sides and bellies. They stand still in groups of eight to twelve. The guanaco population has decreased from a half-billion before the Europeans arrived, to a half-million today, so the indigenous people must not have hunted them seriously, at least not successfully. The long necks of these and the rheas makes me incorrectly assume that the aboriginal choice of hunting weapon, the *bola*, was used to strangle both of these animals whose necks offer such a large target. But actually the bola was thrown at the legs to "hog tie" them. The Patagonian bola was made of two or three braided leather cords, each with a small leather sack filled with pebbles or a wooden ball at the ends of the cords. Gauchos learned how to use bolas from the Indians, and used them on cattle back in the day.

Later, the clouds seem to drop down on us. They are cirrus and nimbus—clouds of high elevation, but they are only a few hundred feet above. It is quite surreal, as if the sky doesn't fit the landscape.

Each time we cross an occasional slough I'm alert to see any wildlife that may visit for the water. There's a big grey goose at one, but I'm not even sure if it's wild, as these sloughs also attract homesteaders, and a little farmhouse is nearby. At times the roadside is thick with daisy-like wildflowers. A healthy carancho tops a fence post and watches us pass. At a road-cut, the exposed subterranean cobbles reveal that this place was once underwater. Blue mountains serrate the horizon.

Some impressive vertical walls stand in the distance. As

we approach El Calafate, I realize that we have indeed gained high elevation, having climbed very gradually on a seemingly flat, but tilted, landscape. When we descend a steep canyon wall into a big valley that holds Lago Argentino my ears pop. We roll slowly in low gear to keep the brakes cool. While looking out the window on the other side of the bus, I realize that the young guy sitting next to the window resembles my older brother when he was the same age—About twenty-one. He also has a wife and two-year-old son, as my brother did then. I consider asking him for his photograph, but decide not to, feeling awkward.

We arrive in El Calafate—named for a thorny blueberry that grows in the area. It's a bit of a boomtown, filled with young tourists carrying backpacks. The locals are doing a good job of developing in a consistent rustic mountain theme. The town sits on the south shore of the huge lake. Eager to get into the mountains, I march directly from the bus to the counter, to buy a ticket to El Chaltén, four hours to the north. In my thirty-minute layover, I find a grocery store and buy bread, cheese and olive loaf cold cuts, then sit on the curb of the terminal parking lot where I can keep an eye on my bus, and make a few sandwiches.

Heading out of town, we pass a glacial erratic the size of a house. It probably fell to the bottom of an ancient glacial lake when the iceberg that carried it melted. Something white is on the other side of the lake, and I'd bet it's an iceberg. After about twenty minutes of backtracking on the single road into town, we hang a left, and leave the pavement, heading north along the eastern shore of the lake, crossing a turquoise river, the Santa Cruz, which drains the glacial waters to the Atlantic. The silvery lake shimmers in the late afternoon sun west of an expanse of sand dunes. Beyond the lake are the Andes, obscured by dark purple rainstorms broken only by sporadic shafts of light. Then we cross another river, this one flowing *into* the lake. The geography is unusual. The next lake to the north, Lago Viedma, is of an equal size as this Lago Argentino. The two lakes are obviously the drowned valleys of huge glaciers from another epoch. They run parallel, from west to east, separated by twenty-five miles of mountains, but the river that drains Lago Viedma, Rio la Leona, runs south through a gap in the foothills of the mountains instead of spilling out onto the pampas as a normal river would. It must have been diverted by a massive terminal moraine at the end of the last ice age. This river dumps into Lago Argentino just a couple miles north of the origin of the Santa Cruz, probably doubling that river's size. I wonder what it would be like to run that river across the pampas to the Atlantic—would there be whitewater, wildlife? The map shows only one little bridge between the lake and the ocean, 140 miles as the crow flies, maybe 200 on the water. We follow Rio la Leona to the north. I see those grey geese again. They must be wild, but I don't see them in my book. Elephant toe formations of sandstone remind me of California desert excursions I've made. The badlands east of Borrego Springs come to mind. Frisbee-shaped lenticular clouds are stacked six-high to the north, like a squadron of UFO's coming in for a landing. Negritos fly from bush to bush.

We exit the mountains and pass the entire east shore of the Lago Viedma, then turn left at a cruz, and head up the north shore for the mountains. The drive takes some time; my excitement, anticipating views of the peaks, probably makes it seem longer than it is. About twenty miles from El Chaltén we pass a shallow pond where I see a large flock of Chilean Flamingos. Though my book told me that they range all over the southern cone, I still find it bizarre to see flamingos out the side window and then turn my head to see glaciers and peaks dusted with fresh snow out the front window. Cottontail rabbits, introduced from Europe, run across the road, just as they do up north, in a way that is enough to make one question Darwin.

The rabbits are well-hidden in the brush beside the road, but when a vehicle passes, they choose to run across the road in front of the vehicle. One may argue that they evolved without the input of vehicles, but it's my guess that they would do the same if spooked by a predator. I could never understand how this helps them to further their genes. One of them doubts its decision to cross the road, and stops. If it remained motionless it survived, with the big bus wheels racing by on both sides. A pair of Andean foxes wanders across the road ahead, and the driver leans on the horn. They split up, one to each side of the road. They're a more squat, dog-looking animal than our sleek foxes, but with coloring similar to the grey fox of North America.

We arrive after sunset, at about 10:30, and my guess is that there will be no room at the inn, whichever one I choose, and I am right. So I hang out at the bar in the big dining room of a busy hostel at the far end of town, closest to the mountains, drink a liter of Quilmes and chat with a few folks before wandering off into the post-midnight blackness to find the area where free camping is allowed.

The road is unscreened gravel, and I occasionally roll my ankle on an oversized cobble that I can't see without the light of a moon or stars. But I do find a sign for free camping, and it directs me down a steep slope, and under a barbed-wire fence. Inside there is a tent village. I raise mine in a space by the fence in a light gusty rain. As I crawl in, the shower begins coming down with force. The tall grass makes a great bed, better than any hostel, and I sleep like a baby, or as a baby should, all night.

In the morning the weather remains unchanged: wind and rain. But after a while, the rain lightens and the sun peeks out from time to time. The wind is a warm williwaw descending from the continental divide where it lets its water content go, gaining heat from the latent energy of that water's previous evaporation. It feels funny. I don't like it. I'm sure it's full of positive ions. I wonder where this water falling on me was when it evaporated. Probably the South Pacific, but maybe a glacier in New Zealand. As I walk across town, waves of dust rise from the road, blowing in the eyes of hikers headed for the trailhead behind me. The big granite peaks are obscured by clouds driven by an angry wind. I duck into a café for tea and ham empanadas, then visit the park visitor's center to register for the backcountry and get an "official" map showing only the "official" trails, most of which radiate from town on routes needed by day-hikers. Already I can tell that I will be spending most of my time off of those.

The Western Union office turns out to be the post office, which is a small room behind another office that is behind the tourist office that is a room in a white house set back from the road. I couldn't find it, but when I asked where it was, the several antennae on the roof made it obvious. The girl behind the counter takes my name and asks me to return later. I try to check e-mail across the street, but the service is so slow and expensive that I abandon it before my webmail page can load.

A girl at the Patagonia Hostel gives me some good information and sells me a fairly good map. It has the "unofficial" trails that will take me where I want to go without backtracking. She recommends that I camp at "El Refugio," on the bank of the river, so I move camp there, where the aging hippie owner tells me they have a hot shower, and most importantly, that they will guard my street gear while I'm in the mountains. It's only ten pesos a day. As I pitch my tent, a flock of parakeets passes close by, chattering excitedly as if they are happy to see me. If they are, the feeling is mutual.

Back in town, the Western Union girl gives me the money from my sister. I pay an exorbitant price at an outdoor store for a pair of wool socks to replace the ones that I now realize still hang in the boiler room at El Gaucho—forty-nine pesos—shop for a bit more food, and find salami and bread, both sold by the 100-gram weight. Then I stop in a "Cerveza Artisana," a microbrew pub in a crowded little rustic cabin, and have a slightly green bock beer, that I appreciate more for it's uniqueness than its flavor. Nearby there's an interesting restaurant with a side of lamb cooking in the front window and a sign reading, "La Casita." After an excellent steak with mashed potatoes and a *copa de vino tinto*, I stop in at the Aires Patagonicos for a nightcap.

CHAPTER 24

The Two Towers

t dawn, frost covers the grass, sparkling in a wintery way. After breaking camp, I cull all the stuff that I won't need from my pack. It's travel stuff. Some of it I need, most of it comes in handy, some of it I rarely use. It reminds me of the amenities of my California life. For the most part they're not really essential. Maybe some are really no more than a burden. It would be a worthwhile effort to simplify my life even further.

I stash a box of this stuff in the office, and ask for the trailhead. The old hippie, reeking of tobacco, even at this hour, tells me, "It's right there," and points across the street. I follow his finger, but the side-street dead-ends with no trail. So I climb a fence and get on a dirt road, and go west at a fork. At a second fork I see a trail up on the slope to the right, and a building on the left, so I decide to go right. That way bends left and takes me to the building, some sort of recreational clubhouse, behind which I find the trailhead. The route climbs through an Oregon desert landscape, with big round reddish boulders and outcroppings that would serve well as an ambush scene in an old western movie.

The trail makes a steady but easy climb. Eventually I get to a viewpoint and in the distance I see the spectacular Cerro Torre for the first time, up a glacial valley and below a waning moon. *El Torre*, "The Tower," is a spike of granite thrusting about 5,000 feet up from the side of a glacier. A thrill buzzes through my body in anticipation of what lies ahead, but I stop here for a bread-and-cheese breakfast, and watch finches and flickers flying by. A packer passes me with two loaded horses behind his own, all in a trot. He's got a mustache and a black beret. His feet fit into foot-holes, above five-pointed stars, in the tops of big iron discs that are his stirrups. I follow him through another enchanted lenga forest where I run into the dreadlocked Basque that I had met in Valdivia, who is hiking out, then I cross a gravel floodplain, and climb over an old terminal moraine before finding the camp, which is full of tents. I pass through the area and take the western-most, windwardmost site, pitch my tent, and sit in the sun with lunch. A guy walks by and asks in Spanish if a bridge crosses the river. I hear his English accent and tell him I don't know, I just got here, in our shared native language, and he continues on.

I pack up for a hike and head to the terminal lake. The view across the lake is more than outstanding. Cerro Torre dominates the landscape as if the entire valley had been constructed with that in mind. I don't think I've ever seen anything this powerful. It is truly majestic, standing 3,100 meters tall (I am below 1000). As seen from the lake, the main tower has two sheer walls of smooth granite. Various ledges hold impressively thick beds of ice. The pinnacle's west side and top are caked with rime ice that I imagine is plastered there by the severe and near-constant attack of the wind carrying vapor from the South Pacific across the Chilean icefield. As that wind meets the tower, I think it gets compressed and shoots upward under pressure. At the peak, that pressure is released and the vapor instantly condenses and freezes, building a bulb of airy ice on the west side of the summit. The majestic tower rises from a jagged, snow-covered ridge running up from the south called the "Cordon Adela." North of the Cerro Torre, is a series of lesser towers, the most prominent is named "Torre Egger," for Toni Egger who was half of the team that may have first scaled this giant spike in 1959. He was lost in an avalanche on the way down, and his camera, which would have contained the proof of their making the summit, went with him.

Not long ago a person could say such a sight is "Awesome." These days that word has been hijacked and rendered impotent. The young cashier at the local market in California tells me it's awesome when I give him exact change. This state I am now in, however—the state of awe—is anything but weak. It could be the most powerful emotion I know... so powerful that it wipes other emotions away, and has the potential to wipe the perceived owner of those emotions away as well. The majesty may bring some to their knees, the glory may cause some to raise their arms as if to shout hallelujah. In my case, I am stunned and stilled. It's a spiritual experience, not different from what I imagine it would be like to see God. My eyes receive the light of the spectacle before me and the image seems to course through my tissues as if to re-educate me viscerally. Each cell of me now knows what Nature is capable of creating—a sculpture of proportions beyond my imagination. My ego has been incinerated by the radiation of splendor. The grandeur has literally blown my mind.

How can a rock do this to a man? Or maybe the question is "Why?" It seems plausible that man would evolve to perceive his environment as beautiful. This would afford him a sense of ease and comfort that would promote health. But what advantage is there for us to be stricken by awe at the sight of a granite tower? It seems like it would only distract an evolving man from conducting the business of survival, and the ability to survive is an ace in the game of furthering genes. Thoughts of my place in society, the role I play and its rewards, are of no concern in this wonderstruck moment. In fact, it is plainly clear that they are unimportant. What *is* important is the vista before me, for it instills a clear awareness free of egoic noise, and in this awareness I find my true self, and an uncontrollable smile. I like the Spanish word for smile, *sonrisa*, because it reminds me of "sunrise." That is the nature of this smile—fresh and radiant. It's like a divine joke has been played on me—like the planet gave me a surprise party. My deepest spiritual experiences have always been like that—humorous—because when you see the Truth, everything else that has been occupying your attention seems hilariously silly.

This experience of awe can only be of use to an organism if there is a spiritual dimension to evolution. Is it by the intention of some omnipresent intelligence that man can experience such ecstasy simply by viewing a huge spike of eroded rock? Or is it by accident—an unproductive and therefore doomed idiosyncrasy of evolution?

Joseph Campbell said, "We are the eyes of the earth, we are the ears of the earth. What else?" Others propose that we are creation's way of experiencing itself, or God's way of experiencing his creation. Of course, I have no idea if there is a God or a Creator, or a Divine Intelligence. But experiences like this give weight to the theory that we are spiritual beings having a physical experience, because I see no use for a physical being to have a spiritual experience. The only possible explanation for the latter would be mental illness. In my view, it is those who are numb to the magnificence of Nature who are insane. Maybe there is one possible explanation: that the experience of awe leads to a reverence for creation that has evolutionary value in that this reverence may provide a means for the survival of a species with the ability to destroy the planet—it's own habitat. That reverence would lead to a view of Nature as sacred, and the destruction of Nature as sacrilege. Again, those irreverent must be insane. But all this would imply intentional evolution, since man has not had the ability to destroy the planet until recently, evolution would have had to have been thinking ahead. If Awe by Nature is an emotion that evolved to prevent environmental destruction, it seems like a failing strategy at this point in time, since we are well on the way to using our destructive ability. This then raises the question, "Can that which drives evolution fail by intention?" Or the better question might be, "Is failure—severe environmental destruction—built into the evolutionary plan as a way to facilitate accelerated change?" It could be that the experience of awe by Nature is a new development for modern man, but that also seems to imply an intention, because those most successful at furthering their genes in recent centuries have not been environmentalists and Nature-lovers, have they? This kind of awe could be a trait of an unfolding spiritual evolution, independent of genetics. The questions are numerous and unanswerable, but interesting to consider.

Over the years I have joked about national parks and monuments being a collection of freak vertical landscapes. We love the sheer rock walls of the Yosemite, Zion, and Canyonlands valleys. We gasp at the tall, sculpted buttes of the Grand Canyon and monument valley, and the exposed volcanic necks of Shiprock and Devil's Tower, wonder at the height of the Redwoods, of Denali, and several other tall peaks surrounded by national parks. The phenomenon might best be revealed by the bizarre totems of the hoodoos that are the only reason for Bryce Canyon National Park to exist. They are vertical oddities. If they were lying on the ground, there would be no park.

A psychologist might point to the church steeple to explain why we hold a reverence for the vertical. It points to heaven—to God. I'm not so sure. It could be that the vertical landscapes make us feel small. Some find that amusing: "Wow, it's so big!" Others find it stunning: "Wow, I'm so small!" The latter are those whose continuum of ego may be fractured, allowing a moment of profound peace to open the heart.

A woman is sitting on a rock at the edge of the lake with a faded orange jacket, which brings that color out of the granite of the tower. It is so right that I ask her if she would like me to take her photograph. She smiles and offers me her camera. She's a pleasant young French woman, Emily, who is working in Cordoba. We skirt the lower lake together and ascend along the crest of the huge lateral moraine on the north wall of the valley. Eventually our progress is thwarted by an avalanche chute that has knocked the moraine down to a steep scree and talus slope. Emily wishes she could get out on the ice, but needs to get back to town. I decide to go on. It is a good thing she didn't come, because it's hairy—very steep and loose. In the soft slope, every step sends sand, gravel and any hunk of nearby talus tumbling down, and also undermines the same material above, inviting it all to meet my shins. It takes me a long time to descend diagonally about 500 feet to the ice, then I meander among hills of loose gravel floating on the glacier, and eventually arrive at the band of level ice I've been seeking. It allows me to cross the glacier between areas of intense seracs. To the north, the afternoon sun is backlighting the seracs, with the tower looming overhead—quite an other-worldly scene. Colors are limited to tones from the whites of ice to greys of granite, and blues from cyan to cobalt. Crevasses reveal that deep glacial cyan that is found nowhere else but in ancient ice. The same color is deep in the heart of the backlit seracs. These cyans proudly expose themselves, compared to other ethereal cyans that appear in the shadowed ice timidly, as if they are sneaking an opportunity to be seen. The clear sky above the Andes is a dark blue you see only in the mountains and out jetliner windows. The glacier sparkles, a cool wind descends from the spires. Ice crunches underfoot.

Across the glacier I run into an ice-climbing class all decked-out in expedition gear, complete with crampons and hats, gloves, and parkas. I ask if there's a trail on this side of the glacier and am relieved to hear "Si." They're headed that way, but they're slow. As I pass the troop in my t-shirt and hiking boots with my wooden staff, the students, who were previously perfectly happy, are wondering why they are adorned with all the paraphernalia. One asks me if it is difficult without crampons, and I offer a way out for their guides by telling them that I'm used to it because I'm from Alaska, which I suppose is in some way true.

I jam by them, but keep stopping to take photos. My eyes are focused on the surface of the ice, two or three steps ahead, so that every time I turn around, the sight astounds me again—the view becoming even more spectacular now that I can see farther up the glaciered valley to other smaller but still dramatic towers (called "needles") north of the monarch. In pools of deep clear water penetrating the profound cyan of the inner glacier, I see occasional small beds of gravel flung on some sub-surface shelf like a spray of jewels. The wet stones seem polished and on display, their golden and rusty colors contrasting with the frosty turquoise. They remind me of sunken treasure—precious.

The trail begins right where it makes sense, and it immediately climbs six hundred feet up into the lenga to get around a big cliff. I lose the route where it gets wiped out every winter in an avalanche chute, now housing a cascading stream with loose scree banks, but find my way following paths made by others who have strayed, and reconnect to the main path, which takes me through taller lenga on the way down to the ridgetop of the southern lateral moraine. From there it's an easy stroll back to the river, and I'm wondering how I will cross it. I never did learn the answer to that guy's question about the bridge. When I get there I see two ropes spanning the spillway of the river, just below the edge of the lake. There is a zip-line on one, sitting at the far side, but tethered to a retrieving line that is festooned from the rope by a series of carabiners. It's a Tyrollean traverse, probably installed by the guiding companies. I reel it in and, since I don't have a harness, I tie two loops to the zip wheel with the retrieving line, put my legs through them, and pull myself across.

It's been a long day. Back in camp I cook pasta and pick up the reggae playlist where I left off. U Roy sings "Top of the Peak." It sounds as if I never heard music before, my senses heightened by the day's experience. Music in the backcountry is a new luxury for me. I brought the iPod for bus trips, but carry it into the backcountry because it's too valuable to leave with my stash in town. And right now the music overwhelms me. It's almost too much. I'm reminded of driving home from ten-day meditation retreats when I would play one song at a time on the cassette deck in my truck. I couldn't handle the over-stimulus of another tune without some quiet time to punctuate and separate—to allow a re-settling to the deep peace I had come to dwell in, and allow digestion of the music I had taken in. Now I endure the over-stimulation and feel an overwhelming pleasure from it. My body is giggling when a light-blue cabbage butterfly passes by happily—or, at least it looks happy, the way it flaps its wings and flutters erratically. For all I know it could be having a shitty day, but it makes me feel happy because it is beautiful.

I'm up at 2:15. Two-thirds of a moon is enough to light everything well in the clear air. I go out into the wind, and hike to the lake to look at the mammoth tower. After a few attempts at long exposures with my camera, I stop and just sit and enjoy. A cold wind is whipping me, and my eyes tear when I look at the tall granite massif glowing in the moonlight like something you'd read about in a Tolkien book. Orion is hanging in the sky over the tower. Down here we see it in the northern sky, and upside down. I think I see the Southern Cross—my uncertainty due to the fact that I don't know what I am looking for—right in the Milky Way. A sudden insight—the image of the Australian flag—reminds me of a fifth star occupying the lower right quadrant of the cross, and the constellation leaps out of the heavens to my eye. It's not the four stars that make the cross, but the fifth, a red star, that identifies it.

At 5:45 the alarm goes off. In a few seconds I convince myself that it's too early for sunrise, but a few minutes later I notice a golden glow on the tent wall and jump up and rush out to see the first light on the tower. As I climb the terminal moraine that is the dam that creates the lake, the top of the tower already glows a radiant gold, and the line of shadow below it slowly drops as the sun rises. The golden light is astonishing. People who never see these things in nature, but only on film, would expect to hear a symphonic soundtrack to this sunrise; something on the order of Strauss's "Also Sprach Zarathustra."

Naturally I take lots of photos, then retire for a few more hours of sleep. When I rise, others are milling around their tents with cups in hand, and I brew some maté for myself and find a boulder to lean back on and enjoy the bird songs, the way I do while sitting on the balcony of my Alaska cabin, listening for the biophany —the local ecosystem's symphony. I listen for the rhythm, the call and response, the layering of high and low notes, and try to open myself to experience a quality I never knew before.

After break-fast and break-camp I visit the lake one last time and pour Aaron Rosewater's water into it. Aaron is a far-out guy I met several years ago who claims to have invented a "machine"—a series of tubes that sends water through several vortexes—that brings water to consciousness. He says his water can bring other water to consciousness simply by contact. So, over the years I have carried small bottles of an ounce or two of his water when I travel, and add the water to special lakes and rivers, glaciers and oceans that I visit. I have no idea about the validity of Aaron's claim, but it is an interesting ritual for me. The point of bringing consciousness to all water is that, since we are over 70% water, this could help humanity evolve to a higher consciousness. I know it's a long shot, but what if he is right? As Martin Luther King said, "We will be able to speed up the day, all over America and all over the world, when justice will roll down like waters, and righteousness like a mighty stream."

I head out on the trail and back-track for a few miles to the next terminal moraine—an older one—where an "unofficial" trail takes off to the north, climbing the spur that separates two glacial valleys, and crossing that spur at a flat point where two lakes meet end-to-end and the lenga surrounding them are dwarfed. Progress along the lake-shores slowly reveals El Chaltén, a 3,400-meter tombstone-shaped monolith that indigenous people dubbed "The Smoking Mountain," also known as "Monte Fitz Roy." Robert Fitz Roy, Captain of "The Beagle," famously giving passage to Charles Darwin, was the first European to see this granite monument. I'm impressed that he made the trip across the pampas, but still I wonder if he deserves having his name replacing the traditional one, given by the Tehuelche people who lived around this monarch for 150 centuries. Certainly Fitz Roy deserves such an honor more than McKinley deserves to displace the Athabascan name of "*Denali*," "The Great One," and certainly "Fitz Roy" seems a more regal name than "McKinley" to my ear, but I will use "El Chaltén" in honor of the aboriginal people.

El Chaltén is every bit as impressive as Cerro Torre, so, sensing that the trail is about to descend, I lunch in a meadow fifty feet above the trail and watch the mountain. Below, people hike by without ever seeing me reclining among the hummocks of grass. I hang out and push my mind towards the insight that I'm looking for—but all I can come up with is that Nature is divine. My mind can't penetrate the unexplored territory without the trail broken before me. I wonder, "Is it the rock itself that is divine, or the processes of volcanic intrusion, uplift, and erosion—the sculptural process—that is divine?" And I realize that it's a moot point—there is no difference between the two. It's all Nature, and it is all divine—an expression of ultimate beauty that the human must be intended to observe.

From here, the path drops down, winding its way through woodlands to the camp. I pass through it and pitch my tent at the upriver end. A rufous-collared sparrow of the southern race checks me in, and a rusty-tailed woodpecker that I fail to identify also investigates this newcomer. As soon as my camp is secure, I head out for the high lake called "Laguna de Los Tres," named by the three French men who first climbed El Chaltén in the early 1950's. It's another scramble up a scree slope, but this time there's a trail and plenty of exposed bedrock to keep the slope stable. At the crest I behold the majesty of the monolith. I don't use the words loosely: "behold" and "majesty" are appropriate in this case. It's as good as it gets: translate that into whatever the word is that means that for you. These granite massifs are works of art—sculptures of Nature. To be in their presence is to be in the presence of a masterpiece. Part of the reason that they are masterpieces is because of the natural composition of shapes and sizes. From the perspective of Japanese aesthetics, which I consider to be the most refined aesthetic sense, these rocks are well-arranged. That is, there is a dominant subject—the major peak—accompanied by a subdominant one. Cerro Torre is accompanied by Egger and Standhardt. El Chaltén has the regal tower called "Poincenot" at his side. A third, subordinate, element completes a composition when the beholder moves and the view changes. It could be a glacier below the peaks, or a bonsai lenga in the foreground, a cloud or the moon in the sky, a dark rocky ridge, or a white boulder in a stream at my feet. The subordinate constantly changes. One appreciates these works of aesthetic mastery by viewing them from different angles and in different light, and in different weather, and with different foregrounds.

Most of us observe Nature fairly regularly if not continuously (even those in the hearts of cities see grass growing from cracks in sidewalks, and pigeons every day) But the problem is that we get conditioned to the experience. In part, we must if we are to get on with the business of survival. It would be overwhelming to live in a forest and be astounded by every tree, every bug, every flower. But in another way we shut ourselves off from the experience of Divine Nature by a process the Buddhists call "the naming of ten-thousand things." That is, we unconsciously name things "tree," "bug," flower," and the naming—the declaration of familiarity—prevents us from seeing the miracle that is right in front of us. When the right mental conditions are present, the sight of a tree, a bug or a flower can jolt us out of our conditioning. Maybe I'm a tough nut to crack. I've usually required big, powerful experiences like an ass-kicking storm, a forest of 360 foot tall trees, or three weeks floating through the Grand Canyon to knock me out of my conditioned mind and into a state the Zen Buddhists call *kensho*. But ten-day meditation retreats, and my first intimate tea ceremony, on a quiet winter morning, brought me to that state of awareness in which the filters on my perception are diminished. In that state, things look more three-dimensional.

I remember a toy I got for Christmas in about 1960 when was only three or four years old. It was a yellow plastic thing that looked like binoculars. You inserted a cardboard disk with stereoscopic slides into it. When I looked through the eye-pieces, Donald Duck or Mickey Mouse leapt into the third dimension. For a such a youngster, the leap from two to three dimensions was almost the same as leaping into reality. Imagine, then, making that same leap from what we think of as reality to a more vivid world. We are always in that world, but we have conditioned ourselves not to see it. In these last two days glimpses of these towering granite spires woke me up.

It occurs to me that people need to see these colossal carvings—to remind them of the sacredness of Nature, and of the insignificance of "I." If everyone could hike alone here, the world would probably be different. I think better. And if they can't come to the mountain, I can bring the mountain to them, through my photographs. I decide to undertake a project: to create a book of photographs of these two sacred, immense sculptures, Cerro Torre and El Chaltén.

The decision feels good. It's an opportunity for me to make a contribution—to help both humanity and the planet. I'm excited.

It's a warm afternoon, and after a few dozen photos I climb out on a rocky point and take a quick dip in the inviting aquamarine tarn at a spot where it is very, very deep. Ice enters the water at the northwest shore where it is fed by a glacier, only a hundred yards away, but the water is surprisingly tolerable. A warm layer, probably in the fifties, must be floating on the surface after a few sunny days.

Before descending, I investigate the outflow of the lake. It falls several hundred feet to the creek that leaves Laguna Sucia, which is in the valley to the south, a few hundred feet below. I'm surprised to see that that lake is green. The name *Sucia* means "dirty," so I was expecting it to be brown or grey, but it's an emerald green, surrounded by granite walls, some below glaciers, some below more granite reaching up to Poincenot. I decide to visit that lake in the morning, and now return to camp to cook dinner while watching the sunset slowly modulate the colors of the thin veil of clouds behind the granite skyscrapers. Again I play with the intense stimulation of music; Coltrane's solo in Miles's "Teo" courses from the earbuds down my spine and my head sways to the "Hallelujah!" of his tenor sax. Afterwards I can't take another tune.

In my tent, I set the alarm for five and fall asleep easily even though the Japanese family camped nearby—who have been napping since my return—are up now and talking loudly. But my mind can relax because I don't understand most of it, and before I know it, the alarm goes off.

The sky looks good, so I put my wind clothes over the long underwear that I sleep in, add a hat and gloves, and I'm off, using the light of the more-than-half moon overhead. I decide to cross the creek upstream, rather than walk through camp and disturb people, and in doing so I luckily stumble upon a trail that I didn't know about. It's on my side of the creek that drains my destination lake, so I follow it upstream. I enter a stunning forest of bonsai lenga, lit softly by the glow of first light as well as the sunlight reflected off the moon overhead. It's a rare and beautiful light with a hint of rose from the eastern sky that makes it different than the blue moonlight I have skied by in Alaska, and read by in the white sand deserts of the Southwest. Above, the bright stars are still blazing in a navy-blue sky over the towers, which are just becoming illuminated by the rosy glow.

The forest peters out, overtaken by the white granite boulders of the glacial outwash plain. This is that kind of granite that has no distinct cleavage. Rather than fracturing easily, it breaks like Styrofoam, and for that reason is very resistant. I once saw men try to blast this kind of rock in Prince William Sound. They had a hard time and ended up overloading the drill holes with explosives to get the stuff to break. They sent one very large doniker a few hundred feet up and out over the bay towards a landing craft that was at anchor. The rumor was that the skipper of the landing craft shit his pants when he saw that massive rock descending towards him, but it landed beside the boat.

The valley bends and gets tighter, and an outcrop pinches the side I'm on so I have to do a little climbing traverse to get around it without getting wet. Still I'm at the lake well before sunrise, so I sit back in the hollow of a comfortable boulder the size of a small truck, and wait. A flock of birds flies by and stops to visit. They act like snow buntings. They wear black masks, are light-bellied and covered with dappled grey and black stripes. I can't find them in my book.

A mackerel sky moves in, and after it receives a deep, dark pink from the sun on the horizon, the eastern edge of each puff is illuminated in a color that reminds me of the fuchsias in Chile. The color lightens and hits the top of El Chaltén, the main tower, and works its way down, shifting to a brilliant gold. When the sun enters a strata of thin clouds in the east, the light flattens. The whole event lasts about fifteen minutes. But then sunlight occasionally finds a line-of-sight through the clouds and strikes the granite in patches for moments, punctuating long lulls of aluminum light. I sit and watch, listening to the thunder of huge chunks of ice falling somewhere above. I hear this five or six times, always searching for the source, never seeing any movement at all on the glaciers.

As I descend the valley to camp, the sun frees itself from the clouds and re-lights the peaks. A young guy with long blonde hair backpacks by while I'm on top of a house-sized rock in the middle of the creek taking photographs. When I hit the bonsai forest, I wander around in it, stopping to admire many of the plant sculptures, and trying to frame a photo, which is not easy because these dwarf trees are on a slope that ascends towards the peaks.

Breakfast eaten and camp struck, I follow the trail heading north along the Rio Blanco, which drains the entire area. In a few miles the trail crosses the creek draining Lago Blanco, to the west. I stash my pack in a cranny and follow the creek up through granite rocks the size of cars and garages, to the small lake in a freshly gorged valley, which looks like it must have been full of ice less than a thousand years ago. Laguna Piedras Blancas is a milky jade. A menacing glacier hangs above it, intensely seraced, and flowing down from the north side of El Chaltén, which is only partly visible, partly hidden by a ridge in the foreground.

Back on the trail, I run into an Aussie who was on my bus from Calafate. We trade stories of our hikes. My route crosses a barbed-wire fence on a boulder pile where the trail leaves the park. The river bends to the east, but I continue following a dwindling trail (it *is* "unofficial" I'm rationalizing), which eventually disappears. I am leaving the wide flat gravel-and-sand outwash plain of the Rio Blanco, and crossing a sand flat with just enough scrub to keep me from seeing too far when I realize I missed my turn, but don't want to turn back to find it. The trail I missed would cut the acute angle between Rio Blanco and the river to its north, which flows east to their confluence. If I just head north, I will eventually cross the trail heading up that river, Rio Electrico. I check my map to be sure I have the right idea, and trudge on in the sugary sand, which yields to my weight and the forward push of my toes. It's mid-afternoon and hot. I run out of water. I am hungry, but want to hit the trail, and the river, and the shade before stopping. I push on with Eddie Grant's "Electric Avenue" in my head, wondering why they named the river "Electric."

Finally I find a horse trail and it's heading to the north-

northwest—just right—but it slowly begins bending to the north, then north-northeast, and then northeast. I grumble while waiting for it to swing back to the west, but finally have to admit I am going the wrong way. So I turn around and head back. After passing the place where I found it, the trail heads off to the southwest, leaving the river. I follow it, grumbling some more, and eventually abandon it because I don't like the southerly trend. Once again I take off through the scrubby forest, heading north for the river. In a few hundred yards I hit another horse trail. I don't remember ever having hit a trail and turning the wrong way in my life, but here I do it twice in a row, which tells me I'm more tired than I want to admit. After a few hundred more yards I come to the river and the trail bends to the east, so I curse and stop for lunch, soaking my burning feet in the icy river.

I'm hungry, so after a couple sandwiches I keep reaching for more dried apricots. Then I do the only thing I *can* do, and turn around to follow this trail wherever it goes. It takes me to the southwest and I mumble protests, but stay with it, thinking it might be circling a swamp. Eventually it rises to the toe of the mountain, enters the forest, and merges with the real trail, which is still an "unofficial" one. At the junction my trail is blocked off with several dead branches, indicating that it's the wrong way to go.

Now I am happier, but the sugar in my dessert of *demascas desecadas* stimulated my pancreas to produce insulin and remove the excess sugar from my blood. The problem now is that it seems to have removed *all* the sugar from my blood, and I bonk. In hospitable grassy woodland, where the trees are tall and a cool breeze is blowing off the river below, I shed pack and boots, and lounge.

A day hiker comes along; a Kiwi, older than I am. We have a pleasant conversation. He must be a doctor because when I tell him what happened, he tells me I'll be fine in fifteen minutes when my blood sugar returns. He's right. After he leaves I get on the trail and feel fine. An easy forty-five-minute walk through the cool green woods brings me to a refugio where they charge four-teen pesos to camp in a fenced yard in the lee of a *roche moutonnée*. The guidebook says it's a huge erratic, but I disagree. The gentle slope facing the retreated glacier and the jagged vertical wall that protects this camp from the glacial wind are typical of a glacial-worn outcrop of resistant bedrock. The glacier wore the upstream side down to a ramp. Water penetrated the cracks in the rock and refroze. As the ice left the trailing edge of the outcrop, it plucked chunks of rock off, leaving this blocky wall that looks like some giant stole the other half of the hill. It is a classic roche moutonnée. The cool grass feels delightful on my bare feet. I was hoping to climb the pass above this place to get a view of the towers from this angle, but my afternoon took more out of me than expected, so I decide to rest and make the climb at 4:30 in the morning. I begin meal preparations in a cook shelter and fall into conversation with the blond-haired kid I saw early in the morning. He didn't miss the trail junction, and beat me here. The confusing thing is that he tells me he is from Chile, but I understand him well.

My bag calls me early, and I set the alarm for four. At 3:58 I wake to the sound of rain, so I return to sleep, waking again three hours later, feeling rested. It's still raining, so I make tea in the shack. After breakfast the Chilean kid comes in, bedraggled. He didn't let the rain stop him, and he climbed the pass at dawn. He said it was so windy that there were times when he had to crawl, but he did get a glimpse of El Chaltén during a brief break in the storm and saw it behind a rainbow. Fortune favors the brave.

It turns out that the reason I understand his Spanish so well is that he is a German who just moved to Chile a year ago to teach outdoor education to kids.

Leaving the compound, I pause at the gate to admire the peaks above when a break in the fast-moving clouds reveals them for a minute. The Danish woman who was camped near me walks up to the gate, so we naturally become hiking partners. She's a social worker in the Denmark winter, a hiking guide in the Greenland summer, and has recently begun to train in aikido because of trouble with drunken clients. She is just arriving to the area, coming down a small road from Chile, where she reports that the traveling was good but slow, hopping from town to town on the single bus that typically runs every other day. I'm back-tracking along Rio Electrico, but after I pass the familiar closed trail junction, I'm on the trail I missed yesterday, which leads me back to a large cairn on the Rio Blanco gravel that indicates the trail junction. I walked right by it yesterday.

I find it entertaining that we never know each other's names. I let it go intentionally, and when we hit the creek to Lago Blanco, I tell her it is worth seeing, and that I'm going to climb the lateral moraine for a view. She opts for the easy route, taking the creek bed, and we never see each other again.

It takes some time to scale the loose scree and talus slope above the creek, but at the top I cross the edge of a forest mat. The climb up the ridge of the moraine in the young forest is steep, but the views are rewarding.

I have lunch on a promontory, a zigzag of the break, facing up-valley with my lower legs hanging off the edge of the forest into the air among roots above the plummeting scree. I see the Dane wandering through the boulders below, and realize she could not see me even if she were looking right at me. My khaki-colored pants and green rain-jacket are the perfect camouflage for my situation. Maybe this is part of the reason that a flock of parakeets flies right at me before they see me and chatter up into the wind above the vast void between the walls of the parallel moraines.

This little valley has two huge lateral moraines pushing into the large river valley at ninety degrees. Both are forested on their back-sides, and completely barren on the inside, where constant decay of the loose scree prevents any vegetation from taking hold. It's not been too long since this gravel was deposited. I imagine it happening—the power of a glacier eating up a mountain and spitting it out. Witnessing the aftermath of such intense glaciation leads me to wonder what it must be like to live in an era of glacial advance, when walls of ice would bulldoze mature forests. The image of old-growth timber being slowly swallowed by an advancing glacier is one I never created before, and it is an awesome one.

Due to global warming, the vast majority of the Earth's glaciers are retreating. A study of glaciers in Alaska revealed that over 98% are doing so. So much ice is leaving the mountains that both NASA and the USGS predict that "The Great Land" will have more earthquakes as the earth's crust rebounds after the released load, and that these quakes will cause more tsunamis.

As the glaciers melt, water collects under them and lubricates them so they travel more quickly, resulting in an even greater rate of melting. When ice melts, revealing rock or dirt, the albedo, or reflectivity, of that area drops dramatically. Ice has a very high reflectivity; rock and soil's reflectivity is much lower, depending on its darkness. The more land that is revealed in a valley, the more heat it will absorb from the sun, warming the valley even more, and melting more ice. The same thing happens in the oceans. The enormous influx of fresh water into the polar seas has changed the salinity so much that it has already slowed the Earth's ocean thermal conveyor current by 30%. This current is driven by once-warm waters that sink after reaching high latitudes in the North Atlantic where they become densely saline after excessive evaporation. The introduction of fresh water from melting ice on land and sea lessens the density of this water, weakening the "pump." Without this thermal conveyor the higher latitudes will cool and the lower latitudes, unable to lose heat via the current, will warm. Glaciers may then begin to grow again, not only in Alaska, but also in Europe, which is ice-free now only because of warm waters reaching it from the tropical Atlantic, the Gulf of Mexico, and the Caribbean. The big problem is that once the conveyor stops, it takes hundreds of years to get going again.

A condor soars high overhead. Fields of sunlight traverse

the slopes of rock and ice as the storm breaks. I climb the ridge towards the ice, crossing a sweet, flat, sandy depression, possibly formed when a buried chunk of ice melted. It would be a fine camp if one were willing to carry water up here. Above, El Chaltén is living up to its name ("The Smoking Mountain") with a plume of white seeming to be anchored to its peak, but actually, being constantly generated at the peak and dissipating at the trailing edge.

I descend, retrieve my pack from the cave where I stashed it, and get back on the trail, feeling great and eating up the trail, my pack minus the weight of a pasta dinner, a little dry milk and cereal, two tea bags, some salami, cheese and bread. I jam back to the double-log bridge crossing the river where a young Israeli stops me, asking for directions. I'm trying to give him the complete lay of the land, but he keeps interrupting me to tell me what he wants to know. I interrupt his interruption and tell him to listen, finish telling him where everything is, and continue down.

While descending, the scene behind me grows more dynamic as the storm clouds seem to be torn apart by a wild, gusty gale, and sunlight splashes the spires, so I clamber through brush off the trail to find a composition. In doing so I discover a pretty little beach below a tiny falls that charms me—a good place to bivouac if one were to climb up here after leaving town late in the day. Knowing this spot might offer exquisite photos in the morning sun, I still try to get some now.

My descent continues through forest, eventually breaking out to the canyon of the big river flowing from the north, the Rio de las Vueltas, which now contains all the water I have seen in the past few days. It looks like a canyon in Eastern Washington or British Columbia. Another classic roche moutonnée hunkers in the valley floor, confirming that my suspicion about the rock upwind from last night's camp is more than justified. I wander out on a promontory, come across some calafate bushes loaded with fruit similar to blueberries, and enjoy a small feast.

CHAPTER 25

Three Sunrises

Soon I'm in town, making camp and getting a shower at El Refugio. I drop in at La Casita for a repeat of the steak dinner I had the night before I left on the trail. I improve it by having a carafe instead of a glass of cabernet. The carafe is a ceramic white penguin. The pony-tailed waiter further improves my dinner by adding a fine salad with shredded carrots and beets on the usual lettuce and tomato. Vegetables! It's crowded, so after dinner I surrender my table to a couple, and retire with the last of my vino to a small table in the back corner where they park their chocolate cake. The smell is too much for me, my resistance being lowered by the wine, and I enjoy a slice on the house, which is excellent with the fruity cabernet that carries a hint of cherry. By the time I'm finished I'm thinking of a cigar, but the Dominican that I've been hauling around is in my tent. So I drop in at Aires Patagonicos for a nightcap.

Cristian, the bartender, asks me to translate his menu. I tell him that that sounds like work, so he fills my scotch whiskey glass. I accept the job, but accepting the pay is a bad idea.

I tell him if he wants to appeal to North Americans and Europeans, he should offer vegetables. He asks me what I mean. I tell him that we're used to eating vegetables, they're important for health, but they're never in restaurants in the southern cone. "What kind of vegetables?" he asks. Rather than go into a long list of produce, I tell him that I was at the market earlier and saw green beans there. Why not offer steamed green beans? They're excellent with a little butter and salt. He makes a note of it, and I get to work on the menu. Some of my translations are not literal so I explain them, like "Hamburguesa Completo," becoming, "Hamburger with the works."

An Irishman enters. He's in his fifties, owns a steel fabrication plant in his home country, and loves to travel and meet people. His name is Tom too, and he takes a liking to me, buys me a drink, explains his motto, his three D's: "Decide, Delegate, Disappear" and looks at me with a satisfaction, as if I now have the key to life. After eyeing the menu he asks me if I know where he can get some vegetables. I call Cristian over and tell him what the Irishman is asking for. The point is well-taken.

Cristian kept filling my glass. Like I said, it was a bad idea to accept the pay. I ended up moving slow in the morning with a *caña*. I guess they use the word because it's like getting hit in the head with a cane.

I get a late start, cross town to the south end, near the park headquarters, and take the trail that heads out towards the Viedma Glacier to the southwest. Another trail branches off of it and heads up to tree line, below a sombrero-shaped peak called "Pliege Tumbado," which means something like "knocked-down fold." My plan is to take this route and make camp below tree line, then climb the peak, but the whole point of the venture is to catch the first light of day tomorrow. A team of pack-horses takes the trail ahead of me. I stay within sight of them 'til the first climb, when the horses open the distance. The trail passes through fields grazed by livestock. I'm reminded of a climb I did in Ansel Adams Wilderness, when I was disappointed to see cow pies on the grassy back-side of the peak.

When I was backpacking in the Owyhee canyons of Southeast Oregon, I realized the degree of devastation inflicted by cattle when I stomped past cattle tracks and manure in sparsely vegetated canyon floors until I hit a natural rock pile blocking the canyon. Beyond the rocks, where the cattle couldn't go, it was another world, filled with tall ferns, rushes, horsetails, and an abundance of herbs. When I returned home I wanted to write a letter to the Bureau of Land Management to complain about the cattle, so I educated myself on the law. On the long list of designated uses for wilderness areas, all are recreational but one: grazing. The cow pies in Ansel Adams wilderness were legal, but the destruction in the remote reaches of the Owyhee canyon network may not be, because the river is designated as Wild and Scenic, and grazing is forbidden on public land along such rivers. It turned out this very issue is the cause for a lawsuit against the BLM by an Oregon environmental group.

It's an easy climb through the forest. The trail follows a stream for a long time then leaves it, and the lenga soon shrink. When I see them begin to spread over the ground, I stop and descend for a minute before heading off the trail to find a tent site. It's not legal to camp here, so I hide behind a thicket. When camp is set, I descend to the stream and fill pots and bottles with water, stash them at camp, put a bottle in my lumbar pack and take off for the peak.

Leaving tree line is like walking out of a house—it's that drastic a break. Tundra takes over for a mile, yields to rock, and from there up, it's a moonscape. A bench on the northern flank attracts me, and I detour by it and get some great views. The reason to ascend Pliege Tumbado is that it has views of both Cerro Torre *and* El Chaltén, and I'm taking in both with pleasure. It's my first opportunity to do so. A climber I met told me he thought of El Chaltén as the masculine and Cerro Torre as the feminine of a royal pair—the king and queen. "Fitz," he explained, "Has broad shoulders and is huge. Torre is slender, graceful and has that hint of an hour-glass shape." It makes perfect sense to me as they stand before me like enormous chess pieces.

Continuing on, I make the peak sooner than expected. A rare event. Usually a climber is fooled by a false summit which, when crested, reveals more climbing. Sometimes this happens more than once. The view from the peak is good, but it's a mountain-top view—there are limited possibilities for creating a composition. The view *is* the composition. Besides, the late afternoon light does not flatter these east-facing peaks, so, unless the clouds are performing well, there is no art to be made. I lounge on the peak with anorak hood cinched tightly around my face to help me endure the wind, and watch the light change as the sun sinks toward the Pacific. When it drops behind the mountains, I drop to camp, making dinner as the sky darkens and the stars brighten, set my alarm for five, and crash. Last night's scotch has me tired, and, as they say in Japan, "Shin da yo ni nemaru"—I sleep like a dead man.

It's a cold morning with stars twinkling in a black sky. My water bottle has a little ice in it. I deny myself the luxury of savoring another moment of the warmth of my bag, and force myself into clothes and boots, take a slug of ice water, leave my headlight on, and head for the high country. By the time I leave the tundra the eastern sky is rosy. Mud at a stream crossing is frozen yet plastic under foot. I reach the bench before the sun reveals itself and set up for the show. When the first rays ignite the peaks, it's not as dramatic as the last two times I saw this because of the greater distance, but nevertheless I'm pleased. Afterwards, I traverse the north slope, westward from the bench for about a kilometer, until I get the composition I want, with a dark jagged ridge—a buttress of Cerro Solo—creating a complementary foreground to the dominant lines of Cerro Torre. Fox tracks cross the sandy scree. On the way down I play with photographing tiny tundra flowers.

After I reach the bottom, while crossing town, a guy with glasses and a red crew-cut encounters me as he exits the grocery store. He asks where I've been, and we walk together on the long north-south artery of the frontier hamlet. He says his name is Antonio. He's from Poland. I guess he changed his name to suit the language here—a trend I could never understand. Personal names don't change when you cross international boundaries. No Hispanic changes from Juan to John when coming north, but most Johns change to Juan when going south. It makes no sense. Antonio is a climber and adventurer. He's waiting for a stretch of good weather to go up Rio Electrico, past its source at the terminus of the Marconi Glacier, and up that glacier to the pass with the same name, where it joins the Great Southern Ice Field. He tells me it's the third-largest ice field in the world after Antarctica and Greenland. He's interested in crossing the length of it, from north to south—a trip of a couple-hundred miles. Right now he just wants to go see it, and spend a night in a tiny shelter some mountaineers built at the foot of a nearby mountain. He invites me to join him, and I take him up on the offer, as the pass will offer views of the granite towers from the northwest. But he wants to wait a few days for the coming storm to pass, so we agree to leave in three or four days. He encourages me to camp at the free campsite where I spent my first night, tells me that the back end is full of climbers as well as guides and porters working for guiding companies, that everyone watches out for each other there, and I can get a shower for four pesos at the big hostel nearby. I feel obligated to spend another night at El Refugio, since they are guarding my gear. But I plan to come visit him in the morning. I make camp behind the old hippie's place, get a shower and try a new restaurant. El Muro, "The Wall," is a very hip place—Beat, I would say—and maybe that's because it's run by an aging woman of that generation. The plate of wood-roasted steak, potato, and onion is excellent. I'm "Belly full and body glad," as a Belizean diver taught me to say, and head back to my tent for the night.

In the morning I visit the free camp, "Madsen," and ask climbers for Antonio and they direct me to the tent of "El Polaco Loco." He's not there, but a neighbor is. She is Evelyn, a sweet

Argentinean with long brown hair and big brown eyes. She offers me maté, so we sit and chat while passing the gourd. We become friends quickly. She's here to work as a porter, carrying supplies in her backpack to remote camps hosting tourists, spending the summer doing what she loves, walking in the mountains. She suggests that I camp beside her and use her kitchen tent to store my gear.

I take her up on the storage offer, but decide to take advantage of the predicted day-and-a-half before the next storm to go up for more photos of The Smoking Mountain.

During the ascent I feel strong. Maybe it's the maté, maybe I'm getting in shape. Probably it's both. At the high camp, just as I move into my tent, a crew of four shows up and camps nearby. One of them is a woman from The States. Not only is her voice the loudest in camp, but I can understand the words without trying, so I plug into the iPod, hit the "Afrojazz" playlist, and cook pasta in minestrone soup while anticipating the sunset. My camera is strapped to a dead lenga branch overhead while I sit and eat with eyes on the peaks. Just as the colors begin, a bank of clouds moves in from the west and smothers the heads of the giants. I just hope the morning is different, and absorb Archie Shepp's version of "No Agreement" like a tonic.

When the alarm goes off, I feel rested, and when I see stars above, I head out for my chosen destination, Cerro Madsen. Like the free camp north of town, it's named for Andreas Madsen, the first *probador*, or settler, in this area. Once I'm out of the trees I see headlights on the switchbacks. Three or four others have the same idea—to be at Laguna de los Tres before sunrise—but they are a half-hour ahead of me, causing me to doubt my timing. So I shift into high gear. By the time I'm half-way up the switchbacks I'm in a T-shirt even though the temperature is in the thirties. At the top, I beeline for Madsen, across the top of the terminal moraine that holds the Laguna. My timing is perfect. I'm on the south flank of Madsen when the light begins. I couldn't have gone any further without the buttress of Madsen obscuring El Chaltén.

My microfleece top and anorak come out of my pack, and the show begins. You can never predict what will happen from the interplay between the distant clouds in the east, which block the sunlight, and the local clouds constantly forming and dissipating around the peaks, often times hiding them. It's a good show even though The Smoking Mountain is living up to its name and maintaining a cloud like a turban around its head. The grand finale surprises me when a horizontal band of copper light sweeps down the massif to its bottom. Just as I think it's gone, it hits the very ground I'm standing on and illuminates the talus I occupy with rich red-gold while the rock above is shaded.

Certain that I got some good photos, my excitement takes me up Madsen like a machine, even though I question the safety of the climb on loose rock and hard, steep snow as much as I do the necessity of this campaign. I remember a long time ago when I ate psilocybin mushrooms and began a long hike to a chosen destination. I don't think I got a half-mile before I realized how ridiculous it was to insist on making the destination. It was clear that the journey was what was to be enjoyed. I spent the day wandering inside of a half-acre of forest, and had plenty to see. Of course, that was in a forest of giant redwoods, but ever since then it has been easier for me to let go of goals if it seems the wise thing to do. This morning I never even consider it. I am too thrilled with the beauty and the anticipation of my photographs and the book I will make. I really feel as if I am in a groove—like I am doing the best thing I can possibly be doing at this time in my life, and that things are falling into place because of it. I express enthusiasm by physically pushing myself and by sharing, and I'm doing both now.

The final eighty feet to the peak requires both hands, so I stash my staff and go up. The hand-holds are good and the climb is easy. The pinnacle is made of two vertical slabs—two halves of the same rock—with one having slid down fifteen feet. The top of the lower one is ninety degrees to the plane of sheer, and both are tilted away from Fitz at about fifteen degrees. The result of this arrangement is a comfortable bench facing the giant. The only drawback is the large deposit of condor guano on half of the bench. I'm sitting at 1,806 meters, 1,056 meters above camp.

The monarch is playing peek-a-boo in the clouds. I have no reason to descend other than a building hunger, and I'm thrilled to be in the presence of the Divine, so I hang out for a couple hours and watch him come and go, and the occasional splash of sunlight that slips between the clouds behind me. All the while I listen to the thunder of calving ice and avalanches. Usually the source of these roars is impossible to find in the vast expanse of ice before me, but today my eye finds a few chunks of ice flying before a black rock wall. With no small amount of luck, a hanging glacier in the same neighborhood releases the volume of a large office building, and I watch it fall to the glacier below and explode in silence. Blocks the size of cars and trucks tumble down the surface of the iceflow, and as they slow, the crack and rumble finally reaches my ear. The sudden realization comes that I never can find the source of the thunder because the action is always over by the time I hear it. This cataclysm was relatively near. Those in the distance have come to rest before the reverberations between the mountain walls reach me. Some black blocks of rock slide slowly down the white slope and disappear in crevasses the way black grains of sand get caught in the cracks of a bar of soap left in an outdoor shower for a few years.

A bank of clouds rises from the west and engulfs the tall granite. At the same time a bitter wind hits my peak. I take it as a cue to descend to my staff and search for an alternate route that is safer than my ascent. Cerro Madsen is a peak on a ridge radiating from the base of El Chaltén. After the cerro, this ridge splits and descends to the valley of Rio Blanco. Retracing my steps down the south buttress seems a bit dicey, so I explore the northern one, but I can't see past a series of pinnacles right below me. Every time I reach a col, I see more loose, steep talus to traverse, more obstacles to skirt, and all this with an incomplete view. The further I go, the less I'll want to abandon this route, which means the more chances I will take to get down this way, so I begin cursing every time I decide to go down without knowing what lies ahead. The route is precarious—steep, loose, slippery and sharp—and demands concentration. I keep telling myself, "I don't fall" (occasionally out loud) and eventually I sneak out of the situation and gain the spine of the ridge, less steep and more solid, where I notice the view again now that the stress is gone. Those end-to-end lakes I took so long to pass a few days ago look like a bootprint from here. Laguna Madre is the sole, Laguna Hija is the heel. Beyond them is Laguna Capri, then a vast sea of pampas stretching to the Atlantic, too far away to see.

Further down I decide to cross a snowfield between the two buttresses. It's steep, and hard, but it faces east, so the filtered sun has already corned the top few inches, allowing my boot's edge to bite. Using my staff as an ice axe, I can arrest a slip before I go into an accelerating slide down to the sharp talus at the top of a couloir far below. Once I'm three-quarters the way across, the fall below me is only eighty yards and ends in glacier-polished outcroppings that don't look so menacing, so I allow myself to glissade to them. They are the color of steel plate that has sat in raging water for years—rusted, yet polished. I'm reminded of fallen trains in whitewater rivers, or shipwrecks on the beaches of the Pacific Northwest.

By the time I reach Laguna de los Tres I am feeling the effects of a fuel gauge on 'E,' but I cross the spillway where the water tumbles down to Laguna Sucia, and explore the high route over the cliffs on the south side of the lake. This is the climbers' access to the base of El Chaltén. I heard it was hairy, so I wanted to check it out. It's nothing compared to what I just did, but it would be more challenging with a full pack. I like the idea of taking this route and climbing the glacier to "Paso Superior," where I could sleep in snow caves and catch dawn's first light on the massif from its very base. But that's another trip—one that I'd like to be roped to a couple of partners for.

While descending, I'm trying to take my mind where it's never been and feeling stuck. I'm wrestling with the concept of earth processes—those responsible for these sculptures—being divine, intelligent, and if the processes are separable from the matter they work on. I can't find a difference. Wind, rain, ice—it's all matter. Vulcanism, evaporation, expansion and contraction, freezing, it's all chemistry and physics. It's all the interaction of matter. I look down at the talus I'm crossing and it's clearly of the same stuff, and probably broke off of El Chaltén. So if El Chaltén is divine, why wouldn't this rock I'm stepping on now be? If this rock is, why not that one over there? The whole scree slope. Why not the whole damn planet, myself included?

My legs and feet are tired when I make it to camp at 3:30. I devour two olive loaf and cheese sandwiches while boiling water for instant mashed potatoes. The five servings of spuds take a while to finish, and then I take a nap.

The sunset hour draws me out of the tent, but dark clouds block any hope for color. On the way back from the outhouse I see a tired man sitting on a log who looks like he could use some cheer. He's got a red hat and red parka on, with a compass hanging from his neck by a red cord. My guess is that he's a North American, so I initiate conversation in English, "Hard day?" Roger is a sixty-five-year-old physical therapist from Medford, Oregon. He loves to travel, and says he figured he better come hike Patagonia while his knees can still take it. They're sore now. He just came up from Lago Torre today, and climbed from this camp to Laguna de los Tres—it's the same trip I did on my second day here. We talk about good hikes in the area. He consults his compass to verify the direction when he points to a place that he knows from the map. When I ask, he tells me he's carried a compass when traveling for years—he can't stand getting turned around, losing his orientation and not knowing which way is north. He broke his foot thirty years ago and it's beginning to bother him on days like this. I've got a dozen injuries that could come back to haunt me as I age. I imagine myself in his situation in only fifteen years. I see myself sitting on that log—white hair, sore knees, refusing to give up. His backpacking days are numbered, but as a whitewater rafter, he will be able to get his wilderness time on river trips for many more years. While we're talking, I see a fresh hawk feather on the ground and offer it to him, but he declines, so I stick it in my hat. We trade cards and will be in touch for whitewater trips in Oregon.

In the morning, the remnants of howling wind and rain on the peaks are tossed at my tent. When the sunrise alarm goes off, I go out to pee. There's no color on the obscured granite. A fine rain falls. All the tents are closed and silent. Two carranchos walk through camp, silently searching for scraps. Now I know where the hawk feather came from. A flock of parakeets dart by while I'm making maté from my tent door.

Soon I'm on the trail. At a swamp crossing, a tiny frog lies in the path, incapacitated by the cold. Maybe my fingers warm it when I move it to the grass. It's a bright green with brilliant yellow longitudinal stripes. That's *one* thing that the many predators here can eat. Yesterday I saw some lizards. There's supposed to be a kind of desert rat here, but the campers in Madsen leave their food in tents with zippers broken by gusts of the pervasive high winds, and no one ever has a rodent problem, so there can't be too many of them. There seem to be plenty of predators but no prey. What do the puma eat? Foxes? What do the foxes eat? Only the introduced rabbit is abundant enough to support these predators, and I suppose the condors clean up after every meal. Strange, though, how those giant scavengers prefer to ride the high mountain winds, far from the rabbits in the lowlands.

In town I make camp in Madsen, and Evelyn invites me to join her and her friends for dinner. Of course I accept, but I know they eat late so go out to El Muro for another fine meal in the late afternoon when most restaurants are closed. I'll eat again with Evelyn and her friends later, in typical Argentina style. I'm happy to be invited by this tall, attractive young woman, but the strange thing is that I feel no sexual energy coming from her at all. I'm not talking about attraction or desire, just the feminine psychic energy that is normally present, exuding from women. And it's as if she's in balloon that insulates her from the masculine energy coming from me. It's fascinating.

At ten, Evelyn and I cross town on foot, in strong gusts carrying sheets of spray, to the internet lounge. Once we began walking together, her gait explains her asexual vibe. She's tight in the hips and legs, with an overemphasized use of the quadriceps and tibialis muscles to initiate the leg's forward swing. Her stride faintly resembles that of the Tin Man. What I sense is that the musculature of her legs is still expressing shock, the result of trauma, after many years. This sense is one that I developed from intense training and then working with hundreds of people as a somatic therapist. It's sad to think that she was molested or maybe raped when she was younger. No wonder that when she told me that she'd never get married I sensed a charge running through her body. No wonder she feels so good when she can use the muscles that wanted to carry her away in flight from her abuser.

We arrive at 10:30, and I meet her friends, Fernando, the owner of the business, and his Australian girlfriend, Tarina. We begin cooking around eleven, and eat pasta in a marinara sauce some time around midnight. In conversation I mention that the wind wears on me. Fernando starts telling stories about the wind. He says that last winter it blew two of his car windows out, and 250 kilometer-per-hour gusts picked up the log benches outside his shop and threw them a block downwind. It's hard for me to imagine.

After dinner we watched a movie. By the time I got in my sleeping bag it was almost three, and I had been up since my pre-dawn alarm, so I slept and dozed as long as I could, then spent the day hanging out with Evelyn and her friend Waldo, a climber from the north of the country who is escaping the intense heat of his desert mountain home, working as a porter here in cool Patagonia. Waldo is an angular man, with broad level shoulders above a wide but trim waist. His face is well-chiseled, with a triangular nose, and his hair, parted well to the side, is combed across the top of his head, making it flat. I get to like Waldo more each time I interact with him. I call him "Señor Tranquilo" because he's one of the calmest, most laid-back and soft-spoken men I've met among adventurers. He plans to climb El Chaltén with his buddy, Indio.

Rain is like static on the tent roof over our conversation which continues for hours. I can't find Antonio. He's not in his tent all day.

After a couple days of hanging with the Argentineans and waiting for the storm to pass, the stars come out, and I still can't find El Polaco Loco. So, in the morning I make a new plan—to hike back up Rio Electrico and try again for Paso Cuadrado. I assume I can hitch-hike to the trailhead, and I would have been correct if I had left at a reasonable hour, but it's almost noon by the time I get on the road, and I eventually realize that there will be no traffic at all. It's an eighteen-kilometer walk on the unscreened glacial till roadbed, in an intense headwind that I lean into. The storm has passed, but around here an intense wind continues to howl for a day after the rain, as if it's chasing the clouds away. I'm tired before I find the trailhead. Luckily, it's an easy hike up the river to the familiar trail . I'm in the same parkland neighborhood of mature lenga that I was in when I had the blood-sugar crash from the dried apricots, this time traveling quickly on the easy trail, when I crest a small hill and see a full-grown puma about fifty yards ahead.

I've heard them a few times—once in the Anza-Borrego desert while reading by the light of a midnight moon in a remote camp. In an effort to describe the sound when I returned from the trip, I concluded that it sounded like a twelve-year-old-boy imitating a woman screaming in horror. Years later I was sitting naked on a sauna step, steaming in the cool night air of the Sierra foothills when I heard it again. "What was that?" My friend thought it must be the new neighbors on her unpopulated road. My mind took about fifteen seconds to remember where I had heard it before, and she confirmed that a lion had been spotted in the area that week.

I saw the ass-end of one as it ran into the bushes while I was driving into the Lost Coast of Northern California, but this is the first time I've stood before a live cat. "Holy shit!" involuntarily leaves my mouth as I freeze and it slinks off for cover. It's big—about five feet from nose to butt, with a long tail drooping down to the ground then curving back. I'm stunned to see that it's the homogenous velvety grey-brown of a Weimariner, with no distinct markings anywhere but on its face—unusual for a wild animal. Its head and torso are slung low from the two scapula protruding from its back as it trots in that cat way that allows horizontal movement without vertical movement—a way that is imitated by Japanese martial artists.

The headwind hid my scent and sound, the hill hid me from the puma's sight, and I surprised it. It almost seemed embarrassed that I caught it in the open, and in a few seconds it's in the cover of the brush near the river.

Standing still for a few minutes, I take in the experience. If it were a bear, I'd be fairly sure that it was gone, but cats are sneaky. So when I begin hiking again I keep an eye towards the brush where it took cover. Once past it, I have to keep turning around a couple times a minute to be sure it's not stalking me. It seems likely that it watched me as I passed. The ground in this park-woods is grassy, but littered with the dead bodies of trees taken down by the williwaws that have ripped down this valley for centuries. Because I'm traveling upriver, the logs lie roughly parallel to the trail, and their grey-brown color is the perfect cover for the furtive feline. I've watched enough house-cats stalk birds and rodents to imagine how the puma would advance behind the logs. I stop and look for a pair of yellow-green eyes burning in the shadows below logs that curve into the air. If I find them, I can intimidate the cat by staring at it— something I would never try with a grizzly. I keep my senses dialed to full power, with my mouth open. I don't know why I do that when I want to hear well. Maybe it lets out the sound of blood racing through my carotid arteries. Even when I decide that it's long gone, like a turkey through the corn, I don't trust it enough to turn my back on it, and I keep turning on occasion to scan for it. I know it would be intimidated by my size with this backpack on, but can it sense my fatigue? I shift my attitude to one of strength and confidence, like I own these woods, and proceed with more and more comfort.

The funny thing is that just a few minutes before this encounter, I was thinking about the lion butt I saw on the Lost Coast, and about a conversation I had the day before with Evelyn about pumas. She has only seen the same—the rear end of one as it ran into bushes for cover. This reminds me of the movie we watched last night at Fernando's, "What the #%* Do We Know?" Part of the film's message is that we have the power to create reality with our minds. Is it a coincidence that I saw a puma just after I was thinking of one? I think so. Once I stood on the bow of an Alaskan ferry telling a friend a story about dolphins playing in the bow-wave of some boat I worked on, and within a minute a pod of Dall's porpoises were below us acting as if they heard everything I said—probably coincidence again, but we had a good laugh because it seemed like I summoned them. Countless times I have told stories of animals or thought of them without their making an appearance, and often thankfully so, since a few of those times, white shark stories have been related to other surfers as we sit like bait bobbing beyond the breakers.

I'm still trying to grasp what the film and many others say about the power of the human mind to create reality.

It occurs to me that the lion may be surviving on fish and waterfowl at the river. I never thought of that food source for them.

At Fraile I set my tent in the same place I did last time, in the lee of the roche moutonnée, and begin cooking pasta. Antonio, El Polaco Loco, comes into the camp with three Argentinean girls in tow. No wonder I haven't been able to find him. He comes over to say hello and give excuses. He's going to attempt to take the girls on the glacier. I'm somewhat entertained, especially that he is carrying everyone's crampons and tents, but disappointed in his character. I thought he was a friend. I thought we were partners on the trip to Paso Marconi. At least he could have left a note at my tent. But all of that is his problem, not mine. I treat him well, but make it clear that I am not happy that he disappeared with no communication. I wish him good luck, and they continue upriver to camp at the terminal lake.

After my belly-full I go searching for the trail I will need in the morning. I can't find it, so I ask the horse packer who's putting horses in a tiny barn for the night. He walks me out and shows me a faint trail in the pasture, which I follow easily, as it grows more obvious with distance from the horses. When it hits the toe of the slope of the valley wall, I return to camp and hit the sack.

The clock reads 4:58 when I wake before the alarm. Outside the stars are moving faster than the wind, and it's dead quiet above the blanket of cold dew. I'm packed and on the trail in just a few minutes. At the toe of the valley wall I look up the steep ascent to see the Southern Cross blazing just over its horizon, and take my first step up. Every step after that is up, crossing tundra, then sharp talus. After an hour there's enough light to turn off my headlight. After two hours I'm at a high, mostly frozen tarn dammed by a tiny moraine, allowing views of El Chaltén. While ascending from there, the first rays strike the summit and I go to work, but I'm not thrilled with the compositions, so I continue up at a fast pace, even though Fitz gets obscured by the massive granite block I pass beneath. This thing must give the pass its name. It's the size of a big city office building. The traverse below it is a steep and rock-solid snowfield. A slip could be serious, especially because I'm using my staff instead of an ice axe. So I step slowly, digging my boot edges into the crust. Just before the pass, the giant comes back into view, framed by the big block on the left, and the jagged stegosaurus ridge of the pass on the right. The framing is perfect, and I wonder if this is the reason it's called Paso Cuadrado. "Cuadrado" literally means "square" and it could refer to either the block of stone or the square-framed view. It must be the huge block. Most people wouldn't notice the framed view. While I maneuver around ice and rock seeking the best composition, one leg breaks through a snow bridge hiding a small crevasse, and my leg goes in up to my crotch and swings freely in the air below—a warning to be careful.

Upon gaining the very col, an alpine fairyland is revealed. The views are immense and imposing. El Chaltén looms above to the left. Cerro Torre and its neighboring spires are spread before me, and the Great Southern Ice Field stretches beyond into Chile, where Cerro Gorra Blanca—"White Cap"—floats in a sea of white several days' travel from here. No wind blows, only the thunder of avalanches, distant and done, find my ear.

I score dozens of photos including several sets of panoramas and a 360 degree panning video.

"Valhalla" is the name I give the ice field near my Alaska home, and this view has the same feeling—that of the realm of the mountain gods. It is a crystalline world, pure, seemingly free of biology. If my memory is correct, the Tibetans referred to this kind of environment as the realm of wisdom.

CHAPTER 26

The Patagonian Wind

I'm nestled behind a big boulder on the south slope of Laguna Torre, just above the terminus of the glacier. The sun is shining on me, but I'm holed-up in the lee of this rock where I'm sheltered from the horizontal rain riding on the relentless wind. I'm hoping the weather will clear, but up the valley, Cerro Torre looks pretty nasty, with an inky dark cloud covering the peak and a veil of rain screening the shaded ramparts below.

The wind howls out on the glacier, and I'm hesitant to travel up the ice as I intended. Already I've been blown off balance a few times. Out on the open ice the wind will be worse, and if it doesn't let up, it will be an Aeolian nightmare to endure for no reason.

I intended to travel up the ice, into the glaciered valley between Cerro Torre and El Chaltén, to get views of the tower from below and from the north. It looks like I'll have to throw in the towel. Too bad. We only had two days of good weather instead of the four that El Polaco Loco thought we would have. Now he's stuck somewhere up on the glacier in this weather with the three inexperienced girls. One might fantasize that this is a good thing, but I'm sure the reality is otherwise.

I burnt up the two days—the first I descended from Paso Cuadrado and went back to town, this time catching a ride in a *remis* (a kind of taxi) that came to pick up a Brazilian couple who were on a day hike. I had promised Evelyn I'd return for her good-bye party, and ended up having another late night with the Argentineans, so the second day I lollygagged with Evelyn drinking maté all morning, watching rufous-necked sparrows (or *chingolos)* hop around camp, and telling stories about the redwoods, how I used to ski the backcountry behind my cabin in Alaska, and about surfing the waves of the Northern California winter. I was hanging out with her because she'd be leaving on the next morning's bus. Work was slowing down, and she's been camped here for over four months, so she's ready to make tracks. In the short time we've spent together we've become good friends. It was noon by the time I went to rent crampons and finally got on the trail to Laguna Torre.

I spent the few hours on the trail learning how to walk. Twenty years ago I was studying human movement and how it was influenced by chronic holding patterns in the muscles as well as habituated misuse and nonuse of muscles. I was fascinated with the psychological origins of many of these patterns, and became particularly interested in the walking gait and explored it. At the same time I was attending Buddhist meditation retreats and spending several long days alternating between walking and sitting meditation. I sought a natural, relaxed gait, discovered it, and analyzed the three-dimensional undulations that are expressed in the spine and hips of a relaxed person taking steps. I thought I knew how to walk. I'm a fast hiker. I like walking. But I just came to the full realization that I do not engage my gluteus muscles as I should, especially when climbing hills. I say "full" realization because now it seems that I have known this for four or five years. How does it happen that you know something for a few years and then realize it?

A few days ago Antonio, El Polaco Loco, told me that his butt was sore from hiking up to the first view-point on the trail to El Chaltén. He had been sedentary for over a week and got out of shape. The thought passed through my head that the soreness was from using the gluteus maximus to hike uphill. I've never had that soreness. Today I paid attention and changed my uphill gate to engage that muscle. But I have to pay attention to each step.

When I was a teenage oarsman I developed strong quadriceps. The front of my thighs were heavily muscled, while the hamstrings behind were neglected. I developed an extreme imbalance of musculature, the consequences of which I am only now realizing. I came to rely on those strong quadriceps to do more that they ought to, and I called on them to push me uphill. It's another version of "your strength becomes your weakness," one of my often-used maxims. Today I shifted my weight towards my heel and worked on drawing my heel back, rather than pushing forward from my toes. The latter is well-known and comfortable—relying on my strength. The former is strange. It makes me feel like the poor farmers in Japanese samurai movies who always run around with tight asses. Maybe I'll get used to it. I hope so.

About three-quarters of the way to the laguna, just after I saw an American kestrel, I noticed that the toe of my right sole had delaminated from the boot. I initiated a search for boot glue, first visiting all the guide camps, then taking the crest of the terminal moraine at the edge of the laguna—a lake with one of the most spectacular views of any lake in the world—to the backpackers camp, and hitting everyone in it for something to stick my sole back on my boot. No glue, but Marius, an Afrikaner from South Africa, gave me dental floss and a strong needle, which I worked with while sitting on a sun-warmed boulder at the edge of the lake, watching the sky back-light the spire at sunset while a *remolinera comun* hopped around the waterline. I protected the threads with duct tape, and all is functional now. After the job I returned the repair materials and hung out with Marius and his wife Genie—people that I felt very comfortable with right away. Marius said he thinks travel is essential to mental health—in order to break a person out of the world-view they create and solidify for themselves just by living in one place, talking to the same people, reading the same newspaper, watching the same TV. He said it's easy to fall into a rut. I said that it's guaranteed: it's human nature.

They invited me to come visit them in Africa, and I accepted. Marius decided to join me at the lake for sunrise, but when we woke it was warm and there were no stars. I went to the lake anyway, and Marius joined me, in case the sun's rays wiggled through a hole in the clouds and lit the peak for a minute. They did. A rosy patch swept the walls of the purple tower for a minute. Three condors spiraled overhead.

After breakfast they headed to El Chaltén and I went to the Tyrollean traverse and crossed the river as I did before, but with my backpack hanging from the taut line by a carabiner in front of me. My legs wrapped around my pack and kept it with me as I laid back and reached behind hand over hand to pull myself across. On the trail up the crest of the lateral moraine the weather began to worsen. I was blown off the trail a few times. The trail climbs high into a lenga forest in order to skirt cliffs and landslides. In the forest I was protected. So were the thorn-tailed *rayaditos*—little chickadee-like birds with long, spiky tail-feathers. When I exited the forest I was ambushed by an aggressive wind wielding big raindrops. A couple of guides were there with a group of disappointed clients. They told me the barometric pressure was dropping. I only went a few hundred yards before taking shelter behind this tall rock, and putting on rain gear.

The guides took the paying customers down to the ice, but I decided it's not my idea of a good time to go down, see how bad it is, and climb back up with my full pack. Any hopes for a photograph are too slim, so I'm enjoying the shelter, Conrad Herwig playing "The Latin Side of John Coltrane" on my iPod, and the ham and cheese sandwiches. Every once-in-a-while I walk around the rock, get blasted by the ongoing gale, and verify that the peak is burdened by heavy clouds. I can't talk myself into continuing. It could easily worsen and be sheer hell on the ice all night in tent-wrecking gusts. But it's hard to quit, and it's comfortable behind this boulder, so I'm waiting for a sign of improvement.

Again I try to understand the powerful effect these big

rocks can have on the human mind. It's as if they can show us the truth, if we are willing to see, just as a saint speaks the truth if we are willing to listen. Maybe, just as few saints walk among humans, Nature creates a few wonders on the planet during any epoch to help us realize the sacred quality of this existence on the physical plane. Who knows, maybe these granite avatars stand here to help human consciousness evolve in this time of human-induced disasters.

While hiking the trail to town I see lots of heumul tracks. Huemul are a large deer that locals call "The Ghost of Patagonia" because they are so rarely seen. By the time I make the streets, the wind is nasty. I'm tired of it. I pass by Fernando's internet lounge and stop in for a visit. Evelyn had brought my street gear here as she promised she would, and I grab it out of his back room. I tell him I want to leave on the morning bus for El Calafate so I can cross the border and see Torres del Paine National Park in Chile. When I complain to Fernando about the wind, he tells me that the wind is why everyone in town wears a wool hat pulled down low—not to keep warm, but to keep the wind out of their ears. Then he offers the use of a small cabin he owns, and I thankfully accept.

On my way across town to the cabin, I see Jesus. He is one of the many high-profile local characters I've met in my travels—extraverted loners who don't fit socially accepted norms. Like many others, Jesus is friendly. He camps at Madsen and knows me because he's passed my tent a dozen times while I'm sitting on the grass. He always says hello to me now, even from a distance. Like a Rasta named Goat who camped on a Caribbean beach near me decades ago, and who used to yell to me every time he saw me, Jesus always sends me a cheerful greeting. He is a hard-working man, finding manual labor on days when there's no work for him as a porter. His face is young but weather-wrinkled around his narrow-set eyes and large nose. A long ponytail leaves the back of his black beret. He's always on a mission when I see him in town.

Later, when I return to have a final dinner with Fernando, he answers my questions and tells stories. He says that the town of El Chaltén exists because the government subsidizes the utilities, making gas and electricity cheaper than it should be. Otherwise the people could not survive the long winter. He says that in order to buy land here you have to live in the town for three years—that is, unless you have connections; after all, it *is* South America. They are just building a firehouse this year. Usually when there is a house on fire, phone calls race around town and everyone shows up, but there's nothing they can do, so they just watch it burn.

When he asks, I tell him stories about my life, and he admits he is envious. He loves to travel, and was about to take off for Spain when the Argentinean peso crashed. All of a sudden his ten-thousand-dollar savings was worth three thousand, and he couldn't afford to go. The economy is recovering slowly. He doesn't know when he'll be able to travel again, but he wants to come to Alaska. I wonder if he'll ever make it, and I wonder how it would feel to earn pesos that can't compete with the currencies of most of the developed world. Anyone coming to Argentina to work would be retreating from the world unless the pay was excellent, or they were involved in some entrepreneurial venture. It seems like the best option is to earn dollars or euros no matter where you spend your time, but of course, that's a bit of a trick. I'm realizing how lucky I am, and I'm realizing once again that I am spoiled.

I fight the wind back to the cabin at a reasonable hour. It howls by the walls all night, and into the morning, when I lay out my gear and get organized and packed—a task that would have been unpleasant if I were camping, or even a guest at a hostel. When I venture out to buy a ticket for a bus to El Calafate, the town seems empty—a ghost town belted by the strange combination of dust and rain, both riding on hit-and-run gusts racing down from the mountains—the dust made by the merciless pressure of ice on rock, and kicked up from the street of glacial cobble, the rain made by the merciless pressure of wind on mountains that force it up where it expands and sheds its moisture, and the odd spray rides the williwaw down to town.

PART 4

CHILEAN PATAGONIA

CHAPTER 27

Natural Beauty

The bus is full. A young Israeli girl with a cold sits beside me. My experience is that communication is poor with Israelis, that they don't listen well. This girl is the same, and like most young Israeli travelers, she's fresh out of mandatory military service.

As I leave my beloved mountains the peaks are completely obscured by a blustery turbulence of billowing clouds like the whitewater at the crest of a thousand-meter tall wave.

Arriving in Calafate, it's early evening and the place is hoppin'. The main drag is full of shopping tourists. The North Americans and British are already looking for dinner. Many restaurants aren't even open yet. I beat the street in a search for shoe glue. All the outdoor stores are tourist-oriented and have nothing for maintenance or repair, just sales. I'd rather stay with my old buddies—the Garmont boots I've had for ten years—than try to buy quality boots in these places. One shop owner gives me a tip and I find the *pegamento* at a ferreteria outside the haunts of tourists. The clerk tells me it's good for rubber even though that material is not among the dozen listed on the label. After I get dental floss at a pharmacy (my natural floss is not thin or slippery enough to sew my boots with), I hike across town to a sewing and knitting store for a few short, stout needles. I know how to ask for them because some of the spires beside Cerro Torre are called needles—*agujas*. With all chores completed, I enjoy Italian food with an Argentinean Malbec, then retire at a hostel.

First thing in the morning, I'm on a bus to Puerto Natales, Chile, the gateway to Torres del Paine. The granite in that park is said to be as spectacular as the granite I just left, so I want to catch a glimpse while I'm in the neighborhood. But even though it's not far as the crow (or condor) flies, I have to take a few long bus rides to get there. I'm hoping for some good photos, but maybe I'll get rained on, like several travelers have described as their experience of Torres del Paine. On the bus I take that refuge, that rest that comes when it's impossible to do anything. I look out the window and let my mind wander, let my brain waves slow. Crossing the pampas in the early morning, when the sun greets grasses and brush that have been rained on all night, the subtle colors seem richer than usual; buff, forest green, sage, maroon and grey. Dark blue clouds break off the storm that's continuing over the Andes and pass overhead, but this landscape is illuminated from the east. The rising sun sometimes strikes directly, sometimes illuminates this land by lighting entire clouds that have drifted downwind from the mountain storm and softened, no longer fighting the sun, but yielding to its power, and accepting the light, and passing it on to the grasses.

All of creation is beauty. I know this.

What do I mean, "all," isn't there ugliness in nature? I don't see it in landscapes. Even hurricanes and forest fires are beautiful. Maybe our perception of ugliness is the result of a psychological reaction to perceived suffering, or to the potential for it. The hurricane itself is beautiful if witnessed from a safe observation point on land, but will the sailor see beauty as his boat succumbs to the fury of the wind-whipped sea? How does the wildfire appear to a man trapped by it before it consumes him? Is the beauty of running game lost when it is taken down by a predator and torn apart as it must be for the predator to survive? Surely there is beauty in that beast's blood to a starving man. Suffering is part of life, contrary to the fantasies of many who wish otherwise. The Buddha made this his first noble truth. And so there can be beauty in it, if we choose to see it—if we choose to detach from a constructed meaning to it all, and from the constructed "I" that is the experiencer.

But we need meaning to organize our lives around. Maybe our idea of beauty has to do with organization. Certainly life *itself* is partially defined by organization, hence the term, "organism." Organization provides comfort. Maybe this comfort is what a human naturally finds beautiful.

Our aesthetics could be influenced by our desire to live. We find a living tree to be more beautiful than a fallen one, rotting and surrounded by broken branches—one losing organization, void of vitality

It's easy for us to see beauty in organization and geometric regularity. The spiral of the hurricane, when viewed from space, is beautiful, but down inside of it the chaos is more difficult to appreciate.

The fact is that all of Nature is organized. It's just that we usually can't see it. Most of it appears as random and accidental. I realized this years ago during a meditation retreat in the desert. After five days of meditation it became apparent that it's human nature to become absorbed into the reality of our own mental ordering. In the following five days I experienced the world with new eyes. Perhaps not so much "new" as our *original* way of seeing the world, but when we learn to see again, it's as if we are in an altered state—one of increased three-dimensionality—and it seems new to us.

The Chinese concepts of "*Wu*" (logical, linear order) and "*Li*" (organic, free-flowing order) had been subjects of my own contemplations before the retreat, so as my eyes began to open again, and as the order of all things began to become evident, I framed the experience with regard to wu and li.

Early in the retreat I was stunned by the beauty of three young junipers growing from behind a low stone wall. The finishing touch that made the scene such a work of art was the way one stone slanted in a different direction than the others. I saw mostly li—the trees and stones—but there was wu in the line of the planting, and in the plane of the wall. As I passed another wall I began to understand the harmony of wu and li. The stones are li, irregular in size, shape and color. But they are set so that their flat sides form a vertical plane—wu. A harmony was created by the artist, the stonemason who chose each stone and decided how to arrange them. Another mason would have made a different wall with the same stones.

Of course, humans are not the only artists on Earth. Beaver lodges, bird nests and beehives come to mind right away. We are able to see this art, this creation of some wu from li, this harmonizing. We recognize the order of the circular lodge and nest, the hexagons of the hive. The order that eludes us is that of li. At the li end of the wu li spectrum is what we see as disorder. The art in this genre goes mostly unrecognized by us. The more a composition approaches the wu, the easier it is for us to appreciate it—for us to find comfort in the organization. The ripples in beach sand and the rows of sand dunes are easier to appreciate than the irregular surface of sand, or sand itself.

It may be that the ordering work of an active agent (the wind in the example of the sand) is easier for us to see than that of a more passive scene. One day late in the retreat I was walking very slowly, maybe one step every thirty seconds or so, trying to keep my attention on every subtlety of the process. As I rounded the corner at the back of the meditation hall I came upon a pile of dry twigs that the wind had created as it swirled where the walls met at right angles. The perfect beauty of it paralyzed me as if I had rounded a corner at the Louvre and encountered a stunning work of a famous master. The wind, the artist, had created a slight spiral to the arrangement of the twigs, hardly noticeable, maybe invisible to my normal eye, but striking in the present state of mind. When I noticed a curl of some hemp-like fiber woven into the work at the top-center and dancing in the wind, I thought, "How bold of the artist."

There are many times when li perfection, though standing boldly before us, is invisible to our eye because we see it as a destruction of the wu that we had created. Various patterns of erosion, decay and oxidation—a decline of organization to our habituated eye, are obviously beautiful when seen with original eyes. But rarely can we transcend the sense of loss of order. Maybe we have a natural disdain for entropy.

An amusing example of this occurred at the same retreat. I was walking again, and passed an old light-blue Ford station wagon. This was the model that had panels of vinyl on the sides that were printed with a wood grain to make it look like an old woody—an obvious imitation of li. But the desert sun had dried and cracked the vinyl so that it contracted, revealing the light-blue below in a gorgeous crackle pattern contrasting with the dark brown and black of the vinyl. The wood print was an attempt to bring li beauty to the car, but it was a mass-produced imitation. Now the car was decorated with an original li design, the work of Nature itself. I smiled and wondered if the owner appreciated it.

For some, beauty may be connected to hospitality. To them, these pampas are a desolate wasteland. This morning's light is incidental. I'm reminded of the joke that locals make on the few gorgeous summer days in Alaska, "It's a good day to sell real estate." We are attracted to a place when the weather is good—when it's hospitable. Many a newcomer to the forty-ninth state, come November, puts palm to brow with the question, "What was I thinking?"

But those mountains behind me are inhospitable, and they are equally beautiful when I am uncomfortable. They are works of erosion—a decline of order, and to enter them is to invite suffering. So all of my thoughts seem to be pages tossed in the waste basket.

On to the next word.

What do I mean when I say, "creation?" Does that imply that there is a creator? We will never know if there is one. The question for me is whether the beauty of Nature is simply an accident or a coincidence, or if it arises by design or expression. Does Nature evolve towards beauty, or do we evolve to perceive it as such, or do both happen in concert? In his book, *Quantum Evolution*, Johnjoe McFadden says that quanta make decisions and in so doing are guiding evolution as they instigate genetic mutation. It's all the product of quantum expression, ourselves included, that is proceeding towards a goal. If so, what is the goal? Is beauty part of the plan? Thinking of my recent realization that all of Nature is divine, now I understand that the common element throughout of all of Nature is the quanta that it is made of. Could it be that it is the quanta that are intelligent—not individually, but as fragments of an intelligence that is omnipresent? ...fragments that are really waves until observed, then materialize ... The *netzutzot*, scattered sparks of divine light, of the Hebrew, and the Aum sound of the Hindu, the *Shabd*, or divine light and sound of the Source, of the Sikh. Speech is organized waves of sound, and in the New Testament John wrote, "In the beginning the Word already existed. The Word was with God, and the Word was God." Heraclitus used the Greek *Logos*, "saying," as both the source and the fundamental order of the universe. Everything, all matter, might be an articulation by the Source.

I think about beauty and art. I might define my own art as the capturing of beauty that one enjoys experiencing over and over, so as to be moved in some way, repeatedly. I could be photographing the pampas this morning. The light is fantastic. I suppose that some fine photographs could be made. But would it move anyone the way the granite peaks move people? It seems I look for the beauty of the beauty. The subject of awe returns. It's that feeling of being dwarfed, of being rendered as insignificant as a pismire, being diminished to a speck, that I am interested in lately. It is an emotion that might lead one to shed the ego, which when confronted with the majestic mount, can be seen for what it is—a desperate mental construct. That is why I've been trying to capture images of those monuments that might evoke awe. Is our awe created by accident? Coincidence? I feel confident in my answer: No.

All of nature is art, but those mountains are of a sacred kind. They may indeed be granite avatars, here to point to the Truth.

The light on the pampas reminds me I live in a divine wonderland, and my only challenge is to remember that, and not be distracted... to experience it fully... to merge with it.

"Immanuel Kant, the leading philosopher of the enlightenment, had argued that reason alone, because it was limited by the senses, could never yield a complete understanding of reality. Aesthetic appreciation must complement pure reason, if one were ever to grasp the true nature of the world."
                                            —*Gerard Helferich*
                                            (*in "Humboldt's Cosmos"*)

CHAPTER 28

Torres del Paine

The weather in Puerto Natales reminds me of Southeast Alaska, and the town has a rough feel to it like most Alaska towns—maybe it's the glacial gravel on the side-walks—but it's poorer. It's a third-world city at fifty-one degrees of latitude—a rarity.

I'm sitting in a restaurant waiting too long for salmon and chips. Maybe they ran out the back door for some fish. Wind drives rain against the windows.

For some reason I'm finding myself among Israelis these days. It's time for me to try to understand why most travelers speak poorly of the Israelis. Well, they don't actually *say* anything, but the phrases, "Popular with Israelis," and "A lot of Israelis" are taken as warnings. I don't get it. I've never heard these kinds of caution before…about people of any nation.

Back in El Calafate, the second person on the bus was a young Israeli tough whose ticket was for the seat beside me. It seemed too awkward not to initiate a conversation, so I did.

"Where are you from?"

"Israel, and you?"

"California. Are you on a long trip?"

"Maybe." He answered without looking at me. End of conversation. We never spoke again for the remaining five hours. I'm sure he's fresh out of the military. Who knows what he went through, who he saw get killed, who he may have killed, what he's wrestling with now.

The bus made the usual two stops at the border: one to leave Argentina, one to enter Chile, and a young Israeli couple broke into the immigration line ahead of others in both places.

I'm feeling an anti-Israeli sentiment arising. No doubt it's in part due to their government, and that is the *last* thing *I'd* want from the world—to be judged by my government.

A few Israelis are at the next table. They seem okay to me.

Before I got off the bus I tried to orient myself according to the guidebook map, but the bus's labyrinthine entrance to town got me turned around. I thought of Roger with his compass around his neck. Mine was in my backpack stored below. My South African friends recommended a hostel, so I decided to try to find it. While waiting for the conductor to get to my pack from the lower baggage compartment, a young guy handed me a brochure for the same hostel. Looking at him I stated, "That's exactly where I want to go." An easy score for him, and lucky for me, because the hostel has no sign; without the address it would've been impossible to find.

It's recently built, with no furnishings to speak of. The décor is reminiscent of a high school boy's garage hang-out. The flag of the region, Magellanes, covers the wall over the stairs. It reminds me of the flag of Alaska—the five stars of the Southern Cross in white on a field of blue above a white zigzag line that must be the snowy caps of the mountains, which are golden below. The linoleum is laid loosely on the floor, like they plan to roll it up at the end of the season. The doors don't close well, and I have to go outside to beat my room's window closed with a piece of scrap lumber. There's not a single clothes-hook or shelf, not even a place to hang a towel or place soap in the bathroom, but the attendants are cool, and it's cheap. My roommate is a good one, Clint, a quiet, coke-bottle-bespectacled man from Michigan.

After my salmon lunch I shop for six-days-worth of food, then return to my room and pack for the morning bus to the park. I'm hoping the weather will improve, otherwise it's going to be a long week.

On the three-hour ride to Torres del Paine, the bus passes below a kettle of condors. There must be forty of them overhead. Anyone would bet that there's a dead carcass off in the brush. At the trip's halfway point is a crossroad named "Cerro Catedral" with two cafes, a handicrafts shop, and a stockyard on its corners. We take a fifteen-minute break at one of the cafés, but it's too windy to wait outside. On board the parked bus feels like it's rolling down a wavy road as it rocks in the wind. I've left the roaring forties and am now in the furious fifties. We get moving again and pass a road sign that reads "Torres del Payne." I thought it was "Paine," so I check the map. It's spelled both ways. Apparently, Chileans are not sure if the place is named for a female Scottish climber named Paine, or the Indian word for the color blue, which is something similar to *payne*. I don't get it. It couldn't have been too long ago that a female Scottish climber came here.

After paying the steep entrance fee of thirty dollars, I walk past almost fearless guanacos to a minibus that crosses a bridge so narrow the driver has to fold his mirrors in to squeeze through, after which he drops me at some building near a trailhead. I've decided to hike up to the towers right away, but have no idea where the trail is, so I take a dirt road to a refugio where I find a trail sign with a map laminated on it. The spot on the map that is rubbed bare from fingertips is where I'm standing. I get oriented and follow the trail markers for a privately owned refugio up a steep valley. The park campground I'm headed for, above and beyond that refugio, is not mentioned on any trail sign. There is no fee to camp there, and it's the concessionaires who post the signs. The trail goes up, rising above the steep walls near the valley's river. Violent winds make the hike less enjoyable than it should be, and my heavy pack doesn't help, but the sun is shining, and lively whitewater rages below, heading south. The east wall is all scree, the west side I'm traversing is full of scrub lenga. Directly below, I see my *left* boot's sole delaminating.

When I make the camp, I make a pot of cream of *zapallo* (a kind of pumpkin) soup, then fall asleep. After waking, I head for the tower feeling disoriented; the soup must have had sugar in it. It's a steep boulder-field scramble to the tarn at the foot of the towers, back-lit by the late afternoon sun. Clouds rage among the peaks of these impressive granite spires. There's a nook among some big boulders where I hide from the wind and study the scene. It's not as moving as the towers of El Chaltén, and I wonder why. Maybe it's because I can't find a good composition through my lens. It's the arrangement of these skyscrapers—too balanced and symmetrical, no dominant, subdominant and subordinate. After the hint of sunset color fades, I'm cold, so I head down. Just after cresting what I now realize is the terminal moraine of big boulders that holds the lake and then tumbles down the valley wall, I meet a tiny Southeast Asian woman who's charging up the scramble like she's in a race. When she asks, I confirm that she has missed the sunset, but it wasn't very good. When I'm halfway down, she passes me. "That was fast." I comment. Her race is to get back to the private refugio, one-and-a-half hours down the trail. She asks if I will be here in the early morning and I say I will. A few steps later she turns again to remember my face so she can say hello tomorrow.

Back in camp the gale sweeps over the dense lenga above my tent, sounding like a jet plane. The trees do a great job of protecting the camp from the gusts while I cook pasta pepitas with an instant basil cream sauce. After dinner I fix my left boot with the glue, take a tiny nip off the airline-size bottle of Old Smuggler scotch I bought to celebrate with El Polaco Loco when we reached the hut at Paso Marconi, then set the alarm and find sleep quickly.

After I turned the alarm off it was hard to trade my cozy bag for the wind I heard roaring in the treetops. It took five minutes to make myself unzip and leave the womb. When I left the shelter of the lenga I realized that it was closer to sunrise than I thought, and got worried I'd miss something, so I shifted into power-climb. Soon layers were being shed. I made the top just in time to photograph the towers illuminated by the rosy glow of the clouds in the east. The gusts came from all directions, but I eliminated half of them by ducking below the crest of the moraine to this platform between two vertical boulders that rise overhead, where I just reclothed myself fully, even adding fleece pants under my nylon ones.

A flat granite rock is my seat beside the slab where my mini tripod is set with rocks weighing down the feet so it doesn't blow over, and I wait. Nothing happens. After a while the granite is sucking the heat from my butt, so I stand and climb to see what's going on in the east. A vast bank of clouds is filtering the light of the risen sun. I return to my nook, and when I glance back to check on the clouds, the little Asian woman appears. When she sees me, she drops down to say hello. She's late because she was on the trail for fifteen minutes before she realized that she forgot her spare batteries. She's from Macau. I know the name of the country from the statistics lists in the backs of atlases, but I have to admit I don't know where it is. My guess is near the Philippines. I'm not too far off. It's a former Portuguese city-colony an hour's ferry ride from Hong Kong. She's Chinese, but her name is Katarina. She grew up in a Catholic boarding school where she was baptized and learned to speak English and Portuguese. Now that Portugal has given the city back to China, she works for the Chinese Government as a translator.

When the sun hits the main tower, it's already well above the horizon and most of its gold light has cooled to white, but watching the continuous play of clouds around the peaks, I keep taking photos while talking to my little friend. When I ask her if she is still a practicing Catholic she says no, and continues for about ten minutes about how she doesn't think she is a compassionate person. Sometimes she doesn't want to help people because she doesn't like them.

Snow begins to fly in the wind, which interrupts her monologue, and she wonders why she is telling me all this—I'm probably not interested, she says. I tell her I am, that I was listening while photographing, and that I think she is more compassionate than she thinks she is. If she weren't, she wouldn't care about it when she has trouble acting with compassion. It wouldn't be important. She just needs to work through the anger that sometimes gets in the way.

Clouds have consumed the peaks, so I decide to leave, and invite her to my camp for tea. She's like a shadow on the way down, no matter how fast I go. So I go with gravity, working my feet quickly over the talus, and enjoy feeling her on my tail. While I'm heating the water, I ask about her travel plans in the park. She says she has a problem because she has no tent. The refugios are not well-placed for a backpacker to day-hike up French Valley and continue on to another refuge in the same day. She wishes she had a tent. I explain that I only have this one-person tent, but at five feet tall, ninety-nine pounds, she's probably the only person who could share it with me—still, we'd have to sleep together. She likes the idea, but doesn't commit a hundred percent, saying that if she sees me on the trail, and if it works out, she would like to do it, then she thanks me for the tea and splits. After I finish my tea, I stand and turn around to see the entire camp has left while we were talking. I make oatmeal and laugh about how nonchalant I am. It's a long hike out of here, and I'm probably going farther that most of those hikers, but I have confidence in my ability to cover the distance—or in my ability to bivouac illegally if I fall short before sunset. I'm headed to Campamento Italia, which is at the mouth of the Valle Francais that cuts the Paine Massif, a huge granitic intrusion, in half. The massif is the block from which *Los*

Cuernos, the famous and frequently-photographed "horns," have been carved by water, wind and ice.

When I pass the refugio, Katarina is sitting by the trail waiting for me. She jumps up and announces that she's decided to come with me. Then she asks me to confirm that I am Tom. With a burst of belly-laughter, I confirm that all of us Caucasians look alike. My pack is lighter by a lunch, dinner and breakfast, and a few ounces of fuel, and I feel strong. The first thing I ask her is why she trusts me so much. She says she can see it in my eyes. I warn her to be careful.

We hike fast. The little firecracker keeps up with me all day, eating chocolate almost continuously. She's thirty-eight, never been married, has had only one boyfriend, and hasn't slept with a man in six years. She likes sports, especially in boats—rafting, rowing, paddling. She just learned how to row a racing shell.

The hike is long, but uneventful. Even though we pass right below Los Cuernos, we can't see much of them. The last half-hour is a grunt, the weight of our packs finally defeating our strength and spirit, but we make Camp Italia before dusk. I set the tent quickly and go right to cooking to use the last light of the day. Kat contributes sausage to my mushroom rice, and I make it soupy to help hydrate our bodies. Afterwards my feet don't want to bear my weight any longer, so I make our bed and realize that her sleeping bag is nothing but a nylon-covered blanket, and she has no pad to insulate her from the ground. She is a strong individual, confident in her physical ability, and craving outdoor adventure, but she is a prisoner in her own culture. I admire her for making it here—to be out in the world as she is. Imagine the spirit it takes to escape her urban Asian environment and go hiking alone in the Andes. Imagine the process of decision-making she went through up to the moment she bought her airline ticket. What emotions did she feel as she went to the airport, on her flight, and when she landed in Tierra del Fuego?

Her courage inspires me. The man who heads the outdoor club in Macau won't let her join because she doesn't subscribe to the herd mentality that typifies Asians even more than the rest of the world's cultures. So she has nowhere to learn, and here she is, in Patagonia, only a novice, and without suitable gear. I try to make this lesson easy by insisting that she buy a sleeping pad while I'm creating an insulating bed for her from stuff sacks and clothes. When I spread out her bag, it reeks of mothballs. I tell her to leave her long underwear on, and I change into mine outside the tent, then we settle in for the night under my bag. I hold her like a kid holding a teddy bear, kiss her forehead, and wait for the fatigue of the day's travel to overcome the discomfort of sleeping with a stranger.

In the morning, I make her tea and oatmeal, then stash her backpack under a tarp at the ranger's cabin near the suspension bridge that crosses the river raging out of Valle Francais. She can hike up the valley with just a daypack, return to the cabin for her backpack, and cross the bridge to head for the next refugio. I give her my e-mail address and invite her to come run a whitewater river with me in the States some time.

After breaking camp, I follow her up the valley, but I never see her again. Strange, but she could have been off the trail looking at something or peeing when I passed. I have to assume she's okay. The trail rises persistently, part of it along the spine of a lateral moraine covered with dwarf ten-foot lenga. I'm crossing a barren knoll when a hanging glacier across the valley, on the east face of Cerro Paine Grande, lets go, and a raging cataclysm of falling ice ensues. The huge chunks are obliterated on the rock below and are soon reduced to the size of sand and gravel, with the finest crystals billowing in the air above the S-curved path dictated by the solid granite wall. The roar is constant. It's a five-minute event, ending in what looks like a waterfall, and is, but none of it is liquid.

In the upper valley, just below tree line, is Campamento Britanica, my home for the night—nothing but some cleared areas for tents. There's no outhouse, which I find negligent of the park, given the amount of traffic this valley gets. Lunch is mortadella. Thinking of the word and what might be its Latin roots, I wonder if it means something like "delicious dead stuff." The mist is getting heavier, so I rest in the dry pod for a while. Later, when the sky brightens a bit, I go up to tree line, but by the time I get there, the mist is real rain and the amphitheater is socked in, so I retreat, cook an early pepita pot and retire with the bossa nova playlist. Celso Fonseca's tune "Meu Samba Torte" surprises me. I don't remember the bass being so soulful. Maybe I never heard it through earbuds before. It moves me. Funny how such a simple pleasure can be so profound.

In the madrugada the rain stops, but the wind doesn't. My eyes open just before the alarm demands they do. A few stars burn in the spaces between clouds, so I take off for the high pass. The eastern sky is hidden behind the cuernos, but I guess it's pretty cloudy, because the dawn is uneventful. Once I'm high in the tundra, some rays sneak through the remnants of the storm and find a granite wall and a series of spires to the west, the highest of which the Chileans call "Cerro Catedral." It seems there are several peaks so-named in Patagonia, and I think of the awe that European peasants must have felt when first experiencing a Gothic cathedral hundreds of years ago. I sit by a boulder, waiting, and get a few shots. In the pause, my sweat chills me in the incessant wind, so I add a layer of fleece, and get moving again. Of course, a minute later the light and cloud combination I was waiting for materializes and I frantically ready the camera, barely catching the scene before it's gone.

It's a push to the pass—a long traverse on loose, sharp granite talus in a bitter breeze. When I make it, I realize it's a false pass, and I lose motivation. The views from the true pass will be to the east, into the sun. I've had no food. My fingers are white. I can't make myself cross another mile of talus, so I head for camp with a pot of Earl Grey on my mind. But I can see that if I return to this place, a good trip would be to travel up the valley from my first camp, across tundra and rock, around the north side of the towers and find this pass from the other side—the northeast. I could then descend into Valle Francais. It would be a memorable hike.

Just above tree line I meet an Aussie who's on his way up—wearing shorts. I yell "What the hell are you doin' up here with shorts?" and he laughs. We converge, and greet each other. I like him right away. I know he's a good man in a few seconds—I'm reminded of the Aussie I met in Bariloche. We could be friends. Funny, how this happens. I pass hikers all day long in the valleys and rarely have an interesting interaction. I warn him about the false pass.

I suppose he felt the same way, because just after I finished my pot of tea he stopped by my camp on his way down, just to say hello. He's on his last day of the big circuit that this place is famous for. It's a week-long hike, or "trek" as they say. I doubt he will make it to Campamento Torres today after hiking up here from Italia, and so does he, but that's where he's headed. He'll bivouac somewhere.

My quiet breakfast is disturbed by a dozen loud Israelis who decide that the log by the trail, about fifty feet from my tent, is a good place to take a smoking break. I wonder again about the cultural attitudes toward the space and privacy of others. My tent is the only one here. Why would they stop here? Is it like a rest stop on a freeway because it is a designated camping area? Is it an urban thing? Would my urban countrymen do the same? Is it a function of the population density of your hometown?

Once packed-up, I head down the trail at a good pace. About halfway back to Italia, a storm descends from the pass I stood in this morning. Rain rides gusts up to eighty miles-per-hour. I hear a clap of thunder behind me, and get into rain gear. From the funky suspension bridge that crosses the river, I head west through scrubby vegetation that offers no overhead protection, but crowds the trail, unloading water on passers-by. It's not an enjoyable hike. I just look at the trail, which is often a trough filled with water, and try to keep warm with the heat of exertion. My mind dwells on the letter I want to write, but never will, to the new Chilean president, telling her about the neglect of these trails and the crazy bridges made of 1x4s that look like a kid built them and that could easily break under the weight of a big man with a pack. I don't mind a rough trail, but I do mind being charged thirty dollars to use it, and I'm concerned for the safety of the less experienced people on this travel circuit.

Seven-and-a-half kilometers later, a newly-built refugio comes into view. I'm ready to call it a day, so I'll camp behind the place. It seems like a good idea to go in and have some soup and get warm and dry, but the soup is tepid and expensive, and there's no fireplace in the new, cold, cafeteria-style décor. When my clothes are dry from my own body heat, I go out back and pitch the pod. An octagon cook-shack is provided for campers, so I use it. A Kiwi engages me while I'm waiting for my pot to cook. Only half of his English is understandable—something about being in Chile on dairy farm business and dropping down here for a week. Once my rice paella is cooked, I escape the cacophony of Hebrew inside, and eat by my tent. The coziness of my sleeping bag attracts me to an early retreat with the bossa nova playlist that's been on my mind. I want to hear it again. During the mellow music some Israelis arrive and begin making camp, clicking tent poles together. My guess is that they rented a tent and can't figure out how to set it up in the dark, so they're arguing about it. Some of them are cooking in the shack and coming out to yell to the ones arguing about the tent. Everyone else in the camp is in their sleeping bags, but these Israelis are oblivious to the fact that they are surrounded by people trying to sleep. It's astounding, and it seems to continue forever. At least we can't understand them. It's just noise poking through the curtain of Brazilian groove. I switch to the boogaloo playlist and turn up the volume.

Once again, I'm surprised by my anti-Israeli feelings. If I ever had such a reaction to a race or nationality, I don't remember it. It's like they're from another planet. While feeling the emotions I realize they are compounded by my recent discoveries about the Zionists—those who strongly and aggressively support the nation of Israel—and their vast influences on world banking, and on the foreign policies of the United States through the lobbying efforts of AIPAC (American Israel Public Affairs Committee), the second largest lobby in the country after the AARP. Also, I recently discovered that there are reasons to suspect the Mossad, the Israeli clandestine force, of setting the explosives for the demolition of the three World Trade Center buildings in September of 2001 (in cooperation with certain devils in our own government).

When I finally relax, I realize that what I don't like in the Israelis is what I don't like in myself—that part of me that is inconsiderate and self-righteous. As I near sleep, I do so with feelings of self-acceptance, then, as I fade, the feeling is that I'm a like a holograph of humanity, containing all of the insanity, as well as all of the enlightenment. It's all OK.

R ain and wind continue all night, but there's a break at dawn, so I make maté and oatmeal and get on the trail south, hoping for views of Los Cuernos. It's an easy eighteen-kilometer hike to Las Carretas camp through flat grasslands with soil as soft as a carpet, and among thin-soiled, glacier-scarred hills covered with low chaparral and high tundra. The first few miles are along the west side of the lake and the silhouettes of peeping grebes float before the light of the rising sun. A perfect fox track is cast in the trail mud. Two flickers inspect me from a dead lenga not far from the trail. A hawk chases a songbird that flies erratically, frantically hoping to make it to cover beyond the edge of the open pampas.

Every day here in Torres del Paine I begin by optimistically stashing my rain gear at the bottom of my pack, and every day I end up taking it out when a light shower intensifies. Today is no different. About halfway to camp I find a wooded hollow between short, steep hills and stop for lunch. While I'm chewing a sandwich, my eyes peer through dead lenga twigs toward a sunlit distant hill, and suddenly I realize that the lenga branches at *sixty-degree angles*, not forty-five. From this perspective, the overlapping twigs are forming hexagons.

I suppose I first began observing the relationship between geometric shapes and intelligence long ago, when I began flying in airplanes. I always requested a window seat, and spent hours looking down at my planet. It didn't take long to realize that modern man demonstrates his occupation of a land through the creation of straight lines and regular geometric shapes. He creates dendritic lines only when building small roads or irrigation canals in hills and mountains. The similarity of a town viewed from 35,000 feet and a circuit board viewed from thirty-five inches led me to the idea that regular geometric shapes are an expression of intelligence, an expression of organization. But *life* is organized. It is *organic*, yet it is rarely geometric, at least to the naked eye. Again, some of the answers to this puzzle must lie in the appreciation of li. Is a highly organized quartz crystal more intelligent than a willy-nilly wee-beast? Why do plants often follow geometric patterns, but never with the accuracy of a crystal?

I've seen no people since I left the refugio, but as I near camp a squad of kayaks floats down the river that the trail now parallels. They beach when I drop my pack, and by the time I find a tent site and am pitching the pod they are upon me, in all their bright primary colors of spray and life jackets and spray skirts, like a troop of clowns in neoprene tutus. And they proceed to act so, taking a look at the cook shack, as if it were an archeological site before wandering back to their brightly colored boats. Again I feel like my personal space is invaded. As they arrived, one of them apologized for doing just that, but I just replied with a soft smile while thinking, "If you are sorry for doing it, then why do you continue to do it?" maybe they are working on a park project.

Just as they paddle away, my camp is set and I'm climbing up to the top of the hill. There's a dense lenga bush to park myself beside to use as a windbreak, and I sit and wait for the cuernos to lift their heads from their wrestling with dark storm clouds. The country below looks like good grizzly country. I've seen land just like this in western Alaska, on the Alaskan Peninsula, and on the shores of Bristol Bay. For every lenga surviving the winds blowing across this high tundra, there is the skeleton of one who did not; some still stand, some lie pointing in the direction of the williwaw that took its life. I pull out the iPod and listen to Sidestepper's "Paloma," and realize that the weather has no intention of changing, so I drop back to the three-sided cook-shack and make an early dinner. Afterwards I'm hangin' out and a horse packer passes, on his way to deliver to the refugio, I guess. He's gone by the time I think to ask for a cigarette—something to help pass the time—and I remember the cigar in my pack, so I find it and light it. It's a "Paloma" that my brother gave me.

I'm savoring the last of it when Sarah shows up. She's a volunteer for the park who comes here from England every summer (her winter). She's checking on the condition of the camp. I show her the trash, tell her about the toilet paper in the stream, and that the water was running brown out of the spigot before I ran it for an hour and cleared it out. I tell her the negative impression I have of the park operation, and she is forced to agree. We both know that those bridges I crossed yesterday, made of 1x4, are an injury waiting to happen, and she knows of some people who have broken through and suffered. I explain that I don't like the other extreme that we have in the United States, where every bridge is built according to Park Service code, of the same overly-stout materials, with safety railings to be sure no one can sue for falling off. I think there should be an element of danger that one accepts when entering the backcountry. People who can't cross a bridge without railings have no business being out on the trail. But when a bridge is so under-built—to the point of being ridiculous—it's not right. And when I bring up the outrageous park fee, I get angry. She tells me that the funds taken in here do not all stay here, but go to other parks too. I don't care what they do with the money as long as they are maintaining this park. It doesn't cost much to do. She says they don't know how to maintain it because they don't know what a park should be like, and that the park supervisor wants to spend the money to provide satellite internet access at every ranger hut. I look at her in disbelief, but it's entirely possible. She tells me that a team of thirty volunteers is here from the United States to fix the trails, and they're doing a great job, but they haven't gotten to the trails I've been on yet. Torres del Paine, she explains, has entered into a relationship with Yosemite to learn how to be a park. Well, I tell her, Yosemite is no model of organization, but the trails are well maintained. Some of the best trails I've ever seen are in the Sierras. Before she leaves, I promise her I'll write a letter scolding the park management for the poor job they are doing and suggesting improvements. Then I spend time reading the graffiti on the cook-shack walls. "Yanqui go home." "Yanqui not war."

CHAPTER 29

My Photographs

In the morning I was up in the hilltops before dawn, but the dawn came to a cloudy sky. The cuernos were not obstructed, but the clouds made a dim, flat light. I hiked over a few ridges before I found a good spot for a composition and waited for a shaft of light to find the cuernos while I watched some diving ducks in a small lake a few hundred feet below. A noisy squadron of parakeets raced by me. The cuernos resemble immense tree stumps, with vertical walls above radiating roots, and spiky tops like the splinters of the hinge a woodsman leaves to direct a falling tree. While the horns themselves are grey granite, these spikes on top are made of a charcoal-colored metamorphic rock. When the magma that became the granite intruded, it came to rest below sedimentary layers and baked them well, increasing their hardness so that they can still stand in the intense winds today. Now that I've gained distance from the horns, I can see the plane of separation between the igneous and metamorphic striking through the massif at about twenty degrees from horizontal.

When rain took over the peaks of interest, I returned to camp following rabbit runs. This area has sand deposits that somehow erode to form sand traps. Maybe these same formations dot the Scottish moors and are the origin of the sand traps of the game of golf. I passed puma scat.

It was a long walk back to camp. I didn't realize how far

I had come, chasing one taller hill after another in order to gain the best view of the cuernos. When I began boiling tea water, the couple who arrived last night at dusk left their tent and joined me. They're good people—a Chilean man and a German woman. I gave them hot water so they could get on the trail early, without setting up their stove. In our introductions I digressed to explain that, no, Alaska is not a frozen wasteland.

Now they've gone. When the rain stops, I'm instantly packed and on the trail at a four-mile-per-hour pace, trying to get out from behind these hills in case light hits the cuernos. After a few miles I'm lucky, and that light comes briefly while I'm in a good place. I'm crossing an area of wide, flat grassland, where the level pampas penetrates the hills to the east. Looking back at the cuernos, I get an almost perfect composition with Cuerno Principal dominant, the cuernos to the right of it sub-dominant, and a wind-pruned lenga standing in sunlit grass before shaded dark hills, subordinate.

In another mile I see the road, and when the trail comes parallel to it, I cross overland so I can hitchhike while I eat my last sandwich and wait for the cloud to part over the cuernos. I wait for an hour before I realize that the one o'clock bus probably would come from the other leg of the "Y" that I'm near, so I rush to the intersection, just a kilometer away, again in four-mile-per-hour mode. As I near the crest of a low rise I see the roof of a bus pass and I curse. At the junction I check my clock and it's two minutes after one. Fifteen minutes later I conclude that I missed the bus. The next one is in five-and-a-half hours, so I begin walking the road, hitchhiking when the rare vehicle passes.

Traffic is just a bit more than nonexistent—a lodge minibus every half-hour that won't stop. At a lake the road crosses an old wooden bridge. The view of the cuernos is good, so I stop and sit on the rail to see if the weather might lift for a minute and let the tops of the peaks out.

A retired German couple comes along in a tiny rental

car. They stop in the middle of the road, and after a brief conversation I'm in the back seat. The bus will stop at the ferry dock in Pudeto, so I'll get out there and hike to the lake to spend the afternoon waiting for shafts of light to pierce the clouds. I've taken my camera off my hip belt, and my map out of the top pocket of my pack, and they're on my lap as we chat and proceed up the road. The couple, Karl and Angela, are friendly people. They now live in South Africa. Karl, a retired accountant, is intensely interested in my stories of the backcountry. Angela is content to listen to us. She's probably in her late sixties, but still beautiful.

The interaction is so enjoyable that I miss my turn-off, and realize it only when we approach the two little lakes that I know are beyond my road. I ask them to stop and let me out, explaining that we've passed Pudeto. I get out of the car and put the map on the roof, weighing it down with my camera. While I fish through my pack for a business card to give them, Karl insists, over an over, that I get back in so he can drive me the kilometer to Pudeto, so, feeling rushed, I quickly close the pack back up and get in. A few minutes later, at the ferry dock, I pull out my pack and realize that my camera is gone. Suddenly it hits me. I left it on the roof. My reality shifts the same way it did in Quintero, Chile, when I lost my wallet. I feel enclosed in a bubble of intense confusion about my situation.

Karl drives right back to the place where we turned around, passing my map lying on the road. We get out and search, but can't find the camera. My head is spinning. Is this all true? Is my camera gone? Did I do something else with it? The map on the road tells me my memory is correct. It was on the roof, and now it's gone. Maybe someone picked it up. Traffic is thin here. A half hour can easily pass without a vehicle, but we were off the road at Pudeto for a few minutes, and maybe someone passed by. Surely, if I were to drive by and see a camera case lying on the road, I would stop to pick it up. There is a little ranger station at Pudeto, so I ask Karl to take me there. He's as concerned as I am and wants to help in any way he can. In an instant my life has changed. All my work of the past three weeks—the endurance of wind and cold, the pre-dawn climbs—all lost, and I am trying to adjust to this version of reality.

I tire of paying such close attention to my belongings, and, in an unusual situation—packed for walking, but riding in a vehicle—I let my attention fade. Now I'm paying the price. All the photos I've taken in the past three weeks are gone. Furthermore, all sense of purpose is gone. Getting the photographs for the book had become my purpose. Now they and the instrument to get more are both gone. The new two-gigabyte memory card in the camera had 600 photos on it that were not backed-up. This can't be true, but no matter how hard I analyze my mental framework of reality, I cannot find another, less hellish scenario to replace this. All my excitement, anticipating the finished products of those photos that I had a good feeling about, all the thrill of wondering how good they will be, which of them may be of the quality I am hoping for—it's all gone.

It's a strength of mine that I'm never late, and I endeavor never to keep anyone waiting for me. That strength has shown to be my weakness both in the cab in Quintero and here, when Karl was waiting for me to get my pack back in the car so he could drive me to the road we passed. This time, that sense of urgency I feel when someone is waiting has brought disaster.

I refuse to admit defeat though, and know there is a way to recover the camera. We drive to Pudeto slowly, raking the roadside with our eyes. Just as we get to the turn-off, a truck-full of Carabineros passes, so I flag them down and explain the situation, hoping that someone picked up the camera and will want to return it. The policeman asks me to write my info in a spiral notebook, the cover of which features blondes in bikinis and high heels. When they drive off, I go to the park guard, but he says I can only report such things at the park entrance, an hour east of here.

Over the years I've noticed that my mind is conditioned to suspect that someone has moved the thing I can't find, and I immediately suspect that the camera was picked up by the single driver who must have passed by in the few minutes we were gone. The strategy I take is to get the word out as fast and as widespread as possible, so that the person with my camera can easily return it if he or she wants to. Karl offers me a ride to Puerto Natales and I accept. It's a quiet ride. I'm in shock. Every time I see something interesting, I think of photographing it, but have to adjust to my situation. Guanacos graze beside the road as if nothing has happened.

At the park entrance I tell my story to the woman at the counter, and ask to give her the info so that anyone who may have found the camera can return it. She says I have to do that at Pudeto—the place where the park guard told me I had to come here. I tell her that, and she says, "No" in a tone that sounds like I am insisting on breaking a park rule. All I want to do is leave my information—the camera type and how to contact me. Finally, I guess to get rid of me, she takes a park entry form, turns it over, and gives it to me. After I write all the info down, she takes the paper and puts it at the bottom of the same stack of forms that she got it from. Without words she's telling me she doesn't give a damn about my camera, and the effort I've made to give her my info has been completely worthless. There's nothing to do but return to Puerto Natales, cameraless.

Back in the hostel I take a badly needed shower and shave, collect my stash of gear from the storeroom and dress for dinner with my German friends. They are kind people, encouraging me to maintain hope all through the steak and beers, and then insisting on paying for my meal.

Afterwards, I don't know what to do, so I go to bed. At six I wake with a bulging bladder. After relief, sleep won't return, so I spend an hour-and-a-half concentrating on the return of my camera. Where is the power of the mind? I can't seem to find it— that other eighty-five or so percent of brain-power that we hear is unused. I think of Fernando showing "What the #$*! Do We

Know" back in El Chaltén. Can I create an outcome to this situation? I try. I also try to pray, which I never do normally. I beseech any guardian spirits—non-physical helpers who are said to watch over us. My camera must return to me. I feel that, with the book project, I was doing what is the best thing for me to be doing at this time in my life. So this shouldn't have happened. What I'm doing is not only pure pleasure for me, but also I believe my photos can be of service, especially combined with a text calling attention to the profound beauty of Nature, the divinity of Nature, and what that means. This kind of thing doesn't happen to me. Well, I do make stupid mistakes, especially when someone is waiting for me, but I remember that the wallet was still in the back of the taxi.

After the provided breakfast of tea and bread, it's still early on a Sunday morning, so I glue my boot together again and leave it by the stove—it's a pretty, old-style wood-burning kitchen stove converted to use natural gas. Afterwards, I go to the station of the Carabineros. A kind officer takes forever to hunt and peck on a computer, misspelling every other word and backing up to correct it. When his report is finally finished, he gets in a disagreement with two others about how to print it. It does get printed, on second try, and I read it and sign it even though it's not the same story I told. I ask for it to be sent to the Carabineros and Guardaparques at Torres del Paine.

Next I take my stinking clothes to a backpackers laundry service. The colorful proprietor, Tomy, with a beard and a bandana around his neck, is sincerely concerned about my situation, and recommends that I put an ad on both radio stations. I do so right away, as they are some of the only businesses open on a Sunday morning. By the time I get that done, an internet shop is open, so I spend time online. I email CONAF, who runs the park, about my camera, let friends know of my blunder, and take a long shot by visiting the website of a lady whose service a friend once recommended. She worked for years as a psychic locating missing people for the FBI. I email her, providing all the details of the event and asking for her help. As I see it, there are three possibilities: the camera is in the hands of someone who wants to return it; the camera is in the hands of someone who wants to keep it; or the camera is still hidden in the bushes by the side of the road. I ask her which is the case.

I print a photo of my camera from a dealer's website, and create a flyer offering a $100 reward. Amazingly, I am told that I made only one mistake in my Spanish. By now a photocopy store is open so I make thirty copies and begin asking tour companies and restaurants to post them. Everyone is very kind and helpful. One bus driver runs down the street after me when he remembers that a road construction crew has been working right in that area—maybe one of the workers had found it. I take the name of the company.

By the time this is all done I'm fading, so I return to the restaurant where I had dinner last night—La Picada de Carlitos, one of those gems you find only occasionally—and have pork chops and mashed potatoes. I can't believe how tasty it is, and tell the matron when she passes, asking her why it's so good. She is proud that she is from the island of Chiloe, and that's why her food is so good. It's head-and-shoulders above all Chilean restaurant food I've had except for that bowl of seafood stew in Valparaiso. Afterwards I'm feeling burnt out, so I return to the hostel to check on my boot and get some rest.

A short rest is all my mind will allow. It's now or never, so I get out on the street to hand out more flyers. At an outdoor equipment shop the owner thinks my chances are slim. I figure it's fifty-fifty. It was in the park, not on the street. There's a different type of person there. He says, "Yeah, but this is Chile." Another kind woman tells me to put an ad in the newspaper tomorrow morning. Everyone is so nice it's hard to believe I won't get the camera back. But it's now been over twenty-four hours since it disappeared, and it seems like someone would have reported finding it by now if they were going to. The hanging out and waiting is going to be hard tomorrow, but there's not much left for me to do but wait, and there's nothing to do in this town but eat, drink and check e-mail.

A cold damp wind is blowing in off La Ultima Esperanza, an arm of seawater penetrating miles inland where it really shouldn't be. Long glacial valleys became flooded after the last ice age, and now the sea snakes its way in, fairly close to the continental divide. I take refuge in another bar with a vinyl record theme like the one in Valparaiso. The bartender in a fedora serves me a schop while Credence Clearwater Revival plays—one of Chile Willie's favorites from high school days in Santiago. It would be appropriate to hear "Oh lord, stuck in Lodi again," but it must have played before I walked in. A free traveler's newspaper lies on the bar. It's name, "Black Sheep" immediately attracts me. It's like a little Outside Magazine, with some good information in it, but it's oriented for the fat wallets—maybe because only the higher-end businesses can afford to advertise. The bartender says I can use a computer upstairs. We climb an ancient, steep, narrow staircase to a little room with a handful of computer stations. There's no news. Nothing's happening in this place, so I walk a block to the happenin' pizza hang-out, and order a pie named *La Guerrillera*, while joking with the waitress about the difficulty of the pronunciation.

In the morning I'm up early with those who are causing a ruckus getting ready for the 7:30 bus to the park. I lie in bed thinking, and trying not to think. It seems to me that in order to affect events the way I need to, it would take more than mere thought. In my effort to concentrate I find myself slightly contracting some muscles in my back, abdomen, and head. That can't be helpful. It's got to be an expansive experience, beyond the boundary of mind and body. Wanting to escape the sounds of the pre-bus rush, I plug into the iPod "Awakened Mind" playlist, which has a half-hour track designed to induce a meditative mental state. I imagine that the camera—specifically the tiny memory card, only slightly larger than my thumbnail—is back in my hands, and I feel the relief and gratitude. They say you have to feel this as if it is a hundred percent true. Like Wilson Pickett said, "Ninety-nine-and-a-half just won't do." I work at overcoming that last half of a percent, but my mind interrupts with the comic image of me still wandering these streets in ten years, refusing to believe that the camera is gone, panhandling for the money to put my 500th ad in the newspaper and post my 5,000th flyer.

At nine I'm on the street. First I make a dozen copies of my flyer—this time with a hundred-dollar bill placed at the top, then I visit the CONAF office. The man there is helpful and calls the park for me. While he's on the phone I realize that I left my originals in the photocopy machine—including the hundred-dollar bill. Maybe the stress is getting to me. The moment he's off the phone I thank him and run the three blocks to the photocopy shop. After two blocks I begin to tire. Is it old age or just two days of inactivity causing me to stiffen up? At the shop the lady has my originals, including the picture of Ben Franklin, in a folder waiting for me. Chileans can be so very kind. How can I not get my camera back?

The posters go up quickly. All the shopkeepers are sympathetic. So I visit another copy shop on the other side of town to make twenty more. The clerk asks if he can post one in his window. At another store the clerk asks for two because he sits on a corner facing two streets. Everyone sincerely wants to help. Most of the country is Catholic. It's hard to believe that the person who picked up the camera is neither kind nor Catholic, but there are plenty such people in Chile. I saw a lady open a restaurant this morning by first removing the iron bars from her windows. You don't need barred windows in a society of kind Christians. But then again, the person driving in the remote park is not the average man on the street. I'm hoping he is wealthier and more sympathetic, so he wouldn't need to keep the camera and have concern for who lost it.

I put an ad in the newspaper. While I'm at the paper's office writing this ad, the radio announcer reads the one I gave him yesterday—strange to hear your name on Chilean radio.

The museum seems like a good spot for a flyer, so I stop in. The ladies there tell me they just heard about me on the radio and wish me luck. After I compliment them on the museum, the oldest lady invites me to enter for free, so I do. There's a display case full of relics, including some skin and hair of the cave sloth that motivated Bruce Chatwin to write *In Patagonia*. There are Indian artifacts and tools of the settlers who killed the Indians off, with no mention of the genocide. I'm fascinated to see a green glass fishing float that looks Japanese, so I ask about it. The older lady tells me they're made in Chiloe, but she doesn't know the origin of the custom, maybe they learned from the Japanese. I tell her about the Japanese glass floats that wash up on the beaches of Alaska.

When the flyers are gone they're all over town. I don't know what else to do, so I walk across town to the hostel. Puerto Natales has cottonwoods growing on some of the streets—Alamos, they're called—and the smell reminds me of various groves in the north, especially in Alaska and in the canyon river bottoms of the Southwest. In the parks, the city maintains cypresses pruned to the shape of giant mushrooms. "Topiary," I think. What a strange word. I'm feeling positive about getting my camera back and am in a good mood. An old lady waits at a street corner, afraid to cross because she is so slow. I help her by walking beside her and stopping traffic—right out of the Boy Scout manual.

Juan, the guy who met me at the bus when I first arrived in Puerto Natales, is at the hostel. He's laid-back and patient, late twenties, I'd guess. It looks like he has rosacea—probably from an abundance of yeast in his body—on his cheeks beside his nose. He is thin, but his younger brother, Ivan, is stocky, round-faced, and a hard worker. For some reason, their little sister lives with them. She has a perpetual pout when she walks by us on her way to high school in the morning.

I'm hangin' out with these guys when a couple of South

Africans enter and we greet each other. When I say I'm from California, the loud one immediately asks if I'm a Republican, which makes me laugh. Then he says he's on a quest to meet a Republican, but he's beginning the think it's impossible. I laugh harder. These guys are just in from the eight-day circuit around Torres del Paine and are obviously out to have a good time, so we arrange to meet at La Picada de Carlitos for dinner. Over bottles of merlot, I'm educated about South African history; how the Afrikaners were defeated by the British, but came back through the simple strategy of reproduction. After a few generations of intentional population growth they became the majority and took control.

The loquacious one tells me he's made a list of forty-one goals to achieve in his life. He believes in the power of writing things down "to make them real." I offer a forty-second goal: "To be able to change your goals." It makes no sense to him. He has big energy, but little receptivity. Maybe it goes in one ear and out the other, maybe it will bounce around inside for a few years and then he'll hear it one day. How long will it take to achieve his goals? Will a forty-two-year-old man still be interested in pursuing a thirty-two-year-old boy's goals? Should he be? I suppose it depends on what the goals are. Some—those that lead us towards true self-fulfillment—should always remain.

A French couple they met on the trail joins us at our table. The subject of conversation comes to the labels placed on people of various nations. It's funny to see the look of surprise on the faces of the French when they learn that they are known the world over as an arrogant people. And I laugh when they say that the French think that about Americans.

No one ever asks anything about me, so I don't have to tell my story, which is some small relief.

CHAPTER 30

The Search

In the morning *la cabeza me duele* from all the wine last night. I make some oatmeal, left over from the trail, and go check e-mail. No word from the psychic, so I e-mail the friend that recommended her and ask him to call her. Other friends have replied assuring me that they are praying and sending out intentions that my camera returns. At the CONAF office there's no word. I don't know what else to do, so I return to my bunk and spend an hour imagining that I have my camera—using the fact that my newspaper ad came out today to support my optimism.

Later when I check mail again, there is the psychic's name. The mouse click on it seems like a drum roll. She tells me she thinks the camera is still out there, on the opposite side of the road from the majority of my searching. My spirits are brightened, and I buy a bus ticket to the park, with no doubt that I will find my camera, and more importantly the photographs it contains, on the other side of the road. On the way back to the hostel I pick up a pair of leather work gloves to protect me from the thorny calafate.

When dawn breaks, the stormy weather of the past week is on its way out—a good day for photography. The light is changing below broken clouds as they head towards the Atlantic. From the bus I see some teal swimming in the salt water beside the road, and then a black-chested buzzard eagle standing on top of an old piling by the edge of the bay. Crossing the pampas, I see the towers from a distance of several miles and am astounded at their beauty and majesty. At their base I was too close to appreciate them. Thoughts come about all we miss—all that we can be blind to—when we are too close to a thing or place. Getting away, gaining distance and a new perspective, often allows us to see more clearly what has been right in front of us all along. Sometimes a horse has to be on the other side of the fence to realize how green the grass is in its own pasture.

My plan is to find the camera right away, then hike out to the lookout at the lake and photograph the cuernos all afternoon until the six-thirty bus.

When we get to the park entrance I show the guards my flyer and tell them I just came to search the roadside for my camera. They let me in, waiving the fee with a slight wave of the hand, as if it were a secret.

When the bus arrives at the ferry dock, all the passengers head for the boat to cross the lake. I walk off in the opposite direction, feeling like I am about to close this chapter. It's windy. My search is casual until I reach the spot where we made our three-point turn. I look for our tire tracks, but the road has been graded, and they're gone. Still, I know within forty feet where the car backed up across the road before driving back to Pudeto. This is the most likely spot for the camera to roll off the back of the car, on the isthmus between two small lakes. Now the wind of the clearing storm is blowing at about sixty miles per hour. You can't stand still in it. Gusts probably reach eighty miles per hour, lifting water off the tops of waves and throwing it at me.

I put on my gloves and get to work, looking around, under, and inside of every bush. Gloves are essential. The thorns of the calafate could have crowned Christ. Other plants are low domes of thorns so dense nothing could penetrate them. To be sure, I test by throwing a camera-size cobble on one and it is repelled. I can ignore those, but I go inside each of the stiff, stunted lenga that grow as chaparral here. In fifteen minutes the entire turn-around area has been searched fruitlessly, but my spirits are only slightly fatigued, and I cross some flat, barren gravel to resume the search a stone's throw down the road. I know I am about to find the camera, so I'm feeling good. I develop a method to be sure I leave no bush neglected, using my staff as a marker. Soon the road is rising on gravel fill towards the crest of a hill to the west, and the slope from the lakeshore to the shoulder of the road is getting taller. It's a steep, forty-degree slope made of glacial till, full of round cobbles. Between the wind, the thorns, and the steep loose slope, it's hard to work. After forty-five minutes of effort, I begin talking to myself. Even if there were a person within a mile of me, no one could hear me over the roar of the wind. My anorak and nylon pants flap with the sound of a baseball card in a kid's bike spokes.

I begin asking to be guided to my camera.

Soon it becomes frustrating to have to look under every single bush on the long slope, because the more I look, the farther I am from the turn-around, and the less likely it is that I'll find the camera because chances are slimmer that it would have ridden this far on an up-hill gravel road. "It should just be sitting here, right in the open," I protest to the spirits on the other side—the ones I've asked to help me. A lightweight camera in a padded nylon case should not have penetrated very far into this thicket, but as anyone who has worked in construction knows, when you drop something, it usually has a way of going into a place where you could never get it to go if you tried. And I'm not planning on doing a second search, so I persist with my meticulousness.

A half-hour later I begin asking out loud why this has to be so fucking difficult. Why must I go through such an ordeal? The wind and the thorns are beginning to get to me, so I mark my place and cross the road for shelter from the hurricane and make a couple of avocado and cheese sandwiches. After the last bite I'm right back to work with determination and confidence, but both begin to wane when I reach the hill. The top of the hill is barren and rocky and flat, so the black camera case should be obvious if it were here, and it's not. Beyond this hilltop, as the road begins its descent, it turns right, so centrifugal force could have encouraged the camera to fly off the roof, and I begin the search again. Here the road-fill is short, but a natural hill covered with tall brush continues down for more than a hundred feet. I climb through every plant on the slope. All this is taking a toll on the skin of my legs, but I don't realize it. I'm focused on recovering my photographs.

As my confidence dwindles, I grow confused. How can this be happening? When I reach the end of the brushy slope, I stop. This side of the road becomes a "cut" (as opposed to the "fill" it has been) from here back to the road to the ferry dock at Pudeto. There's only a ditch beside the road to search and I did that on my way here, four hours ago. So I cross the road and search the other side in a half-hour—it's easy because there's not much vegetation. Then I take another look where I began, and walk the entire area once more, trying to spot something I've missed. I didn't miss anything. I know every damn bush for a half-kilometer. My search is over, but I refuse to give up, so I comb the top of the eight-foot road-cut, where it would be near impossible for the camera to land, in an effort to leave nothing neglected. Six guanacos let me by while I walk through roadside grass, far from the turn-around, approaching Pudeto. I can't imagine its staying on the roof this far, and the map was in the road only a hundred yards from the turn-around—it was weighed down by the camera, so I think the camera must have come off before it did. When I reach the road to Pudeto I turn around and go back on the other side. This is easy because it's thin grass on an uphill slope from the ditch. The guanacos walk ahead of me for a while, then separate and let me through at a distance of twenty-five feet.

Eventually I'm back at the turn-around. I search it one more time because I think it's the most likely place. There's nothing I haven't already seen, but I comb one last time through the entire area to be sure I didn't miss anything. Some of the brush at the bottom of the hill slope was unsearched, so I climb through it. I'm tired. I lie down in the lee of some dense brush and watch the clouds boiling overhead. The burning of my legs and wrists, from all the scrapes, scratches and cuts, finally enters my awareness.

I'm in shock by the fact that I have to admit defeat or risk becoming like the Japanese soldier stranded on a South Pacific island who refuses to believe that Japan has lost the war many years after the fact. I should walk back to the ferry dock, and get up to do so, but wander like an abandoned child back to the turn-around, shuffling my feet without intention. I'm afraid to feel the pain of turning my back on this place. I can't think. I'm shuffling along the road edge when I notice that the gravel is covering the lower branches of the brush. The grader buried the bottom of the bushes. I dig down with my staff and find fresh, green leaves six inches down. Suddenly I remember that when I first arrived at the turn-around, I couldn't see our tire tracks because the road had been graded. Now I know what must have happened.

On the day I lost the camera, I searched the north side of the road, thinking that since we were driving on that side, the camera would be there if it weren't in the road. But Karl didn't pay much attention to what side of the road he drove on, so the camera could have fallen to the south side as the psychic said, just barely off the gravel, stuck in the first bushes beside the road. Sometime in the three days since I've been here, the grader came by and covered my camera with gravel. It's mostly plastic, so a magnetic locator wouldn't pick it up any better than it would the nuts, bolts and bottle-caps that are in any gravel road. I can't dig a kilometer of road shoulder looking for it. I could be standing on it right now.

It's gone.

But I can't stop looking for the camera on my sad stroll to the ferry dock. Just as I give up and surrender to the fact that it's gone, a condor passes about a hundred feet overhead, carving figure-eights in the sky as it tries to make headway into the gale. It's losing ground, but doing so gracefully. I realize that is what I must do as well—accept my defeat and carry on without allowing my mind to be stuck on my loss. Remain positive and enjoy my time on the underside of my beloved planet. I thank the condor and take a deep breath.

The bus is filled with ferry passengers, and on the ride

back to town I see camera screens lighting up as they review the snapshots of their trips.

Back in Puerto Natales I walk directly to La Picada de Carlitos and ask the owner for the best meal of the day. She gives me salmon de pobre—a salmon fillet covered with fried eggs with fried potatoes on the side, and a liter of Cerveza Austral. Back at the hostel the shower stings my scratched skin. I'm punctured by a couple-hundred pin-holes in each leg.

The next day I buy a bus ticket to Punta Arenas, a few hours south of here, and make a reservation for a flight from there north to Puerto Montt, just a few hours south of Valdivia. At an internet shop, I e-mail the Nature Conservancy in Valdivia to expect me in a few days. I'm eager to leave this town and flee from the Patagonian wind. Even though there's more blue sky than I've seen since arriving here, the wind has not relented and I'm tired of it. I'm ready to depart Patagonia and return to the latitudes of lakeside farms and soft late-summer breezes.

Three hours after climbing aboard the bus, we pass fifty-three degrees of latitude, only seven degrees short of Antarctica, just north of the famous Cape Horn. We cross lenga scrub. Half of them dead—succumbed to the weather, no doubt. Then a storm hits, the windows fog, and I see nothing. When it clears, we are in pampas.

Punta Arenas is a real city. It reminds me of Juneau. Just as I get off the bus, a storm approaches and I get only a few blocks before ducking under a shop awning to dig for my rain jacket and pack cover—just like I did every day in the park.

When I get to Hostel Independencia, Eduardo, the young manager, welcomes me. He takes out a city map and gets me all lined-out for food, the Naval and Maritime Museum, and buses to the airport. Then he gives me my own room, with a key.

Taking his advice, I eat at the supermarket's upstairs cafeteria—home cooking at low prices. The Naval and Maritime

Museum is of little interest, just like in Valdivia—model boats, a knot display, brass port-holes, et cetera. But they do ask if I would like to see a film, and I'm happy to watch the voyage of the tall ship "Peking" around Cape Horn by Irving Johnson—a fearless adventure seeker. I've seen it before, but it's a rare film worth seeing again and again. Across the street, I buy a ticket at Transfer Austral to get to the airport tomorrow. The ticket agent speaks so fast that I have to ask her to slow down, which she does for a sentence or two, then her tongue runs away like a freight train. I am trying to understand why the bus leaves at 12:15—12:30, but her answers are unintelligible. Finally I tell her that it leaves at 12:15, but drives around town for fifteen minutes picking up passengers before actually leaving town, ending my sentence with a questioning tone. She tells me I'm right, but that may just be to shut me up and get rid of me. I'll come tomorrow at noon.

Back at the hostel, Anita, the month-old kitten, wanders into my room while I'm resting with the door open to allow heat to enter. My room's window faces the wind and its curtains swing when gusts push through cracks. Anita curls up in the crook of my elbow. She was born about the time Mauro and I crossed that snowy pass and stayed at refugio Italia with Cintia.

The hostel has a bathtub, so I soak in it—an experience I've been wanting for a few weeks—before heading out to a restaurant of Eduardo's recommendation, "Doña Marie." I order Eduardo's favorite, *congrio a la vasca*, and the waiter takes a step back and holds the backs of his hands to his shoulders to indicate that I hit the bulls-eye. I've been wanting to try the *curanto*, a famous dish of southern Chile, but it turns out it is a Friday tradition, and today is Thursday. When the waiter brings me bread and salsa he says Puerto Montt will have abundant curanto tomorrow because it is a dish of Chiloe, which is nearby. The salsa is the same as at La Picada de Carlitos, so I ask about it. He says it's called *peubre*. "It's the best salsa south of Mexico," I compliment, and ask him to write the name with my pen on a napkin. I didn't realize that I was pushing him until I saw him write like a first-grader, barely legible. He likes my Spanish, so he asks me to translate some of the ingredients of the dishes for him so he can explain them to the gringos who always come in but don't speak a word of Castillian. He does well repeating after me, but when it comes to "garlic" it is impossible for him to pronounce. It sounds like his tongue is paralyzed. I wonder what I sound like to him.

It's a good meal, and I walk it off around town, but it's dead quiet except for the wind moaning in the wires, and an alarm blaring from an empty bank. The walk home is into the wind, which bites my freshly-shaven cheeks. At the hostel a crew of French folks have made curanto under the guidance of Eduardo, but they offer no invitation to join them, so I retire with my "blue jazz" playlist on the iPod to obscure the sounds of their party.

Footsteps wake me in the morning and when I stand and yawn, my exhalation condenses in the chill air. The aloe vera I put on my scratched wrists is icy, so in the kitchen I put my wrists over another gas-fitted woodstove and Eduardo asks what happened. I've been waiting for an opportunity to tell him about the road grader, so I launch into my story, beginning by showing him my perforated shins, still punctuated with commas, colons, semi-colons, exclamation marks, and periods all made of dried blood. The story ends with the gravel, and I tell him the name of the company that did the grading, and show him the name in my notebook—Empressa Mansilla Hermanos—adding that I heard they were based in Punta Arenas, and I'd like to contact them to tell them what happened. A typical Chilean, he's enthusiastic to help me. Fifteen minutes later he has called them to explain what happened, faxed them my flyer offering the $100 reward for the memory card, and is asking for more flyers so he can post them. He gives me his card and insists that I e-mail him to check about the camera. I'm happy that now I've taken all possible avenues short of the magnetic locator. I've done all I can do, and I'm off to the bus office.

Upon entering the office, I see the same girl standing with her butt next to the gas heater. It's hot in here, but she's cold.

The French doors must be a hundred years old. They have about an inch gap at the bottom, and don't fit well anywhere else. The wind sneaks through all around. I wonder if they waste expensive gas here, or if it's subsidized like it is just across the border. I have time to think about all the modern weatherproofing materials up in Alaska and how they contrast with Patagonia, how attitudes of energy conservation vary, how things will change here after peak oil.

When 12:15 comes, I'm the only person waiting, but a few more soon dribble in and we wait without a word even though I'm wondering what the hell is going on when the minute hand drops to six. At 12:36 she asks if we all have tickets. Then a van pulls up and I ask if that's the bus. It is, so we all exit the old French doors and board, picking up a few others on the way to the airport.

While checking in with the airlines, I'm taken by a woman Carabinera because of her uniform. The style could be seventy years old; a wool olive-drab overcoat covered with a leather pistol belt that has leather straps crossing her back like suspenders under epaulettes. Under the coat she wears a man's shirt and tie. On top, her bunned-up hair is topped with a hat like officers of the British army wore in India a hundred years ago.

When I ask for a window seat, the lady at the counter asks right side or left, and I tell her "right" so I can see the mountains. When I board I find my seat on the left—it's the right side as you're walking back to find your seat; that's the reason for using "starboard" and "port."

When we pull away from the gate, mixed emotions run through me, like I'm leaving a lover after a quarrel. I feel attachment and loss, but I want to escape and move on.

The plane takes off through a surreal, lenticular cloudscape and then rises above a sea of white vapor. Flight attendants serve a snack of hot dog, cheese and bacon pie, an empanada, and white wine while I read about Chile's plans to harvest electricity from the sea in this nation's version of the Wall Street Journal, *"Estrategia."*

I've forgotten about sightseeing when I look across the aisle and see faces pressed against windows. I bolt to an empty row of seats on starboard side just in time to see El Chaltén. Cerro Torre and accompanying agujas are buried in the blanket rolled in from the Pacific, but I see much of the land that I was walking just a couple of weeks ago. I enjoy spotting specific places where I've stood. Fond memories return.

Soon clouds cover all but the highest peaks. Somewhere below is the valley of Rio Baker, which is slated to be drowned by a Chilean hydroelectric project. I heard that the power is needed for an aluminum smelter. As if drowning the valley isn't bad enough, a 1,200 mile transmission line will be required just to connect this remote place to the grid. It'll cut a wide swath through wilderness forests and National Parks, changing Patagonia forever.

A newspaper on the seat beside me reveals both a lack of censorship *and* the presence of disinformation when it comes to the United States—interesting. There's a front page article warning that global warming could cause the extinction of thirty to fifty percent of all species on the planet. Another says that a new book reveals Kissinger kept secrets from Nixon—an item of strong interest to many Chileans. Down the page a headline says the Bush family and the Royal Family of Saud are close friends, with a photo of George W. walking hand in hand with the Prince. Then, anomalously in the opposite direction, is a disinformation piece linking Saddam Hussein with Al Qaeda. Wouldn't we love to know how *that* article was placed in this paper?

As I stare across the top of the sea of clouds, my mind gravitates to the loss of my camera, and then to the reason I lost it—because I was in a hurry while someone was waiting for me. And an insight comes. The daydreaming slowed my brainwaves and I know something, out of the blue, like it's been suddenly dislodged from a nook in my brain. Suddenly it's clear that my insistence on punctuality, as well as my complete loss of cool when someone is waiting for me, is rooted in an experience I had when

I was about five or six. It was September, and I was out with my parents to shop for school clothes and supplies. Afterwards, I was enjoying one of those nickel amusement rides by the front door while my parents were with the cashier. When my parents exited and passed me on their way out, my father told me it was time to go, but I was having too much fun, and wanted to use all of my nickel's worth. A few moments later, my father blind-sided me with an open backhand to the left side of my head, yelling that he said it's time to go. I remember screaming in terror.

Once I befriended a man at an associated aikido dojo. He was up for his black belt, and I was helping him prepare for his test. In conversation after training, I learned that as a troubled youth, his life was turned around by a psychologist and hypnotherapist, and he became that man's student. It turned out that the man was world-famous and had few other students, so when he died, my new friend became the world's expert in his approach. I was fascinated and had too many questions, so he offered me a session to see what it all was about, and I accepted. All I remember about the session is that in the course of casual conversation—or what seemed like that to me—he asked me to relax totally in my chair and feel any muscular tendency towards movement or contraction. As I relaxed my neck, I felt my head turn about forty degrees to the right, and he asked me what trauma I had experienced that was memorized in those muscles. Immediately I knew, which was strange, because it was only a very distant memory. Now, ten years later, it suddenly pops in my head that I was instantly conditioned always to be on time, and to hurry crazily if someone's waiting—not the worst conditioning, except for the crazy part. It will take a conscious effort to heal—probably with the help of friends who allow me to be late, and who are OK while waiting for me. Or maybe it is more accurate to say it will take a subconscious effort, as it seems I will need to reprogram the subconscious, maybe through hypnotherapy.

PART 5

BACK IN THE HEART OF CHILE

CHAPTER 31

The Valdivian Coastal Reserve

On the bus from the airport to the city of Puerto Montt I study my guidebook, but the hostels I pick aren't on the book's map, nor are the streets that they are on. No big deal: I know that, upon setting foot on the darsena, I will be approached by people offering a room. A kind lady shows me a photo of her place, but it's too far from the terminal. She goes out of her way to find someone representing a nearby hostel, and I follow short, stout, happy Luis to a homey place run by an elderly, devout Catholic couple. Doilies are abundant. Oval mirrors hang in quilted frames. I take *pieza* #3 for five thousand pesos. The hall and stairs are so small I have to carry my backpack sideways in front of me. My door is chin-high. This place was built long ago for the same race of people who wore those little uniforms in the Battle of the Pacific. The inside is covered entirely by narrow boards painted sky blue, with bright orange bedspreads.

Luis offers me a tour of Chiloe. I never have done such a thing, but I consider it only because I've heard so many people, especially Chileans, say they love the island. If Puerto Montt is a little Vancouver, Chiloe is Vancouver Island, home to a subculture of primarily fisher-folk. Marinela used to live there and says it's her favorite part of Chile, excluding Rapa Nui, of course. I could do a whirlwind tour and see it superficially in a day. I consult the guidebook to try to find a reason to go. To see the wooden churches? The houses on stilts over the water? But I can't get excited about it. I'm still not over my loss. The flight was the final act of my abandonment of my lost work. And I'm feeling a little angry tonight—not a good time to be on a minibus with a dozen tourists making small talk. There is a little town on the west coast that is the gateway to a potentially interesting little park, but the chances of rain are high, and I'm just not in the mood for it.

Curanto I'm in the mood for. Before I head out, I ask the old lady, "Until what hour can I ring the doorbell," knowing that these kinds of guest homes have such restrictions. She can't understand me. Is it my correct Spanish, or my gringo accent? She shows me the doorbell and says, "You push it," demonstrating several times, as if I've never seen a doorbell before. I repeat my question twice before she gets it and tells me "Until ten, after that it's dangerous." I tell her I don't have that problem, talk her into eleven, and head west for the port where Luis told me I can find the best curanto. On the way, I feel my anger and let it fill my body. It feels good. I have felt so defeated for the last week that this sensation of power is welcome. God help the thug who tries to fuck with me tonight.

Anger is like that. Because it feels good, we use it a lot to cover the emotion that is really there. In my case, I feel incredibly stupid for losing my camera, and I don't want to feel stupid. As a martial artist, I should have been be paying better attention, so I feel doubly inadequate.

Maybe it's the isolation of Puerto Natales and Punta Arenas that filters out the Latin American flavor of Chile. Maybe those towns are more heavily influenced by Argentina—the most European country in South America. Or maybe the cold and wind drove all the street vendors away from those southern towns years ago. But I'm back in the real Chile now. It's like landing in Tijuana. Street vendors sell cheap stuff—clothes, souvenirs, toys, CD's. Men on the corners opposite the terminal cook skewered chicken over charcoal that glows a deep red in oil drums split lengthwise.

The heat feels good as I pass in the cool air drifting in from the salt water.

The town is dirty and run-down. Wooden buildings are in various stages of decay revealed by the degree of wear on the paint jobs. The worst buildings have lost all their paint, and are beginning to collapse as gravity pulls the wood back to the soil it came from. The puddles in the gutters tell me I am between rains, rains that push the buildings down and invite the fungus that reaches up from the earth to digest them.

While the people are poor, the food markets are full of cheap produce, bringing a comfortable feeling of abundance that I haven't seen in weeks. It makes me think of what I overheard a few weeks ago in El Chaltén, "Argentineans are great people and the mountains are fantastic, but Chile is the place to live." When I heard that I immediately thought of the greenness of this side of the Andes, the lush pastures and farms just north of here. Rain. Rain is what makes Chile the place to live. Over the millennia, moisture-laden winds off the Pacific released rain and snow that wore down the Andes and washed sediment westward, allowing a proliferation of plants that then built thick topsoil. I tend to agree with the guy who made the statement.

It's Friday night. Workers sit on red vinyl seats in bars about as charming as garages while nursing liters of beer at formica tables with loose metal legs. When I get to the port, I'm surprised to see that it's a touristy place—a miniature Fisherman's Wharf. It's late and most of the newly-built shops are closed, but one is just closing, so I ask the pretty woman there where I can get a good curanto. She tells me the restaurant across the street and upstairs is good.

I take a seat and order curanto and a beer. I was told that the dish has shellfish, sausage, meat, chicken and potatoes in a pot of broth, and a pile of dumplings, called *chupaletas*, steamed on top. I'm imagining a seafood stew like a paella. When it arrives at my table, it's a huge oval platter stacked high with the above ingredients: mostly mussels, three clams, a potato, a chicken leg, half a kielbasa, and some kind of smoked and cured ribs with two gummy, flat, round dumplings. On the side are a basket of bread, butter, lemon halves, and a bowl of peubre—more Mexican and less oily than in the south, and heavier on the cilantro. Not what I expected, but not in the least unappealing. After I attack a few mussels the waitress brings me a bowl of broth that has the flavor I was hoping for—the flavors of all those meats and shellfish along with some spices and herbs, the smoke and the garlic. This bowl contains the sensual delight of the meal. The rest is to fill your belly.

I walk off dinner by passing the terminal and heading into the downtown area where poverty suddenly yields to affluence. Banks, pharmacies, big restaurants and hotels, specialty stores selling shoes, sports equipment, electronics, perfume and other such luxuries. There's an internet shop where I check mail, but there's no word about my camera—not that I expected it, but it would be a pleasant surprise. I'm still not in much of a sociable mood, so I return to the hospedaje at ten, which puts a smile on the old lady's face.

Breakfast is quiet. I'm the only foreigner at the table, and when I finish the tea and bread, I'm off to the terminal, but halfway down the block, I feel something is missing. I suppose my senses are heightened after my loss. My lumbar pack is too light, and when I look in, I see my guidebook isn't there, so I make a U-turn and find the book in my room, squeezed between the bed and the wall.

The bus is a refuge where I don't have to interact with anyone. I can sit for hours and watch the land roll by, listen to some music. I don't have to make any decisions. I can daydream, contemplate, or look for insight. It's another cloudy day, so I can't see the volcanoes. I'm looking for Tronador, waiting for it to appear, just as I was while on the mountain above refugio Italia. I saw that mountain only on my first day in the Andes, when I saw the condor at close range. What a treat that was.

In Osorno we take a break, and when I descend to the tarmac, snack food hawkers descend upon *me*. I had forgotten about them while in Argentina and Southern Chile where they don't exist. I've read that the Chilean government makes it easy to create a small business. There aren't a multitude of legal requirements, or licenses and permits required, few hoops to jump through, which I think is good, but it does create a need for tolerance.

The next stop is Valdivia. My pack on my back, I walk from the bus like I know where I am going, so the hostel hawkers let me by. I go directly up the hill to Hospedaje Rios, where, by luck, they have a room for me. Eliana and Roberto are happy to see me, and I tell a few stories about money, mountains and my memory card, then I head to The Nature Conservancy office to inform them that I can begin work at the reserve in the morning. They tell me to catch the 9AM bus out of Corral, and I confirm the time. Everyone in the office agrees that it's a 9AM bus. Back at the hospedaje is a guy who works for Alaska Fish and Game in the summer. Years ago he worked for the Peace Corps in Guatemala and he travels in Latin American countries to maintain his language skill.

There's a big German folk celebration this weekend, and a German folk dancing performance fills the plaza. I pass through the crowd headed for the market, looking forward to a bowl of paila marina, a local seafood specialty. I'm still searching for a dish to rival that one I enjoyed in Valparaiso. The paila marina I'm served is small, so I take the Alaskan's advice and head towards the university neighborhood where there is supposed to be a beerfest, thinking a wiener and a beer will suffice. On the way, I see the parade with Bavarian oom-pah-pah bands on flatbeds. One is actually playing "Roll out the Barrel."

It's a long walk past the university to the fairgrounds. At the gate I pay 300 pesos, enter, and walk across a field to the hall. At the door they want 3,500 pesos. The place is empty. It hasn't started yet. So I leave, giving the girl at the gate a hard time about charging 300 without telling me that it was another 3,500 at the building.

New York Latin Jazz flows from my earbuds on the walk to town, where I check e-mail and call Marinela. She's worried about getting busted for running a speakeasy out of her house. She's just a single mom trying to make ends meet, but the place got too popular. She tells me she and Charly are organizing a seminar for me to teach when I return in a couple of weeks.

At a clothing discount store, I buy a long-sleeved work shirt to protect my arms from brush and bugs. I get a blue one, forgetting that the tabanas like that color. Still thinking of the beerfest wieners, I stop in a sandwich shop and order an "Italiano," because it comes with avocado, cheese, tomato and mayonnaise. After five minutes the proud owner serves me a hot dog smothered in a sauce made of the above ingredients. Not what I had hoped for, but it's okay, and fills me up.

Back at the hospedaje, I talk to Eliana's daughter Patricia for a few minutes about Chile's new female president, Bachelet, who is said to be a touch left of center, part of the South American trend in that direction. Patricia is cautiously optimistic, and so am I.

Sleep is deep but I wake before the alarm, pack, and then have tea before ham and cheese sandwiches with Roberto. At 7:30 I cross town under a heavy pack, which has now gained all the items that I had left with Eliana while in Argentina. At the park where the colectivos pick up passengers for Niebla, there is only one, with only one passenger waiting. Colectivos wait for four passengers before they leave. We wait for ten minutes. I let the driver know I need to catch a bus out of Corral at nine. A minute later the other passenger, an older man, offers to pay double if I will. That way we can leave right now. I thank him and we're off. At the Niebla dock, I leave the car and walk to the boat, swing my pack on the top deck where a deckhand is lashing down luggage, and step on board as they are pulling away from the dock. The oldster from the car sits next to me. He's from up north, and is here to visit his mother. Excitement fills his face, like a child with wrinkles.

It's close to nine when we hit the dock in Corral. Knowing this waterfront from my last visit, I take a shortcut to the road out of town to be sure not to miss the bus. A bus rolls up, and I ask the driver if he goes to Chaihuin. He takes the time to speak clearly and explain that a bigger bus will come in on this road to the terminal, and then turn around and go out to Chaihuin. Just then the bus he is speaking of rounds the bend coming at us, and he says here it is now. I verify that it will pick me up here, and thank him.

While waiting, I watch some seagulls eating scraps thrown in the water by an old fisherman in a ragged sweater who just rowed to shore in one of those yellow dories. He rows back out to an old double-ended sloop with no engine. He is an old-timer still fishing the old way. It's a hard life, I'm sure.

After forty-five minutes, I decide the bus must not be coming, and I'll start hitching, but traffic is almost non-existent. The third vehicle to pass is another bus, which I wave down, then ask the driver about the bus to Chaihuin. He tells me it comes at ten. To be sure, I echo, "It comes at ten," and he says, "Ten or ten-thirty," "*Ma-o-meno.*" As he leaves, I see the roof of my big yellow bus passing through town. I wave to the driver and as he passes, he signals me to push the back door open, then stops with the back door in front of me. The door yields to a stiff push, my pack joins some flour sacks in the back, and I walk up to pay the driver. "Pay when you get off" he says. After a few hundred yards, an old fisherman wearing a black leather Yukon hat, with the visor and ear flaps tied up, waves the driver down from a small yard enclosed by a white picket fence around a little white house. He smiles with three or four teeth when we stop. Then a guy comes running out of the house with a bag and joins us. At the edge of town we stop for an old woman in a dirty apron who instructs a young guy, maybe her son, to put two black oil buckets full of herring-size fish on board. They're next to me, so I ask the guy beside me what they are called. "Picare," he says, just before he falls asleep sitting straight up.

We pass the gorgeous coastline marred by this gravel road, obviously designed to be paved. I read that the government built many oversized bridges on the southern coast, so that there was good reason to later connect them with a wide road, opening the area to logging trucks and development. Environmentalists oppose it.

When we arrive at the out-of-place and over-built bridge at Chaihuin, the bus turns and I jump off. Immediately, tabanas swarm me, but I try to relax as the locals do. I cross the freeway-grade bridge, and enter the reserve. Tina, a woman from Calgary, welcomes me. She has beautiful deep-blue eyes. I tell her that and she ignores me. I suppose it has been hard for her being a single woman here. But maybe she's just at a loss for words when complimented on colored contact lenses. She gives me a few days worth of camping food, explains that I must buy my own produce and meat, and tells me I have to wait till three for a meeting with Alfredo, the manager. I want to get right to work, so I'm disappointed, but let it go and follow her directions to a produce stand and then an empanada café. The café owner says the empanadas are small, so I order four. "How about a half dozen?" she says. I'm okay with that. She makes them from local snails and shellfish. They're a piquant delicacy.

After lunch I stroll down the long deserted beach twirling a hank of rope overhead to keep the tabanas at bay. Six or eight will attack if I stop. At the end of the beach, I walk a short trail that the reserve has just finished, passing through a scrubby native forest on top of rocky cliffs that drop into the sea. A man is snorkeling, probably harvesting the same things I just ate.

I arrive in the office on time, and wait fifteen minutes for

Alfredo to show up. He calls for Erwin, an Indian park guard who is a trail specialist. We go over the idea, the map, the air photos. I'm beginning to get the feeling that Alfredo has his own little bureaucracy going on here. He doesn't have to make any money, so there's little measurement of his performance. Labor is cheap, so as long as he has people working, it justifies his existence. He doesn't really seem to care how much I get done, and treats me like a grunt. I don't like it, but maybe I *am* one. I'm a field worker. He works in an office. Already I'm less than thrilled with the situation. We have to walk a two-mile road to work while a truck remains parked at camp and unused. They've given me backpacking food to eat, and I have to walk into town to get produce, meat, fish or eggs. They won't drive me up to the destination of the trail they want to build—a grove of ancient, rare *alerce*. I'd love to see that grove.

On the other hand, they put me in a bunkhouse with two twenty-five-year-old college seniors on work-study, Pepe and Pablo, who are welcoming, and genuinely happy to share the small cabin with me.

After changing into work clothes, I head out into the woods with Erwin. His stories of winter floods cause me to stay with my plan to locate the trail about twenty feet up on the side-slope of the flat-bottomed valley. We locate more than a kilometer of trail in a few hours, return to base, eat and shower, then joint Pepe and Pablo and head into the little village of Chaihuin for their big annual fiesta. Lucky timing on my part to arrive today.

Dancers in costumes of the early 1800's, with a heavy Spanish influence, step to traditional music, waving white handkerchiefs overhead in a type of square-dance. The men wear flat, circular-brimmed black hats with flat tops. My generation from the States knows this hat from the *Zorro* TV series of the sixties. Bold-striped ponchos drape their shoulders, the neck slot running vertically, like a V-neck. They wear black *pantalones* and boots with big, silver starburst spurs. The women are in typical Spanish dress, roughly 175 years out of date. Maybe the colors and prints are locally preferred. It depends who you ask and who you believe. One of the musicians plays accordion and three play guitars. There is a chorus of female vocals. The crowd loves them, from adolescents to *antiguos*. I enjoy seeing the rebellious teenagers, with punk hairdos and piercings, digging the traditional scene. At the end of the performance, the dancers come to the front row of the audience and take partners. It's surprising how well everyone dances, without any hesitation or self-consciousness. One kid, about seventeen years old and not appearing to have a traditional bone in his body, dances the tradition better than those you would expect to best him; maybe it's because he crosses the line to sexy movement.

The same woman who fed me lunch is frying empanadas in a booth here, and I order another half-dozen to share with my young friends from the reserve. We take turns buying liters of beer, and enjoy the show.

On our way back to the reserve, we cross the bridge, which is like walking the length of a deserted aircraft carrier. There are only a handful of streetlights in Chaihuin, but they are enough to diminish the starlight. Here in the middle of the bridge I stop the crew to look at the stars. The stars are absolutely amazingly brilliant. I've spent plenty of time in the wilderness and have been to many a desert and mountaintop, and the stars right here on this bridge are among the best I've ever seen. Space is a fog of stars, their depth perceivable.

When I was about thirteen and searching for spiritual truth, I laid on the beach one night after meditation, watching the full moon rise out of the Atlantic. That gave me the sensation of being on a rotating planet. Lying on my back, I felt the curvature of the earth in my spine, and realized that, ultimately, there was no such thing as up or down, and that we look *out*, not up. I imagined my spine was stuck to the surface of the bottom of the earth, so that I was looking down into infinity, with a million galaxies full of a million planets each, all underneath me, and it was all true. And it is all true now. I feel gravity holding my feet to the bridge, and hear the sound of the surf. Such stars and surf are a rare combination. The air has to be dry to see this. I never expected it here in a coastal rainforest. I remember the stars I saw twenty years ago in what was then a remote area on the northwest coast of Costa Rica, where offshore winds blew all the humidity out to sea every night. Right now a dry wind is blowing off of the land, doing the same, opening a window to the heavens.

The Chileans confirm that what I have assumed to be the Southern Cross is indeed that. Tonight it's much lower in the sky than it was down in El Chaltén, where it flew almost directly overhead. They say that a line from Orion's belt to the Southern Cross makes a north-south line, their celestial compass in the absence of Polaris.

The next day Erwin and I head into the forest. Like many simple men I've met in my travels, he would be content to walk the two miles to the trailhead without saying a word. Occasionally I break the silence when something attracts my attention: a flower, a caterpillar, a bird… he knows about everything in the forest, and teaches me.

It is a tough day. I battle thickets of bamboo using diagonal sword cuts. I cut the vines that wrap around my limbs with close-distance techniques. The hard work is a good way to release all the frustrations of losing my photographs. I make headway, but at the end of the day, I'm beat. I have to scout ahead many times before deciding where to locate each section of trail. While I thrash around in the brush I leave Erwin at the end of our line to answer "Aqui!" when I yell "Donde estas?" through the thickets. Once I decide where to go, I work my way back to him along the easiest route, hugging the contours of the land. It's a productive day, through dint and severe effort, but it forces me to take it easy after a swim in the river and a meal.

In the morning my body is not ready for another *Dia de Guerra*, and, as luck would have it, Pepe announces that he is driving up to the alerces. When I tell him I've never seen them, he says, "Vamos!" and I kill most of the morning driving logging roads, and then descending a steep straight trail into yet another type of enchanted forest, this one of 3,000-year-old trees that look like miniature sequoias. They are covered with vines that bear dark, fuchsia-pink tubular flowers. Twenty percent of the woody plants in this forest have reddish, tubular flowers. It is interesting, then, to ponder the fact that only three of the thirty-six hummingbirds of the southern cone make it down this far. I like their English names—the white-sided hillstar, the giant hummingbird, and the green-backed firecrown.

By noon we are back at work, at the top of the floodplain, where the valley walls hit the edges of the main stream in the valley, and I'm deciding where to cross the stream. I discover a beautiful route up a natural levee built of boulders washed down from an outcrop upstream. Hundred-year storms have, over thousands of years, pushed these rocks downstream, and where the stream bends to the left, the boulders were thrown to the right, creating a perfect route for a trail heading upstream, with bogs between the levee and the steep valley wall. The levee is covered with ten-foot-tall ferns that bleed red when cut. I cut only a few, just enough to see. They're too beautiful to cut. A *martin pescador grande* flies by. It's a ringed kingfisher, 50% larger than our North American belted kingfisher, and sporting a rusty breast. Ahead, while scouting, I come upon a *huet-huet* who maintains silence and walks away into a thicket. This bird makes the rainforest calls that remind me of old movies about the African jungles. In my book it is written as "hooopooopooopooopooop-ooop…increasing slightly in pitch, volume and tempo."

Again we get a lot done, but I still have some energy left after dinner, so I walk to the last night of the fiesta with Pablo. He had asked Alfredo to borrow the reserve truck to go to the fiesta, was denied, and is feeling a bit disgruntled. He is an Eco-Tourism major, so I ask if he's planning to work for the government, and we begin talking about bureaucracies. He is a high-energy guy—the type who likes to get a lot done when he works, like me, so I warn him that when an organization does not have to make money, but relies on donations or taxes to exist, performance often declines. I know this from experience. I went to work for the Forest Service in Alaska upon graduating from college, but couldn't remain in the bureaucracy, and quit; I'm too production-oriented. There was little incentive to get much done, as it would create more work for the office-folk who ran the show in town. The one reward for my productivity was that I was always welcomed back after I would take off to go run white-water or plant trees for a month.

Alfredo does have his own little bureaucracy here. The reserve has two machetes but no file. Erwin and I had to borrow a file from a visiting firefighter to sharpen our tools. Yet Alfredo uses a new laptop with software that I've never seen before to show me where he would like the trail, which was Erwin's idea, not his. So I figure he treats the truck as if it's his, never to be used on unofficial business by anyone but him. It leads me on to an issue I have been contemplating for several months, that is, the balance of competition and cooperation, and Pablo and I discuss the paradox that neither works well without some of the other.

Too much competition creates an environment lacking compassion. Too much cooperation stagnates creativity. Part of the reason my country leads the world in so many fields is that we honor an individual's creativity and ingenuity. Part of the reason we are leading the world into trouble is our general inability to cooperate. But it could also be said that nations have fallen due to their demand that citizens cooperate and not compete. The creative expression of the individual is essential for self-fulfillment. But fulfillment of the desires of one's ego can be a lethal poison to society. Again, it comes down the degree of identification we as individuals have with our small self we call the ego. If everyone's actions originate from the question, "How can I contribute," we can approach an ideal society previously considered an unattainable utopia. But when our actions originate from the question, "How can I acquire for myself," we are doomed to compete forever, and render our largest commons, our planet, inhospitable to our species. I'm reminded of my yearning for a place to thrive, and realize that what I seek is more utopian that I had thought. My dissatisfaction with The States is based on the economic, cultural and political climate, all of which are the result of intense competition and selfishness. I am not really looking for paradise, but utopia.

Pablo begins talking about Greek philosophy, and my poor Spanish causes me to stumble and fall behind in the conversation, but we then arrive at the fiesta.

It's dragging. A contest for the best empanada, judged by cheering, goes on forever. Finally, the local lady wins, of course, and a cumbia dance contest begins with a "famous" local singing karaoke style, to canned music. I cut my losses by heading back early, thinking of the challenge in the woods tomorrow. Erwin joins me. The others arrive some time in the middle of the madrugada.

The next day is a hard one, searching for a route past a pinch in the valley where a vertical rock wall (the source of the levee material) opposes a steep slope covered with dense vegetation reminiscent of chaparral. The stiff stuff steals my water bottle from my lumbar pack, and my bandana from my back pocket. Twice we abandon our exploration in the frustrating thicket to descend to the relative sanity of the creek bed. Eventually I find a good route below the chaparral. It's a bit of a ledge cutting through a steep forest. After it climbs about fifty feet, it descends to the creek again, and follows the toe of the slope beside a ten-foot rock wall. I like this because I have the hunch that we will have to cross again, but it's late, and I call it a day when we get to the next crossing. Having lost my bottle of boiled water, I lower my head to drink from the creek. The lack of abundant mammals may be the reason all information I receive says that you can drink the water. As I turn away from sucking up a belly full, I see otter (*huillin*) shit on a rock beside me. Then I see *pudu* tracks in the mud. I know that pudu are small deer, but I point to the tracks and say, "baby pudu" to Erwin. He says, "No, adult." The tracks are barely over an inch long. The full-grown pudu stands a mere foot tall at the shoulders, and weighs about fifteen to twenty pounds.

The next day is my last day of work. We go out in the morning and finish by connecting the trail to the road, the section we skipped on the first day when we were wandering around trying to figure out where to go. First, we have to find where we started from, and that takes a little time. We excite a huet-huet who calls its name when threatened.

The trail location turns out well. We connect the trail to the road with the half-kilometer of new, graceful, and natural route that we located before lunch, then head back to base. I'm happy with the job. Erwin tells me he has learned a lot from working with me, and that feels good. On the way home we see an eared dove, Chile's version of a mourning dove, in a tree over the river. He tells me it's unusual to see one alone. They like to be in flocks. I relate stories of the billions of passenger pigeons that once lived in North America—how they would break oak limbs with their weight when roosting, darken the sky when passing overhead. I tell him how it would take two days for a flock to pass by, and how they are now extinct because of the stupidity of the European pioneers who hunted every last one.

Back at the base, I quickly have a shower and lunch, and say goodbye to my friends. Alfredo thanks me and asks if there is anything he can do for me. I've been thinking of visiting the famous mountain resort of Pucon before heading back to Cachagua, so I request that he make a bus reservation for me. I tell him I need to be on a bus to Pucon tonight. By the time I say goodbye to everyone, Alfredo comes back and assures me a ticket will be waiting for me at The Nature Conservancy office in Valdivia.

I cross the piece of misplaced freeway that spans the river and when I walk up to the bus, the driver starts the engine. By the time I reach the top step we are rolling. I wouldn't be surprised if they were waiting for me, but I wonder how they knew.

Leaving town on this fine late summer day, I am admiring the cove, and wondering what kind of wave breaks on the river mouth bar when there is a swell arriving from the winds north of Antarctica. This place is a gem. A hand-painted sign says that a house is for sale. It's on the bluff right above the sand bar. I imagine the possibilities.

When the bus arrives at Corral, I try to get off at my spot to short-cut behind the boat yard, but the driver tells me to wait, then points to me when we get to a spot closer to the ferry dock. I walk along a stinky eddy of the fisherman's cove, reeking of sewage, not fish. I pass old warehouses with disco signs on them. The only indication that they are indeed discos at night is the lipstick-printed cigarette butts littering the path. They probably open the doors at midnight. As I set foot on the dock, a boat unties and maneuvers into the bay with the loading stairs, as if they were waiting for me. It couldn't be possible. I know the routine now, step up on the foredeck to place my pack on top of my staff, against the windshield where it can be lashed down by the deckhand, and then take a seat on the aft deck with the other passengers. As my feet hit the other shore, a bus pulls up, opens the door, and waits for me. You gotta love the transportation in this country. Everyone else takes colectivos because they are faster and the price is about the same, but I'm in no hurry. I have plenty of time before the night bus leaves.

In Valdivia I go to the office, but it's closed for lunch, so I hike to the hospedaje. The family is just sitting down for lunch and they invite me to join them. I accept, and we have pork, rice, tomatoes, pickles and wine. The bankcard arrived yesterday. I feel like that ordeal is finally over until I open it and read that you have to call an 800 number from your *home phone* to activate it. How can the Wells Fargo people be so stupid to send that to me in Chile? We all have a good laugh.

I tell stories about the work in the forest. After lunch, Eliana gives a lecture about education and the importance of enjoying your work. I realize she is on a tangent spurred by thoughts of my volunteering, and the college kids out there on work-study. It's a solid twenty-minute monologue. She loves to talk. It is great practice for my ear. I'm only slightly better at understanding her than I was a month ago, but maybe she is speaking a bit faster now, thinking that my Spanish is better. It would be like her to do that.

She gives me 10,000 pesos that she said she short-changed me the last time I was here, apologizing for her absent-mindedness. She says she went to get change and got sidetracked on another chore, and since I trust her so much, I wasn't paying attention.

Eliana wants to know if I have work with The Nature Conservancy now. I tell her they never offered, but I have to go to the office to pick up my bus ticket, and will see if they appreciated my thirty hours of hard work enough to pay my fare. When I get to the office, everyone is thanking me because they heard I did a great job. I ask about the ticket, and no one knows what I'm talking about. I mention the name of the secretary who was supposed to get it, and she says she forgot. They offer to make a reservation for me, but the terminal is nearby, so I decline.

I buy a ticket to Pucon, then go to the market for *pulmay*, yet another type of seafood stew I want to check to see if it's like the fantastic bowl I had in Valparaiso. Unfortunately, I was too new to the country then to remember the name of it. Pulmay has shellfish, chicken and sausage in it. When it comes it is a big clay bowl filled with mussels, clams, sausage, chicken, and a ham hock. No sauce or broth, just a piece of potato, and a slice of garlic and onion. It's not bad, especially with a bit of hot sauce, some bread and a beer. But it's not the Valparaiso dish. While waiting, I break a sweat in the late afternoon sun reflecting off the river into these second-story windows—the semi-circular tops of tall ones that extend below to the ground, giving the place the feeling of an urban studio flat. So after the meal I go out in the plaza to cool off. A two-man comedy team is performing to a large audience of people walking home from work. I sit on a bench, and from the ornate iron streetlamp above me a pigeon shits on my arm. It reminds me of the pigeons in the remote little towns on the Atlantic coast of Patagonia. I *still* wonder how they got there. Here in the park, the pigeons coexist with the chimangos—the relatives of falcons. The two species intermingle while searching for crumbs in the dirt—the hawk and the dove, side by side.

Back at the hospedaje, I hang out with Eliana for an hour before I get on the bus to Pucon. Leaving Valdivia, the flooded valleys are blooming with water lilies and other plants that initiate the process of this water becoming a marsh, then a bog, and one day solid land again. In the last light of day, regal volcanoes watch over green fields covered by the long shadows of tall hardwoods, and separated by clean sparkling creeks. It's such an attractive environment. I think about living here, realizing that I'd always be an outsider, and never fully assimilate; still, the area invites exploration both to the east and west of this north/south highway. I haven't yet seen the coastal towns north of Valdivia. Putting the seat back to recline position, I plug into the iPod. Us3 plays "Nowadays." "Nowadays it seems we're in the last phase. Maybe it's me."—Just the way I feel right now. It seems like the shit has got to hit the fan soon with all the problems in the world—global warming, peak oil, dying oceans, population growth, farm and soil loss, species extinction rate soaring, et cetera, et cetera. Part of an intelligent search for a new home in the twenty-first century is to take into account the predicted changes. This could be a good place to live when the world takes a stumble. Computer projections say global warming will cause decreased rainfall all through Chile, but that might actually improve this rainy spot.

At dusk, docile domestic animals dally in flooded dells. In Us3's tune "Sheep" the vocalist raps, "Some look at my face and say, 'you're quite absurd,' I say, 'why, 'cause I'm not down with the herd?'"

CHAPTER 32

Pucon

As we roll into Pucon, I'm thinking about emigration on a mythic level because I've been listening to reggae again. The rootsy genre is rife with references to repatriation to the motherland. In "The Border," Gregory Isaacs sings,

> "If I could reach the border,
> Then I would step across"
> and,
> "I'm a-leavin' out of Babylon…
> This place could never be our home."

> And Ricky Grant:
> "Far, far away,
> There is my land.
> That's where I belong.
> I must be there one day."
> And Dennis Brown sings, "Take me to the Promised Land"

My time of roaming through the southern cone, absorbing impressions of the land and the people is nearing its end, and these lyrics remind me of my quest. The Jamaicans' yearning is for their true home, Africa. As an American of Scottish/German/Hungarian/Romanian blood, I really don't identify with any homeland other than North America, a land I love deeply.

My ancestors all left their homes of their free will. They escaped famine, poverty and landlessness, and the threat of annihilation by war, and sought a better life in a foreign land. I contain their genes, not those of a people abducted from the land they loved. The Rastas identify themselves as the lost tribe of Israel, so they become a mortise that accepts the biblical story of the search for the promised land like a tenon perfectly cut to fit them. I don't imagine anyplace being promised to me, and fully acknowledge that what I seek may not even exist. But while the specifics of the songs differ, I've been responding to the soulful expression of the yearning for a home, a refuge from the struggle, the comfort of justice and brotherhood. That yearning was a large portion of the motivating force that brought me here. And I feel that yearning amplified now, with no need to do more than relate to the music.

From the terminal I walk to a hostel recommended by the guide book as a good deal, with good food, Spanish classes, and helpful information, but I find the price up 40%, Spanish classes finished for the weekend, and the owner seemingly exhausted from a long season, with a body language that says, "Don't bother me." Nevertheless, I take a room to avoid the late-night hike around town looking for something better.

My roommate is a young Brit who tells me he just found a good place for almost half the price, so I get directions from him and will follow his move tomorrow. Now my body demands sleep.

By the time I woke, I was ready for lunch and found a burger the size of the dinner plate it came on. Apparently there is a bit of local competition for whose burgers are biggest. Now, belly-full and body-glad, I'm planning on a day of rest, and I've heard that you can swim in the lake, so I walk to it in the strong mountain sun. The famous black sand beach of Pucon is actually black cinder from the volcano. It's rough on my soft feet as I cross the beach. Enjoying the company of a woman would be a nice way to relax, so I turn right, away from the crowds. The woman I'd get along with would probably be at the end of the beach. The last person I pass is an attractive young woman, so I stop about forty feet beyond her. She gets up and dives into the lake, and I ask how the water is. "Super-rico," she says. In a few minutes she asks me for a match. It happens that there's one in my pack, so I walk over and light her roach. It's the first time I've seen a joint in South America. We chat and get along well. When I ask where she's from, she tells me she lives here. "What do you do here?" "I'm studying tourism." I'm surprised that she's a student. She seems older. I'd guess she's in her late twenties. I ask if it's her last year of school, and she says no, it's her first. I'm confused. "But…but, how old are you?" "Eighteen." It doesn't make sense; she seems so much more mature. We laugh at my surprise. I'm careful not to say she looks older, as I know women are sensitive to that—these days so am I. Immediately she asks how old I am and I tell her. Now it's her turn to be surprised. "Are you serious?" "Why would I lie about that?" "I thought you were about thirty-five."

She asks why I travel alone. I explain that there are things I want to do that don't have meaning for others, and that it's easy for me to endure hardship in order to do them. When I'm alone, there is no one to complain about it all, and I'm happy. There are things that I want to do that others can't do because they are not strong enough. Then I wonder if I'm full of shit—if I am operating on old information, refusing to admit that I'm getting older and losing my edge.

She offers me a toke and I decline, so she asks if I smoke, and I tell her no more, I did when I was young, but now it just makes me stupid. Immediately my mind remembers the stupidity of leaving the camera on the roof of the car. I'd be doing that kind of thing all the time if I smoked what Chileans call *pito*. I admit I smoke once or twice a year at a reggae festival or some such occasion. She loves reggae and asks about the festivals. We have some of the best reggae events in the world right in Northern California, and I list some of the greats that I've seen recently. It's interesting that she doesn't know the names of some of the old masters—U-Roy, Gregory Isaacs, Rico Rodriguez, Culture—she never heard of them, so I take out my iPod and turn her on to a dozen tunes. She loves each one and writes down the names.

She's an ecotourism student, but she's not sure if that's what she wants to study because the people in the industry are money-hungry—my experience with Chilean eco-tourism exactly. She's thinking about geography or art history—she likes art and architecture. "What kind of architecture?" I ask. "Rustic" is her perfect reply. We're kindred spirits.

The lake invites me for a plunge in its cool water before the sun gets too low to warm my body afterward. When I return we decide to have dinner together. She suggests eleven, but I convince her that ten will work better, and she gives me her address.

Back at the hospedaje I take a shower and lie down, falling victim to mental self-flagellation. What the hell is wrong with me that I have a date with an eighteen-year-old? In the end I have no use for the numbers. We have a good connection and that includes a disregard for the numbers on both sides. So, at ten I show up at the given address, that is, where the address *should* be, and it doesn't exist. I ask a few of the neighbors to be sure. It's hard to believe that she did this intentionally. I think she was stoned and transposed some numbers, but I guess I'll never know. I'm standing there in the street feeling that vacuousness that I felt when I realized my camera was gone, though not as intense. People like her are rare. Suddenly I'm aware that the aspect of my discontent that causes a yearning for kindred spirits, when boiled down to its essence, is loneliness.

Forcing myself to shrug it off, I head out to eat, and pass a trendy place advertising half-price on Mexican food. It's the first time I've seen either things on a sign outside a Chilean restaurant, so I enter. While I'm standing at the empty bar, talking to the bartender about the menu, an Indian woman with the face of a supermodel walks in and sits beside me. When the bartender leaves, I turn to her, and foregoing all introductions, ask her if she would like to join me at a table out on the deck. She says it's too cold, I should sit right here with her. I'm not going to argue.

She is Marguerita, an MD on a three-month working visit from Columbia. She's answering my question about the exchange program when she stops and asks if I have a problem. I'm caught in a state of mesmerization, taking in only the beauty of her face, and missing entire sentences of her story. She has the most perfect face of any Indian I've seen—damn near flawless—and I'm fascinated with the experience of looking at her, while knowing that it is genetic programming that causes me to respond in this way. I'm a sucker for a stunning mulatta or a fine feminine Japonesa, and I've always thought that even *that* was a program of intentional evolution (just as Latinos and Africanos adore blondes)—the driver of an eventual mixing of the races that will eventually leave us with one race of earthling. She is a work of art—at least her face is. She is conservatively dressed in a way that conceals her body.

I just tell her the truth about where my mind was and she takes it like she's heard it ten-thousand times, so I ask about Chile's heath care system. I'm genuinely interested to know her opinion of this country's social healthcare. She says it's bad. Sometimes people have to wait two years to get eyeglasses, and the dental program is worse. When I tell her that I've seen many people with no teeth, she goes off too fast and with too many medical terms for me to follow, so I just look at her face and enjoy her beauty while eating my enchiladas.

At the end of her tirade, I change the subject by asking what she does for fun. I might have predicted that she likes to dance, and that salsa is her favorite. What about cumbia, I ask. After all, it's Columbian dance music. It's the music of the coastal people, she says. She is from the mountains, and goes on about the music and dancing traditions, about the mountain people and dancing fiestas on religious holidays. I ask if she likes Sidestepper and she dismisses it by stating that she doesn't like music from the United States. "They're from Columbia," I say. Rather than try to explain anything I pull out my iPod and hand her the earbuds while I key-up "Paloma." She likes it. I switch to "Que Sera" and she begins trying to convince me how good the music is, which makes me laugh. When my mug of draft Torobado is empty the bartender asks if I want another, but I decline. I ask for a pen to write the name "Sidestepper" on a napkin for la Columbiana, give the pen back and ask for the bill. While Marguerita is older and more beautiful than the young Chilean, and even though she is sweet-hearted, we have nothing in common, so I'm ready to call it a night. To my surprise, Marguerita asks for her bill too. And after we pay, we walk out together. She wants a cigarette, so I ask to join her and we walk down the street smoking. Everything is cool until all of a sudden she realizes that she doesn't know where she is, or how to get to her hospedaje. When I ask, she doesn't know the name of the place, or what street it's on, just that it is near a park and a gas station. "No problem" I assure her, it's a small town. "We'll just walk until you recognize something."

Eventually that strategy works, and while approaching her hospedaje, she asks to do something together tomorrow and I tell her I will come looking for her in the morning. I kiss her turned cheek goodnight and in my hugging arms I feel a body that has never exercised and is void of the will to do so. I walk away wondering what the hell I am doing again, and by the time I get to the corner I've decided to act without honoring my word; not an easy thing for me to do. But I know that I need to get out of town, into the mountains, away from pretty women. I'll never see her again.

Morning tea is sipped alone in the comodor below my room while the sun rises high enough for a Chilean to open shop. The empanada shopkeeper opens the door for me a few minutes

early, and gives me breakfast and directions to a tourist information office. I find it easily, but the girl at the desk knows nothing
about backpacking trails. She can only direct me to guided tours.
She tells me about a park nearby where there is a trail and shows
me a brochure-style map, but can't give it to me because it's the
only one she has. I laugh and shake my head saying, "Increible."
She gives me the map when I leave, aware that, in a town famous
for mountain sports, I think she and her office are next to useless.

At the bus terminal I get the hours of departures for buses to the park. At the supermarket, "*El Tit,*" I top off my food bag.
At a bookstore I buy a better map. Now I need fuel. I emptied my
fuel bottle in Puerto Natales before leaving for the airport. The
single hardware store in town is located inside the supermarket—a
sign that this town is getting Americanized—and that part of El
Tit is closed on Sunday. Everyone tells me I have to go to *El Mol*
(pronounced "mole"), which is a couple of kilometers out of town.
I have no idea what El Mol is, but I hit the hospedaje, change my
flip-flops for walking shoes, and get on the road with my thumb
out. A guy in a little red pickup truck picks me up and when we
approach another El Tit, he pulls over to let me out. I ask why they
call it El Mol, and he says a Mol is what they call a place with a
lot of stores—it's a *mall*—but the other stores haven't been built
yet. They sell *becina blanca*. I'm not sure exactly what it is, but it's
some kind of cleaning solvent they always give me when I ask for
white gas for my stove. It burns clean, but very slowly. A liter will
guarantee I have fuel for the rest of my time in Chile, and I'm back
on the road with an hour until my bus leaves.

At the hospedaje I pack, check out, and head to the place
the Brit told me about, which is right by the terminal. There I
tell the owner's mother that I am going into the mountains and
will check in here when I return in three days. I ask her to store
my street gear for me, giving her a pizza that I bought at El Tit
in appreciation of the favor. When I get to the terminal, it's a few
minutes before the bus leaves.

The *mini* is filled with campesinos. I'm the only tourist on board. It's not long before the road shrinks and we begin taking side roads to deliver old ladies to their farms. The road becomes a steep, single-lane, rutted route that slams my shoulder into the window as we pass road cuts revealing layers of the same cinders that are on the beach. By the time we drop into the lake-filled valley of the park I'm the only one left on board.

Once again, the Chilean park fees are surprisingly high—4,000 to enter, 7,000 to camp. "That's more than a hotel," I complain. "Yeah, but here you are in nature," the ranger replies, apparently believing his logic. We look at his map and make a plan. Camping is limited to the lakeside at the park entrance or at a refugio in the center of the park, in the next valley, which I can't reach with such a late start. He agrees to store my pack while I hike a nearby ridge today. I'll camp here at the entrance tonight and hike in to the refugio tomorrow. In a few minutes I'm on the trail.

The path goes up. It's a green tunnel through kila, but suddenly the vegetation opens to a sparse ground cover below the canopy of an old growth *coique* forest—large hardwoods with no branches on the curvy trunks for the first sixty feet. Obviously, all of the lower slopes were clear-cut before the kila grew. At a spot with views of the pillars supporting the overstory, I stop for lunch—sandwiches of *Pate del Campo*. I'm a sucker for local foods of the country people, so the name hooked me, but it's nothing but liverwurst. As I climb, the hardwoods yield to pure stands of *araucaria*, a strange pine that must be related to the Norfolk Island pine, since both areas were once united in Gondwanaland. Instead of needles, they have wide triangular spikes that grow out of the branches in a spiral pattern like the leaves of a pineapple—the only connection I ever made between a pine tree and that strangely named fruit. Stepping off the trail, I allow Campesino ladies to pass with sacks of nuts on their shoulders. The eldest says, "No se nada." Either she's anticipating that I'm going to ask a question, or she is illegally harvesting these nuts inside park boundaries. I become intent on finding these nuts.

A carpintero negro visits a trunk overhead, before I cross an open grassy saddle, and the trail enters another araucaria forest, this one enchanted, festooned with long thick pelts of light green lichen, which we call "old man's beard" in Alaska. A buzz overhead must be coming from unseen bees. There is puma shit, human size, but full of hair. The trail is littered with giant pine nuts the size of my little finger. Up a ridge the trail climbs and eventually begins to cross rock outcrops with views. The second such promontory has a stunning vista—a scene from a Chinese ink painting. A granite spur to the east converges with the one I'm on when they both hit the peak to the north; it's covered with ancient araucaria, their trunks cloaked in old man's beard. The dark domes of the branches make them look like giant mushrooms at this distance. To the south and southeast, volcanoes loom in the sky, separated from earth by the haze of smoke from the fires of campesinos. The three ridges below them are progressively darker as they near me. Fronds of araucaria swoop from above like tails of cats, curled up at the ends. And I have no camera.

At a higher outcropping there are views of the central valley to the west. It's covered with low clouds, their tops are lit by the sun, which is low—about at my elevation—but now over New Zealand.

The now-familiar sounds of the forest birds, the chortles and descending whoops, pierce the forest as I descend rapidly, racing the setting sun as the first of those clouds to the west enter the mountain valleys like ships coming into safe harbors. Flocks of noisy parakeets pass on their way to their roost. This is one of the most peculiar forests on the planet. I imagine a person flying directly from the northern hemisphere to Pucon, and immediately coming to this trail, seeing these bizarre trees below floating volcanoes, with these exotic bird calls. He'd be shocked as if he'd landed on another planet.

When I reach the coique forest I'm in the clouds, lit by

the last rays of sun, and the light is magical. I make the road as twilight arrives, and the ranger's house-lights are on, so I stop. There are two rangers, and the man with the key to the office is gone, but the one here at the cabin goes to look for him while I continue down to the office

The guy with the key is laid-back, living a tranquilo life in this quiet park. When he arrives he asks how my hike was and I tell him it was very pretty. When I ask about the araucaria, he launches into a history lesson. The name of the park, *Huerquehue*, means "Place of the Messengers." The Mapuche used to gather up in the grassy saddle for ceremonial meetings in which they honored the araucaria by growing one at the center of a square, each side of which corresponded to four elements. It was known as "The place of the five." The fire element was associated with the devil, whose home was the nearby volcano, Villarica, which is the most active in all of South America. Messengers from all the Mapuche tribes would gather here to establish laws, and return to inform their people of the adopted codes. It's a fascinating story, but while I'm listening I can't help noticing how the muscles around his mouth don't work symmetrically, the left side being quite dead, and I wonder if when he was young he endured some trauma that affected the right hemisphere of his brain. Once, after sitting in the presence of a spiritual master for several minutes, I smiled and felt the asymmetry of my smile dissolve. In the Indian traditions they call it *darshan*, the grace of the guru, that radiant healing that emanates from such a person, in this case healing me of a tweak I didn't even know I had.

When I drop down to the campground, it's on the verge of darkness, but I am surprised to see that it is well-designed and built, as developed campgrounds go. The picnic tables, fences and benches are made of hand-hewn timbers. A material that is impossible to find in The States, but more attractive than sawn timbers or logs in the round. It's the work that makes them both pleasing to the eye, and too expensive to make back home. We don't even use the verb *hew* anymore.

After "Italian rice," I fix my boot again (that glue only lasts a few hikes), and fall asleep to the rhythm of two-inch waves lapping the beach.

G regarious parakeets wake me, and when I unzip my bag, the sound startles a huet-huet, causing it to announce its name. When I exit my tent, I catch the bird exposed in the middle of a clearing, causing it to sprint for cover, leaning forward like a road-runner. They fly about as well as a chicken.

A cloud covers this lake-filled valley like a loose lid. But rays of golden sunshine penetrate the eastern edge and stretch across the valley to light the old-growth forest high on the western slope. At the lakeshore a six-inch-wide beach and a one-foot-high bluff to the forest floor indicate that the water level never changes. A pair of coot paddle by while I cook oatmeal, and I suddenly real-ize that the word *rallado* on the label of the little bag of "grated" coconut is the same word I hear in a sidestepper tune, but never understood because they drop the *d* and make it "rallao." Slowly, very slowly, I am learning this language.

By the time my pot is washed, the sun has burned off most of the clouds and two campesinos are rowing a little boat across the lake. While I'm packing, the first bus of the day ar-rives at the park entrance, and by the time I'm on the trail, I'm behind all the day-hikers who got off the bus, but I pass them all in the first mile of climbing the valley's headwall. Maybe I *am* still a strong hiker. The trail takes me through holly-leafed bushes with red pendulous flowers, and then enters that old-growth that was lit in the early morning sun sneaking under the edge of the cloud. It's a pure stand of big trees with a feathery under-story of kila. Passing a low branch, I realize that the tree is a species of lenga in yet another habitat and form. Here, the most majestic I've seen, almost the complete opposite of the scrub I remember struggling to survive on the pampas north of Punta Arenas.

The trail is not bad, but the signs can be ridiculous. One points at a side trail to a waterfall and, routed into the wood, it says it is 1,050 kilometers away, but the *k* of the *km* is painted over. Another, at a fork in the trail names the two destinations, one above the other, but has no arrows to say which is which. Someone scratched a shallow one in with a knife, and I have to assume it is correct.

The route crosses a saddle between valleys which are dotted with small, almost ornamental lakes, then it passes view spots at the top of the next valley wall. A blue painted stake—that's the local trail marker—is driven between the two diverging trails of a fork, having so little meaning that it's worth a photograph just for the humor in it. I take the wrong fork and end up on cattle trails descending straight down through a steep burned area taken over by kila. A few hundred feet below, I am cursing when I find the trail again, quiet myself, and round the next bend to encounter three cows, two calves, and a bull lounging on the trail chewing their cuds. Luckily, even the bull is docile and they let me by. All the adults have full-grown horns, so I give them a wide berth.

In the bottom of the valley, at a flat between two converging streams where the map and the ranger have both indicated a refugio, there *is* no refugio. It's a small clearing kept mowed by livestock, with a few crude tables and benches, and an outhouse and lean-to, all fashioned from thick and wide hand-hewn slabs. I was expecting at least a hut and a ranger, hoping to ask about the trip to the hot springs, wondering if I could attempt it.

The maps are contradictory. The map I bought in town contradicts *itself.* One side shows a road passing the springs, the other, at a larger scale, shows only a trail, and the area I really need to see—where that trail goes—is covered with an advertisement for the map company. Many of the roads on the map are dead ends. The map is so bad it doesn't even show the road I came into the park on. I consult the map I got at the park entrance, but it's a joke too. The black and blue inks are bleeding through the paper so that it's hard to know which line is on which side. I remember the road to Buchupureo, and think that even if there *is* a road, I'd be walking. Probably for days.

On the park map, I check the table of trail distances to see how far I am from the springs, but this place—the only place to camp legally in the interior of the park—is not listed on the table, while the springs at Rio Blanco, actually beyond the park boundary, are included. For amusement, I study the map and find a house symbol with the word refugio at this spot. The zones of altitude are represented in the typical gradient of colors; dark green for 0 to 300 meters, blue-green for 300 to 600, green for 600 to 900, light green for 900-1200, but then a sky-blue for 1200 to 1500 makes it look like a giant moat occupies those contours, and next, it makes a ridiculous leap to apricot for 1500 to 1800, before returning to a different light green for 1800 to 2100. The trails are dashed lines made of blocks of ink that would be the size of football fields, separated by similar distances. But, it does show a road coming into the park at it's entrance, and one leaving the "thermal baths." The map given to me by the girl at the information office only shows the park, and the baths are outside the park boundary, so they and any road to them don't exist.

When an old campesino passes on horseback, I ask about the road from Rio Blanco. He informs me that there are no buses, and that travel is difficult. I decide not to drop the four miles down to Rio Blanco, and then return to this camp. I make the pea soup that departing climbers left with Evelyn, and that she passed on to me. It's not bad. I knew that it was fortified with nutrients, but only now am I reading on the label that it's formulated for pregnant and breast-feeding women. The shadows of late afternoon are already damp, so everything goes under the cover of the tent vestibule. Argentinean mountaineers know the importance of a tent vestibule, and I'm reminded that they asked me what the English name for it is, so they can deal with North Americans and Europeans who are selling tents. When they asked, the Australian girl was there and I laughed at her expression when I answered. Apparently she had never heard the word. It's one of those words you don't realize is so strange until you try to explain it. I was able to make sense of it by tracing it to the Latin root *vest*, to adorn, which Spanish uses in the word for dress or suit, *vestido*, and said it's a room to take your foul weather clothes and boots off when you enter. I have no idea if I'm correct, but it sounded good.

At sunset the tent welcomes me, but I can't sleep. Outside, the full moon lights the strange araucarias on the rocky ridge to the west, and the stars are sparse in the still, damp, moonlit air. Back inside, I listen to the "blue jazz" playlist, centered around Miles Davis's "Kind of Blue," and I drift off.

The morning sky is a cheerful blue, but the tent is wetter than after any driving Patagonia storm. I have a few drops of condensation inside, which I've never seen before. The air was so saturated that my breath had nowhere to go. The fly is holding as much water as possible, both inside and out. A dark green cow print in the dew-laden grass suggests that the animal passed my tent in the night. Could I have been so unconscious? It's a scary thought. Maybe the crushing weight of the cow somehow causes the grass to shed water, and the print is a day old.

The becina blanca burns so slowly that it takes twenty minutes to boil a pot of water. I'm realizing that this is the stuff they use to mop the floors at the bus terminals. Finally I feel the Earl Grey warm my insides while I wait for the sun to hit the clearing. The outhouse, located on bottomland a mere thirty feet from the stream, is another wonder of hewn members. It is built for some giant, with a high seat that has a one-foot-diameter hole cut into it. The door is the most amazing thing—a single hand-hewn 1x22 inch plank. After my tent dries on a pile of hand-hewn 4x16's at the west end of the field, I pack and climb back up to the lakes, chasing cattle off the trail. A few minutes after I enter the woods up on the saddle, I run into two day-hikers, a grey-haired gringo, and a young Chilean man, who ask about the refugio. I tell them there *is* no refugio, that they should just continue on for a few minutes till they get views up and down the valley, with the araucarias up on the ridges, and then turn around without dropping into the valley, which is burned and infested with cattle.

The gringo, Glenn, tells me they are on they're way to Rio Blanco, and that his wife is going to pick them up there. "What a great trip," I compliment, and perceiving my envy, he invites me to join them; looking at my pack, he adds that if I can't keep up, I can meet them at the hot springs. I tell him it's not a problem.

Glenn is a former science teacher from Montana, but he and his wife spent years teaching in grade schools abroad—Saudi Arabia, Guam, Peru. They were on a trip eighteen years ago when they fell in love with this land of lakes, forests and volcanoes, and never left. Now they have a little hotel that they've made into one of the best in the country.

His science background makes Glenn a wealth of information on the forest. As we hike, he answers all my questions. The holly is a laurel. The biggest araucarias we see are five to six feet in diameter and about 3,000 years old. They are the longest-living things on the planet. Chile has some that are 4,700 years old, beating the bristle-cone pines of the Sierra Nevada, famous for their age. He's an aficionado, I can tell. So I explain to him that I like the way the bark wants to fracture into hexagonal blocks, but rarely makes it to a complete hexagon. This takes me off on a tangent about geometric patterns in nature, the expression of organization and intelligence, the Chinese concepts of wu and li, and my experiences observing Nature while on long meditation retreats. He's stimulated by the conversation and excitedly describes the bark of the roots, where hexagons can be found.

As we drop back down the slope and shoo cattle off the trail, he says he's been complaining to the park for years about the cattle, which are strictly forbidden according to law, but that the CONAF authorities just shrug and say they don't know who owns them. He tells them to kill one and invite all the locals to a barbecue, and they'll find out who the owner is.

At my camp, we stop for lunch. Glenn is celebrating his sixtieth birthday with this hike, and he and his friend Javier enjoy birthday cake after sandwiches. They want to see the lake perched up on the slope to the north before we cross to the east and descend to the *aguas termales*, so I drop my pack in the bushes and we climb through the woods. When we pass what looks like some kind of wild squash with a bright tangerine flower, Glenn warns that it is like a stinging nettle, the only plant in the forest to avoid. The pine nuts are *piñones*, which, he teaches me, can be eaten raw after peeling off the papery husk. It feels good to eat them. My body welcomes the live enzymes after so much processed food in the mountains. At the lake we see last night's campesino and his wife fishing, Glenn gives them cheery greetings, and as we walk away, I tell him that they are the owners of the cattle. He's confused. "Remember the sign we passed that said, 'Pan, 10 minutos' with an arrow down a trail from my camp? They live down there. I saw him ride in last night. So these are probably their cattle."

On the return downslope we spot carpinteros high in the trees, the first Javier has ever seen. I retrieve my pack and we climb the pass and make a long descent on intensely eroded cattle trails eastward to the springs at the edge of Rio Blanco. I have to stop on occasion for those two to catch up. In the last few kilometers we pass an abandoned farm with an orchard of ripe plums that we devour. We arrive at the springs a few minutes after Glenn's wife, pay 2,000 pesos each, and enjoy a long soak in natural pools beside the river. Luckily, no one is around, so I'm able to bathe naked, as all I have is long pants. The pools progressively cool with distance from the scalding source, and I work my way up, but am out of the hottest one in five seconds. Only an old Japanese man could tolerate the intense heat.

The road from the springs is narrow, made of dirt, but in good shape. There is absolutely no traffic. A hitchhiker could be stranded for a day or two.

We head east, toward Argentina. After a half-hour of driving south in a high valley, just west of the Argentinean border, Glenn stops at a ramshackle tiny farmhouse surrounded by chickens and turkeys. He explains that they just bought over 1,200 acres here along with a bunch of friends from both The States and Chile. The idea is to save the old-growth forest from being cut. When he learned that the property was for sale he sent out an e-mail to all his friends, and enough of them actually responded that they were able to purchase this region for 650 thousand dollars. It's not an investment for future profit, but an investment in the future of the planet. I'm impressed.

We all get out and mill about while he has a meeting with the resident of the house, presumably his caretaker, and they make a list of needed supplies. It sounds like they are doing a fencing project. A kilometer down the road we stop at another, nicer house to fix the steps to its deck. There are three CONAF employees there. Glenn's group is working together with them on a conservation plan. I'm laggin' behind, eating crackers out of a box in the back of Glenn's pickup, but when I realize I can ask the CONAF guys to contact the ranger at the entrance to the park and tell him I left the park from Rio Blanco, I walk over, still eating a handful of crackers. When I arrive I notice one of them is the ranger who was at the cabin when I came down from the ridge during my first sunset in the park. I say hello, but when I tell him I'm happy to see him because I didn't want them to be worried about me when I didn't return, my pronunciation of the word for 'worried,' *preoccupado*, sends cracker crumbs spraying at the man. And I burst into laughter while apologizing. Of course they all think I'm crazy, and I suppose it's true, relatively, since, I am not part of this meeting of Latin professionals, but another crazy, wandering gringo. But, it *was* funny.

It's a long backcountry route paralleling the border through alternating environments of clear-cuts, then virgin forest. As we drive, we see as many ox-carts as we see motor vehicles. It's dark when, at a pedestrian suspension bridge, we stop for a stretch and Glenn suggests we cross the bridge. I'm not prepared for the scale of this at all. In a minute I find myself slung over a 300-foot chasm with big trees hanging over the edge and whitewater roaring through the bottom. A full moon rises over the forest canopy on the other side. All I can do is say, "Wow!" with a laugh. What a planet we live on.

Conversation in the cab of the pickup interests me intensely because Glenn and his wife seem to have assimilated well. It is a common sentiment among ex-pats that they never fully assimilate and are never fully accepted as locals, so I ask Glenn about this—if he feels fully accepted or will he always be a gringo. He hesitates, stalls, or is thinking about it, but never answers before his wife changes the subject.

Finally we hit a little town and Glenn has the great idea to stop for a beer at a store. I enter with him, and am amazed at the produce—one cauliflower is a foot in diameter— that reminds me of Alaska's Matanuska Valley produce. Glenn says the soil is so rich they need no chemical fertilizers, or insecticides.

By the time they drop me off at the hostel it's about ten. I tell the owners about my trip, get a shower, and go out for one of those dinner-plate burgers at a corner snack bar. Looking in the beverage cooler, I comment that there are no beers, and the owner, who is in bad need of a nose-hair trim, but otherwise immediately appears to be a good and happy man, without hesitation suggests that I walk a block, buy a beer, and bring it back. His attitude, not an uncommon one, makes me wonder if it is always the affluent who are the greedy. The tour companies are generally owned by members of well-off families. But the average Chilean constantly impresses me with his lack of concern about whether you buy from him or not, as long as he can help you. The image of a Frenchman named Matthew comes to mind. I just met him at the hostel. He's been zig-zagging down the Andes, crossing back and forth between Chile and Argentina. He told me, "Every time

I re-enter Chile it feels good because the people are so nice."

The couple who run the hostel are sweet. They are eager to help we travelers and are not rule-enforcers. I never ask their name, nor do they mine. There is no ledger to sign into with my passport number. The place is quiet, and when I mention that, they say they realize that they're lucky that way. My roommate is Jordan, a young guy from Chicago who's been teaching English in Buenos Aires, and is out on a long trip. He just climbed the volcano, Villarica, with a tour company, and is exhausted. The beer makes me head for the bathroom, and out the window I see a deck covered with propane bottles and lumber. On clotheslines hang drying sheets and a puma skin. When I come back to the room, Jordan is dead to the world, and I follow.

The morning is windy, so I hang in the hostel kitchen, sipping maté. When Jordan comes to life I give him maté and we talk. He doesn't know what an araucaria tree is. He's leaving for Argentina to cut travel costs. I'm hangin' out for another day—not ready to be moving on buses. I mail a postcard, relax in the park listening to Latin jazz on the iPod, do a little window-shopping and read the signs in the tour company windows to get a feel for the local mentality.

Pucon is billed as "The Adventure Capital of Chile." Which means that people come here to pay companies to give them a thrill. Besides paying guides to lead you up Villarica in a long, slow line, you can go white-water rafting, and there is *canopy*, a tour on Tyrollean zip-lines strung high in the over-story of the forest, and *hydrospeed*: running white-water in wetsuits on boogie boards. The whole thing repels me. I quit white-water guiding back in '81 because people were more interested in thrills than they were in Nature. They were looking for a natural roller coaster ride. That was before "ecotourism," a label that allowed some outfitters to progress and mature. But here in Chile that same old buy-a-thrill attitude is being catered to under the label of ecotourism. I wonder if a more mature type of adventure company would survive here. It's a cultural issue that leads directly to the headspace of those who can afford to pay for a guided trip, and the urban environment that both provides access to wealth as well as a separation from Nature.

Stopping under "Cinzano" umbrellas, I have a lomo de pobre and a beer, then return to the hostel for a nap. When I wake the wind has died, so I stroll to the beach. It's fairly empty on this late-season weekday. I have to move because the smell of dog shit keeps finding my nostrils and I can't find the source among the cinders, which are often large and dark-brown. I'm ready for the road again. They're expecting me up in Cachagua in a few days.

Autumn is in the air. Queltehues chase each other off the dormer peaks of a big lakeside hotel in a king-of-the-hill contest. Above them, Villarica is smoking. It last erupted in 1984, and will again when it is ready. This whole town could be wiped out.

CHAPTER 33

Temuco and Puerto Saavedra

Before any one else is awake, I'm in the kitchen, sipping maté in my slow process of waking up. Suddenly there's enough matiene in my blood to allow me to realize that it's 7:21 and there's a bus to Temuco at 7:30, so I dig my insulated plastic cup out of my pack, fill it with maté, zip up the pack, and hike half a block to the terminal. There's no line, and it's 7:29. The darseña is in this region called an *anden*, and there my bus is, ready to roll. Soon I'm sipping maté while passing through the fog of the lake, and then through the attractive resort town of Villarica, and then I re-enter the real Chile.

There's only one foreigner on this bus, and when I descend into the terminal in Temuco, I attract attention. I find a mini heading for the coast; if I take it I can satisfy my curiosity about this section of seashore that I skipped between Lebu and Valdivia, but it doesn't leave for forty minutes. I leave the crowded, dark, greasy terminal, cross streets that have horse- and ox-drawn carts among the traffic, and wander through the huge market tents outside. There are onions like softballs, carrots as thick as my wrist. A kilo of avocados sells for the same price as a single one in California. Prize tomatoes are neatly packed in little wooden crates, even the smallest boxes containing twenty-four. On the seafood side, men and women in white plastic aprons compete to get rid of the day's catch. It's all the same: sierra, salmon, mussels, clams and crab. It's only the sellers who are different. I think the guys who are standing around are customers waiting for the prices to drop. When I pass the spice stall, I see a burlap bag full of a coarse brick-red powder with a little sign stuck in it reading "*Merquen.*" I remember that Jose named one of her schnauzers after this spice, which she told me is the key ingredient of the best Chilean dishes, so I buy a small bag. Mapuche women pass with brightly-colored silk scarves tied so the knot is on top of their head, like a fancy Aunt Jemima. They wear tasseled satin aprons. Their fine dress conceals their poverty. My guess is that they have no more income than the rest of the poor people I see, and I see nothing but poor people, but I wonder if their way of dressing expresses a higher quality of life than the others in old hand-me-downs.

It reminds me of people I've met who seem to embody the Japanese concepts of elegant simplicity and refined poverty, maintaining a clean and neat living situation in the absence of any income beyond survival level. I knew a Garafuna man in Belize who had no money or education, but was always clean and presentable and walked tall, with a kind of nobility. His name was Shine because his skin had a luster like polished ebony. A poor drummer in Haiti always wore impeccably clean whites. In the Central American jungle, an Indian family who took me in when I was stranded kept tidy thatched huts with dirt floors swept several times a day. For some reason poverty usually is accompanied by uncleanliness, but really it is not the cause. Laziness and lack of education are more likely causes for the grub and grime that often accompany poverty, or maybe it's a lack of self-esteem.

Back in the terminal, I work through the chaos to locate the bus I've decided to take, and soon we're out of town and crossing the deforested coastal hills. We stop in a town called Curagua where the island in the main boulevard is lined with a few dozen small, old steam engines with smokestacks from ten to twelve feet tall. This must be how these people managed to cut down every tree as far as they could see. It always amazes me that people can honor such an accomplishment, but at the same time I know the romance of logging, having lived in logging camps of the great Northwest when I surveyed for the Forest Service in my youth, and having cut trees, bucked them and skidded them to a site where I built a log cabin. There's something about it I love, and I understand how any man can love, but there's nothing pretty about a clear-cut. Nothing good accomplished there. While intelligent logging is a beautiful thing, most logging is little more than rape, without respect for the land or the wildlife. So it's difficult to understand how logging towns always take such pride in the havoc they have wreaked. In Fort Bragg, on the Mendocino coast, surrounded by 600,000 acres of forest that has been clear-cut at some point in the last century, logging is celebrated each labor day with the Paul Bunyan Festival. I love the logging games of axe-throwing and log-rolling, but I never attend because I don't share the anti-environmentalist spirit of the thing. Paul Bunyan is the character who said that he wouldn't stop logging until the last tree had fallen. It sounds cancerous to me.

Crossing a one-lane suspension bridge over the river, we enter cool ocean air under a dark marine layer, and follow the lazy river flanked by pastures. At the rivermouth is Puerto Saavedra, a tiny wooden fishing town on a lagoon behind a sand-duned spit, the other side of which is the Pacific coast. The conductor takes me to the base of the spit, where it connects to the mainland at the foot of buffy sandstone bluffs reminiscent of Santa Barbara. The pea-green sea is rough in a California style, with waves breaking on a series of sandbars that extend for a couple hundred yards out. Spray from the waves makes a mist that obscures the view up the beach. Ivory-colored foam rolls up the greasy black sand, and the wet wind curls my hair. I take it all in for fifteen minutes, then turn around and walk the length of town looking for a restaurant with someone in it besides the cook and waitress.

I'm guessing this south side is the tourist and vacation-home side of town. It's abandoned, but not unmaintained. Eventually as I walk, homes become occupied with people who stop their chores to watch me pass. Still, every restaurant is empty. As I pass a market, a man straddling a bicycle addresses me in a voice that makes me think he's announcing my arrival to the crowd of twenty who are loitering out front. I don't understand a single word. His face is mutilated; one eye socket is empty, and it looks like he barely survived a severe burning. The crowd laughs at his words. I laugh and never miss one of my long strides as I hike right by them. Who knows what he was saying. I remember the time I was descending from a ridge after hiking a portion of the Appalachian Trail. It was Thanksgiving weekend, and a school teacher had her small class out for a hike in the autumn leaves. When I came bombing down the trail, one little boy announced, "Look, it's Daniel Boone!" Maybe this guy was saying something like that. Or maybe he was saying, "Look, here comes another stupid gringo looking for a sunny beach with girls in bikinis."

At the very end of town, or I should say, the beginning of town, I find a restaurant that has a family inside, so I immediately enter, as if it was where I was heading all the time. They don't have the *empanadas mariscos* advertised in the window, so I settle for a bowl of paila marina. They only have liters of beer, so I get one and offer a glass to the man with his family at the next table, telling him I can't drink the whole thing. He accepts and asks what I am doing here. After I explain that I just came to see the coast, I ask which is the best bus to take to Temuco if I want to continue to Santiago. He explains all the buses, their departure times, and the terminal where they arrive, and then offers me a ride to Temuco right after we finish lunch. The paila marina is yet another local variation, this one with a teaspoon of hot sauce. Not only tasty, but especially satisfying in this cool damp weather. It's a close second to the Valparaiso dish. You never know where you'll find the best food. Afterwards I leave with the family in their little car and we head back to Curagua, where their home is; they insist that I come in for coffee. While I sip instant coffee, I learn that

Paula is a Jehovah's Witness and is proud that she goes from door to door proselytizing. I remain quiet. Alejandro is not religious. He drove a bus to Temuco for years, but now has a little taxi company with five cars. He needs to go to Temuco for parts, and a few minutes later we're on the road.

The streets of Curagua are the home of a classic collection of *antiguos*—old men. They shuffle around in combinations of scrounged sweaters, sport coats, and hats in an attempt to look dapper, and remind me of old Cubans. I'm inspired to interview them on video. Wondering what words would leave their lips.

While driving, Alejandro gives me the story on the area. Everyone is poor and the men drink too much. When I ask about the wide river, the Rio Imperial that we are driving beside, he tells me it's deep too. Half a century ago, before there was a road to the coast, a riverboat was used for transportation from the city, and it sank, killing about fifty people. Now the river is heavily polluted with sewage, which I assume accounts for the pea-green sea. When we get to Temuco, Alejandro is concerned for my safety because of all the pick-pockets in the main terminal, so he takes me to a new terminal out on the edge of town. Once again, I'm the only foreigner in the terminal. After I buy a ticket for the next all-nighter to Santiago, there's nothing to do but wait for four-and-a-half hours, so I stash my pack at a storage counter, exit, and seeing no name on the terminal, I ask a teen-ager for the name. It takes me three times to get the name—*Rodoviario*—through his Chilean slang. Trusting that I'll remember the name, I take a very long walk into the heart of the city, through neighborhoods of dilapidated houses and mechanic's garages which eventually give way to upscale brake and tire shops. Suddenly I cross some invisible line, and I'm downtown in a sea of humans washing up and down the streets. I search for a music store to buy a CD requested by a salsa teacher I know in California, who heard it while traveling in this country, but the streets are dominated by shoe stores, beauty shops, electronics stores and pharmacies. When my feet begin to complain, I enter a restaurant for a sandwich and a beer. The after-work crowd is here drinking pisco sours and smoking cigarettes. There are a few tables of a more intellectual type—men with beards having serious conversations. I can't hang in the dense smoke, so take to the street again, find an internet shop, and send word to my friends in Cachagua that I'll arrive tomorrow. Glenn is still on my mind, so I send him a note thanking him for the ride, thanking him for buying the forest, and asking again the question he never answered—does he still feel like an outsider? Thinking of all that he taught me, I do some research and learn that araucaria only live to be 1,800 years old—about 40% of the age of the oldest bristlecone pines of the Sierra Nevada. The dagger-like leaves of the ancient tree—the mother of all pines—evolved to prevent dinosaurs from eating them. On a website dedicated to old trees I find this fascinating information: The Colorado Aspen grove I mentioned while marveling at the pure lenga stands filling entire valleys in Argentina has a name, Pando, which is Latin for "I Spread." "It's composed of about 47,000 stems spread throughout 107 acres of land, and estimated to weigh 6,600 tons, making it the heaviest known organism. Although the average age of the individual stems are 130 years, the entire organism is estimated to be about 80,000 years old!"

A taxi gets me back to the terminal and I find a seat on a wooden bench for an hour-and-twenty-minute wait. The terminal is bustling because tomorrow is Good Friday.

I install my earbuds and listen to Jerry Gonzales and the Fort Apache Band while I look at all the signs over the ticket counters. The number of bus lines in Chile is astounding. There are over twenty in this terminal alone. Only a few operate across the entire country. Most are regional. I'd guess the country has three or four hundred companies, and each bus must be maintained. On my walk a few hours ago I passed a deep dark cave of a garage filled with the ring of steel pounding on steel, where men fixed everything from the leaf springs to the chrome trim of buses.

Beside me a man reads an article about UFO's in the magazine *Muy Intersante*. Down here, interest in the subject is widespread, and free of the stigma it has in The States. It's commonly accepted knowledge that occasionally an alien craft crashes and immediately a team from the United States comes to retrieve it. I think of Dr. Steven Greer and the presentation he gave to the National Press Club in DC in May of 2001. Dr. Greer is an emergency physician, but decided to better serve humanity by bringing public attention to the fact that several high ranking military officers, as well as air traffic controllers and defense contractors, have agreed to swear before congress that the United States has alien spacecraft in its possession and has learned enough through reverse engineering to solve many of the world's energy crises in a few years. This especially applies to global warming. But it all is being kept secret. Assumptions are that the energy source may be "zero point," or one that cannot be regulated and sold—therefore the secret. Dr. Greer's organization seeks release of all information on the subject, but of course, the media pays no attention. He did speak to The National Press Club though. There he only spoke for five minutes. He gave the rest of the time to allow each of twenty or more witnesses—military, intelligence, government, corporate and scientific—to present testimony. The video of the presentation, seen by well over a million people on youtube, is impressive, and enough to validate the cliché, "The truth is stranger than fiction."

At 9:15, I board an *Executivo* to Santiago. I made the mistake of accepting seat three, in the front row, when I bought my ticket. It has no legroom. It's going to be a long night. I try to get my legs to extend by putting my feet in the aisle, but the damn steward keeps coming in and out of the door in front of me. Little Louie Vega is my soundtrack for the battle scenes of "The Gladiator" on the TV. It's in Spanish, but I can only hear the words when the actors yell, so there is no point trying to listen. Afterwards my world-music playlist is my lullaby.

CHAPTER 34

Back in Cachagua

I'm happily surprised when I wake up and see the first light of morning. The steward passes out cookies (flour, hydrogenated oil and sugar) on a little tray with a coffee cup. Ten minutes later, when he passes, I ask if the coffee has sugar in it. It does, so I put the whole tray behind the elastic net in front of me and study the world out the window. It takes me a while to decide that we are in Santiago. I know this when the poor decayed urbanscape never ends.

At 8:15 the bus arrives at the same terminal where Marinela had brought me over two months ago. I make my way directly to the Pullman office, not because I like their service, but because I know they have a bus to Zapallar. When the kid at the counter tells me the next bus is at 10:30, I ask if there is another bus line that goes there. He then says he has a bus that leaves at 8:30, in ten minutes. I ignore the fact that he just lied to me because I like the idea of getting on a bus immediately. He issues me a ticket for 4,000 pesos. When I pay with a 10,000 note, he opens a drawer containing a handful of crumpled 10,000 peso notes, looks at it for a few seconds, and tells me he needs to go get change. He'll be back in five minutes. When he returns he doesn't have the change. It's 8:27. He says he'll be right back and goes off in the other direction. At 8:31 he returns without the change. He asks me to go buy something so I can get the change. It's his problem, not mine, I protest. How can he expect to do business like this? He shrugs and says, "It's Chile." I suggest we find the bus and ask the driver for change. We search and can't find the bus. He takes me to another Pullman office, and gets the change, and asks where the bus is. They tell him docks fifty-five to fifty-eight. We go there and there's no bus. He tells me it didn't arrive yet. It's 8:40. Unlike Chileans themselves, Chilean buses are always on time, but figuring that maybe the Santiago terminal is different than the rest of the country because of unpredictable traffic, I wait. After five minutes it doesn't feel right, so I go back to the Pullman office where we got the change and ask about the bus. They tell me it already left. I ask for my money back. It takes ten minutes, but they give it to me.

Beginning again at the Turbus office, I find a bus to Zapallar. The woman asks what seat I want, showing me the plan that is only a quarter full. I tell her it doesn't matter, take the ticket, and walk away. Outside, I check the ticket to be sure of the dock number and notice that she gave me seat three again—the front row with no leg room. I am the tallest person in the terminal. What are they thinking?

Monty Alexander's jazz versions of old reggae tunes help ease my road-weary and frustrated mind. On the ride west, the scenery is monotonous: savanna and sparse woodland under a heavy overcast.

The driver drops me off in Cachagua, and I hike up to Marinela's house. She has a new maid who's expecting me, so I'm welcomed. After a shower, I ask when Marinela will return. "Later" she says. I ask what time, and she says, "In a few seconds." At this point I decide to ask again what time, and she says, "Two o'clock." It's 1:30, so I go to Marinela's bed and take a nap. I wake up at 2:30, stagger out to the kitchen and ask the maid if she knows what time Marinela will return. She says, "I don't know." I'm hungry, so go down the road to a market, but I can't find anything healthy enough for me to eat that doesn't need some kind of preparation, so I get out on the road and begin hitchhiking to Marinela's boutique in Zapallar. Luckily, the few cars that pass don't stop, because Marinela soon drives down the road from her house. She had driven home while I was in the market.

I'm happy to see her, happy that the confusion is over, happy to be off the road. Marinela acts as if I never left, not as if she's been e-mailing me for two months about how she can't wait to see me again. So now I enter a new confusion.

We return to her place for a delicious Chilean lunch: fried fish, mashed potatoes and tomatoes with a chardonnay. Marinela is a seafood-loving island girl, and she offers an urchin roe ceviche as an appetizer. I'm studying her expressions, wondering what's wrong. Finally I ask her if she's nervous, and she admits she is. She has an extraordinary ability to hide her emotions. When we were first getting to know each other, I had no idea that she was even interested in me, but after she invited me to join her on a few trips to run errands in other towns, I asked her. She told me that she couldn't sleep at night because she was thinking of me so much, that it was the first time she'd experienced love at first sight. I had to laugh at the surprise. I was expecting an answer like "A little bit." Now that her emotions are exposed, barriers are dropped and we enjoy being together again in a genuine, open and relaxed way.

The next day, we go on a run to Viña del Mar, to buy supplies for Marinela's bar, *El Clandestino*, that she has moved to a legal location at the polo club. She has a list of calls to make, so she wants me to drive, and complains about my not having an international drivers license. Mine is with me, but it's expired. I thought it was so stupid I couldn't make myself renew it. All I did to get it was to pay ten dollars to Triple A, and they issued a piece of paper that said it was an international driver's license. Ridiculous. She is so stressed because of all that she has to get done (having blown off yesterday afternoon's to-do list so she could be with me) that she asks me to drive anyway. I'm determined not to get stopped by the Carabineros, remembering the astrocartographer's warnings about legal hassles, and the truth is I'm also a bit intimidated by their logo—a shield with crossed rifles—so I drive carefully and don't speed. A mile or two out of town, I round a bend and see a Carabinero truck on the side of the road with an officer standing in the road waving me down. I can't believe it. I've never seen this kind of roadblock in Chile before, and the first time I drive....

Marinela is still on the phone when I'm rolling down the window and giving the cop my license, wondering if the Vedic gemstone is going to work. For some reason she's not the least bit concerned, or she's hiding her emotions again. The cop bends over to my window and looks at my California driver's license like it is an exotic seashell; appreciating the colors in the holographic seal and design more than reading the information. Then he looks up, and with kind eyes, asks where we are going. I tell him Viña del Mar. I'm utterly confused because I'm the only driver he's stopped. The rest of traffic is driving freely. Marinela gets off the phone and they talk in Castillano, which I don't fully grasp, but I'm looking at the guy's eyes and I'm astounded. Every cop I've ever seen in every country I've been in, no matter how pleasant a person, has authority in his eyes. It makes them a little harder, a little less receptive, less compassionate. This Carabinero has the eyes of an angel: soft, sensitive, and caring, full of innocence—what my grandmother called "liebe augen," "eyes of love." Next thing I know, another guy is getting in the back of our four-door pickup. I ask what the hell is going on, and Marinela tells me he is a cop and needs a ride to Viña del Mar. This explains why I am the only one to be stopped—they only needed one ride for this guy. I drive off, still astounded, and relay this to Marinela, who understands the cultural difference. She tells me that once she was on a California freeway and a highway patrol car was behind her with lights flashing. She couldn't understand why the guy wouldn't pass her. Finally he pulled along side and motioned her to pull over. She was speeding, but the cop let her off with a warning and a lecture about stopping on the shoulder of the road when you see flashing lights in the United States.

Back in Cachagua, we set up the polo club for Marinela's opening night. Shortly after she opens I go back to her place and go to bed. I have to teach a small aikido seminar in the morning so I have to miss the party. Marinela joins me toward the end of the madrugada. Her opening was a huge success.

Either the promotional efforts were lacking, or Chileans have little interest in what I have to offer, or maybe both. Only two guys show up for the seminar. One is Charley, who arranged the seminar, and the other is his friend, Eduardo, a famous architect from Santiago. They're both tai chi practitioners. I don't know what they hope to learn in a few days, but I accepted the invitation to teach, hoping I could gauge the local interest in my art. Obviously it's minimal, but I love to teach and they're paying me well, so I make it my priority for three consecutive mornings.

Meanwhile I've settled back into the subculture of this wealthy stretch of coastline. It's comfortable for me here, not unfamiliar, and of course, there's Marinela. She goes out of her way to make things comfortable for me, buys fresh fish and a shellfish, *macha*, to make special Chilean favorite dishes for me, and re-arranges her schedule so she can spend time with me. I feel a bit guilty when she neglects her business and her kids to accommodate me. She makes most of her money in the few summer months, when the Santiagans fill their beach houses, and I want her to make hay while the sun shines.

So, in the next few days I spend time with other people. Jose has just seen a psychic to help her pass through a period of change she is in, and we talk about feeling okay about withdrawing from friends and parties when you need time to be alone, and about having the courage to follow the inner desire to change. Icha takes me surfing on a little beach-break sand bar, lending me a wetsuit and a longboard that turns like a tanker. The waves are small, but the late-summer water is clear and relatively warm for Chile, about 67 degrees Fahrenheit. Afterwards we have a barbecue at his house and he introduces me to his friend, Pato, who wasn't named so because he looked like a duck when he was a kid. His name is short for Patricio. Pato is a recreational chef when he's not traveling around the world directing TV commercials. We get along right away, talking by the brick barbecue grill and drinking beer while he's cooking. He's almost fluent in English. He agrees with Marinela, who told me that I'm lucky to have an audience and clientele for my photographs. It's very difficult to be a fine art photographer in Chile. All artists have a hard time in Chile. In Valdivia, Eliana's daughter Patricia told me that artists and art galleries are associated with the political left who were murdered and tortured by Pinochet, and the culture has not yet rebounded. People are still cautious about associating with artists. I tell Pato that I recently read that while 96% of the population in The States say they appreciate art, only 27% say they appreciate artists. When he hears my camera story he tells me about Francis Ford Coppola's storm of problems while filming "Apocalypse Now." Coppola never quit, though, and Pato insists that I don't. "You have to go back, man. You have to go back and do it again," he says as he hands me a bowl of his ceviche made with gingered shrimp, with no tomato as is common in Central America. After that we enjoy a meal of corvina garnished with sage, and in the end Icha pulls out some Cuban cigars that Pato gave him. Pato assures me that these are *Cohiba*, the very type of cigar that Fidel hands to visiting dignitaries. It's a good smoke, for sure. As we relax on the patio, Icha gets a phone call inviting him to play soccer. He goes for it, and I can't refuse the invitation to join, so the early evening finds us running hard on the polo field with full bellies, surrounded by guys half our age.

I like all these people, and simply want to spend time with them as much as I want to learn about their lives, and their country and culture.

Jose knows I want to give Marinela some space, so she invites me for lunch with some special friends—a yoga teacher and a dream study teacher. I arrive on time, therefore I'm early, and hang out with Mari, the maid, for fifteen minutes before Jose arrives. Mari's cooking lunch. I've always been curious about the glass jar of water that lives on the shelf beside the kitchen door, so I ask Mari about it. It takes a while for her to open up, but she explains that her grandmother was a *curandera*, a shamanic healer, and taught her many things. If a person comes to the door who has a bad energy, the water will absorb it. You know when that happens because the water gets bubbles in it. I check, and there are no bubbles. I guess I'm okay. Mari grates the wood of the *palo santo* tree into a bowl and drops a lit match into the shavings to make them smolder. The smoke is a pungent, soapy incense that purifies the area, like our white sage in California. She asks me if I can find a skeleton *Santo* for her. This is a little figurine common in Mexico, but rare here in Chile. She says she needs it for certain healing rituals. I'm puzzled how she knows about this, but I promise to send one.

Jose arrives excited—it's the first time she's had guests since Christmas, and I feel honored. But that feeling doesn't last long. All of these people can speak some English and proper Spanish, but they choose to speak Chilean Castillano, so I'm left out of the conversation. Two hours go by at the table without anyone speaking to me, so I excuse myself and stroll into the garden, wondering if I could ever learn this Castillano. There, at Jose's pond, is a grey plumbeous rail with a lime-green bill and huge feet that allow it to walk on the lily pads. It thrills me and reminds me of the beauty of the world beyond the social scene—the beauty of the present moment.

Unfortunately, the egoic mind returns when I re-enter the house (someone once said that life would be heaven if it wasn't for other people), and the feeling of alienation returns. So I spend the afternoon alone with the penguins up the beach. Since I was last here they've occupied dens dug into the ochre soil on the lee side of the island, among cacti, where they've reared young ones between outcrops of black basalt dripping with white guano that reminds me of slow-exposure photos of waterfalls. I can't imagine how the penguins dig those holes. I suspect the subterranean homes are passed on from generation to generation and are only slightly deepened by ritual digging at the beginning of every nesting season. They get along well with their pelican and cormorant neighbors, but keep to themselves. When I checked e-mail before lunch, I still hadn't heard from Glen. I'm wondering if he'll ever answer the question—if he still feels like an outsider after all these years in Chile.

In the evening, after dealing with her kids, Marinela comes to me. She is hinting that she wants me to stay. I'm thinking she needs to spend time on her two seasonal ventures to make money now, before a long slow winter. I know about that from the feast-and-famine days of seasonal work in Alaska. Also, I am pretty-well burnt-out on living out of a backpack—as much as I am of trying to understand Castillano. I got involved with Marinela because she told me she didn't have time for a relationship, and she understood that I'd be leaving, but the temptation to extend my stay is not absent. Our evening is filled with a heightened appreciation of being with each other, maybe it's the first wave of sweet sadness we feel about our approaching separation.

At nine-thirty in the morning she calls Icha for me. Icha had told me he'd call at nine, so I was wondering what happened. Marinela explains to him that I'm a gringo and to me nine means nine. He picks me up and we travel to the next town south to surf a heavy and nasty beach-break. It's overhead and closing out, but still it's fun to be in the water. The waves are impressively thick and powerful, but the rides are short, ending in airborne kick-outs just before the waves close out. A clean-up set gets us both and pins me on the bottom for a few seconds. I explain the phrase "clean-up set"—like a broom, it sweeps all the surfers. He says they call it *"mata pajarito."* "Little bird killer"? He clarifies that they call beginner surfers pajaritos, and the occasional big set gets them because they don't know to watch for it. Icha has been surfing longer than anyone in the water besides me.

Sitting outside the break, Icha points to a house under construction and tells me in careful English, "There my friend he build your house, man." Icha always uses the word "your" for "his" or "her," so I understand him, but I consider it literally, and survey the coast, imagining myself living here. The relatively progressive and culturally-creative element here is in high proportion compared to any other place I've been in Chile. Paradoxically, the reason they are here is because they can make a living supporting those of old wealth—unreconstructed conservatives who've been established here for some time. Architects, landscape architects, boutique and spa owners can survive here whereas most of Chile's coast is too poor to support them. These creative people in turn support the artists and galleries. The old money backed Pinochet, and still regards him as a respected leader, while the people I'm interacting with know he was a despot. They refer to him as *"Pinocho,"* Spanish for "Pinocchio," in a play of words that I find perfect, but I doubt they use it in the company of their clientele. Maybe they don't want to bite the feeding hand, maybe the years of torturing political dissenters created a climate of caution that persists today. The good news is that the new president, a former victim of Pinochet's torture, seems to be taking the country in a positive direction, but slowly and wisely. I expect Chile's intensely broken society will slowly mend because of the trend in the neighborhood, with social movements directing the courses of Venezuela, Ecuador, Bolivia, Brazil, and Argentina. At the same time, I expect my own society to break further, with a widening gap between the upper and middle classes that is, unless the people stand up.

The surf's crunching hard now that the tide has dropped, and I'm trying to get a wave in to the beach, but they're all big, hollow, pounding close-outs—the entire thick wall pitches forth at once into shallow water full of suspended sand. Finally I take one, weight the tail of the longboard to make the steep drop, and don't turn. The thick lip leaps forward and detonates behind me, and when the wall of whitewater catches me I dive on the tanker and just ride straight in.

After lunch with Marinela, she asks me to join her on a trip to pay her phone bill. She drives for forty minutes north, then inland, to pay in person because the mail is so unreliable and slow. If her payment doesn't arrive on time, they shut down her phone. We take a coastal route back, and walk out to a jagged point covered with cacti and succulents that are still in bloom. The wind has picked up, and there are whitecaps. Chileans call them *cabritos*, "little goats," she tells me, because they are white and seem to jump. I teach her about the Peruvian boobies that are flying by. A blow-hole gives us great entertainment when the big swells enter a slot in the rock and force a plume of steam out of the top of a chimney about fifty feet overhead. We're happy to be together, and never mention my approaching departure, though it's on both of our minds.

I can't stay. I'm so burnt-out on Castillano that I need a break... My educated friends here speak a dialect as difficult to understand as that of the poor mestizos in the hinterlands. No amount of book-studying makes a difference. I'm frustrated and tired, and losing interest in learning. Besides, I have things to return to, a place I'm paying rent on, and I need to make some money. It would probably be best for Marinela if I left as scheduled. Getting closer to her would make our inevitable parting even harder.

But once again I imagine what it would be like to move here. I have the support of my friends here in Cachagua. That's nearly essential. Imagine the difficulty of settling in a new world with a mysterious language and culture if you have no support. It amazes me that people do it.

I moved to the Mendocino Coast because my intuition said it was right. My former home was ten hours south, in Carpinteria. I just drove into town, not knowing a single person, and slept in the back of my pickup truck. But I was still within my own culture. Within a week I had a place to teach and a cabin in the woods, all in trade for using my skills to improve these structures. I felt I was on track—that I was doing the best thing I could be doing. I had students, and became a student myself; a master of the Japanese fine arts happened to live right in the area my intuitive location meter had homed in on, near my cabin, a place that made my heart sing when I could hear the big surf roaring through the redwood forest.

Life was bursting at the seams in those days, but it began to dwindle when the property where I had my school was sold. I trusted that another space would be provided as the first had been, but it never came, and that was the beginning of the end of my teaching.

I did get a solid education in tea ceremony, calligraphy, and flower arranging, which had a profound influence on my aesthetics and hence, on my photography. But then my teacher began spending semesters away, teaching at universities. He had the same problem as I—the demographics weren't right for either of us as teachers of exotic disciplines. Just as the astrocartographer read from my chart, the Mendocino Coast was very good for me for a few years, but it has been fading ever since.

The astrocartographer. I had forgotten about him. Here I am on the Chilean coast, where he says I will thrive, and I've got support. I listen to my intuition, and I know the timing is not right. It's too soon for me to stay. I need to come back here another time. This place feels familiar, but I still have no evidence that it would be more fertile for my growth here. And the most disappointing aspect is that property values here are higher than they are on the Mendocino Coast. This is the most expensive place on the coast of Chile, for that matter, probably the most expensive residential community on the Pacific Coast of the Americas south of San Diego—another cosmic joke on me. And while one might think that at least there are affluent people around with the time and inclination to train in a martial art, the fact is that most of the rich folks don't actually live here. It's a vacation home community—a remote weekend suburb of the Santiago elite.

On the way home, Marinela answers my questions about the price of real estate in the areas surrounding Cachagua and Zapallar. She says there might be some affordable and hospitable acreage in the hills just in from the coast, south of here, but she expects the prices to go up as more and more people move to the area from Santiago. She says the city's air pollution is so bad that people are getting sick.

In Zapallar we go to the Turbus office and I buy a ticket for tomorrow's bus to Santiago. Before we go home, we visit Jose and then Icha so I can say goodbye. Afterwards, when we stop to pick up a few groceries, her truck gets broken into and her son's electronic game is stolen. It's a wake-up to a reality I didn't know existed in Cachagua. In most Chilean towns you pay a parking lot attendant to watch your car while you shop, but not here in Cachagua—it seems so safe and crime-free. At home in California I usually leave my keys in my truck, rarely lock my locker at the gym, never lock the door of my home. When I walk a quarter-mile out to the headland to check the surf, I leave my board in the back of my truck. Some guys carry two boards, pick one according to the conditions, and leave the other in the back of their pickup, unprotected. There is enjoyment in living with so little crime. It's a pleasure not to have to dedicate a part of one's mind to the protection and safeguarding of belongings—a pleasure I'm so accustomed to that if I were to lose it I would lose a certain quality of life. The sense of conflict and disharmony with the human environment may be a necessary and sane form of paranoia here, but it seems unattractive.

In the evening we appreciate our last hours together with a bottle of cabernet by what Marinela calls the "*chiminey*"—a spanglish name for her stone fireplace.

Mid-morning has me waiting by the market for the big bus with Marinela beside me. She's into her hidden emotion routine again, running through a mental checklist of things I may have forgotten, but I recognize it now and tease her about it. Still she continues so that after my pack is stowed below the cruiser, she misses the experience of our final kiss which I lay on her lips as they are forming words, something about how to get to the airport from the bus terminal. I squeeze her like I'm trying to put our hearts together, while telling her I'll be back.

Sitting in my reserved seat, I feel an emptiness in my heart, and breath deeply as if trying to fill it. "I'll see her again," I tell myself.

Stepping on the bus is almost like stepping out of the Southern Cone. My trip is now in the past, and again I settle down in the rolling refuge to reflect on my rambling, my reconnoitering of the past few months.

Looking out the window, the outstanding feeling I have is one of connection with this place; a sense that it will remain in my life. The people I've befriended here contribute to this feeling, and my connection to Marinela is life-long, no matter what happens and where she is. But what I'm feeling right now is a sense of place. I know I'll return and see this view of the Pacific again.

Of course, I'll surf with Icha, visit Jose. I know I'll see Mauro again, somewhere in the mountains. And Cintia? In me, she has a life-long friend if she wants that. I have friends from down in El Chaltén too: Evelyn, Fernando, and Waldo. Maybe I will see Pablo, my roommate at the forest reserve, again. Thinking of all the people I've met, I remember other travelers too. I know I'll meet up with David, the Australian, and Marius and Geni, the South Africans, one day. When I think of all my travels throughout my life, I can't remember making any bonds like the ones I feel now.

We turn inland and through the window I study the landscape, but notice my reflection in the glass. I'm a different person from the man who bussed out of the Santiago airport back in December. I'm not talking about a new familiarity with two countries. I'm not even talking about the result of my experience of divine Nature in the mountains, which has put me on a new course, instilling a dedication to making photographic portraits of Nature's majesty. I mean I've been humbled. Not by realizing that I am indeed middle-aged, pushing fifty, and slowly sliding down a slope I can never climb again, not by the fact that my mind seems incapable of learning to understand Chilean Castillano, and seems to be getting more forgetful, causing my fuck-up of what seemed like a divine opportunity to photograph the granite towers of El Chaltén. But my humility *is* in some way age related. It may be that the years have softened me, or that I have something more permanent in mind now when I look for a place to live. But lately I'm surprised at the value I place on amenities that contribute to my perceived quality of life.

When I was younger, living abroad for a few years would have been an adventure. I've spent enough time in other countries to *feel* like I've lived there, even though I never extended a ninety-day visa. I've never made the full commitment. Back then I was tougher; living in a cabin in Alaska, chopping wood for heat, carrying water to my kitchen, but feeling a real appreciation for the warmth and every drop of the essential fluid. Back then I could have lived in a third-world country and taken all the inconveniences and every-day challenges as an adventure. Now I don't *want* the routine of daily life to be an adventure. I didn't know that I'd lost my intrepid spirit until now. I thought I was still a Spartan because I survive on so little income, sleep on the floor when I visit a friend, ignore fads and honor the utility of things; because I've never owned a TV or a cell phone; because I dispose of less than a pound of trash per week while the average American throws out four pounds a day. It's not the realization that I'm no longer Spartan that is humbling; it's the realization that the guy reflected in the bus window is spoiled.

I'm reminded of the phrase, "The finer things in life." The average North American would say I lack them, but she'd be assuming the culturally-accepted definition of the word "finer." I have my own definition. So did E.E. Cummings.

The quality of my life in my California town is enhanced by the ability to buy organic and international foods, listen to a variety of music and uncensored information on community radio, trust the mail, fed-ex, and UPS to deliver on time, use high-speed internet access at home, buy used books, music, and cutting edge nutritional products online, pay bills online, work-out in a modern gym, swim in a clean pool, then steam or sauna, stop in at a pub for any of a variety of world-class draught beers and ales, go to a public library and take out a book, access protected wilderness areas with just a few hours of travel, experience the best live music, visit alternative health-care professionals when needed, pay little attention to the security of my home, vehicle and belongings—the list goes on, and the embarrassment I feel when making it causes me to wonder how important these things really are. Really, they are little more than conveniences. I'd give them up if the right opportunity arose, but I don't feel that it has.

If we are the eyes and ears of the Earth, if we are created, designed, or intended to be the instruments through which the Universe appreciates itself, then it seems that my role, for now, is to keep traveling, experiencing the glory of the planet, photographing it, meeting kindred spirits, and looking for the right opportunity. An old Zen saying states, "To be aware of opportunity is divine."

The bumpy road and the dim light make the screen of my iPod hard to read, so I choose the "Rock" playlist, not so much because I want to hear it, but because the shapes of the letters make the short word readable. The list is on "shuffle" setting so that songs play in a random sequence. It begins with The Doors classic, "Riders on the Storm." After the dreamy intro, Morrison sings,

"Riders on the storm
Into this house we're born
Into this world we're thrown
Like a dog without a bone"

Suddenly I realize that, on a subconscious level, I have always agreed with him; that the world is a storm we are cast into—where we have to struggle to survive—and I now consider for the first time that maybe we were both wrong. Staying with the thought, I recognize the possibility that we could have been creating our own reality of difficulty all of our lives simply by living with this fundamental belief. I'm astonished by the insight.

After some thought, I wonder, could it be that my entire motivation for this trip—my dissatisfaction with the United States—is only the result of the cascade of attitudes originating from this basic view, that the universe is an inhospitable place? How deeply is that belief engraved in my mind? Can I simply change my fundamental view and experience life a different way?

In my martial art, a throwing and grappling art, we have to learn how to fall in order to train. A traditional saying is that it takes three years to learn that skill. When I was learning, I realized that I had a deep psychological program that said falling was a bad thing, and that hitting the ground was not pleasant—something to be avoided. I began a process of re-educating myself about the ground and my body's relationship to it. Later I taught students to "make friends with the mat" so they could relax, learn to fall safely, and enjoy the training. Indeed, the ideal of the art itself is to transcend the perception of the attacker as an opposing force—to blend with, or unite, or be in harmony with the attacker; neutralizing the attack becomes possible because of having joined with it, or fitted into it.

My God! The name of the art, "Aikido," can be translated to "the way of harmony with the force and principle of the

Universe." It must be a basic requirement that, in order to attain such harmony, we not see the Universe as something that opposes us. I am humbled

As I return home I begin another exploration; not outward, but inward. I keep up the investigation on my flight.

Buddhists list three "torments of the mind" (*kilesas*). Personalities are usually dominated by one of them: greed, aversion, or delusion (or indifference). I'm an aversion type, more motivated to avoid what I dislike than I am to seek what I like. In a way, the freedom from what I dislike is what I like most. Though Buddhist texts describe the kilesas as "poisons" and "defilements," this had not been my view. But I knew that any motivation, if hidden from consciousness, will keep one stuck on automatic pilot to some degree, leading to missed opportunities for growth, if not directly to suffering.

I thought I was aware of my aversions, and honored them. I was actually grateful for them. The alternatives, constantly running towards what is attractive, or suffering the paralysis of perpetual indifference both disinterested me to the point that they seemed to lack dignity. I did recognize that most of the world's innovations can be credited to greed types, but aren't most of the world's problems caused by insatiable greed, and allowed by indifference? Maybe this was my bias towards aversion—a filter generated by my subconscious mind that justified aversion. Even so, I did recognize that running away from all I had an aversion to would bring a loss of dignity as well.

Now, on the plane flying across the equator, I'm reflecting on the possibility of having an aversion to my very existence. The Buddha taught that life is unsatisfactory. We suffer afflictions, from minor disappointments to deep pain. But he taught that we add an extra psychological dimension of suffering when we react to our discontent out of our natural desire to be free of it. This is not to say, however, that we should not extract ourselves from situations that cause suffering when we can, but simply that we need to be aware of our reactions to what we don't want, and then choose how to act.

Aversion itself I never saw as a problem; I thought of it as valuable. It is a necessary cornerstone of law, ethics and morality. It's also a motivator to extract oneself from poor conditions, as my European ancestors all did, to their credit. Leaving my New Jersey home was certainly the right thing for me to do after college. The potential poison that comes with aversion is an overabundance of discontent, this is the "torment of the mind." So the ability to discern between petty irritations and the feelings that arise from injustices, between having your buttons pushed and facing barriers to self-fulfillment, is the prerequisite to the ability to mindfully still, or to act upon, motivations of aversion. The Buddhist texts do allow that mindfulness of aversion transforms it into "discriminating wisdom." But first one must be aware of the aversion. And I may have just become aware of the mother of all aversions.

While contentedness is certainly an ideal, we don't live in an ideal world. And even if we perceive the Universe as hospitable, I think present global conditions demand some discontent. I am not speaking of a personal discontent, as my ancestors had. After all, I'm not yet *suffering* from the economic/cultural/political climate of my home. I am speaking of a discontent rooted in compassion. In fact, I can say, paradoxically, that dignified content is possible only through some action for change, motivated by discontent. Gandhi and King come to mind, reminding me that *how* one acts for change is vitally important. Obviously the key is in the balance—in the comfort with this paradox. I assume that the degree to which one acts to improve conditions which cause suffering must be determined by the nature of one's uniqueness, and the type of life one is well-suited for. I have a feeling this question of degree will haunt me for some time. It seems the woman who lives her life avoiding all things political and trying to live the best way she can, focusing every day on being fully present in each interaction she has, and the man who dedicates his life to campaigning for some just cause with little regard for his own welfare both lead equally valid lives

Just as we must accept ourselves, yet strive to improve; just as confidence can only be rooted in reality if it is grounded in doubt, and just as wisdom is impossible without an awareness of one's ignorance, true contentment—the satisfaction of self fulfillment—requires that we act with a compassionate attention to the well-being of *others* (people, life, earth). Concern for the suffering of *others* creates a discontent that prevents contentment unless acted on.

Meaningful peace is possible only with a ration of struggle. I suspect it is all part of the human yearning for and movement through spiritual evolution.

So, even though I may have, for many years, been operating on the fundamental idea that the universe is inhospitable, it has also been clear to me, on several occasions, that we inhabit a wonderland that can be called Paradise. Even though it seems likely to me that everything is perfect, just as it is, it is also evident that the truth is paradoxical, and that there are circumstances when I must act, with awareness, on the reasons for my discontent, and that there are other times when equanimity is appropriate.

Taking this trip, pursuing my hope, and not finding what I had hoped for, was more fulfilling than quieting my hope for a South American home in which to thrive.

Cummings wrote, "To be nobody-but-yourself—in a world which is doing its best, night and day, to make you everybody else—means to fight the hardest battle which any human being can fight; and never stop fighting." Did he view the universe as inhospitable?

To be authentically yourself is to feel all the internal dynamics of your uniqueness. We usually think of these as our interests and talents, but it includes our dreams of what is possible, and our yearnings.

 Now I see that my yearning, the yearning that motivated this trip, is really a desire to escape the constant, low-grade "suffering" of fighting Cummings's battle. I do tire of it occasionally, and what better way to recharge one's spirit than to have an adventure in foreign lands, with people of different cultures, and assure oneself that the grass on the other side of the fence, while different, is just grass?

"It's the most wonderful life on earth. Or so I feel."

           —E.E.Cummings

Epilogue

In 2006, when I was writing this story, part of my motivation was a need to inform and alert people, while offering an entertaining story, about the crises (political, social, and environmental) of which the American public was, at the time, still largely unaware of.

Many people are overwhelmed by warnings of crisis, but I've chosen to leave those segments of the book intact as a reminder (that the crises are not going away on their own) and also as a record of the zeitgeist of 2006 for future generations. We are, at this moment, in the most "interesting times" of human history, and our descendants will wonder what the hell we were thinking when they look back to this decade.

Since 2006, Al Gore's "An Inconvenient Truth" opened many eyes to the threats of accelerated climate change, but 33% of Americans still don't believe climate change is real, thanks to disinformation campaigns based on junk science funded by oil companies, and fed to the corporate media. As I write this epilogue early in 2011, the United States still does not have a cohesive plan to reduce greenhouse gas emissions, while Sweden has pledged to be oil-free by 2020, and most of Europe plans to reduce CO_2 emissions by at least 50% in the next forty years. My government continues to ignore international concerns. The American green movement is growing at a snail's pace as it must overcome both the established momentum of our culture of consumption and mobility, as well as the new tangential trajectory initiated by "greenwashing" advertising campaigns that mislead people into thinking they are part of the solution when they are not.

The onset of economic depression, reducing production and consumption, combined with meaningful small steps forward by individual citizens and small groups, has reduced U.S. carbon emissions by 9% since I was in South America.

In the oceans, more than 90% of the large ocean predators – such as sharks, tuna and cod – are now gone, and all fisheries are predicted to collapse within fifty years. Twenty-five percent of the coral reefs of the world have died, and 70% of all living coral is predicted to die in the next ten years. There are now 400 dead zones in the coastal seas of the world. Carbon emissions are acidifying the ocean, with the potential for catastrophic consequences. Fourteen billion pounds of trash are dumped into the ocean every year.

In 2010, an offshore platform operated by British Petroleum (BP) spilled an estimated 206 million gallons of crude oil into the Gulf of Mexico, and then 1.8 million gallons of toxic solvents called "dispersants" were intentionally sprayed on the oil slick, in what some environmentalists argue was an effort to sweep the dirt under the carpet. The combination of the oil and the solvents has created a chemical disaster of a scale previously unseen on Earth (about 20 times the size of the Exxon-Valdez spill in Alaska in 1989). According to Global Access Media, the solvent/oil combination has created compounds that have not been previously studied, so the degree of toxicity is unknown. Many people fear that the solvents can penetrate organisms so easily that they will eventually contaminate all life in the entire Gulf of Mexico. Up to six million people may have been exposed to these compounds, indeed, tens of thousands are already sick, but BP has hushed the subject by plugging information leaks with money. As this book goes to press, the Sun Herald reports that aborted and still-born dolphins are washing up along the Mississippi and Alabama shorelines at about 10 times the normal number.

The population of honeybees in the United States has declined about 30% in recent years. Some point to the pesticides produced by Bayer (a German company with murky past, including strong Nazi ties, and a history of supplying compounds for chemical warfare) as the cause, others think it's cell phone radiation, and others say that fungi and viruses are the culprits. According to the dailygreen.com, if honeybees disappeared, food would become scarce, as colonies of bees stopped pollinating fruit, nut and vegetable crops. And as the plants that rely on bees died off, species relying on those plants will suffer, leading to the decline or death of the species that rely on *them*, and so on.

Early in 2011, a wave of animal deaths swept the globe. Four thousand red-winged blackbirds fell dead from the sky in Arkansas; two million fish died in Chesapeake Bay, 150 tons of red tilapia in Vietnam, 40,000 crabs in Britain, and on and on. "Authorities" said it was nothing unusual, that this happens all the time, but that now we notice it because of cell phone cameras and the internet, and they poked fun at "conspiracy theorists" for questioning the die-offs.

The dramatic rise of oil prices in the summer of 2008 brought increased awareness to the reality of "Peak Oil" and the many challenges we face as we attempt to break our addiction to petroleum, but still, mileage requirements on U.S. vehicles are low. And cars that run on anything other than gasoline are still a rarity in the United States. Of over 250 million cars in the U.S., less than 1% are hybrid vehicles.

Food riots are breaking out in poor countries across the planet, but growing edible crops specifically for biofuel production continues, as does the loss of arable land and soil, and population growth continues to be ignored by just about everyone. With a net increase of 2.5 people per second, or 216,000 per day, by mid-century nine billion humans will inhabit the planet, if we survive that long. In 2009 the number of the world's hungry topped one billion. Agricultural production is threatened by the widespread depletion of groundwater aquifers being tapped for irrigation in arid regions. The one great hope is the discovery of terra preta, the man-made black soil of the Amazon which yielded crops abundant enough to support large population centers there before the Europeans arrived. The United Nations Development Programme's 2009 Arab Human Development Report said desertification threatened about a fifth of the Middle East and North Africa with little effort taken so far to reverse the process. Burgeoning populations and climate change are accelerating the trend.

An alarming portion of the dust of the World Trade Center buildings has been found to contain unexploded, high-tech, military-grade nano-explosives. Polls show that 36% of the U.S. population suspects elements in our own government were involved in the attacks of 9/11, but still almost no media organization addresses the issue. One of the editors of Mother Jones magazine, the source for many of the facts presented in this book, gave "9/11 conspiracy theories" a high "tin foil hat" rating in a 2008 issue. If the letters posted on their website were a good indication of the overall response, the "tin foil hat" rating cost them a substantial number of readers (myself included). Meanwhile, almost 90% of Germany doubts the official story of 9/11.

In 2008, the Army's 1st Brigade Combat Team was assigned to U.S. Northern Command, marking the first time an active unit had ever been given a dedicated domestic assignment.

Such assignment had been illegal until laws changed in that same year.

Half of Americans now think it's OK for the government to eavesdrop on phone and e-mail without court permission if it keeps them safe from terrorism. In 2009, *Popular Mechanics* reported that there were an estimated thirty million surveillance cameras deployed in the United States, with the number growing rapidly as the technology gets cheaper. An *ABC News/Washington Post* poll in July 2007 found that 71% of Americans favor increased video surveillance.

The good news is that, since my trip, the *Reporters Without Borders* "freedom of the press" rating of the United States has risen from a dismal 53rd in the world up to 20th.

In 2008, the U.S. Government bailed out banks that they said were too big to fail. This was such a complicated and convoluted fiasco that I was challenged to put it in a nutshell, so I consulted Omid Malekan's excellent and concise summation on his website, *omidmalekan.com.* It says that the Troubled Asset Relief Program (TARP) used taxpayer money to rescue banks that were "too big to fail" by buying shares of the banks' stock. "Too big to fail" meant that their failure would cause too many home foreclosures and a shortage of home mortgage loans. It's not clear what the banks did with all of the money, but many used funds to buy other banks, making them even bigger. JP Morgan Chase acquired Bear-Stearns and Washington Mutual. Bank of America, owning Countrywide, merged with Merril Lynch. Goldman Sachs was bailed-out because of its failed client, AIG, but it was later learned that Goldman Sachs actually profited from the AIG failure because they had been *"betting"* that AIG would fail. The chairman of the Federal Reserve, Ben Bernanke, refused to loan to Lehman Brothers Bank, allowing them to fail, then he loaned money to Great Britain's Barclay's Bank, so they could buy Lehman Brothers. In the end, the banks invested their money offshore. They maintained low interest, but gave very few loans and very few new mortgages, which meant that customers received very low interest on their deposits. At the same time the banks raised the monthly service fees on the bank accounts of the taxpayers. Almost 2.5 million properties received foreclosure filings in 2009 and the bank executives were awarded huge bonuses. Due to the refusal of the Bush administration and the Federal Reserve to identify the banks on the receiving end of almost $2 trillion in taxpayer loans, I have not been able to determine how many billions of dollars went unaccounted for in this debacle, but after watching Alan Grayson's video "Is Anyone Minding the Store at the Federal Reserve?" on YouTube, in which Federal Reserve Inspector General Elizabeth Coleman dodges the same question about missing money for five minutes, it's easy to come to the conclusion that this was the biggest heist in the history of the planet. And they got away with it, because no one bothered to chase them.

Speaking of billions of dollars unaccounted for, $9 billion of US taxpayers' money, $549.7 million in spare parts, and 190,000 guns, including 110,000 AK-47 rifles, all disappeared in Iraq, according to ABC News. CBS reported the vanishing of $1 billion worth of tractor trailers, tank recovery vehicles, machine guns, rocket-propelled grenades and other equipment and services provided to the Iraqi security forces. Congressional hearings determined that $10 billion was misspent, and the Pentagon concluded that $1.4 billion paid to Halliburton for "military support" was unreasonable and unsupported. But that's all a drop in the bucket of the total Iraq war-spending — about $900 billion through November 2010.

John Pilger's recent comment that 45% of young African-Americans have no jobs while the top hedge fund managers are paid an average of $1 billion a year seems to sum up the situation well. And Mark Provost points to the facts that during the years from 2007 to 2010, the U.S. accounted for half of all job losses in the thirty-one richest countries of the world, and that the U.S. now has the highest unemployment rate among the ten most developed countries. But the GDP of this country has declined *less* than any of those richest countries, besides Canada, indicating a shift of the distribution of income. Meanwhile, nearly two-thirds of U.S. corporations don't pay income tax—a loss of a trillion dollars from the federal budget. At the same time, Obama plans to cut a trillion dollars from the budget by eliminating 200 federal programs, including aid to the poor and to students, and by trimming the environmental protection agency by 12%. Every day it looks a bit more like fascism in sheep's clothing.

Barack Obama was made president, supposedly elected on a platform for hope and change. After two years in office, people who voted for him are losing hope due to the lack of change. Obama campaigned for health-care reform, but then threw the issue into the den of bipartisan bickering in the House of Representatives, who seem to represent insurance corporations more than the population, 59% of whom say the government should provide national health insurance, according to a New York Times/CBS 2009 poll. The U.S. is still the only industrialized country that does not have universal health care for all its citizens.

Although he pledged to end "war" in Iraq and won the Nobel Peace Prize, now, after two years in office, Obama still has about fifty thousand troops in Iraq. He has increased the military budget (larger than the rest of the world combined), and has increased troop numbers in Afghanistan, even though military intelligence inside the Obama administration estimated that there were only about one hundred al Qaeda fighters in the entire country. Wikipedia states that "Opium production in Afghanistan has been on the rise since U.S. occupation started in 2001. Based on UNODC data, there has been more opium poppy cultivation in each of the past four growing seasons (2004–2007) than in any one year during Taliban rule. Also, more land is now used for opium in Afghanistan than for coca cultivation in Latin America. In 2007, 92% of the opiates on the world market originated in Afghanistan. This amounts to an export value of about $64 billion, with a quarter being earned by opium farmers and the rest going to district officials, insurgents, warlords and drug traffickers." Can we guess who these traffickers are?

Nine years after 9/11, Osama Bin Laden is still releasing video commentaries, and he is still the FBI's most wanted terrorist (though the FBI does not list the attacks of 9/11 among the acts of terrorism he is suspected of being involved in)

During his first year as president, Obama has reiterated his commitment to "Seek the peace and security of a world without nuclear weapons," but included $7 billion to expand the nuclear arsenal in his 2010 budget.

In his first ten days in office, Obama appointed eleven members of the Trilateral Commission to top-level and key positions in his administration. Now, many people are thinking that Obama is working for those who rule the world—those who Eisenhower and Kennedy warned us about. In August of 2009 Obama extended the National State of Emergency that George W. Bush created after 9/11 to allow for martial law, the seizing of property (including media outlets), and "Continuity of Government." (If you don't know about Continuity of Government, please research it.) Obama has forbidden the Press to ask any questions about his years of post-college activity with Business International Corporation, which many say is a front for the CIA. The man he appointed to head the Office of Information and Regulatory Affairs is now advocating government infiltration of groups promoting "conspiracy theories" in order to spread disinformation and undermine the efforts of those organizations.

In January of 2010, conservative billionaire Sebastian Pinera, whose brother, Jose, was Augusto Pinochet's Minister of Labour, somehow took the presidential election of Chile, ending two decades of uninterrupted rule by a center-left coalition, and returning power to the same political parties that provided civic support for Pinochet's brutal 1973-1990 dictatorship. Pinera, former owner of a Chilean TV station, has shown disdain for all the populist movements of South America, and is a friend of Columbia's right-wing president Álvaro Uribe.

Chile never withdrew from the School of the Americas (SOA, now renamed WHINSEC), but Venezuela and Uruguay both did soon after I left South America. Costa Rica did in 2007, and Bolivia followed in 2008, making a total of five countries that have left the program.

In June of 2009, masked soldiers armed with automatic weapons abducted Honduran President Manuel Zelaya, throwing him on a plane which refueled at the local US airbase and then flew on to Costa Rica, where it dumped the elected president on the runway, in his pajamas. The soldiers were operating under the command of two SOA graduates: Generals Vázquez Velázquez and Prince Suazo. Since then, over four thousand violations of human rights have been registered in Honduras, including sixty-four political assassinations.

On my first visit to El Chaltén I made the first backpacking trip in this book, camping at Laguna Torre, Poincenot, and Fraile. I was lucky to get some good photographs and my teacher, Dr. Shozo Sato, encouraged me to make a photography book, so I returned the next year. It was on this second visit, in 2007, that I made the other hiking trips written in this book, and then lost my camera. When I returned to Cachagua in 2007, Marinela was in a relationship with the bartender of her short-lived summertime lounge. I stayed with Jose and turned the compost that had been neglected for the fourteen months of my absence, harvesting eight wheelbarrows full of the rich organic soil amendment for her beautiful ornamental gardens, and I went surfing with Icha.

I did return a third time, in January of 2008, with dogged determination to get the photographs I needed, and not lose them, and I succeeded. The book, entitled "The Granite Avatars of Patagonia," is available at my website, www.tomreed.com. When I last left the town of El Chaltén, it had about doubled in size since my first visit, and the road from El Calafate had mostly been paved. Fernando not only offered high-speed internet, but was providing Wi-Fi to the entire town. On that third trip I accompanied Waldo and his climbing partner, Indio, to Paso Superior, where we dug a snow cave and spent two nights. They made an unsuccessful attempt to climb Poincenot (due to high winds) and I photographed Monte Fitz Roy (El Chaltén) from the high pass. I also succeeded in a solo ascent (I did encounter a Fin and a German, and traveled with them for a few hours on the ice) of Glaciar Torre to the base camp for climbing Cerro Torre, "Nipo Nino." From El Chaltén, I crossed into Chile on foot and by boat, then traveled the length of the Chile's Carretera Austral, stopping to photograph Cerro Castillo on a backcountry trip that was thwarted by rain. I returned to Bariloche, where Mauro now lives, and together we crossed the high route from Jakob to Italia at Laguna Negra. On the way to Bariloche, I rendezvoused with David the Australian for a mountain trip, but he injured his toe on the day of my arrival, so I went solo into the mountains above El Bolsón and climbed Cerro Barda Negra for a few photos.

I visited Eliana and her family in Valdivia who all treated me like family again. I saw Pepe, now in the office at The Nature Conservancy, and was not surprised to learn that nothing had been done with the trail I had located in the coastal forest reserve. Pablo met me in Santiago and gave me a tour of the "ceramic town" that was his tourism development project at his job with the government and university. Jose's compost had been neglected for another year, and I worked it again, harvesting ten wheelbarrows for her gardens.

I saw Cintia and Evelyn on both trips and our friendships remain. Marius replied to one of my e-mails and I never heard from him again. Katarina never wrote to me.

In 2008, I saw several California condors at Big Sur, and also photographed one at a distance of twelve feet in the bottom of the Grand Canyon.

In 2009, my father, who smoked cigarettes for half of his life and drank whiskey every day for most of his life, died at the age of 93. Just over a year later, Jack LaLanne died at the age of 96, giving ample reason to question the physiology of longevity.

The insights that came to me on this trip, many while daydreaming on buses and planes, got me interested in the subconscious mind, and eventually I went to school to become a hypnotherapist. That training opened me to the likelihood that the Divine Intelligence of the Universe was even more omnipresent than I suspected. This sounds impossible; how can something be more omnipresent than omnipresent? But our minds are limited in their capacity to comprehend the concept, and I worked to overcome my limitations. I became ravenous for more information, reading books and watching videos on theories of physics, consciousness and reality.

I sat in meditation for 100 hours during another ten-day retreat, where I realized the sacred quality of enthusiasm, which drives us towards self-fulfillment. I had powerful energetic experiences, and opened my heart to a new degree.

Still hungry for a deeper insight, I experimented with a powerful entheogen. I discovered the current wave of interest in Solfeggio sound frequencies, and remain impressed with my experience while listening to chakra-balancing frequencies. I even began exploring astral projection. This eventually led me to Thomas Campbell's Theory Of Everything, which, astounding as it may be, makes perfect sense to me.

It is impossible to study all of these subjects on the internet without exposure to New Age theories, and I took time to investigate some of them, being careful not to throw out the baby with the bathwater. Those who study the Mayan Calendar and other forms of astrology say that next week, on March 9th, a "wave of unity consciousness" will begin. Some say it has already begun, and because my own consciousness has expanded significantly in recent months, I have to admit my experience gives weight to their theory. They claim it is possible that humanity will soon be "confronted with a choice of truth versus tradition."

And today, as predictions of imminent physical cataclysm abound, whether due to the combined effect of all the problems listed in this book, or due to solar flares, shifts in the earths magnetic field, or some other threat, I am sure that many magnificent aspects of my beloved planet will indeed disappear. I have no hope for the survival of the majestic polar bear, and I already grieve for the loss. I have little hope for the rescue of this once-great nation of ours, whether due to the predicted economic collapse, or the continuing increase of disguised fascism, or both. And it has taken me time to come to terms with the losses. But a glimmer of hope has just appeared—at the time of printing this book, late February, 2011—almost all of Mediterranean Africa is in revolution, and the first spasms of uprising here in the U.S. are happening in Madison, Wisconsin (initiated by government employees, of all people).

The entheogen allowed me to realize the meaning of omnipotence, and I now profoundly understand the *truth* that the Divine Universe, which is omnipotent in its capacity for love, compassion, and nurturing, also contains the omnipotent capacity for destruction, horror, and violence, and that all things must come to an end for the Universe to evolve.

As the Universe evolves towards pure omnipresent Love, some of what I love may be destroyed, but new things will begin, and it is my task to evolve by constantly letting go of my attachments to what I have loved (*tradition*), and of my concepts of separateness and smallness, and to work in contribution to the creation of a new era on this planet; an era of increased organization, bringing more cooperation, and a more harmonious existence with each other and all aspects of Divine Nature.

Maybe the next few years will present our opportunity to restructure our societies so they more closely resemble our Utopias, wherever we are.

We certainly do live in interesting times.

"Creatures rise and creatures vanish;
I alone am real, Arjuna,
looking out, amused, from deep
within the eyes of every creature.
I am the object of all knowledge,
Father of the world, its mother,
Source of all things, of impure and
pure, of holiness and horror.
I am the goal, the root, the witness,
home and refuge, dearest friend,
creation and annihilation,
everlasting seed and treasure.
I am the radiance of the sun,
I open or withhold the rainclouds,
I am Immortality and
death, am being and non-being.
I am the Self, Arjuna, seated
in the heart of every creature.
I am the origin, the middle,
And the end that all must come to."

—The Bhagavad Gita

"It is not the answer that enlightens, but the question."

—Eugene Ionesco

"Freedom from the desire for an answer is essential to the understanding of a problem."   —J. Krishnamurti

"When we're deluded, there's a world to escape.
When we're aware, there's nothing to escape."

—Bodhidarma

"Our goal is to discover that we have always been where we ought to be."   —Aldous Huxley

Sources

Facts and figures were mostly gleaned from periodicals, especially *Harpers* and *Mother Jones* Magazines (for chapter 10, I used the MJ article: *The Fate of the Oceans*, by Julia Whitty, March/April '06). Information on biofuels came from, *Starving the People to Feed the Cars: Our desire for mobility could win out over the poor's struggle to survive* (*The Washington Post National Weekly Edition*, Sept/18-24). Some information about Chile came from *Travels in a Thin Country* by Sara Wheeler. Much of the political information was gleaned from various websites. For example, information on the Bush family can easily be found simply by entering "John Buchannan, Bush family" into a search engine. Many independent media sites offer valuable reporting, for example, www.gregpalast.com, www.counterpunch.org, www.commondreams.org. Climate change? Try realclimate.org.

Dying oceans? Try bluefront.org.

Don't forget 9/11truth.org, AE911truth.org, 911blogger.com and all related sites.

No time to read? Download podcasts at tucradio.org.

Like documentary videos? Go to topdocumentaryfilms.com, and trueworldhistory.info

Other sources:

Globalaccessmedia.org—ponerology.com—voiceoftheenvironment.org—

rockcreekfreepress.com—www.zerohedge.com—urbansurvival.com/week.htm—

english.aljazeera.net—worldpress.org—globalvoicesonline.org—huffingtonpost.com—

bbc.co.uk/news—nformationclearinghouse.info/index.html—http://omidmalekan.com—

truthout.org—salon.com—projectcensored.org

Seek and ye shall find. Then share.

Tom Reed, a geographer by education, is a wilderness photographer and author who has worked as a surveyor in Alaska, a river guide in the Western US and Alaska, a sailor, fisherman, somatic therapist, carpenter, artist and a martial artist, and currently works as a hypnotherapist. He is the author of *The Granite Avatars of Patagonia*, a coffee-table book of black and white portraits of Cerro Torre and Fitz Roy, with text excerpted from this book.

His books and photographs are available at his website: **www.tomreed.com**